AF361334

THE PUBLIC PAPERS OF
THE GOVERNORS OF KENTUCKY

Robert F. Sexton
General Editor

SPONSORED BY THE

Kentucky Advisory Commission
on Public Documents

AND THE

Kentucky Historical Society

THE PUBLIC PAPERS OF

GOVERNOR SIMEON WILLIS

1943-1947

James C. Klotter, *Editor*

Edmund D. Lyon and
C. David Dalton,
Assistant Editors

THE UNIVERSITY PRESS OF KENTUCKY

Library of Congress Cataloging-in-Publication Data

Willis, Simeon S., 1879-1965.
  The public papers of Governor Simeon Willis, 1943-1947 / James C.
Klotter, editor, Edmund D. Lyon and C. David Dalton, assistant
editors.
      p.   cm. — (The Public papers of the governors of Kentucky)
  Includes index.
  ISBN 0-8131-0607-9
  1. Kentucky. Governor (1943-1947 : Willis) 2. Kentucky—Politics
and government—1865-1950—Sources. I. Klotter, James C.
II. Lyon, Edmund D., 1943- . III. Dalton, C. David, 1957-
IV. Kentucky. Governor (1943-1947 : Willis) V. Title. VI. Series.
J87.K417   1943
353.976903′5—dc19   87-24085

CONTENTS

CONTENTS

CONTENTS

CONTENTS

HEALTH AND WELFARE   [161]

CONTENTS

STATE GOVERNMENT ADMINISTRATION   [178]

CONTENTS

REPUBLICAN PARTY LEADER, 1944-1945   [203]

CONTENTS

WORLD WAR II   [240]

KENTUCKY AND THE POSTWAR ERA   [257]

CONTENTS

TRANSPORTATION AND TOURISM   [282]

CONTENTS

LEGISLATIVE ACTIONS, 1946-1947   [301]

REPUBLICAN PARTY LEADER, 1946-1947   [336]

CONTENTS

VALEDICTORY   [375]

APPENDIX   [377]

INDEX   [395]

GENERAL EDITOR'S PREFACE

THE Public Papers of the Governors of Kentucky is a series of volumes which preserves and disseminates the public record of Kentucky's chief executives. The series was initiated in 1971, when the Kentucky Advisory Commission on Public Documents, created by executive order, recommended its publication. The commission oversees and manages all aspects of the project in cooperation with the Kentucky Historical Society.

Approximately every two years the public papers of the most recent previous governor and one earlier governor appear in separate volumes, each designed to provide a convenient record of each executive's administration. While the organization of the material may vary from volume to volume with differences in the styles of the governors, available materials, and historical circumstances, the volumes share an overall guiding philosophy and general format.

It is our hope that the series will prove useful to all those interested in Kentucky government, including citizens, scholars, journalists, and public servants. Not in themselves interpretations of Kentucky government and history, the volumes in this series will be the basis for serious analysis by future historians.

R. F. S.

EDITOR'S PREFACE

COMPILING and editing the papers of Simeon Willis proved to be a difficult, time-consuming, and—in the end—rewarding task. I first came to this project when the Kentucky Historical Society asked me to aid John Fred Williams, who had agreed to serve as editor. As Governor Willis's former superintendent of public instruction, he was well qualifed. Under his direction the work began, but only a brief start had been made before his death in 1977. Following that, the editorship went to me. While other projects often intervened, I was fortunate in that two fine scholars aided me in my tasks—Edmund D. Lyon and C. David Dalton have my deep-felt appreciation for their long work and good counsel.

The difficulty with the Willis Papers was not the subject, for he came through the written word as an honorable and a good man. Rather, it was the fact that no significant collection of Willis manuscripts existed. Therefore, to collect his public papers required delving into numerous reels of newspaper on microfilm to try to discover the words uttered by him as governor. Eventually, well over a dozen newspapers produced either whole speeches or fragments. Major papers were examined systematically; local ones were searched when Willis spoke in a particular vicinity. The official journals and documents of the commonwealth produced additional addresses and papers. Investigation in the collected papers of other important political figures yielded a few more. But, in the end, the majority of the materials herein came from newspapers. Often, it was necessary to combine several summaries to get a more complete account; whenever that has been done, it has been so noted. The danger in this, of course, is that, for all their value, newspapers are not always the exact source historians would wish. A comparison of a few recorded speeches with newspaper versions makes that clear. Therefore certain documents herein should be approached with a bit more care than others. Due to the paucity of sources, selected executive orders and veto messages have been included in an effort to present as full a picture of the administration as the sources allow. In all, this volume contains 173 separate public documents and statements.

Once collected, the material was transcribed and edited for consistency. Generally, editorial changes in regard to capitalization, punctuation, and similar grammatical matters have been made without comment. When the editor has intervened to provide other changes, such as paragraphing in recorded speeches, it has been noted. Any omitted material is so cited by ellipses.

Following the editorial work in the document itself, the material was next arranged into topical sections, with cross references to applicable material in other sections. A chronological listing of all documents is provided in an appendix. Footnoting then began, guided by the basic question, "Will this help the reader?" Whenever possible, persons mentioned in the document have been identified fully, as have those events and actions which need clarification.

This book owes much to the aid given by others. I particularly wish to thank the staffs of two institutions—the Kentucky Historical Society and the University of Kentucky. At the former, directors William R. Buster and then Robert B. Kinnaird supported the project fully. Hambleton Tapp, himself once a member of the Willis administration, provided excellent leads and advice, while Thomas H. Appleton, Mary Lou Madigan, and Gretchen Haney all, as usual, contributed and made this a better work. At the University of Kentucky, Paul Willis of the King Library furnished an area for a weary scholar to work and leave materials, while William J. Marshall, Terry Birdwhistell, Anne G. Campbell, William Cooper, Frank Stanger, and others provided, as usual, not only valuable information but also a pleasant and professional atmosphere.

Aid also came from Debbie Skaggs and Dwayne Cox, then of the University of Louisville; Samuel Proctor of the University of Florida; Richard Gassan of Ohio University; Betty Burcham of Ironton, Ohio; Jan G. Burge of Morehead State University; Carol J. Nicholas of the Lexington Public Library; Richard McNeill of the Chicago Historical Society; Richard A. Weiss of Kentucky Wesleyan College; Dena L. Newman of Union College; Dehlia Booth of the Edmonson County Library; Robert A. McCullough of Ashland; and Earl R. Muir, Jr. of Louisville.

But perhaps my greatest thanks must go to Mr. and Mrs. Henry Meigs, the late Ida Willis, and the family of John Fred Williams. On Mr. Williams's death, I was allowed to gather his material relating to Willis for use on this project. After that, Mrs. Willis called me frequently to offer her own often helpful and always candid thoughts on the project. Sally Meigs, following Mrs. Willis's death in 1978, kindly let me gather valuable material from her mother's files. The book is better as a result. To them all, and to unnamed others who helped in many ways, go my deep thanks.

THE CAREER AND ADMINISTRATION
OF GOVERNOR SIMEON WILLIS

Between 1931 and 1967 the state of Kentucky elected only one Republican governor. That man was Simeon Willis. Why? What was it about Willis that made him a successful gubernatorial candidate—and a successful governor?

Little in his background predicted such advancement, for his early life followed an outline similar to many others of his generation and profession. Born December 1, 1879, in Aid Township, Lawrence County, Ohio, Simeon Willis was the youngest of nine children and the seventh son of a seventh son. (His birth certificate contains no middle initial or middle name. He apparently added the "S" later for convenience.) Willis's father, John H., was a Civil War veteran of the Union Army, a farmer, and a contractor in the iron industry; his mother, Abigail Slavens, was also a native of Ohio. The family moved across the Ohio River to Greenup County, Kentucky, when Willis was about ten years old. In that locale he continued the schooling begun earlier and, after courses in a private teacher training school, passed the examination for teachers. Never attending college, "Sim" began teaching in 1898; before he was twenty he served as principal of a small grade school in Springville (now South Portsmouth), Kentucky.

But other professions attracted, and during those same years Willis presented his political ideas through the editorial pages of newspapers in Portsmouth, Ohio, and in Greenup County, Kentucky. He also began increasingly to make his way—often via bicycle—to Ironton, Ohio, where he studied law under the tutelage of Judge William D. Corn. Nearer to his home, Willis received similar private lessons from Josiah Bentley Bennett, a Republican county judge and later congressman. Willis apparently learned well, for he was admitted to the bar on November 11, 1901, and from that time on the law remained as perhaps his real love in public life, even exceeding politics. Whether as a member of an important firm in Ashland, where he moved, or, six years later, as an attorney in his own firm, Willis gained and retained a reputation as a lawyer's lawyer. Much later, when Willis received a citation for outstanding service to the bar, the chief justice of the state's highest court told those assembled, "If books and learning are the tools of a lawyer, then this man's mind is a crystalline library—and . . . whenever opportunity affords, I borrow a volume." Well-versed in his field and financially successful, Willis increased his stature later when he revised and rewrote the respected *Thornton on the Law of Oil and Gas* (6 volumes, 1932).

Yet during all that time the Ashland attorney could not ignore combining the law with politics. In 1905 he ran for city attorney but was defeated; in 1916 he sought election in the Republican primary for a seat on Kentucky's highest court. Later Governor Flem D. Sampson won that race, with Willis third. Finally, successful in 1918, Willis won a four-year term as city solicitor. On the completion of that post, he served an almost six-year stint as a member of the state board of bar examiners. But then, on the last day of 1927, came the action that gave Simeon Willis statewide recognition: Governor Sampson appointed his former opponent to what is now the Kentucky Supreme Court, to fill the vacancy left by Sampson's elevation to the governor's office. The next year Willis won a full four-year term.

But running for office for a Republican was still an uncertain gamble in Kentucky, especially so in the Roosevelt landslide year of 1932. Democrat Alex Ratliff defeated Willis's reelection bid, and in 1933 the former justice returned to Ashland and private practice once more. Over the next decade he held no office but continued to build a reputation as a respected and learned attorney.

Willis's years as jurist had been happy ones; those as lawyer were as well. And the changes that had taken place in his career had been matched by changes in private life. Marriage came in 1920, to Ida Lee Millis, then a deputy county clerk and a forthright and supportive woman, who would be an active participant in party politics in her own right. In 1921 only child Sara Lesley ("Sally") was born. The household she entered was one where the father might play the violin or guitar and certainly would read poetry and history late into the night, the latter so that he could learn, he said, from the leaders of the past. Willis continued his involvement in numerous organizations, including, over his career, the Masonic order, the Benevolent and Protective Order of Elks, various bar associations, the Boys' Clubs of America, and the Kentucky Civil War Round Table.

But in 1943, the organizations and the law took a back seat to Willis's search, once more, for political success. A decade after his reelection defeat, he now sought the Republican nomination for governor. No opposition faced him in the primary, but the general election presented a much different outlook. True, outgoing Governor Keen Johnson had seen his administration damaged by several incidents; and Willis's opposition for the governor's race, J. Lyter Donaldson of Carrollton, was not a strong candidate. In fact, the Democratic primary had, as usual, been bitter, and, as the commissioner of highways, Donaldson had received much criticism. But, on the other hand, Republicans had not won the governor's race since 1927—sixteen years earlier—and it was wartime, when the people might be more hesitant to change.

Standing before a large audience at Mt. Sterling, in his opening address of the campaign, Willis spoke to the concerns of Kentuckians. He told them how he would support rural highways, pour badly needed money into education, plan for the postwar world, and operate a frugal but reform-oriented administration. Pointing to what he pictured as a corrupt Democratic political machine, the man from Ashland said it was time to change, wartime or not; besides, all Americans supported the war effort, no matter what their party. During the campaign, his most controversial program would be his call for repeal of the state income tax.

Before audiences the Republican candidate left a good impression. Over six feet tall, the handsome, white-haired, sixty-three-year-old Willis projected an aura of judicial reserve and dignity, while also presenting a lighter touch as well. He would usually speak extemporaneously and without strong emotion; but that may have been his election appeal in a chaotic, wartime year, when people perhaps sought calm assurance and stability. In reality, his real platform may simply have been his character.

Election day brought a narrow victory to Willis as he garnered 279,144 votes to Donaldson's 270,525. The national attention gained in the important off-year election made Willis an attractive vice-presidential choice the next year, and he would gain some support for that position in the 1944 Republican convention.

But Willis's attentions focused on the state scene in 1943, and there the prospects for success were not bright. First of all, the legislature remained in the hands of the opposition party (the House would be 56-44 Democratic; then at the end of his term, 69-31; the Senate would be 23-15 and 21-17 Democratic). Not only that, but two powerful members of the Democratic party—Earle Clements and Harry Lee Waterfield—controlled each house and were building power for the gubernatorial primary they would enter in 1947. Powerful opponents faced him, eager to capitalize on the situation.

Within Willis's own party all was not harmony and sweetness. Now victorious, the Republicans found themselves increasingly divided by the factionalism so associated earlier with the Democracy. During the course of the administration Lieutenant Governor Kenneth Tuggle, Superintendent of Public Instruction John Fred Williams, and Attorney General Eldon Dummit all had public disagreements with Willis; mountain political leader John Robsion eventually united with a one-time Willis ally, the Louisville Republican Jouett Ross Todd, to oppose the governor as well. Even the governor's appointment of William A. Stanfill of Hazard to fill a short-term vacancy caused by A. B. Chandler's resignation of his Senate seat caused divisions.

But, as the administration opened, all that took second place to the primary concern of winning, on the homefront, the battle of World War II. Nearly a quarter of a million of the state's citizens had left the commonwealth as a result of the war effort. Restrictions were placed on the state government in building and many other fields. And the question of how the commonwealth, and the nation, would adjust to the great changes that would be brought about by war's end, whenever that would be, hung heavy over the heads of the leadership as well.

Yet, if not the best of times, neither was it the worst. The new governor utilized the situation to his benefit. Refusing to instigate a wholesale removal of Democratic office-holders—a move that drew heavy Republican criticism—Willis sought to keep experienced people in office in the personnel-starved war years. He would remark later that he was proudest in his administration of the spirit of cooperation and self-sacrifice he found in state government. In the political sphere that spirit of fraternity proved less present, but even there Willis tried to play off the two Democratic factions against each other, with varying degrees of success.

Frustrations emerged over the four-year term, of course. In the field of higher education, a political struggle related to the presidency of what is now Morehead State University resulted in a brief suspension of that school by the American Association of Teachers Colleges, while an imbroglio at the University of Kentucky involving a young student named Harry Caudill resulted in an investigation there. Other matters—such as the wholesale dismissal of members of the Kentucky Aeronautics Commission—caused brief furors also. A more prolonged struggle arose in the legislative arena, however, as the financially conservative governor had two involved budget fights with the General Assembly. In 1944, citing "uncertain and changing" economic conditions, Willis did not request repeal of the income tax; but two years later he did fulfill that campaign pledge when he made such a request. Twenty-four percent of state revenues came from that tax; the legislature did not repeal. In both 1944 and 1946, and in a special session as well, acrid infighting, mostly of a party nature, took place over finances. Finally resolved, the whole conflict left behind some bitterness. At the end of his term Willis turned over what was to that time the largest surplus in the treasury.

Overcoming the conflicts and the setbacks, however, were the considerable achievements, particularly in education, health and welfare, transportation, race relations, and postwar planning. In the field of education, for example, per capita payments to the schools almost doubled, from $13.49 to $25.66. Similarly, a special legislative appropriation in 1944 of $3 million for teachers' salaries was retroactive to the previous year; overall the average salary for teachers increased 94 percent, from $782 to $1,325 a year. The school term was also extended a month, and the allowable maximum tax rate a county could levy was doubled. At the end of his term an important education study, the Griffenhagen Report, was issued (and, as one writer noted, was "duly reported by the press, then filed away in the State Library"). While education in Kentucky still lagged far behind some of its neighboring states, the Willis administration made tremendous strides to correct the situation.

Although not as spectacular as the educational advancements, improvements in the fields of health and welfare proved equally significant in the long run. Old age assistance increased 65 percent over the four years, while aid to dependent children went 72 percent higher. Tuberculosis, a major health concern, was a chief target, and five new T.B. hospitals were financed—in London, Ashland, Paris, Madisonville, and Glasgow—while an existing one in Louisville was renovated. Major and badly needed improvements were made to the eleemosynary institutions as well.

In numerous other areas, the Willis administration made important advances. One of the most notable of these was in civil rights. The governor created a Commission on Negro Affairs (said to be the first of its kind in the South) in September 1944—a decade before the famous *Brown* decision. Its actions helped Kentucky's generally smooth integration transition a decade later. Willis also appointed a black to the State Board of Education for the first time and supported the act that made Lincoln Institute a state-supported high school and teacher training center. Segregated schools would continue in Kentucky until the 1950s, but the Willis administration greatly increased the meager aid given blacks who had to attend out-of-state professional schools because of segregation statutes. And in state government itself several positions previously denied blacks were opened to them.

Other accomplishments between 1943 and 1947 included the removal of charges from twelve of the thirteen remaining toll bridges in Kentucky and considerable improvement in efficiency within the Department of Highways. Those free bridges and better roads took people to enhanced parks as well, and revenue from that source more than doubled from the prewar peak. *Courier-Journal* reporter Allan Trout, in fact, listed as one of Willis's key accomplishments the fact that "he encouraged the germ of an idea to take root in his administration—the idea that a new tourist economy can be created in Kentucky." In a related area, the administration reorganized the Division of Game and Fish, making it an independent agency more responsible to state sportsmen. A Tax Revision Commission and the Postwar Planning Commission both presented recommendations for future changes; the Willis administration instituted many of the suggestions, while many others would be accomplished in future administrations.

Whether it was educational aid to the young or support for the unfortunate, care for the elderly, better recreation for all, improved roads and free bridges for drivers, increased opportunity for blacks, or simply better planning for the postwar future, the Willis administration left behind a legacy that touched a wide spectrum of the commonwealth's citizens. In an administration unshaken by scandal, Willis departed with a reputation as an honest, reform-minded conservative—one who left the state much improved because of his actions.

At the conclusion of his administration, Simeon Willis returned to his law practice. He ran for a seat on the state's highest court in 1951, but lost to future Democratic governor Bert Combs. It was his last race. From 1956 to 1960, Willis served on the Public Service Commission and, following that, to 1965, on the State Parole Board. He died on April 2, 1965, at the age of eighty-five and was buried in the Frankfort Cemetery.

PREINAUGURAL ADDRESSES

OPENING OF GUBERNATORIAL CAMPAIGN
Mount Sterling / September 29, 1943

FELLOW citizens:

On November the second the people of Kentucky will choose the kind of government we shall have for the next four years. I bear the banner of the Republican party with that deep sense of responsibility which any man must feel when he is fighting for the cause of good government. The success of the cause is vital, and I ask the aid of all voters who share with me the desire to recover for the people the right to govern themselves. This election happens at a time when the country is engaged in a global war which engrosses the energies and the efforts of the whole people. We are united behind our country and its leaders against our common foes.

The first duty confronting the people of Kentucky and the nation is the utter defeat of the Axis powers. To the performance of that duty all Kentuckians have dedicated themselves—Republicans, Democrats, and Independents. If any man for mere political advantage should dare to question the loyalty of the Republicans, or the unity of the American people in the prosecution of this war, he would himself be lacking in patriotism. The fact that Republican governors are giving full support to the war effort without a single complaint from our war leaders, prevents the machine from hiding behind the war to claim a partisan advantage.

Representatives of the Republican party have expressed the attitude of our party when they approved, "the prosecution of the war by a united nation to a conclusive victory over our enemies, including (1) disarmament and disorganization of the armed forces of the Axis; (2) disqualification of the Axis to construct facilities for the manufacture of the instruments of war; (3) permanent maintenance of trained and well-equipped armed forces at home."[1]

The second problem confronting the American people today is that of devising some plan to prevent, if possible, the recurrence of war. Certainly, the future is black indeed if the ordeal we are now suffering must be repeated every quarter of a century. Dare any man suggest that Republicans are less anxious to prevent future wars than any other citizen?

Mr. Donaldson[2] professes to fear the psychological effect of my election upon the successful prosecution of the war, or, in any event, upon the making of a durable peace. What Mr. Donaldson really fears is the devastating effect of my election upon his political machine.

Neither the effective prosecution of the war nor the negotiation of a permanent peace could be affected in any way by my election. My position is that this nation is a part of the world and must be concerned by all that happens in the world. We cannot be safe when there is safety nowhere else. We cannot maintain our honor and our self-respect nationally unless we stand up for our principles everywhere. Such being true, it follows that in peace and for the sake of peace, we must work resolutely with other well-disposed sovereign nations for the permanent maintenance of order and justice. In the governor's office or as a private citizen I shall support any honorable and practicable plan for international cooperation that may promote the peace for which we all pray.

The American people, in cooperation with their allies, will not fail to do all that wisdom may dictate to establish enduring peace. That problem may be left with them.

The immediate problem of the voters of Kentucky is the destruction of the corrupt political machine which has grown up at Frankfort during the past few years. Good government is even more essential in time of war.

The central issue in this campaign is a conflict between two ideas of government. My own idea is that the people should rule and that this should be a government by the people for the people. The concept of machine rule is that the people are to be exploited for the benefit of the machine. It has its favorites who sell their influence and capitalize their friendship. Such men collect campaign funds and enjoy lucrative employments by those seeking government favor. They constitute the so-called invisible government.

The state political machine operates upon that system, which is not only corrupt, but destructive of home rule and common decency. Our government must be clean; it must be honest, and it must be obedient to the constitution and the laws. The evils that create so much resentment among our people are the natural results of that false conception of the function of government by which machines are operated and maintained. The machine system is built upon the idea that nominations and elections to office should be controlled and dictated by the bosses. The recent Democratic primary affords a good example. A group of men, rotating among themselves from one office to another, were chosen in advance to be supported, and no man against the machine was permitted to have a chance. Mr. Wilson,[3] nominee for treasurer, is the only new face on the machine ticket, and already he has shown that his conception of public duty accords with the practices of the machine. He has offered to retain the employees in the treasurer's office if they would contribute to the campaign fund, with the promise to raise their pay in January to match their contributions. The direct connection of the campaign fund with the state treasury is thus flaunted in our faces.

By the same false notion, the appointment and employment of help in all the branches of the state government is regarded as a function of the machine, for which assessments may be exacted for the benefit of the organization. It follows naturally when an employee has paid for his position, or earned it by service to the machine, he feels no obligation to the public. He accepts the authority of the machine and looks to it alone for favors.

The power of the machine is used to obtain state contracts for those who will contribute to campaign funds. This system leads to soap scandals and laundry deals of which we hear, and to countless evils of that character of which we do not learn. Selfish interests have no regard for public virtue.

D.C. Moore[4] exposed the facts about truckers. They contributed to the 1939 campaign fund.[5] Mr. Donaldson handled some of the money, and he failed to report it. Why did the truckers contribute? Moore says they were promised favorable legislation, but the promise was broken. Why did Mr. Donaldson and Mr. Johnson[6] conceal the shakedown? It was contrary to law but was the natural working of a system when public favors are sold.

Our opponents still believe in and practice the system. The recent appointment of a professional lobbyist as finance chairman for this campaign exposes the plan.[7] They are preparing to shake down the corporations that hire lobbyists to prevent legislation they do not like or to promote legislation they seek. Mr. Donaldson may be known by the company he keeps, but his finance chairman is known by the companies that keep him. That act proclaims the purpose to carry on in the future as in the past, and on a larger scale. It is as indefensible as it was arrogant. The pious hope that improvement might be expected is dashed rudely to the ground. So long as the machine is supported, it will practice its own brand of politics. Whoever endorses it supports its crimes and condones its wrongs. The machine grows more arrogant as it wins. It defies the independent voters. Its leaders defy the statutes of the state and disregard the obligations of the oath of office.

The same false philosophy is the source of the sorry spectacle of the governor having to be enjoined by the courts from violation of the very laws he was sworn to enforce.[8]

The attitude of the machine politician is that a road may be built or a building constructed or some public improvement made in a particular locality as a favor to the public directly affected for which the machine should be rewarded. The truth is the people are entitled in their own right to roads and other improvements for which they pay. Public officials should be happy to perform their public obligations and to execute the people's will. Under a proper conception of the functions of government that is always the case. If anybody doubts that the machine is corrupt, or that it means to dominate and control the affairs of the people of this state, let them recall the public speeches of General Meredith, Mr. Kilgore, and Mr. Meyers.[9] Many of the charges were established in court, and the others were not even denied. The only law the machine likes is the statute of limitations.

When the attorney general sued successfully to recover money paid as salary, for work not done, to a relative supported at the time in a state institution, the governor did not discharge the culprit.[10] He promoted him to a better job.

The direct savings in money resulting from suits filed by General Meredith run into large figures. And no one can estimate the indirect value of his watchfulness and courage. The governor may call these wrongs "fly-specks,"[11] but the assaults of the machine on the fundamental principles of government present an issue of profound importance. The people appreciate the meaning of these many exposures. They know the symptoms of corruption when it appears. Certainly they know what to do about it.

It is the system that has prevailed in Kentucky for the past years that has resulted in the corruption of elections and in scandals in the public service. It is the same system used by Hague in New Jersey, by Kelly-Nash in Chicago, and other machines.[12] It is nothing more or less than the Tammany brand of machine politics that believes in selling government favors for campaign funds and common graft. The system must be destroyed. We must have a government of law, based on the simple idea that public office is a public trust. Instead of government by the machine and for the machine, we must restore it to the people.

Those free men and women who fought for principle in the recent Democratic primary were right, and they will finally win. They have lost a battle, but they have not lost the war. They cannot afford to wait four years for another battle with the machine. It will cost the people too much, and it would allow the machine time to widen its grasp and to enlarge its power. It must be destroyed now and not allowed to fatten another four years on the hard-earned money of the taxpayers.

My belief is that it is useless to debate anything else until we destroy the system that glorifies the machine, corrupts elections, and demoralizes the government. It is futile to talk about reform or constructive policies so long as we are dominated by machine rule. First things come first, and until we clean house at Frankfort nothing else can receive just treatment. In my opinion, the people are ready now to make a change. The new administration will be prepared to meet the responsibility and will follow the principles of a true republican form of government. It shall be our constant purpose to give the people the kind of government which they demand. Our program will be positive and constructive.

At the very forefront is the problem of taxation. The taxpayers of this state are staggering under the burdens placed on them in the form of state and federal taxes. On account of the war the heavy federal taxes have been necessarily increased, and this will continue for a long time to come, growing greater every day the war lasts. The chairman of the House Ways and Means Committee,[13] and the chief executive of the nation, have called upon the various states to reduce expenses and lower taxes, in order that the taxpayers might be enabled to meet their responsibilities to the nation. Many of the states have responded to this obvious need, but this state has been deaf to the plea. The proposition now advanced by Mr. Donaldson is for still more spending and still heavier taxes. In his speech at Carrollton in June of this year and again at Madisonville last Saturday, he promised no saving in expenses or reduction in taxes, but asked for additional annual appropriations amounting to $6 million.

It must be remembered that "taxes are paid in the sweat of every man who labors because they are a burden on production and are paid through production." Everyone is a taxpayer, whether or not he knows it. The people are willing to pay the cost of all the essential services of the government. The schools must be maintained, the courts conducted, the charitable and penal institutions sustained; the public health service and the indispensable agencies of the state must be carried on. The constitution has been amended to provide for the aged people unable to provide for themselves and for the afflicted, and the obligation to these wards of the state cannot be denied. These inescapable expenses must be provided and paid, but beyond that there is no right to take the hard-earned money of the taxpayers to fatten a political machine.

The state income tax, under present conditions, is an unjust burden, and the purpose for which it was adopted has been served. It should be the first tax to be repealed, and by its repeal industrial enterprises will be stimulated and encouraged. The collateral damage resulting from this particular tax is far-reaching, and the benefits that will flow from its repeal will be quickly manifested. It has been so in sister states, and it will be so in this state. The loss to the general fund from the repeal of this tax can be replaced by a determined reduction of expenses, by savings resulting from a proper management of the purchasing department, and by cutting the enormous payroll of the state, as any good business manager would slash it. When that tax was enacted, the state had interest-bearing warrants outstanding in excess of $22 million.[14] This has been paid by the taxpayers and a large surplus accumulated. The need for such a tax no longer exists, and justice to the taxpayers and public require its repeal.

The question of taxation is difficult and always will be difficult. Certain objectives must be accepted and a tax program formulated to attain them. The first of these objectives should be a reduction of the tax burden on the people of Kentucky. The next necessity is that the budget be kept in balance, and expense must not exceed income. A pay-as-you-go policy is sound and must be observed. Excessive taxation for the purpose of creating a surplus is indefensible. A surplus dervied from economies, savings, and good management is the kind of surplus that should be sought. The expense of government must be curtailed to the fullest extent possible, consistent with the efficiency of the service.

Similar objectives have been attained in other states, and they can be achieved here. They can be accomplished without the income tax, without a sales tax, and without any additional taxes. The first thing toward the attainment of any objective is the will to accomplish it. The expense of corrupt government is always greater than the people know; and when we get rid of the waste, extravagance, and corruption at Frankfort, our problem will be clarified and its solution found possible.

In seeking revenue for the necessary expenses of a sound and honest administration, the principle of taxing to be observed is the ability to pay, with due consideration to preserving the productive capacity of the people and to maintaining the buying power of consumers. It is high time that consideration be given to the welfare of the state as a whole and that the limits of the capacity of the people to bear the burdens of government be impressed upon those in authority. In my judgment, we have in Kentucky the courage, talent, and capacity to carry out this program. When I am elected governor I shall work with the General Assembly in this, as in all things, to bring relief to the heavily burdened people of Kentucky.

The Department of Highways is headed by a commissioner who has sole charge of the administration of the department. The law creates nine advisory commissioners who are paid $3,000 each per annum and their traveling expenses. They have no authority or responsibility and constitute nothing more or less than political workers for the machine at the expense of the state. It has been the cause of much criticism and source of the corruption of elections. It is common knowledge that the payroll of the highway department is unduly increased just before a primary or general election. There is no reason or excuse for the existence of these advisory commissioners, and they should be abolished. The department should be removed from politics. The construction of roads should be placed in the hands of competent engineers and experienced people specially qualified to build roads.

The only legitimate business of the highway department is the construction and maintenance of roads. That is all the people should pay for at any time. With road building placed on a practical basis in the hands of real road-builders, the scandals at each election will cease.

It is inexcusable that applicants for work on the highway should have to join the machine in order to get a job. Not only must they join up to get work, but they must pay assessments for campaign funds so long as they have jobs. Thus the machine finances itself indirectly from the taxpayer's money, filtering it through the hands of workers, foremen, and contractors. When I become governor, the General Assembly will be asked to remove the highway department from politics and reorganize [it] to build and maintain roads instead of political fences.

The rural roads have been neglected. Many county judges of the state have protested against the mismanagement of the rural road funds. These roads are among the most important in the state. They open up the markets to the farmers and promote the welfare of the communities served. They are an asset of the whole people. Under competent management there will be no difficulty in building rural roads. The county is primarily concerned with these roads, and the counties should have a voice in the administration of this rural road fund.

Under a proper reorganization, the rural road fund can be materially increased, probably doubled. A statute should be enacted giving reasonable control to the fiscal courts over the expenditure of this fund. The state should reserve only such power and supervision as may be necessary to protect the interests of the state and to secure standard construction. This involves a principle of home rule, as well as simple justice, which should be observed at all times in legislation and administration. Insofar as possible each community should enjoy complete home rule, with such state supervision only as subserves the general welfare. The rural road funds should be safeguarded by every means necessary for the purpose.

The employment of workers or contractors in the construction and maintenance of rural roads should be vested in the fiscal court, with sufficient supervision in the state engineering department to require standards to be maintained and to prevent waste or improvidence. The reorganization should be made on the basis of getting the roads built honestly, economically, and with due regard for the rights of citizens whose only object is to obtain good roads at reasonable cost. But since the rural roads are the property of the county, and the people of the county are primarily interested in building and maintaining them, they should have the authority in the counties to get effective action. When politics is eliminated from the roads, and it becomes a mere problem of engineering construction and honest supervision, the needs of the people will be satisfied.

In a representative republic the education of youth is a prime necessity. The impact of war has brought us face to face with the seriousness of the problem of schools. It cannot be delayed; it cannot be avoided. The children must be educated and prepared for the future, and that is a present obligation. I shall urge the General Assembly to make provision to supplement the available money for the school year 1943-1944. This should be at least $3 million and should be retroactive to the beginning of the school year. The distribution should be made to county and independent school districts on the per capita basis, as an addition to the basal monthly salary of the teachers for the number of months of service rendered and to be rendered for the entire school year. For the school years 1944-1945, and for 1945-1946, an appropriation for the common school fund of not less than $15 million for each school will be requested by me. The full 10 percent authorized by the constitution to be distributed as an equalization fund should be allotted. The law should be revised to provide for a wider distribution of this fund so as to help more of the school districts where the schools are entitled to aid.

For several years extensive efforts have been made by educators and other public spirited citizens to obtain federal aid for schools, with the reservation of complete control by the state over its schools and over the distribution of all funds provided for education. I shall do all in my power to secure the success of this plan.

The best brains of the profession are and should be employed to provide a permanent program of gradual improvement, so that never again shall our schools be permitted to lapse into a condition like the present one.

I will strike the hand of machine politics from our schools and rescue their administration from the grasp of machine politicians. The schools belong to the people and should be devoted solely to education.

I am in full sympathy with the general program outlined by the Kentucky Education Association and shall aid in every way possible to promote the welfare of the schools.[15]

The elementary schools, and particularly the rural schools, should be constantly improved. Free text books should be provided, as at present.

The institutions of higher learning are a priceless asset of the state, and we must give them at all times liberal and loyal support.

Postwar problems will have to be solved by educated men and women, and it is not too soon to begin and to pursue a program based on the best thought of our educational leaders.

Education belongs to all, regardless of race, color, or creed, and we should be alert to provide equal educational opportunities for all of Kentucky's children. There should be equality of pay for equal service, and no discrimination on account of race should be permitted. A qualified Negro should be placed in the State Department of Education as assistant supervisor of Negro education or in some similar capacity. High school education should be provided for Negro youths who live in sections of the state where it is not now furnished. This should be done by the establishment and maintenance of boarding school service at the Lincoln Institute and at the West Kentucky State Vocational Training School.[16]

It should be made legally impossible to remove the members of state appointive boards except for good cause, and after a fair trial. The law regarding the appointment of members of the boards of regents and trustees of institutions of higher learning should be observed, and provision should be made to secure its enforcement. The flagrant disregard of the directions of the statute is indefensible and must be stopped. The removal of the schools from the influence of the machine system and placing them solely in the hands of educators interested only in education will enable the people to build an educational structure worthy of Kentucky.

The people of Kentucky amended the constitution so as to provide assistance for aged and dependent people.[17] The legislature has made some provision toward carrying this provision into effect. The act accords with the Social Security Act enacted by Congress, and the funds paid by Kentucky are supplemented by the federal treasury. The administration of this humanitarian act has been inefficient, gross discrimination has been practiced, and the machine has used the funds in an attempt to control the votes of these good people. The aged people resent this dictation and feel that their rights as American citizens have been invaded. This money is not derived from the favor of the machine, but is a right of the aged conferred by their fellow men. The machine has tried to make them feel that they owed something to the machine, and that they were no longer free American citizens with the right to express what they thought and to vote as they chose.

I wish to say to these deserving people throughout the state that when I am your governor you may bring to me any complaints you may have, and you may, with complete candor and without fear, utter any criticism of my administration that you believe justified. Many complaints have been brought to me of prolonged failure to put qualified old people on the list of eligibles. There are many thousands of them. The administration of this trust fund should be removed from politics and placed in the hands of an administrator who has the ability to organize and to carry out the purposes of the law. All discriminations must cease and equality of treatment must be accorded to all eligible to participate.

The waste of this money to pay machine favorites, the accumulation of funds for distribution just before election, the freezing of the lists so as to exclude thousands entitled to the benefits, and other evils that have been practiced will be stopped. This fund must be honestly administered for the welfare of the people for whom it was intended, and every dollar appropriated by the legislature shall be paid honestly and promptly to those who need and deserve it. The amount now provided is very small and should be increased as rapidly as the financial position of the state will permit. Nothing will give me greater satisfaction than the accomplishment of these purposes. The administration of a fund provided by the people for those who have reached a point where they are not able to provide for themselves is a sacred trust. A comparison with similar funds in sister states will demonstrate how this fund has been mismanaged and mishandled in Kentucky. Attorney General Meredith has endeavored to correct many of these abuses, but he has met with opposition and obstruction; and there is no remedy except to defeat the machine and place the control in the hands of men with the correct conception of the nature and purpose of government by the people.

The present machine has persistently violated the fundamental principle of home rule. For example, the power to value property for assessment purposes has been taken to Frankfort. This power should be restored to the people of each county; and the duly elected tax commissioners, as created by the constitution, should be freed from dictation from Frankfort. The only fair thing for the state is such limited supervision as may be necessary to secure equalization of values among the counties.

Power is a dangerous thing and must be kept in control. Every increase of power reduces the liberty of the citizen and increases the tax burden on the people. The tendency toward the extension of power over all the activities of the people must be reversed in favor of greater liberty in everyday affairs.

Another instance of injustice is the power conferred on the state to force citizens in any county to leave their homes and attend court at Frankfort in controversies with the state or some of the departments. The state should be compelled to litigate on equal terms with every other litigant, and the jurisdiction in such cases should be restored to the county of the citizen's residence.

The principle by which we shall be guided is that justice shall be done in every case, and the powers of government shall not be used to oppress and harass our people. The principle of home rule in purely local affairs is fundamental in our form of government and may not be safely infringed. My opponent in his speech in the primary campaign proclaimed his acceptance of this principle, but the course of conduct of the machine administration contradicts the profession. The test of the machine policy is its acts, and not the declaration of its votaries. In view of his statement, however, Mr. Donaldson should join me in securing restoration of home rule in all local matters.

Machine politics must be removed from the schools, from the highway department, from the charitable and penal institutions, from the administration of old age pensions, from the public parks, from the Fish and Game Division, and from every department of government. The sole test of a laborer for the state should be his or her character and fitness for the task and readiness to render honest work for fair pay. There should be no discrimination by reason of race or political affiliation.

Machine politics has involved the whole fabric of our government, and the system has infected all of the activities of the state. This shall be stopped and the government restored to the sound principle of equal rights to all and special privileges to none.

The purchasing department has been found inefficient, negligent, and given to favoritism. It spends millions of dollars every year and no one knows how much the people lost through its operation. It must be radically reorganized and put on a business basis of efficiency and honesty.

The release of large numbers now on the state payroll will relieve the manpower shortage in war work. There are many now living off the state who should be in the army or navy or in some war work.

Men and women who earn their livelihood in the sweat of their brows have a vital interest in clean and honest government. Whether farmers, wage earners, or white collar workers, they are not the type that will give support to crookedness. They resent dictation from any source. I believe in labor unions honestly managed. If not honestly managed, they hurt the laboring men. I am friendly to labor and sympathetic with all measures for the advancement and welfare of workers in all lines of endeavor. As provided by national law, I believe any man or woman has a right to join the union of his or her choice.

It shall be my purpose at all times to promote peace and good will among our people. Friendly relations between labor and management are a condition of the prosperity of all. In candor and good will, differences can be fairly adjusted. Both the wage earner and the wage payer have a common interest in peace and justice, and all citizens of whatever calling desire the prosperity and success of business enterprise. My obligation as governor will be to all the people and in that spirit I dedicate my services to the commonwealth and its progress. I call upon all honest men and women, regardless of occupation or party, to join us in this campaign to smash machine politics and to restore to the people themselves the right to run their own government in their own way.

After the war is over the state will return to peaceful pursuits. Then thousands of men and women who have served in the various branches of the war and war industry will be coming home. They must find their places in a free enterprise system where they may live and shape their futures. Kentucky will never falter in her obligation to these patriots, and everything that can be done to help them will be done. As governor, I shall give every possible aid to every plan for the welfare of the men and women who are serving their country.

The limitations of time forbid a discussion of many subjects of interest and importance. The laws relating to elections, corrupt practices, alcoholic liquor control, fish and game, the disabled veterans, parks and forests, and many others, require revision and improvement in the light of experience and from the standpoint of service to the state. These will be discussed during the campaign and at convenient times and places.

It is sufficient to say now that all these subjects shall be approached in the same spirit I have indicated in discussing other matters. Sound business shall be substituted for political manipulation.

From time to time I shall discuss the various points appearing in the speeches of Mr. Donaldson. On the things about which we agree there need be no argument or misunderstanding. Certainly we all want industrial development. That is a nonpartisan question upon which all Kentuckians can agree as to its necessity. The means to be adopted may result in differences of opinion, but certainly some plan can be devised which will utilize the natural resources of Kentucky and provide work for her people without requiring them to leave home.

As a matter of principle I oppose the creating of commissions and boards at the expense of the state. Insofar as studies may be necessary, I prefer to use experts at the institutions of higher learning and public officials specially charged with duties and possessing qualifications respecting the particular subject matter.

Some of the buildings and equipment of the state institutions have been permitted to become obsolete and to fall into disrepair, and many of them are in a deplorable condition. The reconstruction and repair of all these institutions must be carried to completion.

The farmers of this state represent its greatest productive interest. The legislature should restore to the commissioner of agriculture, labor, and statistics his rightful authority to conduct the affairs properly belonging to that department of government. The state fair should be returned to his supervision and management. In connection with the other facilities provided by the university, he can do great things for the benefit of the farming industry of the state; but he cannot do these things if the hand of politics is continually repressing him. We have nominated a practical farmer who is also a capable administrator for this department. It will be a great gain for the farmers when their department is restored to its rightful position in the state government. What the farmer desired is relief from taxation and from political interference with his normal activities.

The ripper legislation depriving the constitutional officers of their rightful powers should be repealed, and I shall ask the General Assembly to restore to the attorney general full power to represent the state and its departments in all legal matters. The same should be done for the secretary of state and the other officers who have been deprived by ripper bills of duties and powers properly belonging to them.[18]

I take just pride in the ticket that has been nominated with me. It is representative in every sense of the word and fairly distributed over the state.[19] The women are represented by the nominee for secretary of state.[20] That is fitting in these days when the women are sharing in all the hardships of war and of war work. They will be a controlling factor in this election, and to them I look with confidence to stand foursquare in my fight for good government. As you are to meet each of them I refrain from special mention of each one. I will add that when these nominees are placed in the state offices, the public may rest assured that their affairs will be in safe hands.

These are serious times. Our country is engaged in a global war, and the republic is in grave peril. Our armed forces are fighting on all fronts, on land, on sea, in the air, and down under the sea. They are fighting for the fundamental rights of man against dictatorial power, and they are as heroic, as devoted, and as magnificent as any army that ever defended our flag. We who do not share their danger can and will give them all we have—our work, our money, our intelligence, our confidence, our all. America is united as one in support of the war effort, and all that Americans can do to promote its success will be done. Our hearts, our hopes, our prayers are with our defenders; and all that we have and are will be devoted to them and dedicated to their certain victory. They are sacrificing all they have for the honor of our country, and we shall not forget for one moment that the paramount duty of every man, woman, and child at home is to contribute in every way possible everything possessed to support them. Every man, regardless of party, must help to see that everything demanded or desired by the armed forces shall be produced. Kentuckians will not falter in that duty.

Some day millions of men and women of these military forces will return from this war, with the banner of victory over them and ask: "What have you done with what we left?" The answer must be: "We have preserved the right of opportunity in a free enterprise, with a government responsive to the people's will."

---

1. The quotation is from a report on foreign policy adopted by the Republican Postwar Advisory Council meeting at Mackinac Island, September 7, 1943. New York *Times*, September 8, 1943.

2. J. Lyter Donaldson (1891-1960), Kentucky native; county attorney of Carroll County (1921-30); bank president; member of highway commission (1930-36); commissioner of highways (1939-43); Democratic candidate for governor in 1943; chairman of Democratic State Central Executive Committee (1944-48). *Who's Who in Kentucky . . . 1936* (Louisville, 1936), 114; Louisville *Courier-Journal*, August 1, 1943 and March 28, 1960 (hereafter *Courier-Journal*).

3. Holman R. Wilson, the Democratic candidate for treasurer, was a Louisville broker. *Courier-Journal*, August 1, 1943.

4. D.C. Moore (1889-1955), Kentucky native; circuit court clerk and sheriff, Pike County; director (1936-40) and assistant director (1940-43), State Division of Motor Transportation. Frederick D. Ogden, ed., *The Public Papers of Governor Keen Johnson, 1939-1943* (Lexington, 1982), 511n.

5. Moore asserted he had raised money from motor truck interests to aid Keen Johnson's 1939 gubernatorial campaign. He charged that Donaldson (Johnson's campaign chairman) and the governor had authorized him to promise preferred legislation to trucking interests. The charges came out after Moore's resignation in July 1943 to support Rodes Myers's gubernatorial bid. Ibid., 509, 510n.

6. Keen Johnson (1896-1970), Kentucky native; editor and copublisher Richmond *Daily Register*; lieutenant governor 1935-39; governor on A.B. Chandler's resignation on October 9, 1939; elected to that office, served 1939-43; undersecretary of labor (1946-47); vice-president (1947-61) and director (1950-61), Reynolds Metals Company; served on Kentucky Council of Higher Education and Kentucky Board of Education; defeated for U.S. Senate seat in 1960. Ibid., 1-3.

7. The reference is to the appointment of Frankfort corporate lobbyist John Milliken as finance chairman for Donaldson's gubernatorial bid. *Courier-Journal*, October 3, 1943.

8. The state attorney general, an opponent of Governor Johnson, had obtained from the Franklin County Circuit Court a restraining order to prohibit the collection of campaign funds from state employees. The Court of Appeals sustained the injunction and the case went back to circuit court, but the parties never pushed the matter further. Ibid., July 10, 14, 1942; and Ogden, ed., *Papers of Keen Johnson*, 103n.

9. Hubert T. Meredith (1880-1956), Kentucky native; commonwealth attorney (1922-28); attorney general (1937-43). *Who's Who in Kentucky, 1936*, 281; *Courier-Journal*, January 1, 1957.

Benjamin W. Kilgore (1901-51), North Carolina native; associate editor, Kentucky-Tennessee edition of *Progressive Farmer* (1928-32); executive secretary of Kentucky Farm Bureau until 1944; defeated in Democratic gubernatorial primary of 1943; managed Harry Lee Waterfield's campaign in 1947 Democratic gubernatorial primary. Lexington *Herald*, May 30, 1951.

Rodes Kirby Myers (1900-59), Kentucky native; teacher and attorney; commonwealth attorney, sixth judicial district, 1933; state representative (1934-38, 1945); lieutenant governor, 1939-43; state senator, 1948-50; defeated in Democratic gubernatorial primary of 1943. *Who's Who in Kentucky* (Hopkinsville, Ky., [1955]), 243; and Ogden, ed., *Papers of Keen Johnson*, 11.

During the hotly contested Democratic primary in 1943, all three men made speeches attacking the Johnson administration for alleged corruption.

10. Frank D. Peterson, when assistant finance commissioner, had kept his brother-in-law, Shively Whitlock, on the state payroll (at $125 per month) while Whitlock was in jail, the workhouse, and Eastern State Hospital (for chronic alcoholism). On April 2, 1941, Peterson was appointed as business manager at the University of Kentucky. Twenty-six days after that a Franklin County jury returned a judgment of one thousand dollars against Peterson for his actions. *Courier-Journal*, April 29, 1941.

11. Governor Johnson had used this term in a Frankfort speech to the State Central Democratic Executive Committee. Ibid., September 2, 1943.

12. Frank Hague (1876-1956) of Jersey City was a dominant force in New Jersey Democratic politics from the 1920s through the 1940s. *Dictionary of American Biography* (hereafter *DAB*), *Supplement 6*: 265-66. Edward Joseph Kelly (1876-1950) was the political boss and mayor of Chicago (1933-47), while Patrick A. Nash (1863-1943), a sewer contractor, chaired the Cook County Democratic Central Committee. Ibid., *Supplement 4*: 450-51. Together Kelly and Nash controlled Chicago. See New York *Times*, October 7, 1943.

13. Robert Lee Doughton (1863-1954), banker; Democratic member of Congress from North Carolina (1911-52); chairman of Ways and Means Committee (1933-52). *Biographical Dictionary of the American Congress, 1774-1949* (Washington, D.C., 1950), 1098.

14. The state income tax had been established under Governor Chandler in a March 4-25, 1936, special session of the General Assembly. Kentucky *Acts* (Special Session, 1936), 67-101. On July 8, 1943, the Kentucky Tax Research Association had stated that the income tax—imposed to pay off the state debt—was no longer required. Seven states either repealed or reduced their state income taxes in 1943. See Ogden, ed., *Papers of Keen Johnson*, 115n.

15. For the general program of the Kentucky Education Association see *Kentucky School Journal* 21 (1943): 34-38.

16. Lincoln Institute, founded in 1910 and opened two years later, had been set up to provide education for blacks after they had been denied access by law to integrated classes at Berea College. Under the presidency of Whitney Young, Sr. (1935 to 1966) it became a public school and was supported by the state after 1947.

West Kentucky Vocational Training School, at Paducah, had earlier been a normal school and "Industrial College." By 1947, it was in its eighth year as a state school and provided two-year vocational training to three hundred students in such areas as carpentry, barbering, cooking, and sewing. See *Kentucky's Black Heritage* (Frankfort, 1971), 42-43, 64-65; *Biennial Report of the Superintendent of Public Instruction . . . for the Biennium Ended June 30, 1947* (n.p., 1947), 507-8; George C. Wright, "The Founding of Lincoln Institute," *Filson Club History Quarterly* 49 (1975): 64-68.

17. Section 244A of the Kentucky Constitution, which permits the General Assembly to pass laws "necessary for the granting and paying of old persons an annuity or pension," was adopted in November 1935.

18. Governor Keen Johnson's attorney general, Hubert T. Meredith, had long been in conflict with the chief executive; a 1942 act authorized state agencies to hire counsel independent of the attorney general's office, thereby "ripping" power from Meredith. See Ogden, ed., *Papers of Keen Johnson*, 104-5; Kentucky *Acts* (1942), 525-27; *Courier-Journal*, February 26, 1942.

19. The ticket was: Simeon Willis (Boyd County), for governor; Kenneth Tuggle (Knox), for lieutenant governor; Mary Landis Cave (Grayson), for secretary of state; Eldon S. Dummitt (Fayette), for attorney general; Thomas W. Vinson (Jefferson), for treasurer; Elliott Robertson (Henry), for agriculture commissioner; Charles Irvin Ross (Pulaski), for auditor; and John Fred Williams (Johnson), for superintendent of public instruction. *Courier-Journal*, August 1, 1943.

20. As it turned out, Mary Landis Cave was the only member of the ticket not elected in 1943.

INTERVIEW REGARDING ELECTION VICTORY
New York City / November 11, 1943

MANY issues entered our campaign, [including] the restlessness of the people who are resentful against too much interference in their home affairs and who believe sincerely there is too much concentration of power in federal officials.

It is a mistake to assume as some have that Kentucky people voted against the war. We are as much in the war as any other state; our boys are out there fighting whether they are Democrats or Republicans. We are all out for winning the war, and no sacrifice is too much for our people.

The national question was not urged in the campaign, although Senator Barkley[1] and Senator Chandler[2] came into the state and shouted that a vote against the Democratic ticket would be taken as a vote against the president and the war. The people had too much common sense to accept that view and simply laughed it off. To what extent the federal home front regimentation influenced the vote cannot, of course, be determined with any degree of accuracy. I declined to campaign on the Barkley issue.

The people in Kentucky were simply tired and fed up on the high-handed operations of the statehouse band of politicians which has been running the state for many years. The Democratic bosses had become so arrogant through years of power that they finally took the last step and thought they could elect themselves and continue their autocratic control. We have had ward politics in the state. Now that is at an end.

Occupational voting did not control. I had the votes of farmers, miners, businessmen, workers of every kind, women voters, and professional people. Our party carried counties which have been traditionally Democratic for so long none believed they ever would change.

The Democratic machine has doubled taxes in ten years. We have our first income state tax. Our schools are run down and our institutions badly need restoring to efficiency.

Our problem now is to reduce taxes and at the same time find the means to restore our equipment and institutions.

I go into office with a Democratic legislature.[3] I am hopeful that we may lay aside partisan politics and work out a constructive program to help the state. I am not trying to outline such a program until we have gone into conference and talked it all over.

---

1. Alben William Barkley (1877-1956), Kentucky native; prosecuting attorney and county judge for McCracken County; congressman, 1913-27; defeated in 1923 Democratic gubernatorial primary; U.S. senator, 1927-48, and Senate majority leader, 1937-46; U.S. vice-president, 1949-53; U.S. senator, 1955-56. *DAB, Supplement 6*: 34-36.

2. Albert Benjamin ("Happy") Chandler (1898-   ), Kentucky native; state senator from Woodford County, 1929-31; lieutenant governor, 1931-35; governor, 1935-39; defeated by Barkley in 1938 senatorial primary; appointed to U.S. Senate in 1939, following M.M. Logan's death; elected and served as senator 1940-45; baseball commissioner, 1945-51; governor for second time, 1955-59; defeated in later attempts at office. Albert Benjamin Chandler Papers, University of Kentucky Library, and Charles P. Roland "Albert Benjamin Chandler," in Lowell H. Harrison, ed., *Kentucky's Governors, 1792-1984* (Lexington, 1985), 142-50.

3. Democrats held a 56-44 majority in the Kentucky House and a 23-15

margin in the Senate. Kentucky *House Journal* (1944), 5-6; Kentucky *Senate Journal* (1944), 4-5. In 1939, Democrat Keen Johnson defeated Republican King Swope by a vote of 460,824 to 354,704. Malcolm E. Jewell, *Kentucky Votes*, 3 vols. (Lexington, 1963), 2:25.

NEW YORK *HERALD-TRIBUNE* FORUM: "KENTUCKY, A TYPICAL PIONEER STATE" New York City / November 21, 1943

MY right to speak for Kentucky was not derived from the recent election, but it's perfectly obvious that my opportunity to speak came from that happy circumstance.

Kentucky is southern in sentiment and American to the core. It was there that Daniel Boone and Simon Kenton[1] conquered the savage and the wilderness, and laid the foundation for a civilization, and lived the romance that has entertained adventurous boys through the life of this United States.

Down in that state both of the leaders in the Civil War were born, and there lived Henry Clay, who rivaled Daniel Webster[2] in educating the American people to love liberty and union, one and indivisible.

Robert Fulton had a rival in a man named Fitch,[3] who claimed the distinction of having invented the steamboat; and I think some of the residents of one of my towns got an act of Congress declaring that it was actually invented by Fitch and not by Fulton.

So it is that in that central part of the United States the heartbeat of the nation may be felt. Our minds and our hearts and our hopes are with our boys on all the battle fronts of this war. All that we have and all that we are is eternally pledged to their success and to the total destruction of all our enemies.

In that attitude of mind, and with such a problem before us, it is very difficult for us to think about things less dramatic; but it is necessary that we think about things less dramatic than the battle fronts because there are dangers at home as well as abroad. There are dangers that we might lose all that our brave men gain, if we should, by blindness, fail to grasp the effect of excessive government upon the liberties and the enterprise of our people or permit us to break on the rock of economic folly.

It is necessary that the government aid and assist in all the activities of the people, but it is absolutely wrong that the government should undertake to manage and control the activities and affairs of the people.

Nothing better than the history of this country can illustrate the difference between tyranny and liberty. For at least half of the life of this nation we lived under a monarchy; and at the end of more than 150 years the nation consisted of thirteen colonies, with only about three million people, just about the number we have in Kentucky today.[4]

Little progress has been made, except in the knowledge of government, and there has never been a time in the history of the world when so many experts and masters of the science of government lived, and they lived in this country. They formulated a plan of government which would forever protect the people against tyranny and against the encroachments of arbitrary power. And that system must be preserved.

They dared, with enemies all around them, enemies above them and below them, they dared defy the most powerful nation on the earth. And after eight long years of struggle and sacrifice, they achieved the liberty at the end of the Revolution; and when they achieved that liberty they had but one fear, and that was the fear of government. And they so surrounded the powers of government with checks and balances that if that system was honestly and fairly administered and adhered to, there would be no danger to the liberties of the people.

And under that system of government, in a very brief period, no longer than the period we were under the monarchs, this country has made the greatest progress ever made in the history of the world. We have built more schoolhouses, more churches, more hospitals, more railroads, more telephones, more harbors, canals, more of the things that raise the standard of living, than were ever created in a like period in the history of the world. And we created more wealth in the 150 years than was ever created in a like period in the history of the world.

That is what freedom does for people. It releases their energies. It inspires their hopes and faith. It gives wings to the imagination; and the people do the best that there is in them, and they accomplish the most that can be accomplished by people. Now, in all of the planning, and in all of this aftermath which is so essential, the greatest essential is that the powers of government shall be restricted, that the principles of justice shall dominate all plans, because justice is the thing that makes people peaceful and happy, and without it there can be no peace or happiness in this world.

And so all people who are planning—the management of labor, the management of capital, the management of activities of people anywhere—must be alert to see that justice is done, justice to ourselves, justice to our allies, and justice even to our enemies. And I for one would like to be on the jury that tries some of those enemies.

And so it is that we must never forget that the people are the source of all power, and the people are the protectors against all power; and the people, when appealed to, when given the opportunity, will be responsive to the great principles upon which our country was founded, which cost so much of sacrifice, which came to us as a heritage to be held in trust for those who come after us. And so Kentucky salutes her neighbors here and all over the world with this principle:

"For justice, all places a temple, and all seasons summer."

---

1. Simon Kenton (1755-1836), frontier scout and later militia general, a man whose exploits rivalled those of the better-known Daniel Boone. Left Kentucky in 1799 and died in Ohio. Edna Kenton, *Simon Kenton* (Garden City, N.Y., 1930).

2. Daniel Webster (1782-1852). Attorney; member of U.S. House of Representatives, 1813-17, 1823-29; member Massachusetts House of Representatives, 1822; U.S. senator, 1827-41, 1845-50, U.S. secretary of state, 1841-43. *DAB*, 10: 585-92.

3. John Fitch (1743-98); Connecticut native; moved to Bardstown, Ky., around 1796; launched steam-powered boats earlier, received monopoly for that mode of travel, and obtained a patent. Thompson Westcott, *Life of John Fitch* (Philadelphia, 1857).

4. Kentucky population in 1940 was 2,845,627, an increase of 8.8 percent over 1930. It was 29.8 percent urban. *Sixteenth Census of the United States: 1940, Population* (Washington, D.C., 1943), 2: Part 3, 173.

INAUGURAL ADDRESS

INAUGURAL ADDRESS
Frankfort / December 7, 1943

My fellow citizens:

I am very happy indeed to know from the lips of Governor Johnson that he regarded my warriors as worthy foes. And of course I am even more happy that the boys from the banks of the rivers and from the tops of the mountains and from the valleys overwhelmed his cohorts.[1] But equally happy am I that they did not take from him that priceless gift, his sense of humor. And as Governor Johnson . . . goes back to his choice pursuit of his great profession, smiling, we smile with him and give him our very best wishes at all times.[2]

It is a serious responsibility at any time to take up the duties of chief magistrate of this great commonwealth. At the present time, when our boys and girls are giving their youth, their service, and their lives, on all the battle fronts of a world at war, that responsibility is even more serious. I accept that responsibility without fear and with full faith, because I feel very deeply that the people of Kentucky realize their own part in the tasks of our times and stand ready to go forward with manly hearts, giving complete support to our country in all of its trials and to our warriors in their supreme and vital struggle for the vindication of the American spirit and for the victory of American ideals. With a firm reliance upon that divine power which never forsakes or fails a people that humbly seek to know and to pursue the divine plan, our country will not falter in its will to achieve the triumph of peace and justice.

Today is the anniversary of Pearl Harbor, where a sneaking foe struck a treacherous blow at the very heart of America. Then and there, and in the sad days since that infamous day, thousands of our brave Americans have suffered the sacrifices of war in the cause of our country.

Since that moment, all Americans have been as one in the defense of our country. Humbly we thank our heroic men and proudly we cherish their deeds. May we so long and so steadfastly remember our debt to them that our resolution and our endurance shall never fail, and with that debt to cherish, we shall make a better world—a world worthy of the supreme sacrifices of our brave men.

Our objectives for Kentucky have been widely discussed, are very well known, and need not be repeated on this occasion. In order to accomplish our aims and our hopes, we must enlist in the service of the state the very best talent and character available for the purpose.

The productive capacity of our people must be maintained at its best, and no slackening or interruption of the patriotic activities shall be allowed to obstruct the irresistible will to victory among our people. Our full strength must be put into the struggle of the nation for a complete victory in the war. Our highest skill and intelligence must deal with the consequences that flow from war and victory.

The problems, no doubt, will be numerous and difficult. It is not to be expected that differences as to details of administration and means of attaining accepted ends may not arise. But men of good will earnestly seeking the welfare of the state can always find a way to compose differences and to conquer difficulties.

Life is made up of problems. Meeting and overcoming obstacles is the habit of our people. Courage and success is our heritage. The heroic example of our modern young men and women in the armed services affords decisive proof that the pioneer spirit of Kentucky still lives. It must be preserved and kept, not only for us, but for our children.

All of us love Kentucky, and all of us cherish her good name. Let us work together for her good and for her glory. May we forget everything that tends to divide or to destroy and go forward with patience, with tolerance, with courage, and with faith to that bright day when peace shall return and peaceful pursuits shall regain for our people that happiness and prosperity which they so much desire and so richly deserve. Even though we may make errors, we can correct them. That is the secret of the success of a republican form of government. Such governments may stumble, but they need not fall. The will of a great people cannot be denied.

We shall carry on with undaunted faith that mistakes are but stepping stones to better things, and at last, even in our time, we can make the institutions of a free people "shine with beauty and glow with justice."

1. Outgoing Governor Keen Johnson, in a witty valedictory address, compared and contrasted the Republican defeat of the Democrats with the Japanese defeat of the Americans at Pearl Harbor a year before. For a full text see Ogden, ed., *Papers of Keen Johnson*, 511-13.

2. Parts of this passage are garbled on the recording used and do not appear in the printed version.

LEGISLATIVE ACTIONS, 1943-1945

REMARKS TO LEGISLATIVE COUNCIL
Frankfort / December 11, 1943

GOVERNOR WILLIS greeted the council[1] briefly this morning and announced he will submit his message Monday.

"My thought is," he said, "that we should cut expenses wherever possible, but not in any way to impair the essential services of government. Then, when we have determined the irreducible minimums, we should call in the tax departments to see if we have the money to balance the budget.

"Politically," the governor continued, "the majority of the legislative branch is Democratic and the executive branch is Republican, but the matters we deal with are of common interest. I am sure we can work together, that we will be moved by a common purpose. I hope that we will put our heads and hearts into the tasks that lie ahead, as well as our intelligence.

"To me," he concluded, "this is an entirely new line—it is a brand new lawsuit—but I will try to get into it as quickly as possible."

---

1. The Legislative Council, headed by Lieutenant Governor Kenneth H. Tuggle, included eight senators, eight representatives, five members of the administration, and a secretary, Clyde Smith of Barbourville. Frank K. Kavanaugh, *Kentucky Directory* (Frankfort, 1944), 106.

STATEMENT REGARDING TUGGLE "RIPPER"
Frankfort / January 4, 1944

GOVERNOR WILLIS charged that J. Lyter Donaldson, "the man who was rejected for governor by the vote of the people, is in Frankfort directing this sabotage.[1]

"These arrogant men," Governor Willis said, "mean to thwart the will of the people. I want the people of Kentucky to know that the fight for good government will go on. I hope that they will resent this continuation of machine politics and see to it that their mandate is obeyed.

"In these days of such deep concern to all our people, it is most unfortunate that partisanship is ruling when statesmanship is so greatly needed," Willis declared. "The action of the majority in the Senate today indicated a partisan plan to obstruct the orderly execution of the people's mandate.

"The change in the rules, made so as to deprive the lieutenant governor of the right to appoint committees and refer legislation to an appropriate committee is the first step.[2]

"The action in the Senate was wholly partisan; they even refused to grant time to consider the proposed rules and rushed a prearranged program through."[3]

---

1. Donaldson was registered at the New Capital Hotel in Frankfort. *Courier-Journal*, January 5, 1944.

2. A "ripper" bill strips power from an official while still leaving the position intact. A major "ripper" had occurred in the 1934 session when Lieutenant Governor A.B. ("Happy") Chandler had been the target of factional opponents.

In this 21-15 strict party vote in 1944, the Senate "ripped" from Tuggle the power to name committees, refer bills to committees, and employ additional help. Those powers went instead to a three-man committee of two Democrats and one Republican. Ibid.; Kentucky *Senate Journal* (1944), 15-19, 42-43.

3. The Senate majority leader was Earle Chester Clements (1896-1985) of Morganfield. Oilfield worker, 1919-21; football coach at Union County; Union County sheriff, 1922-25; county clerk, 1925-33; county judge, 1933-41; state senator, 1942-44; U.S. congressman, 1945-47; governor of Kentucky, 1947-50; U.S. senator, 1950-57; highway comissioner, 1959-60; consultant to American Tobacco Institute after 1964. Thomas H. Syvertsen, "Earle Chester Clements,"

in Harrison, ed., *Kentucky's Governors*, 157-62; W.R. Jillson, "Governor Earle C. Clements," *Register of the Kentucky Historical Society* 46 (1948): 375-79.

STATE OF THE COMMONWEALTH
Frankfort / January 10, 1944

Lieutenant Governor Tuggle,[1] Mr. Speaker,[2] and members of the General Assembly:

The General Assembly convenes at a critical time in the life of our country. The president has reminded us recently that there are over ten million men in the armed services of the United States. Of these, nearly four million are overseas. Kentucky has about two hundred and fifty thousand men and women participating in the war effort. Every fireside is affected. The hope is justified that the victory will soon be won, but we still have much to face in the way of suffering and sacrifice and personal tragedy. Many costly battles are yet to be fought, and the people must maintain the resolution and effort necessary to final success. It is time for high endeavor, for conservation of all resources, for dedication to a supreme task. It is no time for petty, partisan politics. The production of foodstuffs, war materials, supplies, and weapons of all kinds rests heavily upon the people at home. Nothing can be permitted to hamper this work. The government of Kentucky must be efficient, and everything within our power must be done to win the war.

The first thing to be determined by you is the budget appropriation, with a legislative program for the welfare of Kentucky. The budget must be kept in balance. We cannot spend money we do not have. This is not only common sense, but it is law. Hence, the amount of money to be appropriated by you is the very first problem for your consideration. Until it is settled nothing else can be settled. The Legislative Council and the governor studied the requests of the various units and heard representatives of the several departments. The work was not completed for lack of time, but a comprehensive view of the requirements for each departmental unit was obtained. It was soon apparent to all that the estimated revenues were not sufficient to meet all the requests.

It is a condition and not a theory that confronts us. A budget bill has been carefully prepared by the responsible officials, and it is ready for your consideration. The complete budget report is in the hands of the printer, and it will be on your desks as soon as it can be printed.

The total amount proposed to be appropriated by this act for the fiscal year 1944-1945 is $32,376,700. This includes the provision of $1 million each fiscal year for the institutional improvements. It does not include the disbursements of county fees because these amounts after July 1, 1944, under a new law, will be cleared through the state treasury, without any addition to state income or reduction of expenses.[3]

For the second year of the biennial period the total amount to be appropriated is $32,606,800.00 on the same basis as for the first year. This is an increase over the last fiscal year, when the total was $28,774,207.56, as shown in the last message of Governor Johnson. The contingent appropriation of $3 million for that year which was expended in rehabilitation of the penal and charitable institutions was not included in the total sum mentioned. The largest item in the proposed budget is the $15 million for the per capita school fund, of which the full 10 percent authorized by the constitution is set apart for the equalization fund.[4] The law should be amended to provide for a wider distribution of this fund to help more of the needy school fund that accounts for the increase over last year's budget.

The teachers' retirement fund appropriation is fixed at a figure to comply with the statute. The crisis in which the state, as well as the country, is involved does not lessen our duty to educate our children and our youth. This obligation cannot be postponed but must be continuously met. The amount to be allowed to the common schools has been endorsed by the educators of the state, and I have given my support to the school program. I am confident this program has the approval of the people and of the General Assembly.

As to the institutions of higher learning, the amounts have to be determined from past experience and reasonable expectations as to the future needs. They are now engrossed in war work and the student bodies are very much reduced. This budget makes provision for them on the assumption that normal conditions will return during the period involved.

Capital outlays must be deferred during the war on account of critical materials needed for the war program, and because of the necessity for cutting expenditures wherever possible. The scarcity of materials and the drain on manpower create the necessity for delay in construction which can be done better after the crisis is over and conditions are stabilized. While the work is carried along, plans can be perfected for a postwar program of a permanent nature.

The effort to reduce expenses is complicated by the increase in prices, both of labor and of materials. It would be fortunate if we could grant the requests of the various departments, but that is impossible since they exceed all estimates of possible revenue. A careful study has been made, and reductions as drastic as practicable have been applied. It is not deemed prudent at this time, and with present information, to cut them deeper. Few increases have been allowed over the appropriations for the previous year. In most cases reductions have been made.

The remaining six months of the fiscal year will give us an opportunity to observe the operations of all the departments of government. It may be possible to make greater savings than we now anticipate. When we enter upon the new fiscal year, we hope to be able to save money even out of these proposed appropriations which will be available to take care of needed improvements at the various institutions. You know how difficult it is to prepare a budget today that will fit the conditions six months hence, much less to provide for two whole years, beginning six months in the future. For that reason some flexibility must be allowed, and while we must make the budget sufficient to cover the expenses that appear to be essential, any savings that can be effected will be passed to the surplus. That will help us to go forward with the work of improving the institutions. The surplus fund is a cushion against declining revenues, and it must be kept as large as possible while we are passing through this crisis of war. It should be kept free to meet contingencies that may arise. It is not only unwise but dangerous to encumber or dissipate the whole surplus fund. It should be maintained in a substantial amount as a safeguard against fluctuations in the revenue, and to provide for the necessary work in progress at the institutions.

There are a large number of appropriations that are fixed, and no changes can be made in them. The emergency fund of $250,000 for each year has been retained. The special emergency funds of the last fiscal year have been omitted. It is thought that the above provision will be adequate for all actual emergencies, and it will not be spent otherwise.

The emergency fund for lands and buildings, of $1 million each year, will be sufficient for the improvement of the institutions that cannot well be postponed. The chief engineer[5] advised the Legislative Council that this sum is urgently needed and should be provided if at all possible to do so. It will make useful the improvements now in course of completion which otherwise could not be used until additional provision was made. This includes the mental hospitals, the Feeble-Minded Institute, the School for the Deaf, the state schools under the direct supervision of the State Board of Education, and the Hazelwood Tuberculosis Hospital.[6] In all other cases the claims of the various units have been considered, and the proposed act appropriates to each what was represented as the irreducible minimum to make it efficient.

The physical improvements at the institutional buildings that are in course of construction must be carried to completion. That is expected to require about eight months. As these improvements are completed greater emphasis must be placed on improvements in administration. Some of the work in course of construction was suspended last year, but this has been corrected and that work will proceed.[7] My policy is that all force account work must be restricted within the limitations of the law, and where a contract to be let after public bidding is feasible, it must be done that way. Where conditions have been created which may result in damage if force account work is not continued to a reasonable extent an emergency is presented which requires the state, for its own protection against loss, to do enough force account work to protect its property.

The proposed act appropriates $2,760,000 for the welfare department and $4,250,000 for old age assistance in cooperation with the federal government under the Social Security Act. Additional sums amounting to $102,000 are provided for the Home for Incurables, for the Colored Red Cross Hospital, for the conveyance of lunatics, and for pauper idiots.[8]

The appropriations for the highway department have been continued, and provision is made for the highway patrol.

The proposition to divert road funds to the payment of toll bridge revenue bonds or other purposes is fundamentally fallacious. The road funds are needed to build and maintain roads. Such delay as the war causes in present construction will enable the department to plan for a larger program when the war ends. These funds will be matched by federal funds if applied to road building, but if diverted to other uses the federal money would be lost to the state. The toll bridges are safely financed, and the plan under which they were built should be carried out without disturbance under present conditions. These are the main features of the proposed act, and the numerous other items need not be particularly described. You will have all the details in the budget report soon to be delivered to you. You will note that no provision has been made for the state fair, except for the second year of the biennium.

The next subject of vital importance for your most careful consideration is the revenue which may be expected to meet the expenditures required by the appropriation act. Only the amount of money actually realized can be expended. If the appropriation should exceed the revenues it will be necessary to bring the expenditures within the income, regardless of the amount of the appropriation. The commissioner of revenue[9] has made careful estimates of what may be reasonably expected under the present tax laws. He warns us, however, that these estimates depend upon a number of factors which may change the picture. In explanation of his estimates, the commissioner of revenue stated: "Under stable economic conditions, and in the absence of direct government controls, reasonably accurate predictions for most taxes may be developed on the basis of past performance. But today war is the nation's business. Our war economy consumes 70 percent of total industrial production, according to authoritative sources. The outlook for business in the months ahead thus depends, to a large extent, on federal fiscal and economic policies."

The complete estimate for the first fiscal year of the next biennium, eliminating county fees which do not effect the total, is an income of $30,753,250. For the second year of the biennium the estimate is for $30,645,250. On the basis of these estimates it requires all receipts under the present tax structure, and approximately $3,500,000 additional from the surplus find, to meet the proposed appropriations, including the million dollars each year for the work of rehabilitation at the various institutions. This would carry us through the biennium with a cushion of about four and a half million dollars at the end. The surplus at the beginning of the current fiscal year was approximately $12 million. The budgetary records for the current year's operations indicate, on the basis of the present estimate of receipts, that this surplus will be reduced to about $11 million on July 1, 1944. The deficiency appropriation contemplated for the schools this year will further reduce the estimated surplus by $3 million, leaving, if there are no other deficiency appropriations, a surplus of approximately $8 million. The appropriations provided by the proposed budget act will thus exceed estimated receipts by $3,500,000, which will reduce the surplus to $4,500,000 at the end of the biennium. This results from the increased provision for the schools and the institutions. If the personal income tax alone should be repealed now, and the corporation income tax retained, it would reduce the estimated income to such an extent that a deficit for the biennium of $1,860,000 would result, even after complete exhaustion of the surplus.

In my opening address at Mt. Sterling I said: "The state income tax, under present conditions, is an unjust burden, and the purpose for which it was adopted has been served. It should be the first tax to be repealed, and by its repeal industrial enterprise will be stimulated and encouraged." I said further in the same address: "The loss to the general fund from the repeal of this tax can be replaced by a determined reduction of expenses, by savings resulting from a proper management of the purchasing department, and by cutting the enormous payroll of the state, as any good business manager would slash it."

At the same time, I called attention to the fundamental fact that the budget must be kept in balance, and that expense must not exceed income. I strongly favor the repeal of that tax at the earliest possible date that it can be done without impairment of the services which must be rendered by the government. It will take time to learn the necessities of all the departments and to ascertain where and how much expenses may be reduced without impairment of efficiency. I believe that great savings can be effected, and I shall work diligently with all the officers and agents to that end. But until these improvements in administration and savings in expenses are accomplished facts, we must not impair the ability of the state to carry on in an orderly way.

I am just beginning my administration, but the reduction of expenses will be made as rapidly as possible, bearing in mind always that the efficiency of the government must be maintained. I shall select the most capable men available to carry out this program. Conditions are changing from day to day. Estimates of income are conditioned on these changes. The impact of federal taxes, as well as economic dislocation due to the war, constantly affect income. When the war ends and normal conditions return, the revenues from many sources will return. Just as soon as the revenues which have been stopped by the war revive and the savings and economies which we shall realize produce sufficient funds to balance the budget, I shall ask the General Assembly to repeal that tax. If that time comes sooner than we can now foresee, I shall not hesitate to call a special session for the purpose. It should not be done hastily at a time when it would affect the solvency of the government. With the loss of revenue we have suffered, and with the extraordinary requirements for the schools and for the institutional program, as reflected in this proposed budget act, it is certainly prudent to delay action on the repeal of any tax until conditions are stabilized, so that plans may be made for the future with safety. If any tax was repealed now, and the proposed budget act was passed, it would be necessary to provide some new taxes to produce the additional revenue required to keep the government operating within its income. Otherwise, the expenditures would have to be curtailed. The uncertain and changing conditions make it very difficult to discover a source of revenue that would be reliable and constant. The people are struggling to meet their obligations to the national government in carrying the expenses of the war. The collector of internal revenue has just published the fact that $465,910,065 was collected in this state for the federal government during 1943. This huge sum may be even larger in 1944. It will be a great relief to the people of Kentucky when we are able to cut expenses and improve the revenues to an extent that will enable you to repeal some of the most oppressive state taxes.

In all my public and private discussions of a program of government I have set forth the following objectives to be earnestly sought:

1. The budget must be kept in balance and nothing expended beyond the revenues. Good housekeeping requires that the state live within its means.

2. The essential services of the government must be carried on without impairment and for the welfare of all the people.

3. The schools should have relief, both immediate and for the next biennium, and the crisis caused by the war must be met.

4. That the care of the wards of the state, the sick, the aged, and the afflicted, dependent altogether or partly upon the assistance of the government, has to be maintained and improved.

5. The taxpayers desire relief to enable them to meet the increasing demands of the national government for the necessary expense of the war. No new taxes should be asked, if possible to avoid it, and all taxes hurtful to economic development should be avoided.

These objectives should be attained as rapidly as conditions will permit. I am sure that all of them can be accomplished in an orderly way and within a reasonable time by the cooperation of the several branches of the government. Most of the requests presented to the Legislative Council represent meritorious claims for consideration. The possible revenues under present laws, according to the most reliable estimates, could not exceed $30,750,000, as before stated. Obviously it was necessary to cut these requests to the irreducible minimum consistent with efficient government. After cutting their requests as much as was possible, with our present information, we have been unable to bring the total within the range of the prospective revenue. Of course, they will have to live within the revenue, regardless of the amount appropriated. If conditions should quickly change and revenues revive, we will be able to carry forward the program. It is to be regretted that we cannot today grant all of the requests for revenue and at the same time give immediate relief to the taxpayers, but obviously that is impossible. So long as we are engaged in war we must carry on to the very best of our ability under changing conditions. When the war is over, and normal conditions return, we will be able to accomplish all the objectives for which we are striving.

From time to time I shall request the enactment of legislation.

The constitution limits to two the number of amendments that may be voted upon at one time.[10] I recommend that the right of way be given the proposal to confer upon men and women in our armed forces the right to vote in all elections, wherever they may be stationed. In my opinion the amendment should be broadened for the benefit of absent citizens in the service of the country so as to enable the General Assembly to enact laws to exempt them from taxation while in the service. Certainly the General Assembly should have the power to protect our defenders wherever they may be.

In regard to the highway department, I have requested a reorganization along lines purely constructive and economical. The office of advisory highway commissioners should be abolished. Resignations of the nine men holding these positions were accepted and the places have been left vacant. Bills have been prepared to carry out this reorganization and I trust they may meet with your approval.

I recommend that the attorney general's office be required to handle all the legal business of the state, and the special acts taking away from him certain rights and duties should be repealed. This act will be recommended to you in due course. Likewise an act will be offered on behalf of the Department of Agriculture, Labor, and Statistics. The other legislation which may be required from time to time will be requested in special messages.

Dissatisfaction has been expressed from many sources in regard to the alcoholic control system. A complete study of that subject is being made, and later such information as may be available, with the recommendations I find advisable, will be transmitted to you.

A number of subjects call for consideration and new legislation. These will be submitted to you with recommendations from time to time. It shall be my purpose to propose nothing but constructive legislation for the betterment of conditions. Especially pressing is the proposed plan for the tuberculosis hospitals in the eastern and western parts of the state. I wish to have a representative commission of legislators, citizens, and professional men to prepare and report a plan for the location, construction, maintenance, and operation of such institutions.

I ask the cooperation and support of every member of the General Assembly. I hope that this session may achieve results for the welfare of Kentucky and do nothing to hurt her. You will find me ready to assist and cooperate with you in everything pertaining to the good of the state, and all the departments of the government will furnish you any assistance within their power.

In this time of war in which we are all deeply and vitally concerned, we have a great opportunity to perform a great task in a great way for the welfare of our people. Let nothing distract us from the pursuit of this high purpose. May all the patriotism, energy, and intelligence we possess be united to promote the public interest and the general happiness of our people.

---

1. Kenneth Herndon Tuggle (1904-1978), of Barbourville. Attorney; chairman of the board of bank (1934-53); director in numerous firms; trustee of Union College, Ky.; Republican nominee for attorney general in 1939; lieutenant governor, 1943-47; on Interstate Commerce Commission, 1953-75. *Kentucky Directory,* 118; Hambleton Tapp, *Kentucky Lives* (Hopkinsville, Ky., 1966), 550; Washington *Post,* February 23, 1978.

2. Speaker of the House Harry Lee Waterfield (1911-   ); Kentucky House of Representatives, 1937-46, 1950; lieutenant governor, 1955-59, 1963-67; defeated in 1947 and 1959 in bids for the Democratic gubernatorial nomination; former president of Kentucky Press Association and publisher of *Hickman County Gazette* and other newspapers; president of National Investors Life Insurance Company of Kentucky since 1960. Tapp, *Kentucky Lives,* 571; Robert A. Powell, *Kentucky Governors* (Frankfort, 1976), 8-11; Harry Lee Waterfield Papers, Murray State University.

3. "An act providing for the payment of salaries. . . ," approved March 5, 1942, applied only to counties with a population exceeding 75,000. Kentucky *Acts* (1942), 478-79.

4. Section 186 of the Kentucky Constitution, as amended in 1941, made this provision.

5. Tyler Cutter was chief engineer, Department of Highways.

6. The mental hospitals were Eastern State (Lexington), Central State (Lakeland), and Western State (Hopkinsville). The Feeble-Minded Institute was in Frankfort, the School for the Deaf in Danville, and the Hazelwood Tuberculosis Hospital in Louisville. The name of the Feeble-Minded Institute was changed to the Kentucky Training Home by an executive order dated June 25, 1946. Governor's Papers, Records of the Secretary of State, Public Records Division, Department for Libraries and Archives.

7. For a discussion of the problem concerning finance and construction see Ogden, ed., *Papers of Keen Johnson,* 102n.

8. The Home for Incurables and the Colored Red Cross Hospital were located in Louisville.

9. James E. Luckett (1910-   ) accountant; various positions in Department of Revenue, 1937-43; commissioner of revenue, 1943-44, 1955-59, 1963-71; con-

troller, city of Lexington, 1972-74; comissioner of finance, Lexington-Fayette County, 1974-80. Ogden, ed., *Papers of Keen Johnson,* 180n; *Kentucky Enquirer,* May 12, 1944; statement of Christine Luckett, July 5, 1985.

10. Section 256 of the Kentucky Constitution at that time limited amendments to two.

STATEMENT REGARDING LEGISLATIVE COMMITTEES FOR CONTINUING RESEARCH
Frankfort / February 5, 1944

IN the first place, it is proper to repeat that I favor the improvement of government and the reduction of expense. Any plan that affords a reasonable hope of accomplishing these objectives will have my support.

The bill now offered creating committees on legislative research, audits, and statutes, will not, in my judgment, save any money or improve any of the legislative or executive functions. I do not believe it will tend to lessen expense but will actually increase it. The bill is open to the fatal objection that it is too costly to be contemplated at this time.

The bill has a very distinct partisan flavor which does not commend it to the people who are impartial and who are seeking better service. This is shown by the failure to give the minority party in the General Assembly any representation whatever on the committee. Although the minority has 44 percent membership in the House and nearly 40 percent in the Senate, it is not given any share in the appointment of the committees, [nor is] any provision made for representation of the minority party.

The presiding officer of the House is made a member of the House committee and given the power to appoint all members, while the presiding officer of the Senate is given no right to appoint any member or to serve in any capacity or to have any voice in the matter.[1]

Manifestly the most important feature of the proposal is its validity. It is not based on any section of the constitution and is forbidden by several sections. Section 39 of the constitution, in defining the powers of each house as to rules and conduct, provides how contempt of the house or any of its committees may be punished. Imprisonment, however, is limited to the session of the General Assembly. There is no provision for having permanent committees which could bring private citizens in contempt when the legislature itself is not in session. This section of the constitution is violated by section 7 of the proposed act, which creates a system of contempt under which any citizen of the state could be brought to Frankfort at the instance of any committee or subcommittee or even any employee of the committee.

Section 42 of the constitution limits the compensation of the members and forbids a continuation of the session beyond sixty days; both of these provisions are violated by providing almost a continuous session of the General Assembly through the committees. Moreover, additional pay is provided for members of the legislature, not only equal to the per diem while in session, but including their expenses, which is not allowed during the regular session.

Moreover, under Section 9 of this proposed act, any member or members of the legislature could be employed and put on the payroll. This would be in clear violation of Section 235, which forbids the change in compensation of members of the General Assembly and other public officers during the term for which they were elected.

If it be attempted to defend the act on the ground that it creates new offices, it runs counter to Section 44 of the constitution, which makes each senator and representative ineligible to hold any office created by the legislature of which he was a member, during his term or for one year thereafter. Moreover, the power of the House to employ help is limited by Section 249 of the constitution, which excludes the power to employ others.

The appropriations contemplated equal the expenditures for the whole regular session provided by the constitution. It takes $25,000 at once to be spent before July 1, and then calls for $75,000 for each of the next two years, making a total of $175,000 for the expenses of this committee. This is about equal to the cost of the whole session fixed by the constitution at sixty days.

The appropriation for the present session, made by the last General Assembly, was $181,750. With the extra amounts already appropriated for the present session the extra appropriation for these committees will exceed the entire cost of the regular session.

All material called for or contemplated by this new bill is now available under audits already made by competent men and made pursuant to laws previously enacted. This is a mere duplication of clerical research work, which would not only fail to achieve efficiency, but would actually handicap the work of the regularly organized forces.

There are two separate committees to be coordinated by the chairmen and to employ whomsoever they please without regard to the personnel department created by law for the greater efficiency of the service.

Whilst there is a three-day session provided, it is susceptible to indefinite extension by the committee.

The committee work is a part of the work of the members, and there has never been any provision of law made for paying members of the houses for working on the committees except to the extent they served on the Legislative Council.

There are many other defects in this proposed plan, but the above are sufficient to indicate that it is both contrary to the constitution and harmful and wasteful in its proposals.

I have made the suggestion that the Legislative Council could be preserved as a purely legislative council. The administrative and executive members could be eliminated, and thus the council could become wholly constituted of members of the Senate and House. Incoming members should be made eligible prior to qualification to the offices.

The party representation should be according to the representation in each house. Its work necessarily would be of an advisory character. The presiding officers of the two houses should be co-chairmen of the committee.

If other research is desired, competent persons are available in the public service at this time, so the research work could be carried on without additional expense.

The Legislative Council had an appropriation of only $10,000, and it seems to me that the experience gained by it should be utilized instead of thrown away in a brand new start in an untried field.

The new administration should be given a fair opportunity to demonstrate its ability and purpose to reduce expenses and achieve efficiency.[2]

----

1. See document dated January 4, 1944, in this section.

2. The bill, as finally passed on March 15, and approved three days later by the governor, included several modifications that followed Governor Willis's suggestions. The lieutenant governor, for example, was made ex-officio member and chairman of the Legislative Council, and party representation "in proportion generally" to relative strength was included. Appropriations given by 1945-46 were limited to only $11,000. Several constitutional questions raised by the governor were addressed as well. See Kentucky *Acts* (1944), 317-20, 477.

STATEMENT REGARDING DEADLOCK ON BUDGET
Frankfort / March 4, 1944

THE responsibility for the situation regarding the budget bill rests squarely on the partisan majority in the Senate.[1] The amendments adopted by the Senate made it impossible to pay the teachers the amount of money appropriated for them. By freezing the surplus so it could not be used, expenditures were confined to the estimated income, which is insufficient to meet the appropriations. This would require a horizontal reduction of the appropriations to the actual income. The freezing of the surplus money so that it could not be expended for governmental purposes, and compelling it to be invested in government bonds and held for the next two years at least, deprived the people of the use of their accumulated tax money during that period.

This left the government without any cushion to go through the emergency of war and without any means of adjusting the departments of government, the schools, and the old age assistance program to the fluctuating income. Since there are no new taxes being levied and none proposed, it was a cunning trick on the part of the partisan majority in the Senate to hold out to the people the hope of having the amount of money fixed by the appropriation act, when they knew it would be impossible to pay that amount out of the estimated revenue. The senate amendments killed the budget bill.

If the senators will forget their partisan bias and consent to perform a patriotic service to the people, they will immediately confer with the House leaders and the governor, and pass the budget bill as prepared by the finance department and the governor, with only the amendments recommended by the House committee. The governor assented to the House committee amendments on condition that there be no further amendments.

This budget bill remained in the House committee for many weeks. The committee desired certain additions to the recommendations made by the governor in the budget report, and these were assented to with the definite understanding that the bill as thus reported to the House would be supported by all members of the committee and also by the members from the Senate who served on the joint committee. No sooner had this bill been reported in the House than this agreement was completely forgotten, and several unacceptable amendments were added in the House in violation of the agreement.

The House amendments and the Senate amendments must be rejected, and the House and Senate should agree on a bill as recommended by the governor, with the amendments recommended by the House committee and no more. This would enable the teachers to receive the money appropriated for them. It would enable the departments to function efficiently, and it would enable the agencies of the government to get the amount of money specified in the appropriation bill.

The governor recommended to the General Assembly in his message on January 10, 1944, that the sum of $15 million be appropriated for the common schools, of which 10 percent was to be set apart for the equalization fund. This was embodied in the budget bill as originally prepared, and it was adopted by the House. The Senate also adopted the bill but added amendments which made it impossible to pay the teachers the amount of money they were ostensibly granted.

The attempt to blame the governor is purely partisan and baseless. The governor in his message made his recommendation to all the members of the General Assembly. This message was printed and has been on the desk of every member for many days. Instead of seeking to carry out the recommendations of the governor, the partisan leaders have resorted to measures calculated to harass, hamstring, and cripple the administration. Fortunately these have been defeated.

If no budget bill is passed the responsibility rests squarely on the Senate amendments, which cannot be accepted because of their destructive effect on the appropriations purporting to be made. They merely hold the word of promise to the ear and break it to the hope.

The governor has spent every hour of his time working with the legislature and with the individual members for the welfare of all the people. It is time the people understand where the responsibility rests for the situation is in the General Assembly, and there is yet time. If the leaders of that body disappoint the expectations of the people, the responsibility is theirs alone, and they must answer to the people.

---

1. The executive budget, presented January 10, 1944, increasingly became the focus of a partisan struggle. Senate Democrats presented a budget that exceeded Governor Willis's request and his estimate of anticipated revenue. House Republicans eventually defeated the measure by one vote. The regular session thus adjourned without a 1944-46 budget. Under Kentucky law, the budget for the preceding year would be renewed under such conditions.

BUDGET BILL
Frankfort / March 7, 1944

In a spirit of the utmost good will, I come before you to suggest solutions of the pending problems. The program which I shall suggest to you is clear and uncomplicated with any collateral considerations. I ask nothing for myself or for any political party. I ask only that you serve the cause of education, and the welfare and institutions of the state, by providing ample pay for the teachers, ample protection for the wards of our commonwealth, and provision to make secure the old age assistance now being given.

It is not too late for the General Assembly to enact a sound and constructive budget law. Despite all difficulties and obstructions, let us consider the reasonable course, with the sole desire to do right. In such a spirit, let us examine the situation existing, how it may be relieved, and the consequence of failure to meet the demands of the occasion.

In an address to you at the beginning of this session a budget bill was presented with the request that first consideration be given to it. I explained to you then that until that matter was settled nothing else could be settled. At the same time you were advised of my readiness to assist you, and to cooperate with you, in everything pertaining to the problem; and, on behalf of the administration, the services of every department of the government were offered to you. As you know, I had but the short period of one week after the Legislative Council dissolved within which to write the budget act and to prepare my original message to you. With the assistance of the finance department and the attorney general's office, the task was accomplished. My time for many days during the sessions of the Legislative Council was required to get the suspended work at the institutions resumed. The council knew this fact, and the members were in accord with the work which had to be done and had to be done then. In fact, the Legislative Council was so impressed by the seriousness of the situation created by the stoppage of the work at the institutions that they sent a committee to request me to act in the matter. I had, in fact, already acted and had completed my part of the task. The suspended work was quickly resumed and is being prosecuted diligently. I worked with the Legislative Council in entire harmony, and a tentative budget was agreed upon without controversy. The tentative agreement as to every point was fully respected by me in completing the budget report and in preparing the budget bill. The budget bill was referred to the appropriations committee of the House on the twelfth of January. Hearings were conducted, and the Senate committee participated in the hearings. The bill remained in that committee until February 8, when it was reported to the House with certain amendments. The chairman of the committee, Honorable J. Lee Moore,[1] worked with me in complete harmony at all times. Some of my suggestions, made necessary by developments after the bill had been introduced, were accepted and incorporated by committee amendments in the bill reported. In the same spirit I cooperated with Chairman Moore and agreed to the requests of the committee given to me by the chairman in a letter dated February 5 and delivered to me on February 7 and caused no delay whatever. It was my understanding, and it was Mr. Moore's understanding, as he stated it to me, that a majority of the members of the House committee would adhere to the recommendations of the committee, and oppose any new amendments that might be introduced from the floor. The bill was reported as stated on February 8 and remained in the House until February 25, when it was passed with several amendments added which were not acceptable to me. The Senate declined to remove the House amendments and added other amendments which were even more objectionable. They had the effect of restricting the surplus fund for particular uses and making it unavailable for the purpose of meeting the obvious requirements of the bill itself. They froze the surplus fund, except for the single purpose specified. Moreover, the Senate took out of the budget bill the contingency fund of $1 million for each fiscal year, which was necessary to continue the rehabilitation of the institutions. The effect was to cut every appropriation to the new income. In my message to you on January 10, I referred to this emergency fund of $1 million set up for each year, for the improvement of the institutions. The chief engineer had advised the Legislative Council that such a sum was urgently needed. Without it some of the improvements now in course of completion will be rendered useless, and will remain useless, until additional provision shall be made. The Senate amendments did not repeal or reduce the appropriations for the essential needs for the government, or for the educational program, or for the institutions, including Hazelwood, or for the old age assistance, or for the needy blind, or for the dependent children. What the Senate amendments did was to make it impossible to expend the money except in the way and for the purpose specified. It sealed up the surplus fund so that the new income alone could be used to meet the appropriations for the recurring expenses of the government.

The estimated income is based on the best calculations that can be made in advance, but the income may not be as high as we expect. The report published Saturday shows that a decline in revenue over the previous eight months' period, as compared to the same months of the preceding year, amounted to $1,723,346 for the general fund, and $1,495,309 for the state road fund.[2] The warning thus given us cannot be lightly brushed aside. The effect of the Senate amendments was to require a horizontal reduction of each appropriation, including the appropriation for the old age assistance, for the schools, and for the institutions. These appropriations were made, upon the best information obtainable, to provide the irreducible minimum required to carry on the services. Under the Senate amendments, if the revenue did not revive and improve beyond all expectations, there would be a horizontal reduction of every appropriation. This would have deprived every one of the institutions and departments of that much of the money nominally appropriated for them. We are therefore confronted with the situation in which a new budget bill must be adopted or we must operate under the 1942 appropriation set for the last fiscal year. This will not carry with it the emergency appropriation of $3 million for the rehabilitation of the institutions, including Hazelwood, because appropriations for extraordinary expenses and capital outlay are excepted from it. In this situation there would be no provision whatever for Hazelwood, and the improvements at Hazelwood would be useless until another appropriation could be made. The effect of the present situation, unless something is done immediately, will be to return us to the appropriation set for the fiscal year next preceding, limiting the schools to the same appropriation given that year and depriving the institutions of any emergency aid.

I think it is entirely practicable for you to solve the problem. First, take the budget bill, as recommended by the governor, with the amendments added by the House Committee on Appropriations and assented to by the governor, omitting entirely all amendments added by the House and all amendments added by the Senate. This would carry out the full school program and take care of the institutional needs that are pressing.

Some apprehension seems to exist that additional funds may be needed for the old age assistance, aid to the needy blind, and aid to dependent children. This apprehension is not without some basis. Although no one knows, we are very hopeful that it will not be necessary. But, in order to provide for such an emergency, an emergency fund of $450,000 for each of the fiscal years should be provided, to be used in case the emergency actually occurs, in order to maintain the present level of welfare assistance.

It is the purpose of this administration to economize and to save in every place that it is possible, but we cannot in advance cut the appropriations. What we save will be carried to the surplus and will be available for use when it is needed in the operation of the government.

If the General Assembly is unwilling to accept this suggestion and desires the present administration to go back to the last preceding budget, then, as an alternative, I suggest that you relieve the schools, the welfare program, and the institutions by special bills, as follows:

1. Adopt a bill appropriating the money to carry out the school program as presented in the budget report, with the amendments agreed to by the governor and the appropriations committee of the House, without either of the amendments added in the House or in the Senate. This would take care of the schools, and under the law it would supersede the budget act for the preceding year for the schools alone, and the old appropriation act would apply only to the other subjects of the appropriation not covered by the special act.

2. Create an emergency fund of $1 million for each fiscal year for the prosecution of improvements at the institutions on the same terms as was provided in the last budget act, which set up $3 million for the purpose. That would put into effect the provision stricken out of the budget act by the Senate. In either event, the emergency appropriation for old age assistance should be made.

Either of these suggestions is entirely practical, and if the members of the General Assembly will proceed at once to carry out these purposes there need be no difficulty whatsoever in accomplishing it. The members skilled in parliamentary law can find the way to do it.

When I appeared before you on January 10, I had expected that the budget bill would be promptly passed and that the various bills relating to the highway department, to the attorney general's office, and to the commissioner of agriculture would be enacted. Some of these bills have been acted upon, but there are others which require further action by one or the other of the houses and in some instances by both branches of the assembly. They are good bills which ought to be passed, and I hope you will enact them.

In view of the legislative situation that has existed for some time, I have not deemed it prudent or advisable to make further recommendations or to attempt to urge the passage of particular bills. For that reason I have not made any further recommendations regarding the various subjects mentioned in my first address. I have avoided the introduction of controversial subjects.

I trust that the selected leaders of this assembly will aid in a solution of our problems. I believe you have the skill and the purpose to accomplish it. I thank all who have helped and cooperated and commend them to their constituents.

Constant criticism is leveled at the governor in order to arouse opposition, prejudice, and resentment. You need not worry about that. Criticism based on facts may be helpful, but criticism manufactured and without basis in fact accomplishes no good. Let no such criticism discourage you. In my former message I set forth the main objectives for which I am striving and for which I shall continue to strive while I am governor. Such objectives cannot be accomplished without the cooperation of the General Assembly and the support of the people, and even then they cannot be accomplished instantaneously. Your experience proves to you that improvement in administration and in the processes of government is one that must be accomplished by patient effort and constant trial. I have endeavored to work with every member of the legislature and have been available to every one of you at all times for assistance and consultation. I have not tried to impose my will upon any member or upon the body, and I shall not attempt to do so. My purpose has been the long-range one of accomplishing for Kentucky the improvement in government which is so much desired. I have been willing to share the credit for accomplishments with all who would help, regardless of party. The situation which now confronts us was not created by me. The solution is in your hands, and in your hands alone. The responsibility rests with you. I am ready, willing, and anxious to cooperate and to give you every aid within my power. Nothing recommended in this message could possibly give a partisan advantage. It deals only with the vital business of the state. Every member should be concerned to see that the schools, the aged, the blind and helpless, as well as the institutions, are properly financed and supported.

I appeal to you, regardless of party, to help solve these problems and to give your best thought for the remainder of the session to work which is so important. Let us forget all extraneous issues and concentrate all efforts upon the completion of our task. In that spirit, and with such purpose, we cannot fail.

---

1. J. Lee Moore (1899-1949) of Franklin. County attorney; state senator, 1935-39, 1947-49; state representative, 1939-47; chairman of Kentucky House Appropriations Committee, 1944. *Courier-Journal*, October 5, 1949.

2. As assistant director, Division of Accounts and Control, and budget director, Warren M. Van Hoose issued a report on March 3, 1944.

BUDGET BILL
Frankfort / March 10, 1944

To the General Assembly:

There is yet time to pass the special bills for the benefit of the schools and to create emergency funds for old age assistance, aid to the needy blind, and aid to dependent children, as well as for the further rehabilitation of the institutions.

In order that the General Assembly may be advised of my position, I wish to state that I have no intention of calling an extraordinary session of the General Assembly for the further consideration of a budget bill, and there will be no special session for such purpose.

I trust that with this information the General Assembly will proceed to pass the bills above mentioned. I hope that all extraneous issues may be forgotten and only the welfare of the people as a whole be considered. The serious need for the passage of these bills cannot be emphasized too strongly. All other considerations should be put aside. The sole responsibility for the solution of this problem is upon the General Assembly, and only the General Assembly can be entitled to the credit when it is solved.

INTERVIEW ON BUDGET BILL
Frankfort / March 11, 1944

GOVERNOR SIMEON WILLIS said today in an interview he believed there was time in the remaining three days of the legislative session to enact a budget bill thereby relieving the stalemate between the Republican executive department and the Democratic legislative department.

Governor Willis revealed a cautious inclination to compromise in a last-minute effort to prevent reversion to the old budget July 1 if a new one is not enacted. The new biennial budget, passed by Senate Democrats and defeated by House Republicans, calls for expenditure of $66,628,950. The old budget totaled $57,329,124.

On his willingness to give and take with the Democratic leaders,

Governor Willis said: "I would be willing to accept any sort of compromise which resulted in keeping the government sound, rendering the essential services, living within its income, and making ample provisions for the schools, institutions, and welfare assistance."

Governor Willis was presented four questions framed to give an index to what may prove to be long-range Republican strategy in refusing to yield to the Democratic version of the new budget. While his answers were not as pointed as the questions, they revealed his insight into what the questions meant.

"Do you believe," Governor Willis was asked, "there is time in the remaining three days of the session to reconsider the budget bill and enact it into law?"

"Yes," he replied. "If the Senate would recede from its amendments and pass the House bill, it could then be adopted by the House. The right of a legislative body to express its will cannot be taken away by the rules. The rules are in control of the House. Any rule to the contrary can be repealed or suspended at any time."

"From your experience as the Republican governor with the Democratic legislature, do you believe it is possible to reach a compromise in the budget stalemate?" the governor next was asked.

"I regret to say," he replied, "that I have not found some of the leaders of the House and Senate hospitable to any sort of compromise.

"I have insisted upon only such a budget as would prove practicable. I object to an appropriation without the ability to pay it. If the legislature would pass a budget bill and fix the appropriations substantially within the income it would be acceptable," he added.

"If it would provide for the excess of appropriations over actual income to be paid from the surplus, that would be acceptable," the governor continued. "It is impossible for the government to pay out more money than comes into the treasury. The only possible means of meeting excess appropriations made was from the surplus, which was forbidden.

"I would be willing to accept any sort of compromise which resulted in keeping the government sound, rendering the essential services, living within its income, and making ample provisions for the schools, institutions, and welfare assistance."

The governor next was asked: "Assuming that the budget bill could be resurrected in a give-and-take spirit by both sides, to what minimum extent are you willing to recede from the objections you have stated with reference to the bill the Senate passed and the House defeated?"

"I cannot recede," he replied, "from the position that when an appropriation is made the people will expect it to be paid, and if the money is not provided the appropriation has to be cut down to meet the actual money. For that reason it is unfair for the legislature to appropriate money ostensibly for some purpose and then provide conditions under which it cannot be paid, thus misleading the expected beneficiaries. Such a day-to-day living would obstruct the operations of the agencies and prevent planning of their work on a successful basis for the whole year."

"In what respect, if any," the governor was asked, "do you believe the people would be injured by automatic continuation of the old budget July 1?"

"The vital differences," he replied, "are in the benefits we proposed to confer upon the common school system and for the continuation of improvements at the institutions. As to old age assistance, I had hoped it would be possible for us to get along on the [old] appropriation [of $4,250,000 a year], but if an emergency should arise I was prepared to call a special session to deal with it. I stated this in my letter to the chairman [J. Lee Moore, of the House Appropriations Committee] on February 7."

"You have stated," the governor next was asked, "you do not intend to call a special session for consideration of a new budget for the next biennium. Do you likewise have no intention of calling special sessions for relief of education, welfare, and the institutional reconstruction program?"

"It would be useless," he replied, "to have a special session for the consideration of a new budget bill. Men who would not give me a reasonable budget bill in sixty days of the regular session certainly would not help me in a special session.

"This, of course, does not preclude the calling of a special session for any emergency which may arise during the remainder of my administration. What may constitute such an emergency will be for my decision at the time it arises."[1]

The next question was the first of four which attempted to find confirmation of what the Republican strategists may have in mind in being more willing to revert to the old budget than to accede to a new one framed by the Democrats.

"Do you believe," he was asked, "this stalemate between a Republican executive department and the Democratic legislative branch will justify you politically to ask the people to give you a Republican legislature in 1946?"

"I think," he replied, "the action of the Democratic leaders was sufficient to justify me in asking the people to give me a Republican legislature in 1946. I will say, however, that the Democrats who supported my program were just as earnest and faithful as any other members, and I certainly shall commend them to the people for their courage, loyalty, and intelligence."

"If the old budget is automatically renewed July 1, and no tax laws are repealed," the governor next was asked, "are you aware that the cash surplus may be from $20 million to $25 million by June 30, 1946?"

"It is possible," he replied, "that operating under the old budget without any special appropriations for emergencies may increase the surplus considerably, but I do not believe it will reach the figures you have mentioned."

"If the people give you a Republican legislature in 1946," he next was asked, "have you considered the possibilities of a gigantic public improvements program in the 1946-48 biennium, sponsored by a complete Republican administration and financed by the possible cash surplus of $25 million?"

"If I should have a Republican legislature in 1946," the governor replied, "I would ask it to carry out my program already advocated before the people. I would want to advance the cause of education, meet the requirements of the schools, including the Negro educational program, and all features of my educational program.

"I would also advocate the continuation of a constructive program of improvements at the institutions and urge constant betterment of the old age assistance program. If that left a margin of safety, I would then recommend a repeal of taxes in order that the people might be relieved of the tax burden so far as possible."

"As the head of the Republican party in Kentucky," he was asked finally, "do you or not see political advantage for your party in the next governor's race if the Republicans are able, in the 1946-48 biennium, to inaugurate and finance a magnificent program of public improvements in the fields of health, education, welfare, parks, and highways?"

"As head of the Republican party in Kentucky," the governor replied, "I do not seek any political advantage from the program which I advocate. I ask the people for support of the public improvements which I advocate in the fields of health, education, welfare, parks, and highways, but I do it on the merits of the proposition. If we can accomplish our program, which I have advocated and which I think commands the confidence and support of the people, then our party should be benefited to the extent it supports the program which I advocate. But I do not seek political advantage in executing the duties of my office, but seek solely to promote the welfare of the people.

"It is my belief that the party is served best by its adherents serving the country. After all, the credit for public improvements belongs to the people who pay for them," he concluded.

1. Governor Willis at this time sought to force the Democratic majority to pass his budget bill by suggesting that, if they did not, no special session would be called. As usual, however, he differentiated between a special session for education and one for the budget and did not preclude a session for an "emergency" situation. See also the message dated March 17, 1944, in this section.

BUDGET
Frankfort / March 16, 1944

THE refusal of the General Assembly to cooperate in enacting a budget bill to take care of the needs of the common schools compels the government to operate under the budget act of 1942 for the fiscal year 1943-44.[1]

The General Assembly failed even to consider the special bills recommended by me for the benefit of the common schools. Other special bills recommended by me were likewise denied consideration, although they related solely to welfare assistance and rehabilitation of the institutions.

This situation presents an emergency immediately affecting the common schools, as the time for employing teachers is rapidly approaching. The schools cannot afford to lose any more trained teachers, and efforts should be made to bring back as many as possible of those who have heretofore left for higher pay and other callings. The first consideration is the proper education of the children, and that should be our greatest concern.

In view of the seriousness of this problem, I believe further effort should be made for the enactment of the common school program. As early as possible I shall call a special session of the General Asembly for the consideration of the subject of an appropriation of funds to carry out the entire common school program, which I have heretofore recommended to the General Assembly. When this first task shall have been completed the other emergency bills will be recommended.[2]

---

1. The actual fiscal year was 1944-45.

2. A special session devoted to education funding was called within two months. See message dated May 15, 1944, in this section.

BUDGET
Frankfort / March 17, 1944

IN order, if possible, to prevent misrepresentation and distortions, I restate the facts of the record. It is not possible for me to correct every misstatement that may be made by those who do not desire to be accurate, but in dealing with the public business it is important that the people understand exactly the situations that are presented and the reasons which require them to be dealt with as they arise.

It is my policy to ignore misrepresentations in gossip columns and editorials, trusting the news columns of the papers to report the facts. It is the facts upon which public opinion is formed, and when the facts are fully understood the people will not be fooled.

Much of my program has been accomplished, both in the enactment of laws, and in the defeat of many efforts to undermine by indirect action the constructive program of my administration. The perversion of my message to the General Assembly, in which I stated that no extraordinary session of the General Assembly for the consideration of a budget bill would be called, is not to be excused.

The message was submitted on March 10, at a time when the partisan leaders in the legislature who desired to hamper the administration were trying to smother legislation then being requested by me, in order to force a special session in which a free hand at the whole budget might be given them. To forestall that plan, the General Assembly was definitely advised that there would be no such special session. There will not be any special session for the consideration of a new budget bill.

As stated by me, in an interview with Mr. Allan Trout,[1] published in the *Courier-Journal* on March 12, this did not preclude a special session to consider some specific problem of an emergency nature, such as an appropriation for the schools, or one for the institutions, or one for welfare assistance. Notwithstanding these very clear statements, there is now being made an effort to confuse the two things. In an editorial this morning the *Courier-Journal* said: "The special budget session which the governor said just a week ago today positively would not be called, but which he said yesterday will be called was made inevitable by his tactics."

Such attempt to confuse the public is indefensible. The difference between the two is all important. The legislature had ample opportunity to grant my requests at the regular session, but the leaders in control stubbornly refused to permit consideration of the general budget or the special bills. Under the constitution I have the right to call the General Assembly in special session for the consideration of a single subject. I propose to do just that, and the single issue of granting or denying the school program will have to be met. There can be no evasion or subterfuge.

The same men who refused to reconsider the budget bill prevented consideration of the special bills. They knew in plenty of time it was the last chance they would have to pass a general budget bill reasonably meeting the demands of the occasion. They cannot evade the issue that will be presented. The responsibility will be placed squarely upon them. When that issue is met we can proceed to deal with other problems of an emergency nature that may then remain to be decided.

The special session which I propose to call to take care of the schools will not have for consideration a new budget bill, or any budget bill. It will have no power to consider anything except relief for the schools.

In fighting for the objectives which I have undertaken for the benefit of the people, I am compelled to proceed step by step until all of them are accomplished facts. None of these objectives have been abandoned, and none will be. The fight will be carried forward until the victory is finally won. The effort to delay or defeat us by misrepresentation will not succeed. We will not be diverted from our purpose. I think the people will understand that we have fought to promote the welfare of the state and not to play politics.

Fortunately, there were enough independent Democrats in the legislature to prevent the success of the schemes devised to impair our program. I appreciate the cooperation given by these high-minded and independent Democrats, and I know they have the support of public opinion.

Let the public understand once and for all that this administration is striving for the achievement of the objectives already approved by the people and will not permit these objectives to be obscured or diverted in partisan uses.

---

1. Allan M. Trout (1903-1972). Tennessee native; journalist for the *Courier-Journal*, 1929-67; state board of education, 1968-72. *Courier-Journal*, December 8, 1972.

VETO OF HOUSE BILL NO. 243
Frankfort / March 21, 1944

In a message concerning the veto of House Bill 243, the so-called Roadhouse Bill, the governor said it was not necessary to eliminate the sale of beverages at roadhouses, as the act creating the new department (House Bill 305) "takes care of this question at least as well as does House Bill 243 and no need for duplication exists."

Governor Willis said that the value of postponing the elections until that time "was debatable."

He added it was "the very essence of a republican form of government that elections be held in order that the people may express themselves. . . . Elections have always been held during war and other crises. The people have a right to vote whenever they desire and are jealous of that right."[1]

Under terms of the bill, voters could say whether they favored sale of whiskey and the sale of beer by the drink or the package. Willis said: "The splitting up of the questions to be submitted to the voters into four points is of doubtful value," and that it might be "impossible to determine the will of the majority."

He also said that provisions of the bill enabling a city to vote wet while the county was dry was "a drastic departure."

The governor also vetoed a bill which would have amended the state inheritance and estate tax laws to provide exemptions ranging from $5,000 to $25,000. Willis said the Department of Finance had advised him the bill would result in a loss of from $300,000 to $500,000 annually in taxes. He said that with other state revenue decreasing, he had no alternative other than to veto the bill.

Another bill vetoed was one which would have required the state finance department to furnish quarterly reports to members of the General Assembly, showing names, addresses, titles, and pay of state employees. Willis said the report would have involved unnecessary expenses, that it would serve "no useful purpose," and that the requested facts were available at any time.

---

1. Proponents of the law had contended that men in the armed forces had a right to vote on local option and that such elections should be deferred to at least 1946. *Courier-Journal*, March 22, 1944.

PROCLAMATION FOR SPECIAL SESSION
Frankfort / May 15, 1944

To all to whom these presents shall come:

WHEREAS, the regular 1944 session of the General Assembly of Kentucky adjourned without enacting an appropriation bill resulting under existing law in requiring all the governmental agencies and departments to operate under the appropriation act for the fiscal year 1943-1944; and

WHEREAS, the provision thereby made available for the common school educational system is not sufficient and creates a crisis in the schools, making it imperative that special provision be made for the common school system created and maintained under the mandate of the constitution:

THEREFORE, in consideration of the facts and conditions mentioned, and by virtue of the power vested in me by the constitution of the state to convene the General Assembly of the commonwealth of Kentucky in extraordinary session, I, Simeon Willis, governor of the commonwealth of Kentucky, do hereby issue this proclamation convening the General Assembly of Kentucky, in extraordinary session at the seat of government at Frankfort, Kentucky, at two o'clock P.M. on the nineteenth day of May 1944, for the sole purpose of making appropriations from the surplus and general fund for education as follows:[1]

1. Common School Per Capita Fund. For the payment of teachers' salaries which shall include interest on state school bonds.

2. Equalization Fund. For equalization of educational service in the common schools as provided by law.

3. Free Textbooks. For the purchase of textbooks, as provided by law.

4. Lincoln Institute of Kentucky. For ordinary recurring expenses of operating a practice teacher training high school in accordance with a contract between the State Board of Education and the board of trustees of Lincoln Institute.

5. College Tuition for Negroes. For extraordinary expenses of paying college tuition for Negro students required to go out of the state to obtain higher educational training.[2]

6. Teachers' Retirement Fund. For administering and complying with the obligations of the state under the Teachers' Retirement Act, KRS 161.220 and 161.710.

7. And for ordinary recurring expenses of operation for 1944-1945 and 1945-1946 of the following other divisions and subdivisions of the

Department of Education and educational agencies under the control
of the Kentucky State Board of Education.
   a. Superintendent of Public Instruction
   b. Division of Certification
   c. State Board of Education
   d. State Textbook Commission
   e. Vocational Education
   f. Vocational Rehabilitation
   g. Kentucky State College for Negroes
   h. West Kentucky Vocational Training School for Negroes
   i. Kentucky School for the Blind—White
   j. Kentucky School for the Blind—Colored
   k. Kentucky School for the Blind—Workshop for the Adult Blind
   l. Mayo Vocational Training School
   m. Public School Lunch Program
You will there assemble in accordance with this proclamation at the
seat of government at Frankfort, Kentucky, in extraordinary session on
the day and date above written to act upon the subjects herein named
and only said subjects.
   GIVEN UNDER MY HAND, this fifteenth day of May 1944, by the
governor.

To all to whom these presents shall come:
   WHEREAS, in the governor's proclamation of May 15, 1944, convening the General Assembly in extraordinary session, provision for
the Kentucky School for the Deaf, including both white and colored,
was inadvertently omitted; and
   WHEREAS, the emergency which has arisen concerning education
affects the Kentucky School for the Deaf,
   THEREFORE, in order that the General Assembly may consider the
whole subject matter sought to be submitted, according to the power
vested in me by the constitution of Kentucky, I do issue my proclamation amending and adding items as follows, to wit:
   To provide for the ordinary recurring expenses of operation of the
Kentucky School for the Deaf, white and colored, and this addition will
be treated by the General Assembly the same as if in the original
proclamation.
   GIVEN UNDER MY HAND, this seventeenth day of May 1944, by the
governor.

---

1. Governor Willis had declared that he would not call a special session unless assured of Democratic cooperation. After a series of meetings with legislative leaders in early May, he decided to limit the call to educational matters only. See *Courier-Journal*, May 5, 9, 16, 1944.

2. Under the Anderson-Myer State Aid Act of 1936, black students received up to $175 tuition annually for courses not available to them in-state as a result of Kentucky's segregation statutes. Five thousand dollars were appropriated for that fund for 1937 and 1938. Kentucky *Acts* (1936), 110-12.

SPECIAL SESSION
Frankfort / May 19, 1944

I HAVE called you in extraordinary session to meet an extraordinary situation. The failure at the regular session to enact an appropriation act has required us by the force of existing law to operate the government under the appropriations for the last fiscal year of the current biennium. As a result, every department of the government will operate within the limits of expenditure provided by the act of 1942 for ordinary recurring expenses. The appropriations under the act of 1942 for capital outlay and emergency expenditures are not continued in effect. We can operate for the present under the last budget insofar as all the departments are concerned, except in the educational department. The amount appropriated by the act of 1942 for the schools proved insufficient. This fact was recognized by my predecessor, who supplemented it from an emergency fund which he had but which I do not have. In addition to that provision by Governor Johnson from one of his emergency funds, you provided $3 million from the surplus to supplement the 1942 school appropriation for the current fiscal year. Moreover, the $400,000 equalization fund has been spread more widely, and that means less to the counties that participated therein last year. The schools, therefore, are not in as good condition as they were during the fiscal year 1943-1944.

The crisis of the schools which has been approaching over a number of years has been accentuated by the impact of war and the failure to maintain for next year provision equal at least to that for the current fiscal year. For these reasons I have deemed it necessary to call you together to deal with this single subject. I have limited your consideration solely to the schools because of the emergency that called for immediate action. Furthermore, I deemed it wise to remove the subject from every extraneous consideration.[1] The single subject presented is the adoption of a bill for the relief of the schools.

The peril of the schools is facing us now. There is a shortage of competent teachers and a threat that many schools may be without teachers. I have heard from every part of the state, and I am convinced that the whole educational system will be greatly impaired if these proposed appropriations are not made. The act proposed is believed to be sufficient to solve the problem of the present crisis. The leaders of educational thought unite in advocating it. The amount of money required is available, although it requires the use of a part of the accumulated surplus. I see no reason why the surplus should not be used to the extent that may be necessary to meet these appropriations for education. The surplus belongs to the people for public use and was accumulated during the years when the appropriations for the common schools were certainly not sufficient. I can conceive of no emergency more pressing than the emergency of the schools to justify resort to a part of the surplus in the treasury. The very purpose to be served by a surplus, as I stated in my original message to you on January 10, 1944, is to take care of situations resulting from the impact of war, the fluctuations of revenue, and other conditions resulting from emergencies. I do not now propose, and have never proposed, that any part of the surplus should be used for current running expenses of the government. But relief for the schools is not of that character. It is no fault of theirs that they are not here to assist. They are rendering the paramount service required of all citizens. Some teachers have left for war work where the pay is higher. Certainly they should not be blamed because the work which they are rendering is essential. But the education of our children cannot be postponed or delayed. It must be carried on each year. All we can do about it must be done, and certainly we can make the provision deemed sufficient by the educational leaders of the state.

Many requests were addressed to me to include other subjects for your consideration. The importance of many of these subjects is apparent, but they cannot be introduced at this time. The program for the tuberculosis hospitals has been launched. The General Assembly at its regular session enacted a law which will be effective on June 13, 1944, directing the governor to appoint a commission for the purpose of devising plans for the construction, financing, and operations of several tuberculosis institutions.[2] This plan will be carried on in an orderly way and without delay, but it required no further action by the legislature until the report and recommendations of the commission shall be received. The provision for the repairs at the institutions now being carried out will be completed in a few months. At the end of that time we will know what further improvements are imperative, what manpower and materials may be available for further construction, and what money may be required. That situation can be dealt with when the time arrives in the light of conditions then existing. In fact, all other subjects which have been suggested, however important, are not of such nature as to require immediate action.

I recommend the adoption of the bill which will be offered to meet the present emergency. It will, in my opinion, promote the general welfare, and meet the reasonable expectations of the people. It will reflect credit on all who have part in the achievement.

---

1. Governor Willis responded in this way to majority leader Earle C. Clements's attack the day before the special session opened. Clements accused the governor of abandoning an earlier agreement that would call for an expanded session, covering the entire budget. Willis, in turn, stated that no agreement was made and later called another Clements communication "a low-grade letter." *Courier-Journal,* May 18-19, 23, 1944.

2. House Bill 147, "An act making provision for State Tuberculosis Sanatoria," created a commission of twelve members, appointed by the governor. They would, within a specified time, recommend sites for new TB hospitals. Kentucky *Acts* (1944), 174-79.

EDUCATION BILL
Frankfort / May 31, 1944

I HAVE received a copy of your resolution requesting me to enlarge the call for the present special session so as to include several additional subjects.[1]

When I issued the call for the special session I explained the necessity which compelled us to eliminate consideration of all other subjects except the schools. In a published statement I said:

"I have called a special session of the General Assembly to meet at two P.M., Friday, May 19, for the purpose of making appropriations for the common school system, asking that any extra amount required over the income for any fiscal year be taken from the surplus. It seems to me that the crisis in which the schools are now involved requires relief which can be met only by a special appropriation. If the income should be inadequate, then I think the surplus should be used for the schools to the extent of the deficit. I can conceive of no possible contingency calling for resort to the surplus of greater importance than the maintenance of the school system.

"There are many other subjects which have been suggested to be embraced in the call, but these matters, however important, can be taken care of from time to time and do not require immediate action of the General Assembly. So far as these other subjects are concerned, they will be dealt with from time to time as action may be required. If an emergency should arise which requires legislative action in the future, a special session can then be called. Any action now would be predicated upon prophecy, and it is better to await events and deal with real situations. The only emergency requiring immediate attention is the schools, and I am limiting the session to that one subject so that it may be considered impartially and without being involved in other considerations."

As I explained to you in my message on May 19, at the opening of the session, I fully appreciate the importance of each of the subjects suggested in your resolution. Many people have mentioned these subjects to me, and thorough consideration was given to each request before the special session was called. I conferred with many senators and representatives, and I reached the conclusion which I know is sound—that relief for the schools should be considered before undertaking to solve any other problem. First things come first. The schools will open early in July, and immediate relief is demanded. The condition of the schools constitutes a pressing emergency, and that subject is now before you for consideration.

The bill which has been introduced was carefully prepared, and it is regarded as sufficient to take care of the schools. That bill has not been passed, although ample time has elapsed for its passage. It is not only the most important subject, but it is the only subject before the General Assembly. It serves no useful purpose to propose new subjects so long as the one pressing problem remains unsolved. It would require but a few days to pass the school bill, and I trust it may receive your prompt, favorable, and undivided consideration. The schools must have relief now. The other subjects will be considered in their own proper time and order, and appropriate action recommended.

I explained these matters to you in my message on May 19. In that message I said:

"The program for the tuberculosis hospitals has been launched. The General Assembly at its regular session enacted a law which will be effective on June 13, 1944, directing the governor to appoint a commission for the purpose of devising plans for the construction, financing, and operation of several tuberculosis institutions. This plan will be carried on in an orderly way and without delay, but it requires no further action by the legislature until the report and recommendations of the commission shall be received.

"The provision for the repairs at the institutions now being carried out will be completed in a few months. At the end of that time we will know what further improvements are imperative, what manpower and materials may be available for further construction, and what money may be required. The situation can be dealt with when the time arrives in the light of conditions then existing. In fact, all other subjects which have been suggested, however important, are not of such a nature as to require immediate action."

I have also explained it in public addresses. In an address to the Kentucky Education Association I emphasized the needs and demands of other branches of the government.[2] When the time comes to take action upon any other subject, I shall call upon you for such action.

With due respect to your opinion, as indicated in the resolution, I am convinced that the introduction at this time of any additional subjects would be the signal for additional delay and debate. Confusion of many things should not be allowed to delay action for the solution of our present pressing problem, which cannot be delayed. The attempts we see on every side to spread confusion, when you have but one subject for consideration, is sufficient to show what might result if the field were broadened and other subjects brought before you. The issue is simple, plain, and unclouded. It is just this—shall the bill offered for the relief of schools, including sufficient of the surplus to meet any deficit in revenue, be enacted?

I recommend most earnestly that the proposed bill be adopted without further delay.

---

1. On May 24, 1944, by a 30-2 vote, the Senate supported an Earle Clements-sponsored resolution which called on the governor to amend his call to include a full budget revision. Specifically, attention was directed to tuberculosis hospi-

tals, conservation, veterans assistance, and old age assistance. Kentucky *Senate Journal* (1944), 3244-46.

    2. Given April 14, 1944. See "Education" section.

MEMORANDUM TO SENATOR MOSS
Frankfort / June 1, 1944

I HAVE considered the tentative act appropriating money for the operation of the state government which you[1] handed to me last evening.[2] A corrected copy was sent to me this afternoon. The bill is not satisfactory to me.

    1. Let the General Assembly pass the school bill now pending before it without change or amendment.

    2. When that is done let the proposed bill be corrected in the following particulars:

    a) Make provision for the supplementing of old age assistance if the provision of the old budget should prove insufficient. There is apprehension that this result may happen. Under the proposed bill all of the income and all of the surplus funds are disposed of so that if an emergency should arise in the future in respect to the old age assistance, there would be no way of caring for it except by new taxes and a special session of the General Assembly. In the first proposed bill which you handed me there had been written, and then cancelled, an emergency fund of $250,000 for each year of the next biennium to take care of a possible emergency requirement of the old age assistance fund, including funds for dependent children and aid to the blind. Undoubtedly this emergency provision should be made in any bill that I am to consider.

    b) The provision for the tuberculosis sanatoriums departs from the plan already adopted by the General Assembly. This conflict should be eliminated. I do not intend to be placed in a position of having two conflicting laws on the subject of the tuberculosis sanatoriums which would create confusion and possible delay. The appropriation for the tuberculosis sanatoriums should be made in accordance with the existing statute which will be effective June 13, 1944, or the legislature should clarify the situation, giving a single plan for this purpose. The board should contain representative men from different occupations, and should not be limited to the medical profession or any other single profession.

c) The funds set apart for the repair of the institutions should be made on the same terms that were contained in the act of 1942 respecting the $3 million. I do not think it should be frozen at the top so that no cushion would be left for emergencies. I see no reason why this fund should not be provided for the next two years on the same terms that it was provided for the past two years. If the money is to be invested in United States bonds during the period when construction work is not practicable, the language should be changed so that the bonds could be converted into cash when construction contracts were made. In other words, the money should be available to comply with existing laws as to the making of such contracts, and the money should not be frozen for any definite period, but free to be used as soon as construction materials and men are available.

I have repeatedly stated my reasons why the schools should be taken care of before anything else is undertaken. It is an emergency that is upon us now. As soon as that emergency is satisfied and the members of the General Assembly sign an agreement to enact such a bill, we can then complete the entire subject matter. There will be ample time to resolve differences of opinion and to reach a definite conclusion, but until the school bill is passed it is a waste of time to discuss these other questions. I hope the school bill can be passed at once.

---

1. Ray Bingham Moss (1889-1979) of Pineville. Republican state senator, 1931-50; minority floor leader under Willis; *Courier-Journal*, September 21, 1979; *Who's Who in Kentucky, 1936*, 295. Republican Whip Claude L. Hammond of Corbin read the memorandum publicly and placed it in the Kentucky *Senate Journal* (1944), 3322-24.

2. Even though a full budget was not included in the call for a special session, legislators had drafted a proposed budget very similar to the Democratic version earlier defeated in the regular session. Governor Willis's specific objections to that maneuver and the proposal continued his earlier criticism. *Courier-Journal*, June 3, 1944.

STATEMENT URGING SUPPORT
FOR EDUCATION BILL
Frankfort / June 3, 1944

THE attempt to confuse the issue by changing the discussion from the one subject of relief for the schools to all other subjects of government is now apparent.

On January 10, 1944, shortly after the General Assembly convened, the governor presented a general budget bill which was referred to the proper committees in both houses. The appropriations proposed by that bill were substantially within the estimated income. Hearings were conducted and the two committees worked together for a time.

Some amendments were agreed upon in the House committee which were accepted by the governor and which increased the appropriations substantially. The amount, however, was still within the range of a balanced budget.

The bill, with the committee amendments, was reported to the House. Amendments were added by the House which increased the appropriations in excess of $2 million, and with these amendments the bill was adopted by the House. The Senate retained all the House amendments and added others which still further increased the total and surrounded it with impracticable restrictions.

It made the appropriations but prevented the payment of them. It required a horizontal reduction all along the line, affecting every department of the government, including the schools and old age assistance. This made the bill so objectionable that it was defeated in the House.

The governor appeared before a joint session, when there was yet time, and proposed the passage of the budget bill as recommended by him, with the committee amendments or restrictions. If that was not acceptable, he proposed that the government operate under the old budget, as required by law, but that special bills be enacted for the relief of the schools, for the benefit of the institutions, and for the protection of old age assistance.

These proposals were not acted upon by either house. The majority of the senators remained silent and refused to vote. The fifteen Republican senators voted for the plan.

The General Assembly adjourned without passing any sort of a budget bill. This remitted the government to the 1943-44 budget. The state can operate under that budget for the present, but it will not be sufficient for the schools. It leaves them where they were last year, without the special help given. The governor announced that he would ask, as soon as possible, that a special session grant relief to the schools. A great many suggestions were made, and some with insistence, that other subjects be included.

In view of the experience at the regular session, it was clear that the introduction of other subjects would lead to delay and confusion which might endanger the school bill. This is again made clear by the present discussion. The condition of the schools called for immediate relief. All other subjects could wait further experience, to be dealt with when and if a new crisis arose.

Opinion appeared to be strongly in support of the proposal to grant the schools $15 million, with the full 10 percent for the equalization fund. The surplus was available to make up any deficit resulting if the income proved insufficient. After careful study and mature deliberation, the governor decided to call the special session limited to a consideration of the one problem of the schools.

The reasons for this position were explained in a statement to the press when the call was issued. In the governor's address to the General Assembly on May 19 the subject was restated and the facts presented why the single recommendation was absolutely essential. Days passed without action. Each house adopted a resolution requesting inclusion of several additional subjects. The merits of these subjects were appealing, but the reasons for not including them were compelling. In response to these resolutions the governor restated the issue.

In the meantime, Senator [Ray] Moss had sought to work out the problem. He believed that he could obtain a bill satisfactory to the governor, with an agreement signed by all of the legislature to pass such a bill and adjourn. No such bill has been prepared or agreement signed.

Senator Moss advised the governor that absolutely nothing would be done by the opposition, in any event, for old age assistance and other needs for the dependent. The tentative bill exhausted every dollar of estimated revenue and estimated surplus, so that nothing would be left for the old people whatever crisis might arise. The governor will not consent for the door of hope to be closed in the face of the needy old people, the dependent children, or the needy blind.

A copy of a proposed bill was given to the governor Wednesday night. A corrected copy was given him on Thursday afternoon. As soon as the governor considered this bill he advised Senator Moss that the bill was not satisfactory and pointed out:

1. That the General Assembly should first pass the school bill pending before it without change or amendment or restriction.

2. When that is done, let the proposed [budget] bill be corrected so as to provide for old age assistance, if the contingency arises, and to carry out the program already under way as to tuberculosis hospitals.

In regard to the institutions, the work which has been initiated is being carried forward. That was the program of the governor during the campaign, and it was included in his budget bill, and it is what the public demands.

There can be no good reason for changing the plan or terms of the appropriations relating to the institutions. The governor should have the same authority under any new law that the former governor had under the 1942 act.

This protracted discussion of a whole budget problem is not designed to obtain a bill, but it is intended to create confusion and divert the issue. It is planned to get complete control and to defeat the school program. At the present time the General Assembly can consider the school bill. It can with propriety consider nothing else because the only subject before it is the school bill.

The bill pending in the House and Senate does not encroach on the surplus farther than is acceptable to the opposition. This is proven by the earmarking in the tentative bill of $3,319,050 of the surplus to make up any deficit in the estimated income. It is necessary for the relief of the schools.

If persons interested in the schools, including the teachers themselves, will stand by this bill and insist upon its passage, success will be assured. If they permit the continued discussion of numerous other subjects not up for legislative consideration, they will defeat the whole purpose of the special session.

The attitude of certain leaders has demonstrated both publicly and privately that the sole purpose is to defeat the school program, regardless of its effect on the schools. They desire to tie the governor's hands in carrying on his administration. What they fear to try directly, they seek to accomplish by indirection.

Those who favor relief for the schools must back the school bill with all their influence. If they cannot pass the school bill by itself, they certainly cannot pass it when complicated with many other subjects. The schools need relief today. All other subjects can be dealt with hereafter. There is no reason for delay. The public expects the General Assembly to proceed at once to pass the bill for the relief of the schools.

PROCLAMATION FOR SECOND SPECIAL SESSION
Frankfort / June 12, 1944

To all to whom these presents shall come:

Whereas, the extraordinary session of the General Assembly of Kentucky, which was called pursuant to proclamation of the governor on May 19, 1944, has duly enacted a bill appropriating money for the operation, maintenance, support, and functioning of the state government of the commonwealth of Kentucky, including appropriations for the various offices, departments, boards, commissions, institutions, and subdivisions of the state government, and for the Department of Highways, and designating the sources and funds from which said appropriations are made, more fully set forth in Senate Bill No. 3 passed unanimously by the Senate and by the House;[1] and

Whereas, the original proclamation specified particularly the purpose of the special session as being for the sole purpose of making appropriations for education and for the different educational funds; and

Whereas, some doubt has arisen as to the validity of the appropriations made for public purposes other than for the schools; and

Whereas, it is the desire of the executive and legislative departments that said bill shall be valid in all respects and that said appropriations so made are necessary and proper for the carrying on of the state government;

Therefore, in consideration of the facts and conditions mentioned, and by virtue of the power vested in me by the constitution of the state to convene the General Assembly of the commonwealth of Kentucky in extraordinary session, I, Simeon Willis, governor of the commonwealth of Kentucky do hereby issue this proclamation convening the General Assembly of Kentucky in extraordinary session at the seat of government, Frankfort, Kentucky, at 11:30 o'clock P.M. on the twelfth day of June 1944, for the purpose of passing an act appropriating money for the operation, maintenance, support, and functioning of the state government of the commonwealth of Kentucky, including each of the various offices, departments, boards, commissions, institutions, and subdivisions of the state government, and the purchase of record books as provided by Section 28.130 of the Kentucky Revised Statutes of 1942, judiciary and court costs, Confederate pensions, the Frankfort Cemetery, Jefferson, Kenton, and Harlan county fees, and for defraying the expenses of all other state obligations for (a) the fiscal years ending June 30, 1945, and June 30, 1946 (b) the fiscal years of the Department of Highways ending March 31, 1945, and March 31, 1946; designating the sources and funds from which said appropriations are made, and providing for the establishment of certain revolving funds and the investment of certain funds; providing for money refunds; prescribing certain powers and duties of the commissioner of finance, the governor, the state treasurer, and other public officials, institutions, boards, commissions, and agencies with respect thereto; and providing for funds for the State Tuberculosis Board; authorizing and empowering the commissioner of finance with the approval of the ·governor to limit, restrict, and supervise expenditures of all money appropriated by the General Assembly in the second extraordinary session of 1944, and to reduce or adjust each of the appropriations; to provide for certain appropriations to be limited to specific purposes and barring the use of appropriations for certain purposes; repealing all blanket and continuing appropriations and appropriations made by any previous act or acts of the General Assembly of the commonwealth of Kentucky, and repealing all laws or parts of laws in conflict with any of the provisions of such act; enacting each section and each subsection as a separate or specific appropriation.

You will therefore assemble in accordance with this proclamation at the seat of government at Frankfort, Kentucky, in extraordinary session on the day and date above written to act upon the subjects herein named and only said subjects.

GIVEN UNDER MY HAND, this twelfth day of June 1944, by the governor.

---

1. In defiance of the governor, the General Assembly had passed a complete budget bill, which included the subject of schools, the only item covered in Willis's proclamation of the first special session. Constitutionally, the legislative action was questionable, but since the budget met most of the governor's requirements, he agreed to another special session, thus ensuring the budget's constitutionality. On June 16, 1944, the budget bill was passed, enrolled, and signed by the governor. *Courier-Journal,* June 10, 1944; Kentucky *Acts* (1944), 522.

A REPORT TO THE PEOPLE
Louisville / June 23, 1944

Six months of this administration have passed and the people are entitled to know the progress that has been made. It is sound policy to let the people know the facts. With the facts, they can be trusted to reach sound judgments. Mutual confidence is essential in a government of the people, by the people, and for the people. A government attuned to the aspirations of the people is the ideal, and freedom from governmental interference, except where absolutely necessary, is a safeguard of liberty. It shall be the policy of this administration to keep the people fully informed at all times of all activities.

Despite statements to the contrary by the opposition, the program of this administration has in large part been accomplished, and unexpected situations have been dealt with promptly and effectively. Immediately after the inauguration the suspended work at the several state institutions was resumed. This work is being prosecuted diligently, and the bad conditions at the institutions are being corrected.

The welfare department has already established a record of fine achievement. The plans for the future are being developed, and the many problems attending the administration of the institutions, old age assistance, and the prisons will be the constant care of faithful and devoted public servants.

The men and women appointed to office have been carefully chosen. The administration has secured the services of $10,000-a-year men for $5,000 positions, and also $300 per month quality has been obtained on a $150 salary basis.[1] Our gratitude is due these men and women whose loyalty and patriotism prompt them to make personal sacrifices for the public good. The appointments for responsible places where service without compensation is required have met with general commendation. In fact, the appointments generally have established confidence in the honesty, efficiency, and high purpose of the administration.

The General Assembly authorized the appointment of a Youth Guidance Commission to make a comprehensive study of the problems of youth and for the discovery of ways and means to prevent youthful delinquency. The governor has selected a commission of five men and women, especially qualified and deeply interested, to make this study.[2]

A new parole board of high-minded and able men and women has been set up to carry out the policy of rehabilitation of the prisoners.

This board is devoting much time and outstanding ability to its task.

A new Department for the Control of Alcoholic Beverages has been established under an act of the last General Assembly. Men specially qualified have been put in charge of this important and exacting task. This carries out a long-cherished plan to separate the enforcement of liquor laws and regulations from the Department of Revenue.[3]

An act creating a board to locate, plan, construct, and manage tuberculosis sanatoria was recommended by the governor and passed by the legislature. An appropriation of $1.5 million for this object is included in the budget bill. This commission will be selected shortly, and the important work will receive the most competent and careful consideration at all times. It is one of the objectives advocated by the governor for many years, and the people are greatly concerned that the humanitarian purpose shall be achieved.

A postwar planning board will be selected to give comprehensive study to all the needs of the people and particularly the soldiers, returning now and after the war is won.

A complete tax program is not practical when conditions as a result of the war are constantly changing.[4] Fluctuations in values and the transfer of peace activities to war purposes constantly affect sources of revenue. A board of competent men will be selected to make a special study of the whole subject for the purpose of recommending to the General Assembly a comprehensive program of tax reform.

The governor recommended, and the legislature passed, an act submitting to the people an amendment to the constitution authorizing the General Assembly to provide for voters in the armed services, or necessarily absent from the state, a means of participating in all elections.[5] The governor approved several bills for the convenient handling of the business and property of those in the armed services while serving their country.[6]

The program for the highway department has been largely accomplished. The roads are now in the hands of an accomplished engineer who is devoted to the construction and maintenance of a first-class highway system. Against violent opposition this program was put through and preserved, and the people are to be congratulated on this achievement.

From information furnished by the Division of Records of the Department of Highways, the saving in administrative costs for the first four months of 1944 over the first four months in 1943 is approximately $100,000.

Elimination of useless jobs, such as guards on bridges, gasoline checkers, and investigators, which are not carried on the administrative payrolls, produced a saving for the first four months of 1944 over the same months of 1943 of approximately another $100,000. By a closer check on toll bridge collections, the total toll collections for the first four months of 1944, compared with the same months in 1943, show a total of approximately $35,000 advance in toll collections.

Projecting these figures for four months for the entire current year, at this rate of saving on administrative cost in the department, as brought about by the reorganization under the present administration, there should be a total saving in the administration of the department of approximately $300,000 per year. This figure does not include a multitude of economies that have been effected in the field in the elimination of unnecessary jobholders and useless jobs, where the cost heretofore has been charged to the construction and maintenance departments, and are not reflected in the figure of administrative cost savings just mentioned.

In the reorganization of the department, nine advisory highway commissioners and one rural highway commissioner have been eliminated. A large number of jobs and jobholders have been eliminated, either by outright elimination or consolidation, such as, for instance, eighty bridge guards, a number of gasoline checkers, toll bridge supervisors, investigators, and the like, who were riding around the state in state-owned cars and performing very few governmental duties. All of which, in addition to the saving in administrative cost, has effected a saving in the maintenance and construction funds of approximately an additional $25,000 per month.

The net result of reorganization in the highway department is that there should be a saving of approximately $50,000 per month or $600,000 per year, in administrative, construction, and maintenance cost. By reorganization and more careful supervision of the toll bridges, there will be collected and turned in to the toll bridge fund an estimated $100,000 more than was turned in last year, even though traffic this year is running approximately 5 percent below 1943.

The Department of Highways, under present conditions, with its reduced revenue and federal restrictions, cannot undertake any construction except the most urgent small projects that may be necessary or vital to the immediate transportation needs. The department is devoting its energies toward the maintenance and upkeep of the present system and is now engaged in the making of surveys and completing the plans on a large reservoir of road projects that are ready to draw from, and the work may be put under construction immediately after the war is over. This department now has plans completed on projects which contemplate a cost in excess of $10 million and is planning additional projects at the rate of approximately $10 million a year. We may look forward with confidence to the initiation of a well-planned and intelligent program of highway construction in Kentucky, beginning as soon as the war is over.

If the federal legislation that is now pending is approved, the Kentucky program will be of considerable magnitude and will include improvements of the main federal system of roads, construction and improvement of feeder roads, and construction and improvement of the connecting links of the main highways through towns and cities.

A complete budget bill has been adopted which is satisfactory to the legislative and executive departments and is believed to meet public approval. It is a fitting time for a report to the people of the facts regarding the long struggle over the budget. When the General Assembly convened in January, the governor presented a general budget bill. That proposed bill cut expenses in practically all departments, except those relating to welfare and education. The necessity for increased appropriations for those purposes was plain and urgent. The bill was referred to the proper committees in each house. Hearings were conducted and the committees worked together for a time. Certain amendments were agreed upon in the House committee which were accepted by the governor. The bill, with the agreed committee amendments, was reported to the House on February 8. During this period, from the introduction of the bill until it was reported to the House, the governor worked with the committee in complete harmony and urged constantly that action on it be taken. The bill remained in the House until February 25, when it was passed with several amendments added by the House and which were entirely out of line with the recommendations of the governor and the House committee. With these amendments, however, the House adopted the bill. The Senate retained all the House amendments and added others that still further increased the total amounts appropriated and, at the same time, put restrictions in the bill which made it impracticable and unworkable. It made appropriations but prevented the full payment of them. It was so constructed as to require a horizontal reduction all along the line, affecting every department of the government. It was absolutely harmful to the schools and impaired old age assistance, which could not operate under any reduction. The irreducible minimum had been provided in the bill for these objectives. The Senate and House amendments made the bill so objectionable that it had to be defeated. The governor then appeared before a joint session while there was yet time and proposed the passage of the budget bill in proper form. If this was not agreeable, he proposed that the government operate under the old budget passed in 1942, but that special bills should be enacted for the relief of the schools; for the benefit of the state institutions; and for the protection of the provision for the old people. These proposals were not acted upon by either house. Attempts to bring out the bills were frustrated. The majority of the senators remained silent, but the fifteen Republican senators voted for the plan. The General Assembly refused for many days to consider any provision for the operation of the government and adjourned without passing any sort of a budget bill. This remitted the administration to the 1943-1944 budget. It operated with special hardship upon the schools and left them in worse condition than they had been before. The last General Assembly had provided $3 million additional pay for the school teachers during the fiscal year 1943 and 1944. Former Governor Johnson had given them additional money from an emergency fund. This could not be done by the present administration, as no such fund was provided for it. The governor announced, upon adjournment of the legislature, that he would ask, as soon as possible, that a special session grant relief to the schools. A great many suggestions were made for additional subjects to be considered. In view of the experience at the regular session, it was perfectly clear that the introduction of other subjects, however important, would lead to delay and confusion which might endanger the school bill. This was made still clearer at the special session, when every effort was made to confuse the issue presented by the demand for the relief of education. The conditions of the schools called for immediate relief. All other subjects could wait developments to be dealt with when and if a new crisis arose. Public sentiment was strongly in support of the program for the schools. The surplus was available to make up any deficit resulting if the income proved insufficient. After careful study, long deliberation, and many conferences with representatives of both parties, the governor decided to call a special session limited to the consideration of the problem of the schools. The reasons for this position were explained in a brief statement issued with the call. When the special session assembled, the governor restated the importance of the subject and recommended that nothing else should be allowed to confuse the issue. Days passed without action. No attempt was made to consider or act on the matter before the legislature. Efforts to bring out the school bill were defeated. Finally each house adopted resolutions requesting the governor to broaden the call to include several additional subjects. The merit of these suggestions was appealing, but the reasons for not including them were overwhelming. The governor responded to these resolutions, repeating the reasons already advanced. In the meantime the Senate leaders of both parties endeavored to work out a bill upon which agreement of all the parties could be secured. A tentative bill was prepared, but it was not satisfactory to the governor. It included the school bill, but it failed to protect the program for the assistance of the needy old people, the dependent children, and the needy blind. The governor then explained, if they would pass the school bill and correct the proposed bill in several particulars specified, he would accept it. These corrections required provision for the protection of the old age assistance program, a workable plan for constructing tuberculosis hospitals, and clarification of the appropriations for the construction of improvements of the state institutions when the war was over. The senators then reformed the bill by amendments so that it was satisfactory to the governor. Immediately upon the passage of the bill by both houses, the governor announced his approval and congratulated the General Assembly and each member. Obviously the act was valid only as to the schools, but in view of the agreement of both houses on the bill, the governor expressed a willingness to broaden the call so as to include the subjects embraced in the bill, but not embraced in the call. This was accomplished in five days and the governor signed the bill. The result is that the budget bill which the governor had recommended was finally adopted, with additional provisions which were proper and useful. This bill, moreover, provided for the investment of surplus funds in government bonds until such time as they can be used. It contained the school program in full with sufficient of the surplus to meet it. It is clear to all at this time that the results achieved could not have been reached in any other manner, or any earlier, or without the expense of an extra session. As late as May 8 the opposition was determined to defeat the program outlined by the governor. The justice of the cause and the pressure of public opinion brought about the happy solution of the controversy. To all who aided the consummation, the thanks of the governor and the appreciation of the people are due. The result proves that men of principle can work together for principle. This constructive program for the schools has been adopted for the next two years. It will revive the spirit of the school people. A solemn obligation rests upon all school teachers and educational executives to see that the people are not disappointed in their demand for improvement of educational opportunities for our children.

The vocational educational program and plans for vocational rehabilitation of handicapped civilians and returning soldiers holds out great promise for the future. Vocational training will develop increased earning power and promote the common welfare. The provisions for Lincoln Institute will redound to the welfare of our Negro youth and provide for them opportunity for high school education.

Every department of the government will be constantly admonished to be on the alert for saving and for improvement in service. The whole program of economy and efficiency will be carried into effect as rapidly as conditions will permit.

Every officer will strive for the good of Kentucky. The support and cooperation of the newspapers, public speakers, educators, radio, and ministers who have access to public attention is requested. Distortion of facts and petty faultfinding should cease. Great constructive effort for Kentucky is what is demanded of all Kentuckians. In these fateful days, when such heroic sacrifices are being made for human welfare, people should rise above all littleness and attain a height worthy of Kentucky's valiant sons in all the fields of endeavor.

----

1. Section 246 of the constitution limited state salaries of all but the governor to five thousand dollars. An amendment to overturn this limitation had failed in November 1943.

2. House Resolution 32 (Chapter 187) provided for *nine* members, one from each congressional district. It had been approved March 17, 1944. Kentucky *Acts* (1944): 411-12.

As of the date of this speech, eight members had been appointed from all the congressional districts except the fourth: W.B. Moser (Murray); Landern Childers (Henderson); Luther R. Stein (Louisville); Edward G. Klosterman (Covington); Mrs. Frank Murray (Lexington); John Fred Williams (Paintsville), vice chairman; Joshua B. Everett (Maysville), chairman; and Clark Bailey (Harlan). *Kentucky Enquirer,* June 14, 1944.

3. Approved March 20, 1944, Chapter 154 (House Bill 305) created a Department of Alcoholic Beverage Control, consisting of a commissioner, appointed by the governor, and board. Kentucky *Acts* (1944), 329-45.

4. One of Governor Willis's campaign planks had been elimination of the state income tax.

5. Chapter 5 (Senate Bill 26), also known as the Blake, Swope, Moore, and Howard Act, was an amendment to section 147 of the state constitution. Among its provisions was one allowing the filing of absentee ballots with the county clerk. Approved by the legislature on March 14, 1944, it was endorsed 157,654-30,548 by the voters in the November elections. Kentucky *Acts* (1944), 6-78; *Courier-Journal,* November 9, 1945; and Executive Orders, Secretary of State's Records.

6. Chapters 38, 100-3, and 134 of the Kentucky *Acts* were among those dealing with veterans. Kentucky *Acts* (1944), 83-84, 190-95, 282-91.

A SECOND REPORT TO THE PEOPLE
Louisville / August 31, 1944

KENTUCKIANS very properly are interested in the accomplishments of their state government. It is the purpose of the present administration to keep the public informed, both as to the things done and as to the plans for further action. In order to do this, reports will be made from time to time. In this manner, and by this method, the facts published at intervals can be brought together and presented as a unified and connected pattern. The whole picture is what the public desires to see and upon which the judgment of the people will be passed.

Every Kentuckian is happy that the state fair has been restored and is now being held at Churchill Downs. The fair is a cherished institution of the farmers and their friends. It brings the people closer together and promotes the interests of agriculture and stockbreeding. It stimulates thought and excites ambition, which is good for the development of the state's resources. Friendly rivalry in attaining excellence in the products of our state advances the interests and promotes the welfare of each and all. The great contribution of the farmers to the war effort has thrilled the patriotic fervor of Kentuckians everywhere. The legislature gave ready and vital cooperation to the fair. The commissioner of agriculture, Churchill Downs, and all organizations and individuals having a part this year in making the state fair a success deserve the thanks and grateful appreciation of all fair-minded men and women.[1]

The governor is happy to report that the administration of the agency for the conservation of wildlife has been taken out of partisan politics and placed in the hands of the sportsmen of the whole state. Both the organized and the individual sportsmen have been recognized and consulted. A competent and earnest group of nine men has been selected from a list of forty-five names chosen by the sportsmen in the various congressional districts to constitute the Game and Fish Commission. That commission has taken over the management of the division and is now in complete control. An outstanding director has been chosen, and the long-cherished dream of the sportsmen has been brought nearer to realization.[2] The employees of the division have been put on a merit system, with their tenure of office depending solely on honest and loyal service. The governor congratulates Kentuckians generally, and the sportsmen particularly, on this achievement in self-government. The active assistance and cordial cooperation of the public in making this experiment a success is needed and desired. It is for the sportsmen to furnish the people a demonstration of successful conservation, and certainly they will not fail to make good in that task.

The public is aware of the work done by this administration for the relief of the schools and for the advancement of education. The entire school program is now in operation, and the teachers and executives in charge of the educational interests of the state are exerting their best efforts to render the children of Kentucky the finest possible service. The state is to be congratulated on the progress that has been made, and the educators of the state should be commended for the service they are rendering. The education of the youth of the state is vital, and it must be given constant attention.

The highway department has been reorganized and placed in the hands of outstanding engineers interested in the construction of highways. The partisan political setup has been abolished. The economies that have resulted are but a forecast of still greater savings to be realized. The reorganization of the highway department will be finished only when competent engineers and technical men in sufficient numbers can be secured; but great progress has been made, both in promoting the work of the department and in reducing the administrative expenses. The future field for this department is broadening, and its importance in the postwar program cannot be overestimated. The aviation fields to be constructed after the war will be connected directly with the highway department and included in its plans.

The important finance department has been reorganized and its administration improved. Drastic reductions in expenses have been made all along the line. The purchasing department has been placed in the hands of honest and competent men who possess the confidence of the public, and a new spirit prevails in the state's business. The saving of money effected in that department is most gratifying, and the businessmen of the state are cooperating fully to give the state good service.

The assessment of state employees for political purposes has been stopped, and favoritism among those who deal with the state has been abolished. The state now gets full value for every dollar spent. This is a consummation long desired. Any employee of the state, as any other citizen, who believes in the restoration and maintenance of good government is free to contribute to the necessary and proper expenses of maintaining party organization, carrying on political campaigns, and preserving the gains we have made. But all such contributions are absolutely voluntary and without any strings attached. Indeed, all good citizens, whether employees of the state or otherwise, should be glad to help according to their ability, to promote and to preserve good government. It is essential that the fight be carried on, and the expense of the fight must be provided by those who believe in the cause. The administration welcomes the help of all who share its philosophy of government and who desire to see it succeed.

The welfare department is carrying on the work of rehabilitation of the institutions, and ambitious plans for the future are being perfected. Announcement from time to time of progress will be made. One enterprising newspaper now has some of its best staff reporters investigating the work being done in this department, and the facts in detail will be published in the near future. The people are justly proud of the achievements of the present commissioner of welfare and of his predecessor in the office, who remains with the department as chairman of the welfare board and who is rendering outstanding services to the commonwealth in this long-neglected field.[3]

The governor, in his first press interview after he decided to be a candidate for the office, announced, as a matter of principle, that the alcohol control authority should be separated from the tax-collecting agency. Moreover, in the same interview the abolishment of liquor sales at places where no sufficient police protection was provided was advocated. Both positions are undoubtedly right. Both objectives are now accomplished facts, and the undivided attention of able and experienced men of integrity is being given to the enforcement of the liquor laws and regulations.

In every department of the government we have obtained the services of qualified and honest men who are striving to render the people the best service at the least cost. It is the purpose of this administration to maintain the high standard which has been established.

The last General Assembly created two statutory commissions to serve humanitarian needs. One is the Youth Guidance Commission for the purpose of aiding the youth of the state and to find ways to prevent delinquency, which has been a growing menace. The other is the Tuberculosis Sanatoria Commission, which is to make the selection of sites for hospitals in the various districts and to formulate plans for the structures to be built. A well-considered plan to combat the great plague of tuberculosis has been launched, and it will be prosecuted to a successful conclusion. The governor has appointed to these commissions men and women of high character and ability who have at heart the welfare of the youth of the state and whose concern for those suffering from tuberculosis has been fully proven.[4] It is most encouraging that businessmen and women from all parts of the state are able, ready, and willing to give of their time and talent for the assistance of their fellow citizens. The governor is confident that great and lasting good will result from the work of these commissions.

It is a source of satisfaction to be able now to report to the people that the government is being operated in accordance with the constitution and the laws, and that the hand of machine politics no longer impairs the efficiency of the public service.

Turning now from the objectives attained, let us consider some definite plans for important work to be done in the immediate future.

The governor intends to create by executive order three separate public commissions to be composed of citizens specially fitted for the tasks to be performed. It is necessary to investigate and study the various plans that are being suggested for postwar development by students of the subject. In all parts of the country far-seeing men of labor, industry, scientific, and other activities are making plans to meet, insofar as possible, conditions that will confront the country when the war is over. The heroic achievements of our armed forces and those of our associates in the war bring sharply to our attention the inevitable approach of victory. The prayers of the whole people are that this victory may be speedy and complete. Even so, we know that great effort and sacrifice yet remain before victory can be won, and the resolution of the nation must not be relaxed for one moment. We know also that victory will bring in its train a number of problems affecting the physical, economic, mental, and moral well-being of our soldiers and sailors, as well as of our people generally. The present planning bodies in the various departments of government are limited in the scope of their work. The governor's cabinet has a limited jurisdiction. The highway department can deal only with roads and bridges and allied activities, while the educational and welfare departments are restricted to construction suitable to their purposes. The fact remains that broader planning must be done in many other fields. The governments all working together can provide but a small part of the necessary employment, probably no more than 10 percent, while private industry must take up the other 90 percent of the volume. A commission composed of representative citizens to make a careful study of all plans will be of great value in fixing the public policy to be pursued after the war. Such a body can ascertain the physical and human resources of the state. It can formulate definite plans and make recommendations for the development of our resources. Such planning will be helpful to agriculture, labor, mining, manufacturing, transportation, conservation, and to all the work to be done. It can render real assistance to private enterprise with the knowledge gained from its own investigations, as well as from the consideration of the reports of investigations made by others. The governor has received acceptances from many of the men desired to serve on this commission, and it is hoped that a complete announcement can be made very soon.[5]

This administration has sought to promote the interests of our Negro people in every possible way. The fine cooperation of the Negro citizens in the fight for good government, their patriotic participation in all of the nation's war efforts, and their devotion and loyalty to our common country afford every incentive for us to aid them in the consideration and solution of their problems. In order that a better understanding may be secured and that proper consideration may be given to all problems, the governor proposes in a short time to appoint a Commission on Negro Affairs, to be composed of outstanding citizens of the two races especially interested in the welfare of our Negro citizens. It will be the province of this commission to study the civic, economic, educational, housing, health, and all other needs of the Negro people of Kentucky and to propose definite steps to be taken to meet such needs.[6]

During the war the state has been deprived of practically all revenue from the production of alcoholic liquors and from the sale of motor vehicles. This has amounted to several million dollars. At the same time it has been necessary to increase the expenditures for the common schools and for the further rehabilitation of the neglected institutions. Economies in administrative costs have been effected in practically every one of the departments of government. Intensive efforts in that direction shall be pursued unceasingly during this administration. The permanent improvement in state properties and the acquisition of new properties for the pressing needs of the state are nonrecurring investments which will be completed in due course. But after all, when the war ends and all the sources of revenue are available, it is the belief of the governor that many taxes can be removed and a sound tax structure established.

During the month of August permission has been granted to produce beverage alcohol. This will bring into the state treasury a considerable sum of money, probably $750,000. This money will be paid into the general fund. It is not possible for the governor to earmark money, but money that goes into the general fund can only be spent to meet appropriations made by the General Assembly. Every effort will be made to keep all departments of government at the lowest practicable expense so as to save as much money from the appropriations already made as may be possible. Such savings will pass to the surplus fund at the end of the fiscal year, and the experience gained during the fiscal year will be helpful in providing means of financing the government without any oppressive taxes. It is the general opinion, in which the governor shares, that the income tax, under present circumstances, retards the development of the resources of the state. The inheritance tax act needs radical revision, and many other taxes operate adversely upon the economy of the state. These subjects will require much consideration, and the facts upon which to base sound judgments must be assembled. A scientific study of the tax question will enable the General Assembly to shape the tax laws so as to promote the development of our agriculture, labor, manufacturing, transportation, mining, and other interests, and at the same time provide sufficient revenue to finance the necessary and proper activities of the government.

To meet this problem, the governor will appoint a Tax Revision Commission to study the tax structure of the state and to make recommendations as a basis for the governor's recommendations to the next session of the General Assembly.[7]

The problem of taxation is a difficult one at all times. It is especially hard now because of the great burden of federal taxes which our people must bear. When it is recalled that Kentucky's federal tax-take for the past year was $553 million, the burden upon our taxpayers can be appreciated. That was an increase over the previous year of more than $67 million. Taxes are paid in the sweat of everyone who labors, and everyone is a taxpayer, directly or indirectly, whether or not he is aware of it. The cost of war has been so great that every field of taxation has had to be explored. The essential costs of the state government also must be met, and everyone knows that our whole tax structure will have to be revised when the war is over and conditions become stabilized. The problem is one for the consideration of all the people, but there must be some agency where the thought of the people may find expression and through which their purpose may be translated into action. The obvious need is a competent Tax Revision Commission to survey the tax structure of the state and to recommend a program of a comprehensive nature. Nothing is more vital to the employment of our workers, the advancement of our agriculture, the development of our industrial life, and the prosperity and happiness of our people than a sound, just, and equitable tax structure. The governor will appoint to such a commission citizens especially qualified to master the subject. The ablest and most representative men available will be sought for the task. A comprehensive study and survey of the whole field will be recommended, and the commission will be asked to give the governor a broad plan of taxation which will produce the revenue necessary to provide for the essential services of the government, economically administered, and, at the same time, protect the people from unjust, excessive, and oppressive exactions.

Neither the statutory commissions heretofore appointed nor the commissions formed by the governor, will involve any expenditure of public funds. The work will be done by patriotic persons willing to serve the public at a personal sacrifice. It is evidence of the success of representative government that such services can be obtained, and the thanks of all of us are due these outstanding citizens who render at a real personal sacrifice great service to the state.

At the end of this war, the workers of Kentucky will be able to return to peaceful pursuits for the production of life's necessities and conveniences. Having met the terrible responsibilities, and having suffered the awful sacrifices of war, Kentuckians will not shrink from grappling with the problems of peace. The task of maintaining justice, of providing the general prosperity and happiness of our people, and of keeping step with the march of civilization, will not be unwelcome. The difficulties, however great, will be approached with the confidence, the courage, and the forward outlook that is the heritage of Kentuckians. Grateful that we have been able to accomplish so much for Kentucky, we face the future without fear or doubt. When the work outlined in this report shall have been completed, the main objectives of this administration will have been accomplished.

The sniping of low-breed creatures who have no faith in their fellow men must not be permitted to mislead the people or be allowed to discourage public officials in the struggle for good government. In order to succeed we must have faith instead of cynicism, good will instead of malice, and the whole truth in the place of distortion and misrepresentation.

The renewed interest of so many people in the work of government is stimulating and encouraging to those charged with official responsibility. A sound and wholesome public sentiment is the best antidote for evil practices and the perfect climate for constructive achievement.

Notwithstanding the progress that has been made, much remains to be done which will need the support, the confidence, and the cooperation of all good citizens. Confident of that cooperation and support, this administration will continue to work for the full realization of all its objectives. The friends of good government have a right to rejoice in the successes we have won. They have every reason to carry on the battle with confidence that still greater victories will be achieved in the days to come.

1. No state fair had been held in 1942 and 1943. In both the next two war years a fair was held. Churchill Downs was selected as the site because the fairground was being used as part of a war defense plant. See Lawrence A. Cassidy, *Kentucky Fairs, 1816-1957* ([Lyndon, Ky.?], 1960), appendix, v.

2. Governor Willis appointed five Republicans and four Democrats to the commission: George Long (R-Benton); J.B. Miller (D-Williamsburg); Errol W. Draffen (R-Harrodsburg); O.W. Thompson (R-Pikeville); W.G. Buchannan (R-Corbin); W.H. Washbourn (D-Beaver Dam); H.M. Bertram (R-Louisville); and E.H. Pohn (D-Horse Cave). The director was Stephen A. Wakefield of Shelbyville. Frankfort *State Journal*, August 13, 1944; and *Kentucky Directory*, 111.

3. Joshua B. Everett (1895-1985) of Maysville. Connected with Bankers Trust Company in New York, 1926-39, vice-president at departure; involved in Maysville grain elevator and agricultural supply firm; commissioner of welfare, 1944; chairman of Board of Welfare and active in other commissions; acting superintendent of Kentucky Children's Home, 1947-48; president of Kentucky branch of English-Speaking Union, 1961-83; involved in numerous civic and cultural organizations. *Courier-Journal*, January 18, 1944; May 7, 1985.

4. Headed by state health commissioner Dr. Paul E. Blackerby, as ex-officio member, the sanatoria commission included G.L. Simpson (Greenville), O.F. Hume (Richmond), C.C. Howard (Glasgow), Edward W.M. Seaton (Ashland), Joshua B. Everett (Maysville), state representative William G. Biggers (Prestonsburg), state senator Cass R. Walden (Edmonton), Charles H. Cook (London), Claude L. Hammons (Corbin), Lawrence Ashmore (Madisonville), and Mrs. Bert R. Smith (Bowling Green). Everett, then chairman of the State Board of Welfare, was elected chairman; and Dr. Hume, secretary of the commission. Lexington *Herald*, August 1, 1944; and Frankfort *State Journal*, August 11, 1944.

5. See the section entitled "Kentucky and the Postwar Era."

6. See the section entitled "World War II."

7. See the section entitled "State Government Administration."

STATEMENT REGARDING PUBLIC ASSISTANCE
November 1944

I HAVE talked with a majority of the members of the legislature and I have corresponded with still other members. I wish to confer with the remaining members as soon as possible. Most of the members, Republicans and Democrats alike, express an earnest desire to see the problem of public assistance satisfactorily solved, but no such solution has been suggested.[1] Resolutions are sent in from time to time from various organizations requesting additional aid for the aged, but none of them has indicated how such additional aid could be financed.

The telegram from Speaker [Harry Lee] Waterfield and other official leaders of the Democratic majority in the legislature asked for a special session to make an additional appropriation without the levy of any new taxes. They must have known that all of the money in the surplus fund and all of the estimated revenue had been appropriated by the last special session. In fact, they know that the appropriations actually exceeded the estimated revenue to the extent of $3,319,050, for they earmarked that amount of surplus to prevent any cut in the appropriations. It was provided by the appropriation act that if the revenues actually became sufficient to pay the appropriations, then the full amount of the emergency expenditure fund should be restored. The effect of the budget act was to freeze the emergency expenditure fund of $3,319,050 to the end of the biennium, which will be June 30, 1946. The remaining $5,300,000 of the surplus was required to be invested in bonds and held intact to meet the programs for the tuberculosis hospitals and capital outlays for the other institutional repairs. The actual amount required to maintain the present level of public assistance payments to June 30, 1945, is estimated to be $875,000; and for the next fiscal year it is estimated to be $1,900,000. There is not now available or unappropriated sufficient funds to make such payments possible. The actual collections of revenue must exceed the estimates by more than $3,319,050 before the frozen surplus could be freed for use again, and that cannot be known until the end of the biennium. Money for old age assistance must be available before June 30 to be paid in May and June, and we cannot appropriate money that has already been appropriated, without reducing all the appropriations in accordance with the budget act.

An additional appropriation now without providing the money to meet it would require the finance department to cut all the appropriations so as to bring them to the actual revenue received. This would derange the programs now in operation and would create many new problems no less serious than the one presented by the public assistance needs. No one has dared to suggest that we disturb the school program, the institutional repair work, the tuberculosis sanatoria, or any of the work of the various departments which are rendering such outstanding service to the public. No one could be more anxious than I am to maintain the present level of public assistance. Even that is low compared with other states, but it must be remembered that we have a larger number in proportion to population sharing in the assistance, which necessarily reduces the amount that can be paid to each from the amount made available by the legislature.

I am determined that the financial condition of the state shall not be crippled. It is absolutely essential to maintain solvency and efficiency in the state government in this emergency. I hope to see Kentucky go forward with a long-range program which will more nearly meet the obligations which her people have assumed by the constitutional amendment putting upon the General Assembly the obligation to provide a pension or annuity for needy old people.

In studying the problem, all its phases must be considered. I propose to appoint a Tax Revision Commission which will study the whole tax program, as well as the amount of money essential for carrying on the functions of the government and for the discharge of all the obligations of the state. This is to be the long-range solution of the problem, but the immediate task of raising sufficient money to meet the present problem is one that deserves the careful consideration of every citizen and particularly of every legislator. I am hopeful of finding a solution which the leaders will accept and agree to carry out without delay. I shall continue my conferences until I have completed them. This problem was not solved by previous administrations, but it was aggravated by certain incidents which occurred. By the freezing of the program a great many deserving people were kept off the rolls, and when that large number was released, by court order, it increased the burden to be met.

The programs for the needy blind and dependent children were held back by various circumstances until recently, and this administration has had to bear the full load of these two additional programs. It is a problem which the governor can only recommend to the General Assembly, where the responsibility for it rests. The amount appropriated for this fiscal year by the General Assembly was $4,400,000. At the same time all other available funds were appropriated for expenditures definitely set by the legislature. I called attention at the time to the fact that if the public assistance program required more money, there would be no place to get it without new taxation and a special session. The leaders of the majority party have definitely stated that they would oppose any new taxes, but they have not indicated where they could get the money without new taxes.

The inequalities, discriminations, and other administrative evils that were discussed during the campaign have all been eliminated; and every dollar appropriated by the legislature is being paid directly to the persons entitled thereto, and that is all the administrative departments can do.

As soon as my conferences are completed I will announce my conclusions and recommendations and see if [it is] possible to obtain an agreement for their adoption.[2]

---

1. The 1944 budget included $4.4 million—an increase of $150,000—for public assistance programs. Welfare commissioner John Quartermous announced in August that these levels of funding would not support continuance of the present programs for 1945. *Courier-Journal*, August 24, 1944.

2. This funding problem eventually resulted in a special session of the legislature that began April 23, 1945. See message of that date in this section.

INTERVIEW REGARDING FIRST
YEAR IN OFFICE
Frankfort / December 2, 1944

GOVERNOR SIMEON WILLIS, discussing today his first year as Kentucky's chief executive, said all objectives advocated in his campaign speech at Mount Sterling had been put into operation with two exceptions, revision of the state tax structure and repeal of the income tax.

Willis, who will have completed his first year in office next Thursday, said the "whole philosophy of government has been changed back to the principles of the constitution and the laws" under his administration.

"The government is now being operated for the benefit of the people rather than a political machine," he declared.

First steps toward revision of the tax structure will be taken soon, he said, with appointment of a tax advisory commission to study tax problems for every approach.[1]

"This is the only part of my Mount Sterling address that I have been unable to carry out so far," he said, "and this has been due to the war."

Governor Willis has encountered three distinct crises since he took office. The first, prevailing at the time of his inaugural, found rehabilitation work at all state institutions at a standstill under executive orders of former Governor Keen Johnson, who had taken the action after Hubert Meredith, then attorney general, said the work was not being done legally. Acting under his emergency powers, Willis ordered work resumed on all emergency projects immediately and on all others when contracts could be let.

His second crisis was a budget stalemate during the regular session of the 1944 legislature which carried over through two special sessions. Differences with the Democratic majorities in the House and Senate were settled and a compromise budget [was] passed.

His third crisis is the present shortage of funds to keep public assistance payments at their current level. Although additional money ($150,000 a year) was appropriated for the needy aged, indigent blind, and dependent children, the latter two programs have been expanded to such a degree that a reduction in individual benefits has been declared necessary unless supplementary money is appropriated.

He said today that all public assistance was being distributed among the needy fairly and equitably as prescribed by statutes. He remained noncommittal on possibilities of a special session but said:

"If it is possible to get more money, we want them [benefit recipients] to have it."

He outlined the chief accomplishments of his administration as follows:

1. Full resumption of rehabilitation work at state institutions, with repairs and renovations carried as far as possible.

2. Assessments against state employees for political purposes discontinued.

3. Administration costs in almost every department of government substantially reduced, with the most able men available holding the key positions.

4. Elimination of the positions of nine advisory highway commissioners.

5. Accomplishment of a rural road program which gives the counties greater authority in spending funds allocated by the state and [permits] them to retain any funds that remain unexpended at the end of the year.

6. All educational aims outlined at Mount Sterling carried out, including increased pay for school teachers.

7. Parks, soil conservation, and forestry programs placed under the direction of the most efficient men available, with plans calling for extensive improvements.

8. Commissions for study of problems relating to postwar planning,

youth guidance, Negro affairs, and establishment of five new tuberculosis hospitals appointed.

The governor said he had visited almost every part of the state for addresses to build up good will and unity among the people and to promote education, industry, and other causes.

As for next year, Governor Willis said he planned to "carry on with the same objectives for continued improvement."

---

1. The commission was appointed some three months later, on March 19, 1945. See *Courier-Journal*, March 20, 1945.

STATEMENT DENYING CHARGE
OF DICTATION TO LEGISLATURE
Frankfort / December 8, 1944

MY approach to the problem presented is not "dictatorial."[1] It is just the opposite. Instead of telling the legislature what to do, I ask them to agree upon a program or plan of action.

Unless substantial agreement can be reached in advance, it would be a useless waste of money to have a special session. The taxpayers do not desire to pay for a futile and dilatory debate upon various and sundry suggestions.

It is for the chosen leaders of both parties to determine details and to achieve agreement. When agreement on the essential points is accomplished, the method of carrying out the agreement can be arranged.

I think the suggestion that the agreement would not be binding is a reflection on the legislators. If agreement is once made, there is no room to doubt the members would keep their pledges. I am seeking the views of the members of the legislature. I am not seeking to impose any other views. When I have completed my survey of the whole field my views will be stated.

The individual members of the legislature are free to express their views in their own way and at such time as they may desire. I reserve the right, and request the opportunity, to express my views in my own way and at the proper time, both to the public and to the leaders of the two parties in the General Assembly.

---

1. Pike County Republican representative William E. Justice had told *Courier-Journal* reporter Allan M. Trout that Governor Willis's plan to receive advance agreement on public assistance before any special legislative session was "dictatorial." *Courier-Journal*, December 8, 1944.

PROCLAMATION FOR SPECIAL SESSION
Frankfort / April 19, 1945

To all to whom these presents shall come:

WHEREAS, the General Assembly, by an act approved June 12, 1944, made an appropriation to the Division of Public Assistance for ordinary expenses of operation and cooperation with the federal government under the Social Security Act approved August 14, 1935, including adjustments of prior year or current year accounts necessary to comply with federal regulations and for the administration of old age assistance, KRS 205.010 to 205.080, including the cost of printing checks for recipients of the public assistance program, and, also, for the administration of the statutes pertaining to aid to dependent children and to aid to the blind, which appropriation has been used to maintain the same level of payments that had been established theretofore and which will be practically exhausted by the payment for the month of May 1945, leaving the last month of the present fiscal year without an appropriation to make such payment; and,

WHEREAS, there is sufficient money unappropriated in the treasury resulting on June 30, 1944, from the lapse of prior appropriations to provide sufficient funds to maintain the same level of payments for June 1945; and,

WHEREAS, the federal government has provided, or may provide, certain benefits for men and women who have served in the armed forces of the United States or in war activities, including minors and their wives and husbands, which benefits require the making of contracts which cannot now be made by minors under the law of the state of Kentucky; and,

WHEREAS, an emergency situation exists in regard to improvements at the Greater Cincinnati Airport owned by Kenton County and located in Boone County, which requires legislation to enable the improvement to proceed;[1]

NOW, THEREFORE, in consideration of the premises, I, Simeon Willis, governor of the commonwealth of Kentucky, do hereby issue this proclamation convening the General Assembly of Kentucky in an extraordinary session at the seat of government in Frankfort, Kentucky, at 7:00 o'clock P.M. on Monday, the twenty-third day of April 1945, for the following purposes and no other:

1. To appropriate from the money now in the treasury derived from lapsed appropriation as above recited sufficient to supplement the appropriation to the Division of Public Assistance in an amount required to make the regular payments for the month ending with June 30, 1945;

2. To pass an act enabling minors entitled to benefits under any federal or other legislation to make valid contracts in respect thereof, and to perform legally all acts necessary to obtain the benefits of such legislation for said minors;

3. To pass an enabling act for the Greater Cincinnati Airport owned by Kenton County and located in Boone County for the purpose of carrying out its plan of financing, whereby the obligations for the improvement may be liquidated out of revenues derived from the operations of such airport.

The members of the General Assembly will, therefore, assemble in accordance with this proclamation at the seat of government at Frankfort, Kentucky, in an extraordinary session on the day and date above written to act upon the subjects herein specified and upon no other subjects.

GIVEN UNDER MY HAND, this nineteenth day of April 1945, by the governor.

---

1. The "emergency situation" to which Governor Willis was referring apparently concerned overcrowded conditions at the airport. He sought a bond sale to finance additional buildings. See *Courier-Journal*, April 19, 1945.

SPECIAL SESSION
Frankfort / April 23, 1945

I HAVE called you together at this time to enact legislation deemed necessary and important. I have endeavored to communicate with all members in advance of the session to make certain that the proposed legislation conform, so far as possible, to your judgment and wishes, and meet fully the public needs.[1]

The public assistance program has been carried forward at the same level previously approved by you. The appropriation made at the last special session will not be sufficient to carry the regular payments to the end of the current fiscal year. The details of administration and distribution of the funds will be given to you by the officials in charge of the program. I am advised that the minimum amount required to continue the regular payments through June 1945 will be $350,000. This estimate is based on the actual experience through the nine months of the current fiscal year, and it is believed to be as accurate as can be made in advance of actual developments. It is sufficient to allow a reasonable margin of safety.

There is available in the treasury unappropriated money sufficient to take care of the proposed supplemental appropriation. It represents the unexpended balances of appropriations made in 1942 for the fiscal year which ended June 30, 1944. The amount left in this fund not appropriated by you will remain in the surplus fund [until] June 30, 1945, and be subject to appropriation by the General Assembly at future sessions. It may not be expended for any purpose until appropriated by you.[2]

It is not necessary at this time to deal with the program for the next fiscal year. If the amount which you have already appropriated for that year should prove less than you desire to have distributed or allocated to the public assistance programs, it can be considered and disposed of at the regular session. The next fiscal year will begin July 1, 1945, and the next regular session of the assembly will begin in January 1946.

The disability of infancy, under state law, has resulted in a denial to many of the young men and women of our armed forces the immediate benefit of national legislation. In order to obtain the money that was intended for them, it is necessary that valid contracts be made. I have, therefore, included in the call a provision to enable you to enact such [a] bill as you may deem proper to remove disabilities from the young men and women entitled to benefits under the acts of Congress, including, of course, wives or husbands of those embraced by the national law. They should be empowered to make contracts in respect thereto as fully as if twenty-one years of age. It is not deemed wise to remove the limitations on the contractual powers of infants generally, but certainly no reason exists for denying these thousands of young men and women the power to contract for benefits which the Congress of the United States has provided for them. I trust that you may pass appropriate legislation to achieve this end without withdrawing any proper protection from the contractural [*sic*] powers of persons under twenty-one years of age.[3]

It is apparent that aviation will play an important part in the transportation problem of the future. There is immediate need for the construction of airports in Kentucky in order that our state may keep abreast of progress in that field. I have included authority for you to enact appropriate legislation for the financing of airport facilities, and I hope this legislation may meet with your approval.[4]

These matters are of great public interest, and I feel certain that each of you appreciates the urgency which has justified this extra session. The governor's office is ready to render you every assistance possible, and I trust your work may be facilitated in every possible manner.[5]

---

1. The special session of the General Assembly met from April 23 to May 11, 1945. There were 10 vacancies in the 138-member, two-house assembly, 6 due to resignations, 3 to deaths, and 1 to the armed forces. One of those missing from the previous session was Democratic floor leader Earle C. Clements, now in Congress. His successor was T.C. Carroll of Shepherdsville. Paducah *Sun-Democrat*, April 22, 1945, and *Courier-Journal*, April 25, 1945.

2. State revenues for the first six months of the fiscal year had exceeded appropriations by 7 percent, leaving a large surplus. By unanimous votes, the legislature transferred $331,956.82 from this surplus to the Department of Welfare, thus covering the regular payments. Chapter 4 (House Bill 5) was approved May 4 and went into effect immediately. Kentucky *Acts* (1945), 7-8; Kentucky *House Journal* (1945), 76; and Kentucky *Senate Journal* (1945), 130.

3. Passed unanimously by both houses, approved May 4, 1945, and entitled "The Kentucky G.I. Bill of Rights," House Bill 6 (Chapter 2) extended loan and credit rights of war veterans below the previous age limit of twenty-one years. Kentucky *Acts* (1945), 2-3; Kentucky *House Journal* (1945), 99-100; and Kentucky *Senate Journal* (1945), 132-33.

4. "An Act Relating to the Issuance and Retirement of Revenue Bonds for Airport Facilities . . . ," approved May 9, 1945, set up specific guidelines enabling governmental units to borrow money and issue bonds for airport construction. Chapter 4 (Senate Bill 5) passed both houses unanimously. Ken-

tucky *Acts* (1945), 2-8; Kentucky *House Journal* (1945), 142; and Kentucky *Senate Journal* (1945), 166.

5. Governor Willis, in remarks not in the prepared text, also noted the interest concerning the capture of Berlin and the upcoming world security conference. He expressed his hope that the legislature "will not disappoint the expectations of our great people." Richmond *Daily Register*, April 24, 1945.

PRISON INVESTIGATION
Frankfort / April 30, 1945

I AM informed that a joint resolution has been introduced and is about to be debated in each House of the General Assembly purporting to authorize the appointment of a committee for the purpose of conducting an investigation of the prisons at LaGrange and Eddyville.

I deem it proper to call your attention to the fact that this is a special session of the legislature convened by proclamation stating the subjects to be considered, which subjects are:

1. The appropriation of money for the payment of public assistance through June 1945 in order to carry the regular payments to the end of the fiscal year.

2. A bill to remove the disability of infancy from men and women of the armed services entitled to the benefits of federal legislation.

3. An airports bill.

By the express terms of Section 80 of the constitution you are prohibited from considering any other subjects. This section of the constitution is mandatory, as has been held by the Court of Appeals repeatedly. The legislature at a special session has no power to consider any subject not specified in the proclamation convening it. Any act of yours at this session beyond the subjects named in the proclamation would be absolutely void. Any consideration of such outside subjects is a waste of time and of the taxpayers' money.

Moreover, the investigation you propose to make is wholly unnecessary. The executive department is conducting an investigation under the direction of Mr. Beverly Waddill, a qualified, able, and experienced investigator.[1] This investigation must not be obstructed or delayed by any outside interference. It is being conducted thoroughly, honestly, and completely; and it will include, before it is finished, both the LaGrange and Eddyville prisons.

When the investigation is concluded, the facts found and the evidence adduced will be made available to the General Assembly at its regular session.

The legislature may not appropriate money for the purpose of paying the expenses of an unauthorized investigation. In making appropriations, it is limited to the subject assigned in the proclamation convening it. The proclamation does not include the subject matter of this pending resolution. Any committee appointed under such a resolution would have no power to employ anybody, or to expend any money, or to conduct any lawful investigation. It could serve no purpose, except to interfere with, delay, and obstruct the present investigation. There can be no reason for partisan interference in this independent administrative investigation.

This investigation is being prosecuted with diligence. A trustworthy and able representative of the press, Mr. Allan Trout, has observed the proceedings from the start and has had access to every fact developed by the investigation.

The taking of testimony from day to day will be open to representatives of the press, and all the facts developed will be available to the public through the newspapers.

The subject matters submitted to you for lawful action are important. The aged, the blind, and the dependent children, as well as the young men and women of our armed forces entitled to benefits provided for them by Congress, look to you to give prompt and favorable consideration to the measures for their relief. That is the only business before you, and it is worthy of your attention.[2]

---

1. The executive order formally appointing Workmen's Compensation Board member Beverly B. Waddill of Madisonville "to make a full and complete study" of conditions was signed four days later, on May 4, 1945. See Secretary of State's Records.

2. The demands for an investigation were stimulated by newspaper accounts telling of the premature release of LaGrange Reformatory convicts through the use of forged records. After receiving the governor's message, and despite his warning, the House by a 54-35 vote called for an investigation of penal conditions. A few hours later the Senate, by a 22-9 margin, adopted a similar resolution. See *Courier-Journal*, May 1, 3, 17, 19, 1945; *Kentucky Enquirer*, May 1, 3, 20, 1945; Paducah *Sun-Democrat*, May 2, 1945; and Owensboro *Messenger*, May 3, 1945. For Governor Willis's veto and subsequent actions, see the veto message of May 9, 1945, in this section.

AMENDMENT TO SPECIAL SESSION
PROCLAMATION
Frankfort / May 3, 1945

WHEREAS, by a proclamation issued April 19, 1945, an extraordinary session of the General Assembly was convened to pass an enabling act for the Greater Cincinnati Airport, owned by Kenton County and located in Boone County, for the purpose of carrying out its plan of financing whereby the obligations for the improvements may be liquidated out of revenue derived from the operations of such airport; and

WHEREAS, it was the intention to include all other airports similarly situated so that a general law was necessary to be passed to cover all parts of the commonwealth;

Now, in order to make clear that intention, the said proclamation is amended so as to enable the General Assembly to pass a general law applicable to all airports in the state, and to enable them to adopt a plan of financing whereby the obligations for the improvement of airports might be liquidated out of revenues derived from the operation of such airports.

GIVEN UNDER MY HAND, this third day of May 1945, by the governor.

VETO OF HOUSE RESOLUTION NO. 3
Frankfort / May 9, 1945

I HAVE received House Resolution No. 3, which purports to provide for the investigation of the administration of the prisons at LaGrange and Eddyville. I regard this resolution as invalid, unnecessary, and calculated to interfere with the investigation being conducted at the present time. It violates three sections of the constitution. By the express terms of Section 80 of the constitution you are prohibited at a special session from considering any subject not designated in the proclamation convening it. This section of the constitution is mandatory, and any act done outside the subjects specified in the proclamation are absolutely void and of no effect. There is nothing in the call to authorize an investigation at the prisons or elsewhere. The attempt by this resolution to make an appropriation is also invalid. The resolution was not embraced by the call, and it did not receive fifty-one votes in the House of Representatives on the final roll call. The resolution contains an emergency clause and attempts to appropriate money. By Section 46 of the constitution any act or resolution for the appropriation of money, on its final passage, must receive the votes of a majority of "All the members elected to each house." One hundred members were elected to the House, and this resolution on its final passage received but fifty votes. By Section 55 of the constitution an emergency clause likewise requires the concurrence of a majority of the members elected to each house.

The proposed investigation is wholly unnecessary and improvident. The welfare department started an investigation immediately upon discovery that forgeries had been committed by prisoners working in the reformatory at LaGrange. This investigation has been proceeding with diligence under competent direction and with complete publicity. No one has been or will be spared, but every branch of the prison will be investigated and the evidence taken and preserved so as to be available to the General Assembly in due time. If any evidence of criminal conduct is disclosed, it will be laid before the commonwealth attorneys of the districts where the jurisdiction is vested to prosecute and punish. Every effort is being made, not only to correct evil practices, but to formulate a system which will prevent, so far as possible, evil practices in the future.

We have obtained the services of General Roy Easley[1] as director of corrections, and he has complete charge of the reorganization of the prisons. His long experience and high character [are] sufficient evidence to the public of the sincerity and earnestness of the purpose to correct any and all evil conditions at the prisons.

We have also obtained the cooperation of the Federal Bureau of Prisons and will continue to do so. This investigation must not be interrupted or interfered with by partisan attempts to pervert and obstruct it. Such an investigation would be no help. If the legislature had shown a willingness to cooperate and assist the present investigation it would have been welcomed, and arrangements would have been made to have utilized assistance of that kind. But no sort of cooperation has been offered. If this investigation discloses the need of legislation there will be time enough to enact it at the regular session next January. Long before that time both the General Assembly and the public will have all the facts.

For these reasons House Resolution No. 3 is hereby vetoed.[2]

---

1. Roy W. Easley (1891-   ). Frankfort native; chief of police, city of Louisville, 1926-30; Louisville director of safety, 1930-34; sales representative for Frankfort Distilleries, Inc.; colonel, Kentucky National Guard; defeated for mayor of Louisville, 1945.

2. The House, by a 49-35 margin, voted to override the governor's veto; the Senate did so by a 20-11 vote. Kentucky *House Journal* (1945), 150; and Kentucky *Senate Journal* (1945), 189-90. A ten-man legislative committee, chaired by Senator Richard Maloney of Lexington, met on May 18 and decided to use part of the $10,000 appropriation to hire a penologist to study Kentucky's prison system. *Courier-Journal*, May 19, 1945.

STATEMENT TO LEGISLATIVE COUNCIL: BUDGET
Frankfort / October 23, 1945

I MET with the Legislative Council at the beginning of its session and explained the reasons why I have nothing to submit to it until after November 15. I am willing to repeat these reasons:

1. The budget cannot be made up until after the change which may be effected by the vote of the people on the constitutional amendment. (If this amendment, to prevent diversion of road funds to other purposes, is ratified by the people, it will shift some $2 million a year from the general fund to the road fund.)

2. The official estimates of income will not be submitted to me until the fifteenth of November, as provided by statute. After that date budget requests will require conferences with department heads concerning the appropriations they are seeking for the several departments.

3. The Tax Revision Commission is giving exhaustive consideration to the whole problem, and its report has not been completed.

K.R.S. 7.070 provides that the governor may send messages to any session of the council containing his recommendations and explaining the policy of the administration. For the reasons set forth, up to this time I have not deemed it necessary to send any messages to the Legislative Council.

The fact that the meetings of the Legislative Council have been unnecessarily prolonged by the Democratic majority under the leadership of [Vice-Chairman Harry Lee] Waterfield, obviously for the purpose of political gain, and at the same time this Democratic leadership has been holding political caucuses in different parts of the state, does not change the situation insofar as the governor is concerned. When the interests of the state make it desirable that I appear before the council, the council will be advised.

STATEMENT REGARDING TAX POLICY
Frankfort / October 25, 1945

THE charge of the Democrat members of the Legislative Council that this administration has a secret financial policy in the form of a 3 percent sales tax, or any other tax, is wholly false and utterly ridiculous.

The Democratic majority of the Legislative Council is sitting in Frankfort at the taxpayers' expense, and about all they do is guess this and guess that, trying to find a way out of the dilemma, which is of their own creation, by trying to fix their policy before they can know the financial facts, estimates, and needs in the manner provided by statute.

I recommend, therefore, that the Legislative Council adjourn and save the remainder of their expense budget until after November 15, when, and only when, work of a constructive nature can be accomplished.

The type of politics which is being played by the Democratic majority is proving to be nothing more than the furnishing of sensational headlines for their newspaper organ.

Many Kentuckians believe that this sort of political maneuvering does more to cause disunity and lack of progress in Kentucky than any other one thing.

PHILOSOPHY OF GOVERNMENT

BOYD COUNTY BAR ASSOCIATION
Ashland / December 4, 1943

"The administration of justice is the noblest profession of all mankind," Governor-elect S.S. Willis told members of the Boyd County Bar Association at a dinner in his honor here last night. . . .

"Much of the confusion of our land will disappear if justice can be performed; it is up to the bar of our nation to see that our country retains the things for which it was founded," Willis said.

"The world has become as one, and distance is nothing. We are in a big world living close together, and we must all conform to the divine plan. The simple plan of the Master is one which we must all live, and then we may have peace."

KENTUCKY PRESS ASSOCIATION,
ANNUAL MIDWINTER MEETING
Louisville / January 20, 1944

Governor Simeon Willis addressed the group at a dinner-dance given by the Louisville Board of Trade, the Brown Hotel, the *Courier-Journal*, and the Louisville *Times*.

"The press is an arm of the government which is absolutely indispensable," Governor Willis said. "Government depends upon the press and hopes that it will be fair. Please give us the facts in your news columns—and if you give facts there, your readers will have no trouble in understanding your editorials."

REDEDICATION OF MOUNT ZION CHURCH
Perry Park / May 7, 1944

At this time Mr. Perry[1] introduced Governor Willis, who in a short address said in part, "I know that everyone must be inspired with the significance of the occasion. People have been forgetting special phases and worthwhile things and leaning on the material things. We see self-destruction and the accumulation over these years of materialism being destroyed, but back of all is God keeping his watch. We do have the divine laws, the whole purpose of life, to improve God's church. It is the home, the churches, and the schools all over the world and the higher institutions of learning that make our people great."

---

1. John Holliday Perry (1881-1952). National counsel to major newspaper chains; owner and publisher of several newspapers and radio stations chiefly in the South, including the Owenton (Ky.) *News-Herald*. On May 11, 1944, the latter paper noted that Perry was a "frequent visitor" to his three-thousand acre estate at Perry Park, site of his ancestral home. At that time his residences were in Florida and New York. *Who's Who in Kentucky, 1936*, 315; Owenton *News-Herald*, May 11, 1944; and New York *Times*, December 5, 1952.

DEDICATORY SERVICE,
BROADWAY METHODIST CHURCH
Paducah / September 15, 1945

The church has the greatest opportunity in history to spread true gospel throughout the world, and there appears to be no doubt about it being prepared and unafraid to face the challenge squarely, Governor S.S. Willis declared Saturday night in an address at Broadway Methodist Church.

"The entire world is looking at America, and the nation can provide an example of a country building year after year upon a foundation of citizens who believe in God," he asserted.

Governor Willis said he believes the future of the world is bright, as regards possibilities that lie beyond the shadow of present difficulties. He predicted religion will be strengthened by the faith of veterans who have learned to know God while facing death in foxholes and [of] the home front which learned to seek and depend on divine guidance during the war.

"We must keep faith and face the future with the courage of our forefathers. I am impressed with this generation, which was branded by some as soft but which went on in this war to show that it is worthy of the great traditions of America," the governor said.

"The building of character is the purpose of life, and character cannot fail. As we build character we build a nation. I assure you now of my absolute faith in the church," Governor Willis declared.

He pointed out that a great moral organization for peace can be built by the same persons who built America's war-winning machine, and that the world must be taught to handle power so it will be of benefit to mankind instead of a destructive force such as Germany, Japan, and Italy formulated.

He called the war the result of failure of some men to obey the laws of God. "Whoever forgets God ultimately comes to destruction," he asserted.

Inventions have brought peoples of the world close, and through this unity Christianity can be made to secure peace, the governor said.

STATEMENT READ TO
FEDERAL POWER COMMISSION HEARINGS
Charleston, West Virginia / April 11, 1946

EXPRESSING "apprehension" that the natural gas act of 1938 is "but a first step toward federalization" of the gas industry, Governor Willis said "the conservation of natural gas, like that of any other resources, is a function of the state. . . ."[1]

"In my judgment, the federal activities should be restricted to the legitimate regulation of interstate commerce in natural gas and leave the state absolutely responsible for all other activities in regard to it.

"I trust that the hearings will result in a recommendation that the national government be not allowed to interfere in any way with the production, use, conservation, or movement of natural gas within the state," and, the governor continued, "that its activities be restricted to a fair and reasonable regulation of purely interstate transactions."[2]

Willis said that the "trend" in the direction of ultimate federalization "should be arrested at once and the exclusive jurisdiction of the state recognized and respected."

---

1. Chapter 556, an act "to regulate the transportation and sale of natural gas in interstate commerce," was approved by Congress on June 21, 1938. Among other provisions, it allowed the Federal Power Commission (FPC) to adjust those rates subject to the commission's jurisdiction, if such rates were found to be unreasonable, discriminatory, or preferential. *United States Statutes at Large . . . 1938* 52 (Washington, D.C., 1938): 821-33.

2. The Natural Gas Investigation, instituted by an order dated September 22, 1944, involved eight hearings (including the Charleston one), more than three hundred witnesses, and some 14,435 pages of testimony. In recommendations issued October 15, 1946, the Natural Gas Industry Committee suggested that FPC rate regulatory control "shall not extend to any part of the business or activity . . . of production and gathering, whether carried on by a pipeline company or others." See *Twenty-Sixth Annual Report of the Federal Power Commission . . . 1946* (Washington, D.C., 1947), 66-69; *Twenty-Seventh Annual Report of the Federal Power Commission . . . 1947* (Washington, D.C., 1948), 102; and "Brief and Recommendations of Natural Gas Industry Committee," in *Hearings before a Subcommittee of the Committee on Interstate and Foreign Commerce, United States Senate,* 80th Congress, 1st Session (Washington, D.C., 1947), 207.

KENTUCKY RURAL CHURCH COUNCIL, DINNER MEETING
Lexington / May 7, 1946

GOVERNOR SIMEON WILLIS, who also spoke at last night's dinner,[1] declared that "the strength of our nation has been recruited from the rural areas," and charged the rural ministers with their responsibility in molding and shaping the lives of the oncoming generation, stating that "no one knows where genius will bud." He expressed the belief that today's problems and those of every generation can be solved by faith, courage, and intelligence.

---

1. The dinner was held as part of the Rural Leadership Institute at the University of Kentucky Agricultural Experiment Station. Among several other speakers was the Right Reverend William R. Moody, bishop of the Episcopal Diocese of Lexington. Lexington *Herald*, May 8, 1946.

LABOR DAY PROGRAM
Berea / May 14, 1946

[THE governor] expressed his pleasure in speaking to a Berea audience and said that he wished he knew more about the institution. Launching into his particular message for Labor Day, Governor Willis said that anything worth having is worth working for. The value is not always in the goal, but in the gaining of it. "Work," he said, "is the condition of happiness of every human being."

He pointed out that one of the results of work is education, and the main purpose of education is to build character, for no matter how intelligent a person may be, "if he uses that intelligence in the wrong way—to the detriment of human welfare rather than for good—he is worse than useless."

Education, or the building of character, the governor declared, begins in the home and is later taken up by the school, the church, and the community in which one lives. He said that each generation has two distinct obligations: that of meeting and trying to solve the problems of its day and that of training the next generation to do the same.

"Things change as we go along. Each generation has its problems. . . . The whole purpose of life among free peoples is to educate, a problem that carries over from generation to generation.

"Work is the foundation of all success. . . ." Today a boy on the farm must know about machinery and chemistry. Advancement through the years has increased the complexity of problems. Knowledge is power; therefore the problem is the developing of good men and women who will use that power beneficially. Development of character begins in the home and is sustained by church and school. "By a sterling citizenship is the future of our country assured."[1]

---

1. This document is a composite of three versions of his talk, taken from the Berea *Citizen*, May 16, 1946; the Richmond *Daily Register*, May 15, 1946; and the Frankfort *State Journal*, May 15, 1946.

JOINT CONVENTION, AMERICAN ASSOCIATION OF SCHOOLS AND DEPARTMENTS OF JOURNALISM AND AMERICAN ASSOCIATION OF TEACHERS OF JOURNALISM
Lexington / January 10, 1947

GOVERNOR SIMEON S. WILLIS, speaking before a joint convention banquet of two national journalism education associations here last night, declared that "an acknowledgment is due on behalf of the government to the press of this country."

"The debt of the government to the press and reporters is great. It is the press that enables government to accomplish most of the good things that we do accomplish," the governor told 150 delegates of the American Association of Schools and Departments of Journalism and American Association of Teachers of Journalism meeting in the Phoenix Hotel.

"The press prevents many government wrongdoings by means of publicity. It is a great power and a dangerous one. The great principle for journalist-educators to teach is the use of this great power."

Speaking on the topic "Covering the Capitol Beat," Governor Willis defended his own press relations policies and advocated that reporters of public affairs get better acquainted with the public servants and get the true facts about proposed legislation before reporting it.[1]

---

1. This version appeared in the Lexington *Herald*, January 11, 1947. For a slightly different account of the talk see the *Courier-Journal* of the same date.

BOYD COUNTY LINCOLN DAY BANQUET
Ashland / February 8, 1947

GOVERNOR WILLIS, also a speaker on the program, declared the principles of Lincoln, if properly observed, will preserve this country for all time.[1]

"Many men have written beautiful words—but that is not the reason why his memory lives—he freed the slaves—but that is not so important—he saved the Union—and it is not any one of these things—it is all of them which brings a great love for his character," he said.

"I never lose my zest for Lincoln Day banquets. I attend more and more each year and upon every occasion such as this I am further impressed by the reverence which is shown by people of all races, colors, and creeds for this great American," Governor Willis emphasized.

"We today face our problems the same as he did. We have the same courage, the same resolution, the same patriotism—every generation will have just as good and bad results—but in the end we will have no fear, for we will maintain the faith of Lincoln," the governor related.

The governor said in conclusion that he had tried to keep faith with the people of Kentucky.

"Like Lincoln, I have tried to fight a good fight—I have kept the faith."[2]

---

1. Recently elected Senator John Sherman Cooper of Kentucky, the main speaker, praised Governor Willis's administration in his talk.

2. This version is a combination of two accounts of the talk, taken from the *Courier-Journal* and the Ashland *Daily Independent*, both of February 9, 1947.

LINCOLN CLUB
Louisville / February 12, 1947

GOVERNOR SIMEON WILLIS in a brief talk paid tribute to Abraham Lincoln as a man whose character, sense of justice, and faith in his country had won worldwide acclaim and devotion. "As we look into the future," he said, "and see the problems that face us, we must realize that they are problems such as have faced every generation, and we must bring to these problems the principles held by Lincoln. Just so far as we have departed from his precepts, so we have suffered; and so long as we remain true to his principles, we will be true to the people of Kentucky and of the United States. . . . Whatever we do for our country, we do for the greatest country ever inhabited by the common man."

100th ANNIVERSARY OF
KENTUCKY FEMALE ORPHAN SCHOOL
Midway / May 21, 1947

GOVERNOR SIMEON WILLIS attended the exercises and was the principal speaker. He said that all Kentuckians must rededicate themselves "to truth, religion, and the righteousness that exalteth nations."

Kentucky, Governor Willis said, "believes in the moral forces that make for good Christian life and must maintain her interest in the character and spiritual life of her people.

"If the individuals making up a society are strong, then that society will be strong," the governor declared. He said the past 100 years can be described as a "training ground for the accomplishment of even greater achievements in the years to come."

THE JUDICIAL PROCESS
AND THE EXECUTIVE FUNCTION
Lexington / October 2, 1947

Part I
Introduction

GOVERNMENT is a necessity wherever people live, work, and associate together. In every civilized society, and even among savage tribes, some form of government must exist to maintain tranquillity, to settle disputes and conflicts of interests, and to preserve the rights of each member of the society, as well as the authority and security of the society itself. Countless forms of government have been tried, and many systems are in existence today. Government is power; and power may be used for evil and destructive purposes, as well as for good and productive results. The problem is to create and delegate sufficient power to protect and maintain the security of the governed without fostering a breed of tyrants or destroying the essential liberties of the people.

The struggle for justice, after centuries of trial and error, finally culminated in the great experiment in this country of a written constitution, defining the powers of government and defending the rights of each individual member of the society.

Government in its nature consists of three functions, viz: (1) the making of law; (2) the execution of law; (3) and the determination of what is law in any case. When these powers have been centered in one person, tyranny and oppression have resulted. *The Federalist* thus expressed the thought: "The accumulation of all powers, legislative, executive, and judiciary, in the same hands, and whether hereditary, self-appointed, or elected, may justly be pronounced the very definition of tyranny."[1]

The founding fathers desired to frustrate the arrogance of power and the tendency toward tyranny and to forestall forever the encroaching nature of arbitrary power by a definite separation of the powers of government, confiding each to separate bodies of magistracy and forbidding each to exercise any power within the province of the other, except as expressly permitted by the Constitution. John Marshall, the great chief justice,[2] put the distinction in these plain and precise words: "The difference between the departments undoubtedly is, that the legislature makes, the executive executes, and the judiciary construes the law." So long as that principle is preserved in all its purity and power, and each department fulfills its function, it does not seem possible for government under a written constitution to fail in its great objective—to establish and maintain justice and liberty for all.

My assignment in this series of studies of the processes of government is confined to the judicial and executive functions. References to the legislative power will be incidental, although necessary, because of the overlapping and interlacing of the carefully separated, but closely allied, operation of the distinct bodies of magistracy.

Part II

The Judicial Process

The first consideration will be given to the judicial process in the determination, interpretation, and administration of law.

Justice Cardozo,[3] in his introduction to his discriminating book on the *Nature of the Judicial Process,* thus posed his problem:

> What is it that I do when I decide a case? To what sources of information do I appeal for guidance? In what proportions do I permit them to contribute to the result? In what proportions ought they to contribute? If a precedent is applicable, when do I refuse to follow it? If no precedent is applicable, how do I reach the rule that will make a precedent for the future? If I am seeking logical consistency, the symmetry of the legal structure, how far shall I seek it? At what point shall the quest be halted by some discrepant custom, by some consideration of the social welfare, by my own or the common understanding of justice and morals? Into that strange compound which is brewed daily in the caldron of the courts, all these ingredients enter in varying proportions.

The business of the judge is to find and to apply the law to the facts of the controversy, not forgetting for a moment the consequences of his work or the limits within which his power may be exercised with safety and propriety. What is law? How is it evolved? What is the judicial process of finding it? Definitions abound, but in seeking the goal of the jurist, it is apparent that the broader subject must be circumscribed by the elimination of much that might be accurately described as law. Fundamentally, law is the principle that controls the operations of the materials and forces of which the universe is composed. It is omnipresent, omnipotent, and pervades all things that can affect the senses.

> The very law that molds a tear,
> And bids it trickle from its source,
> That law preserves the earth a sphere,
> And guides the planets in their course.

It is a conception of the uniform order of sequence, as when we speak of the laws of motion, of growth, of gravity. Law in that sense inheres in the nature of things and dominates the physical world. It is eternal, changeless, created "in the beginning," and is merely discovered, not made, by man. The uniformity is in the nature of things, and there is no law outside of them to be consulted or obeyed. As physical beings we are subject to physical laws. In a similar sense we are governed by moral or spiritual laws, whether or not we are conscious of it. We find ourselves in the clutch of elemental forces that brook no disobedience and depend upon no human sanction, of which we think as the laws of our being.

But laws of that character are quite apart from the conception of law with which courts are concerned in their work and about which lawyers contend in their daily grind in the ordinary administration of justice. If our statutory and judge-made laws be sound, they must be consistent with the others mentioned and, to a large extent, the work of unseen hands and derived from imperceptible sources. It is in some such sense that the saying is true that we do not make laws but merely discover them. Passing the law of natural things, the sway of moral principle, and the axioms of experience which have the force of law, we approach in a practical way the consideration of law as enacted by legislatures and as evolved by judicial reasoning from accepted standards. Such laws are necessary for the disposition of concrete social conflicts and for the regulation of human action in an organized society, where disputes necessarily arise. The idea of law with which we now concern ourselves relates to the origin and application of the rules and regulations that govern the status, transactions, and relations of men, formulated or accepted by duly constituted authority, and enforceable by established agencies of government. There are, indeed, laws that affect the lives, liberties, and properties of persons; and the purpose of the judge is to seek the sources of those laws and to find the foundations upon which they are erected. It is obvious that the law does grow, and its growth is watched and nurtured by the judges more than is generally realized.

"Law is anything," said Judge Hough,[4] "that is effectual in depriving any person of life, liberty, or property, provided it emanates from a national governmental agency or from a state."[5]

The judicial process in the evolution of the law is the application of the results of experience and the effects of legislation to the problems presented by particular cases. As put by a writer in the fourteenth edition of the *Encyclopedia Brittanica:* "It is proposed to define law for the jurist as the sum of the influences that determine decisions in courts of justice. This will be found to satisfy the conditions of a working definition." What are the influences that determine decisions? And how are they discovered, developed, and applied?

The motives, springs, and purposes that underlie the law and actuate alike the legislator and the judge are at the very threshold of such an inquiry. The great Demosthenes,[6] with a freshness that defies time and a finality that approaches revelation, thus defined it:

> The design and object of all laws is to ascertain what is just, honorable, and expedient, and when that is discovered, it is proclaimed as a general ordinance equal and impartial to all. This is the origin of law, which, for various reasons, all are under obligation to obey, but especially so because all law is the invention and gift of heaven, the sentiment of wise men, the correction of every offense, and the general compact of the state, to live in conformity with which is the duty of every individual in society.

Proceeding from purposes of the exalted character thus described, the law must be found by the jurist in an atmosphere of precedent and tradition that not only affects, but to a certain extent molds, his decisions. The great body of professional opinion, as well as public opinion in general, operates directly, albeit unconsciously, upon the mind of the judge in choosing the path he must pursue. The law journals to a limited extent are the organs of this opinion. The reported cases mark the progress of authority. Dissenting opinions are addressed primarily to the judgment of the profession, and if they possess any value, it is derived from the power of convinced minds to influence the thinking of the judges and lawmakers until a new supplants the old opinion. It is not very common, but sometimes a minority view ultimately becomes the controlling one. It is this fact that gives vitality to the maxim that no question is ever settled until it is settled right. The former Chief Justice of the United States Charles E. Hughes, in his notable book on the Supreme Court, says; "A dissent in a court of last resort is an appeal to the brooding spirit of the law, to the intelligence of a future day, when a later decision may possibly correct the error into which the dissenting judge believes the court to have been betrayed."[7]

Actuated by the purpose to find a just rule, animated by the desire for fair play, alive to the duty to render every man his due, and affected by the pressure of the prevailing professional and public opinion, the judge is far from being free to impose upon the law his personal views or individual convictions. Yet the philosophies of the judges, the experiences upon which they depend for enlightenment, the individual social attitudes are not entirely submerged, but may affect and color their interpretation of the influences that enter into the formation of judgments. Overemphasis easily may be placed on the political, social, or economic views of judges. Conviction is a characteristic of every strong man. Without it no judge could worthily fulfill his function. But responsibility and study are apt to sober the most radical, as [they are] likely to liberalize the most conservative of men. But after all, a judge, like every other reasonable man, "must measure himself by his own rule and standard." If the judge has character and capacity for growth, if his tendency is toward self-improvement, and if his fundamental conceptions are sound, little fear of his superficial predilections need be entertained. And it must be remembered that the prevailing opinion in any state of society is influenced by history and tradition, and the views of judges will vary as their knowledge of the background of the law varies. The law has been likened to a great pool gathered from the fountains of justice. Every legislative act and every judicial decision raises the level of that pool and affects the quality and content of the whole; but it is equally true that the new legislation and the latest decisions are themselves affected by the fusion with the existing body of the law. Hence the law, slowly evolved through the ages, is the composite result of many factors and is seldom traceable to the mere will of the actors. Indeed, as Alexander Hamilton observed, "the judiciary may be truly said to have neither force nor will, but merely judgment."[8] The function of administering justice thus becomes an agency in the working out of principles, and it is impossible for it to be a mere instrumentality for the expression or enforcement of the personal will or wish of the judges, or of the legislators, or of both combined. And it can never become the manifestation of a dominant desire or will, unless it possesses the permanence to enforce itself upon all the influences that enter finally into the formulation of the accepted postulates of justice. This thought is implicit in a statement of Judge Cooley:[9] "The time will never come when all laws will be in the form of statutes, never a time when the judiciary law, which is evolved in, and constitutes the very act of, administering justice, will not form a part of our legal system. It is only a question at any given time how far it is necessary or expedient to transmute the judiciary law into statutory form."

But even the enactment of statutes does not end the constructive work of the courts. Indeed, a study of the adaptation and interpretation of statutes and their effect upon the development of the law will demonstrate that the work of the judges, although sometimes aided, has just as often been retarded by the necessity of assimilating a vast amount of ill-considered legislation. Perhaps many legislators, untrained in the law, are surprised, if not shocked, at the results accomplished by their work after it passes through the refining process of judicial interpretation. The influence of the Roman or civil law in the slowly expanding body of the common law is apparent in some instances, and especially in certain localities.

We may put aside as foreign to our purpose the simple cases in which the result is foreordained, and which are disposed of as a matter of course, without the necessity of pausing to reexamine the foundations upon which their determination rests. Such cases form the mass of judicial pronouncements, rest upon accepted authority, and seldom touch the field where divergence of opinion is likely. But the rare cases that offer opportunity for choices among several possibilities afford debatable territory and furnish the great battlegrounds of the law. How do the courts proceed to determine such cases? It need hardly be noted, of course, that all judges do not consciously proceed from one expedient to another, following a system of selection and deduction, until a decisive formula is found. There can be no such thing as compartments in the law where parts may be found to fit every need. But actually all judges are subject in some degree to the various forces that underlie all law and operate on all agents and agencies having to do with its administration. Individual defects will be discovered. Some judges may be so committed to legal theories that decision for them is impossible, unless the problem may be assigned to some definite doctrine established by precedent or suggested by analogy. Others may not be ingrained in the philosophy and history of the law and stand ready to determine every decision from an individual sense of what immediate justice or apparent interest seem to require.

These two types of judges produce two types of critics that are always abroad in the land. One set of critics are apt to say that the judges who dare to advance new doctrines, or to extend old ones, are remaking the law and effacing, if not destroying, its landmarks. Even Lord Bacon[10] inveighed in some such vein, and we hear it to this day.

The other class condemn the courts as archaic, oblivious to the demands of justice, and bewail that the rights of modern men are being crucified upon some ancient formula that may have been all right in its time but which no longer can be serviceable. The two types of judges and critics represent the "falsehood of extremes" and accentuate the inherent difficulty in working out justice with due respect to new ideas and experience, and with proper deference to time-honored precedents. Both types may be found in nearly every jurisdiction and doubtless serve a useful purpose in keeping the institution of the law alive to its duties, as well as aware of its difficulties. But it is easy to divine the chaos that would come if either were permitted permanently to control. The true principle will be found in picking and choosing wisely from the good that has been established and assimilating it to the new things that are found to bear the tests of truth. "Prove all things; hold fast that which is good," is eminently sound and is both progressive and conservative, however paradoxical that may sound. The critical function, however precious, must always be subordinate to the constructive capacity of creative jurists.

Mr. Justice Cardozo in his work, to which I referred, on the *Nature of the Judicial Process* formulated a fourfold division of the forces to be followed and the methods that must be applied in the best judicial work. These four methods he thus classified:

1. The method of philosophy.
2. The method of history, tradition, and sociology.
3. The methods of sociology; the judge as a legislator.
4. Adherence to precedent; the subconscious element in the solution of social conflicts.

In his later work dealing with the growth of law, he referred to the earlier classification he had adopted and, notwithstanding some acknowledged overlapping, adhered to it as practically sufficient. In the later work he said:

> Our fourfold division separates the force of logic or analogy, which gives us the method of philosophy; the force of history, which gives us the historical method, or the method of evolution; and the force of justice, morals and social welfare, the mores of the day, with its outlet or expression in the method of sociology. No doubt there is ground for criticism when logic is represented as a method in opposition to the others. In reality, it is a tool that cannot be ignored by any of them. The thing that counts chiefly is the nature of the premises. We may take as our premises some preestablished conception or principle or precedent and work it up by an effort of pure reason to its ultimate development, the limit of its logic. We may supplement the conception or principle or precedent by

reference to extrinsic sources, and apply the tool of our logic to the premise as thus modified or corrected. The difference between the function of logic in the one case and in the other is in reality a difference of emphasis. The tool is treated on the one hand as a sufficient instrument of growth, and on the other as an instrument to cooperate with others. The principle of division is a difference, not of kind, but of degree. With this reservation, the fourfold classification of methods has sufficient correspondence with realities to supply a basis of distinction. The judicial process will not be rationalized until these methods have been valued, their functions apportioned, their results appraised, until a standard has been established whereby choice may be directed between one method and another. We may find the subject to be such that the hope to rationalize it fully, at all events in our day, will have to be dismissed as futile. That is not a reason for refusing to do the best we can.[11]

The purpose of the law is the solution of problems which perpetually arise and are always debatable. Such problems come with every new conflict of principle, albeit in a more complex form or in a more complicated field. Principles are not changed by the changes in material things. The effort to stabilize conduct and to fix right must not be allowed to hamper progress or to hamstring enterprise. The pool must not be permitted to become stagnant or caused to break its bounds. Activity must not become violence, and conservation must avoid inertia. Neither the judicial nor the legislative mind can visualize in advance every variety of human action or every phase of the conflict of interests, nor formulate with certainty a perfect rule to fit every exigency. We must forever wait on experience and bear the loss of that necessity. On the checkerboard of events all the moves cannot be foreseen. The eternal struggle of the law is to maintain stability and yet to avoid static; to make progress without producing violence or uncertainty. Stability without stagnation and motion without destruction are the horns of a dilemma between which the course of wisdom must be charted. The difficulty may not be denied, but the struggle is insistent and unavoidable and constitutes the supreme task that vexes all judges. Any principle, to possess permanence, must work only good. And even though good may appear in some situations to result from the operation of a rule, it may not do so under more complex conditions. A fair illustration may be found in the history of the fellow servant doctrine in damage cases growing out of the relationship of master and servant. In its origin it obtained wide acceptance as a fair and just rule. But as the conditions of its operation became more widespread it encountered conflict with accepted conceptions of what was just, resulting first in its judicial modification and finally in its legislative overthrow. The Supreme Court of the United States adverted to this subject in these words:

> Regulations, the wisdom, necessity, and validity of which, as applied to existing conditions, are so apparent that they are now uniformly sustained, a century ago, or even a half a century ago, probably would have been rejected as arbitrary and oppressive. Such regulations are sustained, under the complex conditions of our day, for reasons analogous to those which justify traffic regulations, which before the advent of automobiles and rapid transit street railways would have been condemned as fatally arbitrary and unreasonable. And in this there is no inconsistency, for, while the meaning of constitutional guaranties never varies, the scope of their application must expand or contract to meet the new and different conditions which are constantly coming within the field of their operation. In a changing world it is impossible that it should be otherwise. [*Euclid* v. *Ambler Realty Co.*, 272 U.S. 365.]

The changing circumstances in this changing world demand a vigilant study of the processes of justice and the operation of the rules formulated to promote it. And the duty of adjustment is not obviated by the accumulated experience of the ages.

The problem of the lawyer is to predict the conclusion the court will reach and to present the facts, arguments, and authorities that tend to produce it. Indeed, the late Justice Holmes declared that, "The prophecies of what the courts will do in fact, and nothing more pretentious, are what I mean by the law."[12]

The definition is striking but not entirely satisfactory, without many assumptions and numerous limitations. It tends to belittle the search for principle, supposed to permeate all things and transactions and which ennobles and enriches the study of the law. If it presupposes the presence of a principle whose reasoned result on any given state of facts may be foreseen and predicted, if the court itself be true to tradition, it may not be so far afield. But the theory of Judge Cooley and the older jurists that a decision upon a point arising in any given case ought to be followed because it constitutes the highest evidence that we can have of the law applicable to that point, is more consonant with our accepted conceptions, and more nearly expresses reality. As evidence of the law, persuasive in every case, and conclusive when founded in sound reason and fortified by experience, the decisions of the courts afford a standard for the lawyer in his search for the intangible something that is understood to be the law. In one sense, although somewhat ironic in its suggestions, "A legal duty so called may be nothing but a prediction that if a man does or omits certain things, he will be made to suffer in this or that way by the judgment of a court"; but in reality a legal duty is not so easily described nor dependent upon a foundation so precarious. A legal right is one which the organized power of society may be employed to enforce and defend. But what will that power enforce or defend? Duty is determined by an innate and prevalent sense of fairness and right, or by a positive enactment springing from that source, and it depends upon the circumstances as well as the social attitude of the time. Such duty, when sanctioned by the prevailing agencies of authority, will be enforced for the benefit of those to whom it is due. Undoubtedly there are social duties, moral duties, and legal duties which have a higher sanctity than the mere supposition or expectation that a court will inflict certain compensation or suffering for a breach of them.

Edmund Burke,[13] whose profound mind and felicitous expression contributed so much to enrich the law, said:

> For if there were not some principles of judgement as well as of sentiment common to all mankind, no hold could possibly be taken either on their reason or their passions sufficient to maintain the ordinary correspondence of life. It appears, indeed, to be generally acknowledged that with regard to truth and falsehood there is something fixed. We find people in their disputes continually appealing to certain tests and standards which are allowed on all sides, and are supposed to be established in our common nature.

If a court fails to act in favor of it, a legal right is not destroyed. It endures despite the error of the court. It is the court, not the duty, that has failed. It is a fallacy to predicate the existence of rights and duties upon the mere means designed to protect and promote them. If one means of protection fails another will be found, if the right is still respected and the duty continues to be recognized. If the means of vindication are inadequate or feebly pursued, the right itself may be impugned; but sound thinking will not surrender the substance because of a failure of the form designed for its preservation. The duty, if it is real, will survive a court that denies it.

The interest of the lawyer in the processes of the judges is a practical and continuing one. Naturally the business of the lawyer is to win cases; and the impulse is to put forth the factors and the features of the case that seem to hold the greatest promise of achieving the result desired. That fact affords the very reason why the methods of judges must be appreciated by the lawyer. The lawyer must put himself in the position of the judge and put forth the influences that tend to produce in the judge the conviction the lawyer entertains. If there be a controlling precedent, you need go no further than to show its applicability. If one be cited against you, perhaps it may be differentiated in its facts or distinguished on principle. If you chance to be in direct opposition to an authority which must be overthrown in order that you may prevail, your sole hope is in demonstrating its fallacy. It is then that you subject it to all the tests of philosophy, history, tradition, social justice, and the tendency of it to conflict with other and more compelling precedents. It will not do merely to criticize or denounce it. It is essential that some substantial reason be advanced for its disregard. Here is the forum for the intellectual effort that distinguishes the true lawyer. Precedents are modified, and even overthrown, under the searching analysis and careful criticism of lawyers. It may be relatively infrequent, but the list of overruled cases is an imposing one. If a case does not accord with the dictates of reason and justice it will be subject to assault, until it is brought into a harmonious relation with the system that must work justly in order that it may endure.

The variety of circumstances under which human conduct must be judged, and the multitude of cases that must arise, require the skillful work of lawyers and judges to keep and maintain the proper adjustment. We must have carpenters and mechanics, however perfect become tools and machinery. The bar serves the bench, and unless good work is done by the lawyers, no better may be expected of the judges. Webster's arguments at the bar were the forerunners of Marshall's opinions. The work is ceaseless as time. Models may be found, guides may be fashioned, but the burden of work remains. The multiplication of books does not lessen the obligations or burdens of the bench and bar—rather the reverse.

After all the factors of reason, logic, philosophy, experience, social aims, and legal standards have served their offices, the final responsibility rests upon those who carry one; and the perpetuity of the system depends upon the success they may attain. Our system of law at last rests upon the tacit understanding that the verdict of the jury and the judgment of the court constitute the law because under them one man's property is taken and bestowed upon another, and men themselves are taken from their families and fellows and confined in durance vile, and sometimes they are put to death. These judgments must be founded upon the innate sense of justice which is the intuitive gift of the great masters of our law.

Theorists may speculate, and philosophers may dispute, but in practical life it is the operation of principles and processes upon people and their possessions that determine[s] ultimately their justice and fix[es] their durability. The words of former Chief Justice Hughes are apt:

> In our system the individual finds security in his rights because he is entitled to the protection of tribunals that represent the capacity of the community for impartial judgment as free as possible from the passion of the moment and the demands of interest or prejudice. The ends of social justice are achieved through a process by which every step is examined in the light of the principles which are our inheritance as a free people.[14]

In leaving this branch of our subject, the words of Daniel Webster in his eulogy of Mr. Justice Story are appropriate:

> Justice, Sir, is the great interest of man on earth. It is the ligament which holds civilized beings and civilized nations together. Wherever her temple stands, and so long as it is duly honored, there is a foundation for social security, general happiness, and the improvement and progress of our race. And whoever labors on this edifice with usefulness and distinction, whoever clears its foundations, strengthens its pillars, adorns its entablatures, or contributes to raise its august dome still higher in the skies, connects himself, in name, and fame, and character, with that which is and must be as durable [as] the frame of human society.[15]

Part III

The Executive Function

We turn now to a consideration of the executive function, which embraces the execution of the laws in obedience to the enactments of the legislative power as interpreted, supplemented, and explained by the judicial power.

The federal Constitution says simply that the executive power shall be vested in a president of the United States, and proceeds to designate his powers and duties.

The constitution of Kentucky invests the governor, who is called a chief magistrate, with the supreme executive power. He shall take care that the laws be faithfully enforced, and he is given certain specified duties and prerogatives. The various powers are peculiar to each department, as their designations import: the legislature makes the laws, the judiciary expounds them, and the governor sees that they are faithfully executed; but even in this duty, the executive is restrained in some degree, because laws must be enforced according to the constitution, and not at his will and discretion, and only with the means provided by law.

"It may be stated as a general rule inherent in the American constitutional system, that, unless otherwise expressly provided, or incidental to the powers conferred, the legislature cannot exercise either executive or judicial power; and the judiciary cannot exercise either legislative or executive power (Kentucky Constitution—27-28). The existence in the various constitutions of occasional provisions expressly giving to one of the departments powers which by their nature otherwise would fall within the general scope of the authority of another department, emphasizes, rather than casts doubt upon the generally inviolate character of the basic rule" (277 U.S. 200).

Mr. Justice Brandeis,[16] in his dissent in the Myers case (272 U.S. 107), thus explained the situation:

> The separation of the powers of government did not make each branch completely autonomous. It left each in some measure, dependent upon the others, as it left each power to exercise, in some respects, functions in their nature executive, legislative, and judicial. Obviously the president cannot secure full execution of the laws, if Congress denies to him adequate means of doing so. Full execution may be defeated because Congress declines to create offices indispensable for that purpose. Or, because Congress having created the office, declines to make the indispensable appropriation. Or, because Congress, having both created the office and made the appropriation, prevents by restrictions which it imposes, the appointment of officials who in quality and character are indispensable to the efficient execution of the law. If, in any such way, adequate means are denied to the president, the fault will be with Congress. The president performs his full constitutional duty, if, with the means and instruments provided by Congress and within the limitations prescribed by it, he uses his best endeavors to secure the faithful execution of the laws enacted.
>
> Checks and balances were established in order that this should be "a government of laws and not of men."
>
> The doctrine of the separation of powers was not to promote efficiency, but to preclude the exercise of arbitrary power. The purpose was not to avoid friction, but, by means of the inevitable friction incident to the distribution of the governmental powers among three departments, to save the people from autocracy.

The purse was placed in the control of Congress; the sword in the hands of the president to be exercised pursuant to law; and the power of judgment and reason was enthroned in the judiciary, without other sanction than the power of reason and judgment.

The legislative and the judicial powers are distributed to bodies containing many men, the executive power is reposed in a single individual, with subordinates. This is because of the nature of the executive function, which requires authority commensurate with the action expected of the executive. It is the executive branch of government that carries into effect the laws, and sees to the due performance of the work outlined by the legislative and judicial powers.

The chief executive powers of the nation are diplomatic representation and negotiation, commandership of the armed forces, supervision of the execution of the laws, appointments to office, removal from office, and the management of the properties and services of the government.

The Constitution confers a veto power on legislation and authorizes the president to advise on legislation. The part the executive is permitted to play in respect to legislation is an enlargement of the executive function.

In the states the executive powers are also enlarged to the extent the governor is empowered to act in respect of legislation.

The state assumes a responsibility for the construction and maintenance of roads and bridges; for the regulation of many activities; for the education of the youth; for the maintenance of law and order; for the punishment of crime; for the custody and treatment of the mentally ill and other dependent persons; and all of these and other governmental responsibilities are discharged by the executive branch of the government. In brief, all the services and control which the state exercises over its people are administered through the executive departments and agencies.

The executive can make no law, levy no tax, make no appropriation, or perform any judicial or legislative functions other than in the limited and restricted sense of ascertaining and executing the legislative will as construed in the judicial decisions.

The legislature sits for sixty days every two years and the courts have vacations between regular sessions. But the executive department is on duty at all times, night or day, and renders continuous service.

The executive may call special sessions of the legislature and specify the subjects that may be lawfully considered; but he may not adjourn them except for a limited time, under conditions rarely existing. The executive has the appointing power and the power of removal under regulations prescribed by law.

Chief Justice Taft,[17] in the Myers case, gave an exhaustive review of the development of our doctrine of the separation of powers. He said:

> The vesting of the executive power in the president was essentially a
> grant of the power to execute the laws. But the president, alone and

unaided, could not execute the laws. He must execute them by the assistance of subordinates.

As he is charged specifically to take care that they be faithfully executed, the reasonable implication, even in the absence of express words, was that as part of his executive power he should select those who were to act for him under his direction in the execution of the laws. The further implication must be, in the absence of any express limitation respecting removals, that as his selection of administrative officers is essential to the execution of the laws by him; so must be the power of removing those for whom he cannot continue to be responsible. It was urged that the natural meaning of the term "executive power" granted the president included the appointment and removal of executive subordinates. If such appointments and removals were not an exercise of executive power, what were they? They certainly were not the exercise of legislative or judicial power in government as usually understood (272 U.S. 117).

Underlying the fears was the fundamental misconception that the president's attitude in his exercise of power is one of opposition to the people, while the Congress is their only defender in the government, and such a misconception may be noted in the discussions before this court. This view was properly contested by Mr. Madison and others in the first Congress.

The president is a representative of the people just as the members of the Senate and of the House are, and it may be at some times on some subjects that the president elected by all the people is rather more representative of them all than are the members of either body of the legislature, whose constituencies are local and not countrywide; and as the president is elected for four years, with the mandate of the people to exercise his executive power under the Constitution, there would seem to be no reason for construing that instrument in such a way as to limit and hamper that power beyond the limitations of it, expressed or fairly implied. . . . (272 U.S. 123).

The resemblance of this description to the situation of the state governors, as respects the General Assembly, is so obvious that repetition would be superfluous. The power of removal from office, as applied to administrative subordinates required to execute the policies of an executive, and in securing efficiency and loyalty, is essential to successful performance of executive duties.

But the reasons for sustaining such power do not apply to boards or commissions of an independent nature that may be charged with administrative responsibility apart from the general administration and enforcement of the laws.

In performing the administrative functions, peace officers may be removed by the executive for dereliction of duty, but the power is hedged about with many restrictions. If the legislature passes an act, the governor may veto it for any reason deemed sufficient; but in Kentucky a constitutional majority of the whole body may pass the act notwithstanding the veto. If the governor believes an enactment does not constitute law, because of a violation of the constitution, he must, nevertheless, enforce it, unless his view of invalidity is sustained by the courts.

There is, and always has been, a tendency of any given power to augment itself. But the profound respect in which the principle of the separation of the powers of government has always been held has had a retarding effect on such tendency. Yet the people are apt to look to the executive to provide a remedy for any evil conditions, which has seemed to give ascendancy in popular esteem to the chief executives. But in reality, the solid sense of the people respects the dignity and majesty of the judicial office, and the creative power of the legislative function leads many able men to prefer legislative or judicial work to that of the executive.

The range and extent of the executive work brings that department in closer contact with more people, which fact accounts for the larger number of people looking to the executive branch for every possible governmental service.

The qualities of character required for all governmental service are quite similar, but the executive has more frequent need for the hardihood to say "no" because of his single responsibility in so many instances.

The power of pardon is given to the president and to the governor; and it is a power capable of abuse, as in any power. But the institution and development of the probation and parole of prisoners has relieved the executive to a great extent of the immense pressure that formerly vexed and burdened him. It is not so much power as it is arbitrary power that must be watched and feared. The multitude of duties and obligations that rest upon the executive call[s] for constant attention; and the enlargement of the executive departments has multiplied the occasions for his supervision, even though it enables him to carry on a much larger volume of public business. The number of state employees has increased over the years; and the very magnitude of the executive work has required an improved system of selecting and qualifying state employees. One of the gravest problems is the enlistment of competent help at the scale of compensation the state has been accustomed to allow. Undoubtedly some improvement along this line is necessary and will have to be provided.

The rewards of private employment are so much greater that many competent persons who would appreciate public service cannot afford to make the sacrifice required to render it. The lack of continuity in carrying on much of the work of government, because of frequent changes in personnel, has a tendency to impair the efficiency of the service. This problem can be solved by reasonable tenure based on experience and qualifications, and by providing more adequate compensation for those who really prepare for the work.

But change in personnel is not an unmixed evil. The introduction of new blood stimulates initiative and ambition, while a feeling of security may tend to create arrogance in petty officials and cause stagnation in the public service. The policy to be found is one that assures a reasonable tenure to the worker, without impairing the sense of responsibility to the public.

The courts have recorded precedents and the legislatures have the published laws and journals to guide them. The executive worker has not such advantage, and the experience of one administration may be completely hidden from the new executives that take over the task. But the Council of State Governments has practically overcome the disadvantage. This well-organized and efficient agency has developed a service that is rendering invaluable aid to good government and to the science of administration.

Students will discover many instances of the mingling and overlapping of the separate powers; but this can be traced to the compromises made in formulating our system of written constitutions designed to meet the exigencies of peculiar situations with the proper checks and balances. Implied powers are not classified apart from the express powers from which they may be implied and which give rise to the doctrine of implied powers. They are based on necessity because it must be presumed that an express power was given to be exercised; and when it cannot be exercised effectively without some incidental or implied power, it is reasonable to conclude that such power was included in the express power.

In the last half century administrative agencies have developed to perform many functions of government. The tasks assigned to them partake of the character of legislative, executive, and judicial work and should be the subject of separate and distinct treatment in this series of studies of governmental processes.

Every student is bound to be impressed with the diligence, skill, and care of the founding fathers, who created a form of government of such great power and yet restrained it within such rigid limits that justice may be achieved under it and the great blessings of liberty preserved for every generation. Our reverence for the founding fathers and for their handiwork is but a spontaneous tribute for their sacrifices, their wisdom, and their great love for free institutions.

It is reasonable to believe that if their spirits could communicate with us, their command would be for us to preserve and perpetuate forever the greatest liberty under impartial law so that the best in men should find opportunity, and the least gifted of our race should have safety.

---

1. A series of essays written by James Madison, Alexander Hamilton, and John Jay, *The Federalist* first appeared in book form in 1788. Governor Willis was quoting from Madison's No. 47. In the original the correct word is "elective" rather than "elected," which Willis uses. See Benjamin F. Wright, ed., *The Federalist* (Cambridge, Mass., 1961; orig. pub. 1788), 336.

2. John Marshall (1755-1835). Revolutionary War officer; attorney from 1780; delegate to Virginia House of Burgesses, 1780, 1782-88; delegate to Virginia convention to ratify U.S. Constitution, 1788; congressman, 1799-1800; U.S. secretary of state, 1800-01; chief justice of the United States, 1801-35; author of *Life of George Washington*, 5 vols. (1804-07). *DAB*, 6:315-25.

3. Benjamin Nathan Cardozo (1870-1938). Attorney; author of several respected legal works; justice of New York Supreme Court, 1913; justice of New York Court of Appeals, 1913-32; U.S. Supreme Court, 1932-38. *Ibid., Supplement* 2:93-96. Governor Willis quoted correctly from Cardozo's *Nature of the Judicial Process* (New Haven, 1921), 10.

4. Charles Merrill Hough (1852-1927). Attorney; U.S. district judge, 1906-16; U.S. circuit judge, 1916-26; president of Maritime Law Association, 1919-27. *DAB*, 5:249-50.

5. Quoted from Charles M. Hough, "Due Process of Law—To-day," *Harvard Law Review* 32 (1919):219.

6. Demosthenes (384 B.C.-322 B.C.). Greek orator and statesman. *New Encyclopedia Britannica*, 15th ed., 30 vols. (Chicago, 1983), 5:578-80.

7. Charles Evans Hughes (1862-1948). Governor of New York, 1906-10; U.S. Supreme Court justice, 1910-16; defeated Republican presidential candidate, 1916; U.S. secretary of state, 1921-25; chief justice of the United States, 1930-41. *DAB, Supplement* 4:403-7. The quotation Willis correctly cites is from Hughes's *Supreme Court of the United States* (New York, 1928), 68.

8. Alexander Hamilton (1757-1804). Aide-de-camp to George Washington in Revolutionary War, 1777-81; member of Continental Congress, 1782-83, 1788; delegate to Constitutional Convention; coauthor of *The Federalist*; U.S. secretary of the treasury, 1789-95. *DAB*, 4:171-79. The exact quotation, from No. 78 of *The Federalist*, is, "It may truly be said to have neither FORCE nor WILL, but merely judgment." Wright, ed., *The Federalist*, 490.

9. Thomas McIntyre Cooley (1824-1898). Attorney; Michigan supreme court reporter, 1858-65; state supreme court justice 1865-85; also in law department (1859-84) and history department (1884-98) of University of Michigan; Interstate Commerce Commission, 1887-91; author of numerous works, including *A*

Treatise of the Constitutional Limitations which Rest upon the Legislative Power of the States of American Vision (1868). *DAB*, 2:392-93.

10. Francis Bacon (1561-1626). English lawyer, courtier, statesman, philosopher, lord chancellor of James I. *Encyclopedia Britannica*, 2:561-67.

11. The quotation is correctly taken from Cardozo's *Growth of the Law* (New Haven, 1924), 62-64.

12. Oliver Wendell Holmes (1841-1935). Civil War soldier; attorney; editor of *American Law Review*, 1870-73; author of numerous legal works; Massachusetts supreme judicial court, 1883-1902; U.S. Supreme Court, 1902-32. *DAB, Supplement 1*:417-27. The quotation is from Holmes's *Collected Legal Papers* (New York, 1952; orig. pub. 1920), 173.

13. Edmund Burke (1729-1797). British statesman, political writer, orator, and Whig member of Parliament. See Carl B. Cone, *Burke and the Nature of Politics*, 2 vols. (Lexington, 1957-64).

14. The quotation is from Hughes's *Supreme Court*, 241.

15. The quotation is from Webster's eulogy of jurist Joseph Story (1779-1845) and appears in *Writings and Speeches of Daniel Webster*, 18 vols. (Boston, 1903), 3:300.

16. Louis Dembitz Brandeis (1856-1941). Kentucky native. Attorney since 1877; author of several important legal works; U.S. Supreme Court justice, 1916-39. *DAB, Supplement 3*:93-100.

17. William Howard Taft (1857-1930). Attorney; Superior Court of Ohio justice, 1887-90; U.S. solicitor-general, 1890-92; U.S. circuit court justice, 1892-1900; president of the Philippine commission, 1900-01, and civil governor, 1901-04; U.S. secretary of war, 1904-08; U.S. president, 1909-13; Yale University professor, 1913-21; chief justice of the United States, 1921-30. *DAB*, 9:266-72.

LAW AND POLITICS
Danville / November 14, 1947

THE topic of this evening, I am informed, concerns the broad theme of "The College and Government." In such an atmosphere, it seemed most appropriate that my remarks should be addressed to that phase of the subject in which I had been most experienced. My own life work has been devoted to the law, and my brief excursions into the political field have been purely incidental. I am told that certain politicians have been willing to concede that I was competent to advise in regard to the law; but no one has reassured me that I possessed any particular qualifications to advise on the political side. I venture upon that branch of my topic purely upon my own. The selection of my subject derived from a suggestion of President Taylor,[1] of the University of Louisville, in his address at the centennial celebration of that fine institution. He mentioned that the first chair in law at Transylvania [University] was entitled "Law and Politics," and he thought it was time to revive in the courses of study an expanded development of political science and government.

The long list of judges, governors, senators, and other eminent public officials graduated from Centre College attests the presence here of a sympathetic climate for such a discussion. It is recognized everywhere that Centre College has exerted a commanding influence upon the life of this state and nation. Not alone in public life, but in the private lives of countless men and women can be traced the teachings of able, earnest, patient, patriotic, and devoted men who shaped the character of this institution and inspired the work of its students.

Never before was it more important that law and politics be better understood or more ably advocated and capably administered. The world affairs of today seem to be disordered by problems almost too complex for mastery. Such a condition is a challenge to the best that free institutions can produce.

The basic of systematic reasoning lies in a definition of terms. Hence we must first know what is meant by law and what is comprehended by politics, before we may hope to understand the relationship between them.

Law has never been defined to the satisfaction of the philosophers and writers who have delved into its history, origin, and objects. Indeed, some great writers have doubted whether it could be defined. Anything that is known can be defined, and to say that law can never be defined is equivalent to saying that it can never be known. But it is possible to know what the law has been at any given time; and if room be allowed for the growth of the law through the added experience of each generation, a reasonably adequate definition is certainly possible. Of course, we cannot follow those who adhere to the doctrine of the cynic who declared that law was anything positively asserted and plausibly maintained; nor even the fellow travelers of the same school who think that the law is but the last guess of the highest courts. We prefer to seek the true principles deduced and declared by the great men of the law. It is easy enough to define statutory law simply as the product of legislation, prescribing conduct deemed for the general good or forbidding acts deemed detrimental. Many of the writers emphasize law as rules of action emanating from a sovereign authority and operating upon the citizens or subjects. Another school of thought insists that law is derived from nature as the gift of the Creator and is merely discovered by men. Still another class of writers, adverting to the vast body of law not enacted by any lawmaking body, or emanating from any authority, or discoverable in the natural sciences, insists that law is derived from the usages and customs of society; and all the written law, legislative enactments, and judicial decisions are but evidence of that intangible and elusive something that governs all human conduct. Without attempting to pursue these interesting discussions to their logical conclusions, it is sufficient for our purpose to know that law is the sum of the forces sanctioned by society that govern and control human conduct and relations, whether derived from custom, legislation, or other source. The subject is great enough to engage the best and noblest minds and important enough to enlist the energies and labors of those who wish to contribute to the establishment and to participate in the administration of justice.

Slowly but surely, lawyers, politicians, and students of sociology, are becoming conscious of the fact that civil liberty and individual freedoms prosper or perish upon economic foundations and policies. Many fine objects and noble aspirations have foundered on the rocks of economic fallacy. Never before was it more necessary that we have a broad understanding of all the forces that hasten or hinder progress towards a higher and better standard of living for ever-increasing numbers of men and women. Knowledge is power; but power may be abused as effectively by evil men as it may be used constructively by good men. Therefore, it is clear that the great and supreme need of the world today is the training and development of good men and women in great numbers to control the powers that govern all things and regulate all human conduct.

On the other hand, we find the definitions of politics fairly satisfactory and without much divergence. It is the science and art of government; the science dealing with the organization and administration of a state in both its internal and external affairs; it is, in short, political science. Historically, it was that branch of ethics which dealt with the ethical relation and duties of states or social organizations. It is otherwise explained as the theory or practice of managing the affairs of public policy or of political parties; hence it embraces political affairs, principles, convictions, opinions, sympathies, or the like. We cannot overlook that the word sometimes is used in the bad sense that evil men have visited on a beautiful science, giving a notorious name to a high calling. It is in such sense that politics is deemed a selfish seeking of office and power by artful or dishonest means or management to secure success or private profit at the expense of the public treasury.

It cannot be denied that many people regard the very name of politics with aversion and suspicion. It is this sinister aspect of political efforts and accomplishments that deters so many good people from participation in so-called politics and from willingness to be candidates for office. This condition of public opinion increases the facility with which bad men are able to take over and exploit the powers of government. When you realize that politics is the science of making, construing, and enforcing law and the means by which policies are determined and enforced by agents clothed with full authority, you cannot escape the responsibility, or the desirability, of enlisting the best talent, the firmest character, and the highest intelligence in the hard work and constant sacrifice involved in participation in politics. To those apathetic citizens who refuse to be interested in politics, the words of J.B. Priestly[2] are peculiarly fitting:

> Politics shapes our lives. It takes us in and out of wars. It decides whether men will have steady jobs, women will have decent homes, children will have a chance to grow up healthy and fit for adult life.
>
> You may take no interest in politics, but, you may depend upon it, politics takes an interest in you.
>
> So if you do not want to be a miserable pawn on the board, pushed around to suit somebody else's convenience, make up your mind to take a keen interest in politics.

Politics will be no cleaner or better than the men and women who are engaged in it. If politics be truly the science of government, it must follow that good politics is the sole means of attaining good government. If you seek to escape from participation in politics, you necessarily defeat the purpose of a government by all the people. When the citizen abdicates his powers, they will be exercised by someone for him. If we expect anything approaching the ideal, we must pay the price in loyalty and effort, whch alone can realize ideals. Sufficient effort and adequate numbers can redeem politics from the sneers of the cynic or the jeers of the wicked and enthrone statesmanship, which can be depended upon to treat politics with thought and imagination, with the one great object of serving the best interests of the country. The evil politician thrives upon the apathy and indifference of good people and is enabled to gain power for himself and profit for his faction at the expense of the country and to the discredit of government itself. Certainly the lawyer should understand and practice politics, even though he has no desire to be a candidate for office. Every man has an interest, indeed a vital interest, in seeing that suitable men and women do become candidates for office and fight for sound principles. Indeed, an alert, advised, and courageous public opinion is the very condition of lasting good government and will sustain even an ordinary public official in carrying on faithfully the duties of public office. On the other hand, even a great public official cannot succeed indefinitely without such sustaining help.

It so happens that we are living in a period of history when the direction of human affairs is confused by powerful forces operating in political, economic, and social thinking. Elemental forces are striking at the eternal verities. The underlying issue is crystal clear. It is simply whether individual man is to acknowledge his failure and submit to totalitarian forces; or shall he assert his mastery and prove his mettle by maintaining individual freedom and eternal justice against any power and under any assault? This confusion and conflict of ideas did not flow from the last world war. Indeed, the sway of the dictators in many lands flourished before the war and was the direct cause of the war. It arose from the failure of the people in those lands to establish justice and economic freedom. The distress and dissatisfaction of people affords a fertile field for demagogues and dictators. The slow process of establishing justice in reestablishing peace must not discourage the ministers of justice or the advocates of liberty or the adherents of stable economy. Humanity has groped through the ages for the formula for the attainment of peace with justice and the preservation of individual freedoms. We believe that the secret was found in liberty, regulated by law, predicated upon the consent of the governed. This is attainable only by free people, constantly alert and intelligent, deserving the rights they have and daring to maintain them at whatever cost.

Education of the people universally, and of the leaders particularly, is the sole hope for the solution of all our political, social, and economic problems. It is essential to the maintenance of human liberty. That education must embrace the development of the highest potential capacities of the great number of people; and it must extend to the whole range of human conduct, activities, and relations. In studying law and politics, the teacher and the student will find a field as broad as human experience, as high as human aspiration, and as important as civilization itself. It calls for the highest qualities of human achievement. In pursuing them in his future life, the lawyer and the layman in whatever activity he may engage will find opportunity for the accomplishment of the greatest good, and for the linking of his name and fame with the noblest and the finest minds that have gained immortality by serving their fellow men. As a great industrialist has said in addressing a graduating class of young Americans:

You have the mental equipment and the training to become outstanding among your fellows in capitalizing the opportunities your country
offers. From your ranks the nation obtains its professional leaders in
industry, the sciences, and government. Your opportunity for leadership
is great indeed. But with leadership goes responsibility. You face one of
those challenges in America destined to stand in history. It is a challenge
that calls for supreme effort and great wisdom. But the objective is
becoming clear. Before you is the responsibility to keep freedom in
America. At no time in the history of the world have the stakes been
higher. To preserve the dignity of individual man. To remove the fear of
want and oppression. To preserve these United States as a rock of
material and spiritual strength in a world of chaos. To bring eventual
peace with well-being for all people.

No generation of young Americans ever had a greater opportunity or
a greater responsibility.

In conclusion, I leave with you the prayer of a devout Christian who
spent his life in China: "Give us the strength to accept serenely those
things which cannot be changed—Give us the courage to change those
things which can and must be changed—And grant us the wisdom to
differentiate the one from the other."

---

1. John Wilkinson Taylor (1906-   ). Kentucky native. Various educational
and administrative positions at Columbia University, 1927-30, 1934-38; professor and assistant to the president, Louisiana State University, 1938-40; in
military in World War II; University of Louisville, 1947-50; deputy director-
general and acting director-general, UNESCO, 1951-54; executive director,
Chicago Educational Television Association, 1954-71. *Who's Who, 1980-81*, 3258.
On the question of the "centennial" celebration of the University of Louisville,
see Dwayne Cox, "How Old is the University of Louisville?" *Register of the
Kentucky Historical Society* 81 (1983): 59-76.
2. John Boynton Priestly (1894-   ). Born in Great Britain. Veteran of World
War I; delegate to UNESCO conference, 1946-47; chairman of International
Theater Conference, 1947-48; member of British National Theatre Board,
1966-67; author of numerous plays and books, beginning in 1922 and including
his autobiography, *Instead of the Trees* (1977). *Who's Who, 1982-83* (British), 1790.

EDUCATION

125th ANNIVERSARY OF CENTRE COLLEGE
Louisville / January 21, 1944

FELLOW Citizens of Kentucky:

It is a rare privilege, as governor of the commonwealth, to speak on behalf of the people of Kentucky. It is a privilege even rarer to be able to utter sentiments which we know will command universal approval. Such an occasion is now presented in the celebration of an important date in the life of Centre College. For a century and a quarter, old Centre has been a potent factor in the cultural, spiritual, and educational growth of this state. The influence of the college, and of those great spirits that gave it character and leadership, has been felt throughout the state and in all parts of this great country. The pride of the whole state in this institution has been equalled only by the devotion and loyalty of the teachers and students. The contribution Centre College has made to education has been noteworthy. The uplift given to the general advancement of society has been inspiring. Celebrations of landmarks in the life of an institution are helpful and constructive. They mark the progress that has been accomplished and point the way to still greater progress in the future. In a free country, where the dignity and worth of the individual is the supreme objective, education is vital. It is the one factor that preserves the strength of free society. It is the basic essential of a strong citizenship.

Education brings to the people the leadership and the character that prevents decay and assures growth. It is a law of life that when growth ceases, decay begins. The people are the repositories of all power and the source of all advancement. Power in ignorant or evil hands is dangerous and destructive. Wisely used for noble purposes, it is an instrument of progress and achievement. Education is power. Religion assures its proper use.

The education of the people is a perpetual task, and its performance is our sole dependence for future security. Fortunate is that people great enough to know how its greatness is preserved. It is the glory of Centre College that it has held the banner high and kept the rudder true. It has struggled through the years to maintain and advance the cause of liberty, justice, and righteousness. From the achievements of the past, we derive courage and faith to carry on to great ends. Tyranny and liberty always have been and always will be at war. Tyranny thrives on ignorance and prejudice. Liberty flourishes where intelligence and faith abide. It is a prime aim of the present administration to promote in every way the advancement of a sound educational program.

With high hopes and with serene confidence, Kentucky congratulates Centre College on her past and bids her Godspeed for the future.[1]

---

1. This address was broadcast over WHAS radio. Other speakers on the program were James H. Hewlett, acting president of Centre College; and Fred M. Vinson, director of the Office of Economic Stabilization in Washington, D.C. See *Tributes to a College* (Danville, 1944).

KENTUCKY EDUCATION ASSOCIATION
Lexington / April 14, 1944

THE proper education of the youth is one of the most important problems facing civilized society. Particularly is that so with a people who have chosen to govern themselves through a republican form of government. The founding fathers and those who laid the foundations of our republic well knew the part education must play in the life of our nation.

The Father of Our Country admonished his countrymen to "promote—as an object of primary importance, institutions for the general diffusion of knowledge." He believed that "in proportion as the structure of a government gives force to public opinion, it is essential that public opinion should be enlightened."

James Madison[1] thought that "a popular government without popular information or the means of acquiring it is but a prologue to a farce or a tragedy, or, perhaps, both." "Knowledge will forever govern ignorance," said he, "and a people who mean to be their own governors must arm themselves with the power which knowledge gives."

Midway between Washington and our present day, that great Kentuckian and martyred president, Abraham Lincoln, stated that education "is the most important subject which we as a people can be engaged in." Continuing, he said that he hoped "to see the time when education, and by its means, morality, sobriety, enterprise, and industry, shall become much more general than at present," and he stated that he should be gratified to have it in his power "to contribute something to the advancement of any measure which might have a tendency to accelerate the happy period."

Two American presidents of more recent times have forcibly expressed themselves upon the importance of education. Woodrow Wilson, himself a great educator,[2] thought that "without popular education, no government which rests upon popular action can long endure." "The people must be schooled," he maintained, "in the knowledge, and if possible, in the virtues, upon which the maintenance and success of free institutions depend."

Herbert Hoover felt that "if we were to suppress our educational system for a single generation, most of our people would die of starvation, and intellectually and spiritually, we should slip back four thousand years in human progress."

The early Kentuckians showed an acute interest in education. In 1821 the legislature of the state appointed a committee of eminent Kentuckians to collect information relating to the feasibility of public education in the state. A statement or two from the report of that committee will show how our forefathers felt about education.[3]

"Popular education," said that committee, "is the prop which sustains free institutions, and the lever which overturns the oppressor's throne. Happily, we are not laboring to undermine a fabric of despotism; but to remove the rock on which tyrants build. While monarchs and usurpers understand and pursue their own interests by extinguishing the lamps of knowledge, and punishing with death the free expression of opinion, let us not be blind to the means of preserving and perpetuating our own liberties. Bind the minds of men in chains of ignorance, and it requires but a moderate portion of art and talents to enslave their bodies. Wherever these chains exist, let us break them. Let us wage on the citadels of ignorance a perpetual and exterminating war. Let us remove every fragment upon which ambition can seize to erect his gloomy edifice. It is the first of our political duties—we owe it to our principles, to our institutions, to our posterity, and to mankind!"

This movement was in the field of public education. We must not, however, overlook the part which the church played in the development of schools in our state. The early settlers of Kentucky were, as a rule, religious. Early schools were church-related or church-supported schools. Without the foundation work which the churches gave, it would have been impossible to introduce our system of public education.

Education helps to make men free. If we say that a man has freedom to worship and fail to teach him how he may practice his religion in the service of his fellow men, we have not truly given him the freedom to worship. If we say a man has political freedom and fail to teach him the principles for which he may feel the urge to cast an intelligent vote, we have denied him this freedom. If we say a man has the freedom to earn a living and fail to teach him how to earn a living, we give him only the freedom to starve. If we say that in America people have a free public school and fail to house that school in a sanitary, well-equipped school plant, fail to support that school for a standard term, and refuse to support the employment of a qualified, conscientious teacher, we have failed to guarantee the freedom to learn; but on the other hand we safeguard ignorance—the food on which despots gorge themselves.

The constitution of Kentucky was begun in the spirit of prayer. The preamble was a prayer—listen! "We, the people of the commonwealth of Kentucky, grateful to Almighty God for the civil, political and religious liberties we enjoy, and invoking the continuance of these blessings, do ordain and establish this constitution." It was said as if the convention was on its knees! It may have been, for it was the foundation of a government that was set up that the people might be free. Free to do what? To worship, to vote, to earn, to learn; to enjoy life, liberty, and the pursuit of happiness.

The constitution sets up machinery whereby the people might be guaranteed the freedom which is basic to all freedoms—the freedom to be educated. The state and many of the communities have gone forward in many directions toward the realization of the great dream which was born in the 1892 convention.[4] But we have not gone far enough.

There are still seventy-five counties in which the elementary school children have the opportunity to attend school only seven months out of each year. There are still too many of our young people of high school age who are not in high school due, for the most part, to the fact that there is no high school accessible which meets their needs. There are still too many schools which make no provision for teaching young people the dignity of work and how to earn a living with their hands. There are still too many schools which are housed in buildings not suited to learning.

Too many schools do not have properly qualified teachers. It is an axiom that there cannot now be, nor has there ever been, a good school unless there was a qualified teacher. Kentucky teachers have educated themselves to meet the high standards of competence set up by law—twenty-five thousand meet minimum state standards, but eleven thousand are not available for teaching. Why? Because the salaries are too low. The increase in teachers' salaries has not kept pace with the increased cost of living. The percentage of increase in teachers' salaries in Kentucky from the beginning of the war until the meeting of the 1944 legislature was approximately 8 percent, while the increase in the cost of living over the same period was from 22 to 25 percent. During that period the average salary of teachers in Kentucky was almost one-third below the average for the nation. The result has been that today only about 77 percent of the children are attending a school in which there is a teacher with a regular certificate.

We have waited too long in taking bold steps to carry out what was in 1892, and is still, the will of the people. We have waited too long in actually meeting the demands of republican government. We are suffering now because too many single men have been rejected by the army on account of lack of adequate education. If the physical and intellectual welfare of all the children in all parts of the state had been given adequate attention, the drafting of fathers would not have come so early.

What can a well-organized, well-staffed, and adequately supported school system bring to our state?

1. It can develop in the minds of every person that "the individual human being is of surpassing worth." Education will make us all recognize that our children are more precious than the earth on which they live, the food they eat, the clothes they wear, the houses in which they live, the banks in which the gold rests, the factories where things are made. If education does not do this, it is not education. People must feel that this is true.

2. Education can develop in the mind of everyone the feeling that all the earth with all its culture belongs to all men regardless of whether they are of high or low estate. "The earth is the Lord's and the fullness thereof." The culture, the freedom, the blessings, the privileges, the

responsibilities, belong—not to one man, one group, one race—but to all men, all races.

3. Education will lead us to the conviction that the human mind can be trusted if it is set free. Freedom does not mean license. It does mean that the mind set free to learn can be trusted. It means that if learning is not provided, the mind cannot be trusted. Education will forever refute the contention of the despot that the people cannot be trusted and that only the anointed can govern. Truly, slavery of body follows slavery of mind. Education helps men to believe this.

4. Education can teach us that men should be their own rulers. They must know, and the school must teach every man, the truth of the statement that government by the consent of the governed is the tenet which can live with free people. The home, the school, the church, the state, the nation which provides such training that the talents of its members may be used to the fullest in its development, will live. Those who fail to exploit the potential strength will always be second-rate.

5. Education will teach people that differences are more easily settled through peaceful means than by war. Wars are caused by failure to understand the other man's point of view. Education will help men reason. "Come, let us reason together," says education. "Let's fight it out on this line," says the ignorant.

6. Education teaches us to tolerate, respect, and value racial, political, and cultural minorities. Only the ignorant—the spiritually unlettered—become intolerant. Education need not cause us to adopt political, cultural, or racial patterns; but every person who believes in democratic-republican life must give every man the right to his choice of racial, political, or cultural pattern.

Education should do this and more. Our schools must develop every individual so that he may make the most of himself, live peaceably with his fellow men, earn his living, and assume civic and religious responsibilities. The forward step in this direction in Kentucky must be a bold one—we must wage total war in defense of these rights of our children, the citizens of tomorrow.

Today, Kentucky does not hold an enviable position, educationally speaking. In 1940, forty-four states had longer average school terms than did Kentucky; forty-six states had a larger percentage of pupils of high school age enrolled than had our state; only nine states had more functional illiterates. In the same year, 117,000 children between the ages of six and eighteen in Kentucky were not enrolled in any elementary or secondary school. In the same year, the average annual salary of Kentucky county school teachers was $611. This is only $11.94

per week, no more than that received by unskilled laborers or char-women. This was the situation before the war. The impact of the war has made conditions worse.

The state administration which I head stands committed to a program calculated to improve the schools of this state. Early in the regular session of the legislature which has just closed, I recommended to that body that it appropriate $3,000,000 to be used as an emergency fund for the payment of teachers' salaries for the current school year. A bill was immediately introduced in the lower house, was passed by both houses, and signed by me.[5] The money from this appropriation has long since been distributed to the teachers of this state, and information reaching me is to the effect that it has had a salutary effect on the morale and spirit of the teaching forces. At the same time I recommended to the legislature that it appropriate $15,000,000 to the general school fund, $13,500,000 on a per capita basis and $1,500,000 to be used as an equalization fund. Provisions for the appropriation of these two items were incorporated in the general budget bill, which, as you know, failed to pass the legislature.

Fifteen million dollars is not an exorbitant sum for state support of education. Our sister state of North Carolina appropriated, for education during the past year, $28,728,000; Georgia, $19,000,000; Louisiana, $18,496,374; Alabama, $17,000,000; West Virginia, a state with a population much less than that of Kentucky, $18,775,000; Indiana, in round numbers, $20,000,000.

I have committed myself to calling the legislature into extraordinary session for the purpose of giving aid to the public schools of the state—to appropriate $15,000,000 to the common school fund and to make other appropriations needed to carry our educational program forward. In the very near future that call will be made.[6]

It is a genuine pleasure to have the privilege, early in my administration, of meeting this great assemblage of school people. Through the cooperation of all, teachers, executives, administrators, supervisors, legislators, and state officers, real progress can be made in the elimination of ignorance in this state. I take this opportunity to pledge to you my full support during my term of office. No greater honor could come to me than to have it said, upon my retirement as the chief magistrate of the commonwealth, that I had been a governor friendly to education.

---

1. James Madison (1751-1836). Fourth president of the United States, 1809-17.

2. Thomas Woodrow Wilson (1856-1924). Twenty-eighth president of the

United States, 1913-21, had served as professor at Bryn Mawr, Wesleyan University, and Princeton University. He was president of Princeton, 1902-10.

3. A committee of William T. Barry, J.R. Witherspoon, D.R. Murray, and John Pope presented an elaborate educational plan to the 1822 General Assembly. The report included an accompanying statement by George Robertson and letters of advocacy from John Adams, Thomas Jefferson, and James Madison. It was not until 1838, however, that the legislature established a general system of public education. Lewis and Richard Collins, *History of Kentucky*, 2 vols. (Covington, Ky., 1874), 1:502-3.

4. The constitutional convention convened on September 8, 1890, and the resulting constitution was signed April 11, 1891. Voters ratified the constitution in August 1891. After that ratification, delegates reconvened September 2-28 and made several additional changes. The document was signed again and proclaimed completed. A court case validated the procedure. The convention, then, was properly the 1890-91, not 1892, convention. See Hambleton Tapp and James C. Klotter, *Kentucky: Decades of Discord, 1865-1900* (Frankfort, 1977), 263-64.

5. House Bill 9, introduced by Ed Marcum (R-Manchester) and Adron Doran (D-Wingo), had passed by 95-1 and 37-0 margins. It went into effect February 1. See Kentucky *Acts* (1944), 110-11; Kentucky *House Journal* (1944), 391; Kentucky *Senate Journal* (1944), 638.

6. The call for a special session was made a month later, on May 15, 1944. See discussion of the issue in "Legislative Actions, 1943-1945" section.

STATEMENT REGARDING SPECIAL SESSION
Frankfort / May 15, 1944

I HAVE called a special session of the General Assembly to meet at 2:00 P.M., Friday, May 19, for the purpose of making appropriations for the common school system, asking that any extra amount required over the income for any fiscal year be taken from the surplus. It seems to me that the crisis in which the schools are now involved requires relief which can be met only by a special appropriation. If the income should be inadequate, then I think the surplus should be used for the schools to the extent of the deficit. I can conceive of no possible contingency calling for resort to the surplus of greater importance than the maintenance of the school system.

There are many other subjects which have been suggested to be embraced in the call; but these matters, however important, can be taken care of from time to time and do not require immediate action of the General Assembly. So far as these other subjects are concerned, they will be dealt with from time to time as action may be required. If an emergency should arise which requires legislative action in the future, a special session can then be called. Any action now would be predicated upon prophecy, and it is better to await events and deal with real situations. The only emergency requiring immediate attention is the schools, and I am limiting the session to that one subject so that it may be considered impartially and without being involved in other considerations.[1]

---

1. For a discussion of the special session, see "Legislative Actions, 1943-1945" section.

KENTUCKY WESLEYAN COMMENCEMENT
Winchester / June 5, 1944

GOVERNOR WILLIS pointed out the disciplinary values in the educational process. Education, he said, is "an uphill climb all the way." Whether it be work in the classroom, the library, or the laboratory, we make these values our own through application and hard work. A college education is, therefore, the governor said, a means of character development and brings rewards in personal satisfaction to the individual student.

Education is, moreover, of supreme importance, the governor emphasized, in the successful achievement of democratic government. Government by the people carries with it education of the people in the interest of intelligent government and government for the people. In fact, an educated citizenry is absolutely essential to safeguard democratic government; without an educated people, [a] republican form of government cannot be the beneficent form that it ought to be.

Governor Willis paid his tribute to Christian education and its cultivation of the spiritual potentialities of the life of our nation. Faith in one's self and faith in one's government, he said, need to be founded upon faith in God and in the power of His church. He congratulated the members of the class of 1944 upon their graduation from Kentucky Wesleyan College, which is making its contribution to American education as a small liberal arts church college.[1]

---

1. This account is from the Winchester *Sun,* June 6, 1944. For slightly different versions see the Frankfort *State Journal* and Lexington *Leader,* both of June 6.

INDEPENDENCE DAY CELEBRATION
Morehead / July 6, 1944

GOVERNOR WILLIS, making his first appearance in Morehead since his election to the governorship last year, expressed his pleasure at being asked to appear on the program and termed it a "homecoming" for him to be back in this community.[1]

Governor Willis declared that "the people of the world must be educated to liberty, and then they will not question it." He spoke of the part which all educational institutions play in the education for a better world, emphasizing the importance of each insignificant rural school and pointing up his remarks with the statement that "the greatest people rise from the common masses."

"Without education a people are ignorant," the governor said, "and it is commonly known an ignorant people will perish in an incredibly short time." He discussed history and its proof of the necessity for high morals and good character in the building of a worthwhile world. He challenged his audience to work towards high ideals, reminding themselves that "man is created in the image of God, and that in developing our facilities to the highest we are not only completing an individual accomplishment . . . but that of a higher destiny as well.

"Education," he said, "is a perpetual problem, and all we have done is only a beginning of what we will have to do to win the war."

1. The "homecoming" reference is to the fact that Morehead State Teachers College was the normal school nearest his home of Ashland. The talk, like so many of Governor Willis's, was delivered extemporaneously. Morehead *Independent*, July 13, 1944; and Lexington *Herald*, July 7, 1944.

EASTERN KENTUCKY EDUCATION ASSOCIATION
Ashland / November 9, 1944

"LET us resolve that we will never close the door of opportunity to the barefoot boy of America," declared Governor Simeon S. Willis. . . .

In urging the development of the future citizens of Kentucky to the utmost of their ability and capacity through proper education channels, the governor pledged himself to do all that he could to aid the cause of the teacher and the schools.

Governor Willis said that the hope of Kentucky is not centered in its vast store of natural resources but in its people, who are almost exclusively native American stock, and that "Kentuckians are the trustees of the heritage handed down by our forefathers . . . the things we have today were given by them; let us pass them on unimpaired."

The governor compared the first 150 years of the colonists under tyranny to 150 years under liberty, in which the original thirteen colonies have been enlarged to forty-eight states with a population of 130 million people.

"The primary requirement for advancement of the men and women of tomorrow is character," Governor Willis declared, in urging the teachers to carry on the banner of freedom with the spirit, "I shall be worthy of it."

FOUNDERS' DAY
Lexington / February 22, 1945

Citizens of Kentucky should compete to see who can do most for the state, not to the state, Governor Simeon S. Willis told approximately 250 alumni and friends at the first annual Founders' Day banquet.[1]

In our type of government, he said, it is the individual who counts, and all of the people must be educated to their best capacity. A university, to serve the needs of the people, the governor continued, must be capable of leadership and must keep the people up to the highest standards. Great states have developed with great universities, he added.

There is no politics in education, Governor Willis said, and there should be none. For those who wished to learn the relationship which should exist between a university and a state, he recommended the book *A University Is a Place . . . A Spirit,* by Dr. Frank L. McVey, president emeritus of the university.[2]

Declaring that the university must have adequate tools for its work, Governor Willis said that a fieldhouse would be built at the university "as soon as materials and men are released." The building of the structure was settled six or eight months ago, he added, when money was appropriated and put into bonds.[3]

In his tribute to the men who founded and built the university, the governor said, "The way to honor our great men is to go forward and accomplish deeds worthy of their heritage."[4]

---

1. Designed to recognize the builders of the University of Kentucky, Founders' Day was celebrated on the date in 1865 when the Kentucky legislature established a state institution of higher education under the Morrill Act. Lexington *Herald,* February 23, 1945.

2. Frank LeRond McVey (1869-1953). Ohio native; high school principal in Iowa, 1891-92; professor at University of Minnesota, 1896-1907; president of the University of North Dakota, 1909-17; president of the University of Kentucky, 1917-40. His wife, Frances Jewell McVey, collected and arranged *A University is a Place . . . A Spirit* (Lexington, 1944). See *Courier-Journal,* January 5, 1953.

3. Appropriations for what became Memorial Coliseum were made under three governors—Keen Johnson, Willis, and Earle Clements—and by three General Assemblies—1942, 1946, and 1948. The total cost was approximately $4 million. Dedication of the edifice took place on May 30, 1950. See Herman L.

Donovan, "An Investment in Youth," *Bulletin of the University of Kentucky* 42 (1950): [4-5]; and "Memorial Coliseum" clippings, Buildings File, University Archives, University of Kentucky Library.

4. This account is from the Lexington *Leader,* February 23, 1945. For slightly different versions see Frankfort *State Journal, Courier-Journal,* and the Lexington *Herald* of February 23, 1945.

BALD KNOB HIGH SCHOOL COMMENCEMENT
Bald Knob, Franklin County / May 25, 1945

At Bald Knob, Governor Simeon Willis told the graduates that education in its broadest and best sense means the full development of the potential capacities of each individual. "It embraces intellectual, spiritual, moral, and physical development of new ideas; and the progress of invention will constitute a continuing challenge to the sufficiency and the soundness of our systems of government. It is essential that our people know and understand the history of our country and the success of our institutions."

Governor Willis declared that the future belongs to those who prepare for it and that America must maintain her leadership in the world in the mastery of making and the management of machines. He also declared there must be unity and understanding among ourselves as well as with all nations and all peoples. This unity can come from understanding, and understanding comes from knowledge, he said.

EASTERN KENTUCKY STATE TEACHERS COLLEGE COMMENCEMENT
Richmond / May 30, 1945

"Education is absolutely essential to the perpetuity of a free republic," Governor Willis said. "There can be no successful government by the people unless the people themselves possess character, intelligence, and a high concept of responsibility not only to themselves and their family but to their community and their country."

Referring to the four teachers colleges[1] and the University of Kentucky, where teachers are trained, the governor said that he looked forward "to a steady advance from year to year in the strength, usefulness, and achievement of our higher institutions."

"The influence of the teacher," he stated, "is second only to the home, supplemented by the church in determining the character and citizenship of our people."

---

1. The four white teachers' colleges were Eastern Kentucky State, Western Kentucky State, Morehead State, and Murray State.

FOUNDERS' DAY
Lexington / February 22, 1946

HENRY STITES BARKER lived almost seventy-eight years. He spent twenty-eight of those years in important public service; and he left the impress of his thought and character on the moral, judicial, and intellectual life of his time.

He was born in Christian County, Kentucky, on July 23, 1850, the son of Richard Henry and Caroline M. (Sharp) Barker. He was educated in the public schools of Louisville and in the Kentucky University. He was admitted to the Kentucky bar in 1874 and practiced in Louisville for many years. He was married May 22, 1886, to Miss Kate Sharp Meriweather, who now resides in Louisville.

Judge Barker was city attorney of Louisville from 1888 to 1896. He was circuit judge the first time from 1896 to 1902; judge of the Court of Appeals from January 5, 1903, to January 2, 1911; president of the University of Kentucky from January 1, 1911, to 1917; and again circuit judge in Louisville from 1922 to the time of his death on April 23, 1928. He was chief justice of the Court of Appeals during the final year of his term.

In all these responsible positions he displayed great natural ability, untiring energy, and unswerving fidelity to the noblest ideals of a noble profession.

When we pause to consider what it is that endears men to their fellows and causes them to be enshrined forever in the halls of fame, we recognize that it is because of one or more of three things—what they did in the field of action, what they wrote or spoke upon the burning issues of their time, and, most important of all, what they were as individuals. And when we come to estimate the character, the writings, and the work of Judge Barker, we know that he measured up in all the three conditions of a lasting fame. His contribution to literature consists of opinions written by him as judge of the highest court of the state, after-dinner speeches on many important occasions, and memorial and cultural addresses on special occasions. The volume of his writing is very great, and it is to be hoped that his works may be published and made available to students everywhere. It is not likely that any Kentuckian ever excelled him in the beauty and dignity of his diction, the elevation of his thought, and the majesty of his philosophy. . . .[1]

The addresses, articles, and tributes to deceased friends cover a wide range, and all were filled with sentiment, enriched by learning, and adorned with beauty.

These include memorial addresses on Abraham Lincoln, Professor Scovell, James G. White, President Harding, Aaron Kohn, Alex P. Humphrey Jr., and James P. Helm;[2] several addresses to the General Assembly of Kentucky; arguments before the Court of Appeals; and many occasional addresses of distinct merit and permanent value.

His university addresses were aimed at the improvement of the moral and cultural conditions surrounding the education of young men and women, and his appeal always was for high ideals of living, devotion to country, and for lives of virtue and service by all who came within the sphere of his influence. He felt profoundly the necessity for good men and women to perpetuate the liberty and happiness of mankind.[3]

These opinions are but samples of the several hundred delivered by Judge Barker while a judge of our highest court. They will be found, beginning with Boreing v. Boreing, 114 Ky. 522, 72 S.W. 431, and continuing for eight years, and running through some twenty-nine volumes of reports.

As president of the university, difficulties were met, but his work was successful. He is to be judged, as he requested, by his work.[4] He was not afraid of change. During his administration the roster roll of four-year students doubled. But increase in product is not the sole or even the best test of the quality of the school. The graduates reached high positions and took their place in the world among the best. The test of trial proved the mettle of the graduates and the standing of the university, and that stands true to this very day.

In 1917 a special investigating committee from the board of trustees took President Barker's testimony. He thus explained his attitude, purpose, and objectives:

> What I have done here is on record. To say that I have or haven't made mistakes to intelligent gentlemen like you would be absurd. To say that I came here from the bench with little or no knowledge of how a university should be run would be of no use to you gentlemen, for of course you already know that. But I accepted the presidency of this university under the conditions I have detailed to you, and I have done the very best that I could with it. I have been honest and faithful, and I have been just to every man on these grounds. Every man has had his opportunity—there has been no effort ever made to break a man down because he has been progressing too far. I have undertaken to build this university up, and when the time comes I am going to lay my cards down on the table and let you read the record.

> I want to say to you gentlemen that I want to be judged by the work I have done. I don't want a man to come here and say he didn't do it this way like it had been done, but he undertook to do it this way. I am not comparing myself to Napoleon, but I want to say this—in his day the old generals and men in charge used to call him a fool because he never fought a battle on the old lines, because he was always breaking the rules of good strategy; but the answer to that is that he conquered the world, and I make this point because possibly I have broken some of the old rules of strategy and procedure at the university. I want you to take the university as it is, what it was, and then compare them. How has it grown in the five years of my administration—in five years its roster roll has doubled of four-year students. I don't mean some of the courses, like special students, but I mean men and women taking the four-year courses, those taking four years leading to a degree—they are the backbone of the university, and I will show you by the records that in my administration they have doubled. I will show you, as I have said before, that when June comes we will have graduated more students than were graduated during all of the previous forty-four years. That is for numbers, but I will go further than that, for I propose to show you what has become of the product. I will show you mechanical engineers, chemists, men of physics, men educated for teachers, holding high and responsible positions, taking their rank in the world. I will show you that when I came here there were twenty students in the Agricultural College taking courses leading to a degree, and today there are more than two hundred. I will

show you those graduates taking high rank as county agents, doing great work in building up the agricultural interests of the state. What is being done at the university, what is being accomplished, is it getting results?—that is what I want you to look into.

Judge Barker was a magnanimous as well as a just man. He was considerate, generous, and charitable. When he was preparing to leave the presidency, he said to the trustees, in June 1917:

> I came to this university relying more upon the wisdom of those who elected me than upon my own. When I leave in September 1918, it will be with no bitterness of heart and no wound of spirit. It will always be my sincere desire to forward this university and its interests in every way possible. I shall rejoice in its success without regard to who causes or promotes that success. I shall ever be ready to give every man the credit that is due without envy or jealousy that his work has been superior to mine. When you elect my successor and install him into my office, the first duty that I will discharge to myself, to the commonwealth, and to you, will be to put my hand in his and ask him to tell me how I can advance his interests and the interests of the great institution over which he presides.

He was admired and respected by all, but he was truly loved by his close associates because of his true manliness, his courteous bearing, and his genuine character.

His writings disclose an intellect of the noblest dimensions, an orator of masterly accomplishment, and a judge of supreme excellence. Judge Barker's work for the moral and intellectual advancement of the youth of our state—what he called "the most precious jewels in the casket of her glory"—was the grand ideal which he never ceased to serve, and to advance which he never ceased to strive.

When we reflect upon what Judge Barker did, what he contributed to the law and to the literature of this commonwealth, and what he was in character and accomplishment, the tribute he paid to a brother lawyer who had passed on seems most fitting: "His life was gentle, and the elements so mixed in him, that Nature might stand up and say to all the world, This was a man!"

---

1. This address, in printed form, covered eighteen pages, the majority of the text being excerpts of Barker's addresses and judicial opinions. Much of the quoted material has been omitted. For a full text, see *Henry Stites Barker: An Address by Governor Simeon Willis* ([Lexington], 1946).

2. Melville Amasa Scovell (1855-1912). New Jersey native. Chemistry instructor, 1875-76, assistant professor, 1876-80, and professor, 1880-84, University of Illinois; director agricultural experiment station, 1885-1912; and dean, College of Agriculture, present-day University of Kentucky, 1911-12. Lexington *Leader*, August 16, 1912.

James Garrard White (1846-1913). Native Kentuckian. Instructor of mathematics in what is now the University of Kentucky, 1869-70; professor, 1870-75, and head of the department, 1875-1913; dean of College of Arts and Sciences, 1889-1908; vice-president, 1909-13; acting president, 1910-11; dean of men, 1912-23. Faculty/Staff Biographical File, University Archives, University of Kentucky.

Warren Gamaliel Harding (1865-1923), twenty-ninth president of the United States.

Aaron Kohn (1854-1923). Louisville native. Attorney; partner with Henry S. Barker for eleven years; prosecuting attorney for Jefferson County for four years; elected to Louisville Board of Aldermen in 1880, serving three terms; member of Board of Public Works beginning in 1894. Jewish Historical Society, *A History of the Jews of Louisville, Ky.* (New Orleans, [1901?]), 51.

Alexander Page Humphrey (1848-1928). Louisville native. General counsel for numerous corporations; member, Board of Charities and Corrections, 1921-25. "In Memoriam," 225 *Kentucky Reports,* vii-xi; Benjamin LaBree, ed., *Press Reference Book of Prominent Kentuckians* (Louisville, 1916), 245.

James Pendleton Helm (1850-1910), corporate attorney. Active in political affairs. William E. Connelley and E. Merton Coulter, *History of Kentucky,* Charles Kerr, ed., 5 vols. (Chicago and New York, 1922), 4:73-74.

3. Omitted here are some ten printed pages of material, almost solely quotations from Barker's speeches and judicial decisions. See note 1.

4. For a historian's interpretation of the Barker years see Charles G. Talbert, *University of Kentucky: The Maturing Years* (Lexington, 1965), 24-47.

STATEMENT REGARDING DR. W.H. VAUGHAN
Frankfort / May 22, 1946

THE chief executive told the delegation, three World War II veterans,[1] that the Morehead regents would choose a capable man to replace Dr. Vaughan[2] and urged them to go back to their studies and help make the institution a better one.

The governor said later he told the delegation that "politics went out with Dr. Vaughan, and there'll be no politics in the school while I am governor." He added that the Vaughan case was "settled."[3]

Governor Willis also declared he appointed the board of regents and that the board was responsible for conditions at Morehead.[4] He praised the regents and declared, "There is not a politician among" the four appointed members.

"I want the public to understand," Governor Willis continued, "the place [as president of Morehead] is open to all available talent." He added neither he nor the regents knew now who would be selected.

In answer to assertions by the students that the Southern Association of Colleges and Secondary Schools might cancel Morehead's accredited standing, and that if that happened many students would not return in the fall, the governor declared there is nothing to investigate until a new president is named. Any inquiry by the association, he indicated, would have to be based on the qualifications for the president of the man chosen as Vaughan's successor.[5]

---

1. Members of the delegation were Morehead Club of Veterans' president Arthur L. Howard of Paintsville, Robert L. Siles of Ann Arbor, Michigan, and Carlos C. Page of Cincinnati. *Courier-Journal*, May 23, 1946.

2. William Hutchinson Vaughan (1899-1972). A.B., Georgetown College, 1923; A.M., George Peabody College, 1927; Ph.D., Peabody, 1937; instructor and principal, Louisa schools, 1924-28; principal, dean, Morehead State Teachers College, 1928-40; president, 1940-46; registrar at Peabody after 1946; author of *Robert Jefferson Breckinridge as an Educational Administrator* (1937). *Who's Who, 1962-63*, 3218; Ashland *Daily Independent*, May 1, 1940; Cratis Williams, *William H. Vaughan* (Morehead, 1985), 60.

3. Supporters of Democrat Dr. Vaughan argued that his dismissal resulted from political motives; his opponents countered that Vaughan's political actions as president had no place in an academic setting and that his dismissal thus removed politics from the institution. *Kentucky Post*, May 10, 1946; *Courier-Journal*, May 24, 1946.

Dr. Vaughan was considered a friend of Democratic congressmen Fred Vinson and Joe Bates. See W.E. Crutcher to Tom Underwood, May 23, 1946, Thomas Rust Underwood Papers, Box 23, University of Kentucky Library.

4. The board of regents included Democrats William H. Keifer of Ashland and Mrs. Allie W. Young of Morehead; Republicans Roy Cornette of Morehead and J.M. Rose of Olive Hill; and ex-officio member, Superintendent of Public Instruction John Fred Williams. Young, Cornette, and Rose were considered anti-Vaughan. *Kentucky Post*, May 10, 1946; *Courier-Journal*, May 24, 1946.

5. Vaughan's successor, William Jesse Baird (1890-1951), received a B.S. degree from Berea College in 1919, a M.S. from Cornell University (1924), and a LL.D. from Berea (1944). He served as president for five years, until his death in

1951. Previously he had been at Berea as director, Department of Agriculture (1925-30), and dean, Foundation School (1925-44), as well as president of Berry School, Mt. Berry, Georgia (1944-46). "General Catalog, 1949-50, 1950-51," *Bulletin of the Morehead State College* 19 (April 1949): 5-6; New York *Times*, February 21, 1951; *Who's Who, 1950*, 120.

STATEMENT REGARDING POSSIBLE INQUIRY AT MOREHEAD
Frankfort / May 23, 1946

TEXT of comment made by Willis:

"Dr. Vaughan's contract expires June 30, and the board of regents decided not to renew it. The board designated Dr. Warren C. Lappin,[1] dean, to conduct the affairs of the college as acting president until a president can be found.

"The American Association of Teachers [Colleges] is welcome to visit here and to investigate the administration of Dr. Vaughan and of this administration on the subject of education generally.[2] One thing they will find is that this administration has not and will not play partisan politics in the schools, and will not permit the enemies of the administration to play factional politics any longer.

"The members of the board of regents have stated they were seeking the ablest and best qualified man for president, and no other consideration would affect the choice. This policy meets my approval.

"The friends of Morehead College will support the board of regents. What others do is not the responsibility of the regents or of the administration."

---

1. Warren Curtis Lappin (1900-1975). A.B., Transylvania, 1920; A.M., University of Chicago, 1929; Ed.D., Indiana University, 1941; principal, Morehead High School, Breckinridge Training school, 1920-40; interim president at what is now Morehead State University, 1946, and again in the early 1950s; twice mayor of the city of Morehead; dean, registrar, professor of education, 1940-71. Lexington *Herald*, July 24, 1946; "General Catalog, 1949-50, 1950-51," *Bulletin of the Morehead State College* 19 (April 1949): 6; "1953-54, 1954-55," ibid. 21 (April 1953): 11; Morehead *News*, August 14, 1975.

2. Leslie R. Gregory, president of the American Association of Teachers Colleges, telegrammed that his group had ordered an investigation of Dr. Vaughan's dismissal. Headed by Dr. W.P. Morgan, president emeritus of Western Illinois State Teachers College, the investigating committee interviewed the chief figures in July. Gregory's committee in accrediting and classification reported to the association in 1947 that "there is serious need of legislation to make possible a better system of control for the colleges of Kentucky," and recommended that Morehead be dropped from membership in the association "until such time as laws are enacted which give reasonable assurance that the colleges will have the stability likely to result from wise and nonpolitical, nonfactional control." That recommendation was adopted. *Courier-Journal,* May 24, 1946; Lexington *Herald,* July 24, 1946; *American Association of Teachers Colleges Twenty-Sixth Yearbook, 1947* (n.p., 1947), 138.

REMARKS REGARDING GRIFFENHAGEN AND ASSOCIATES' SURVEY OF EDUCATION
Frankfort / July 22, 1946

GOVERNOR WILLIS stated he had employed the Chicago firm of Griffenhagen and Associates to conduct the survey and that he expected to put into effect by the end of this year such necessary changes in education as he could by executive order. Those that require legislative action, he added, can be taken up by his successor and the 1948 General Assembly.

Griffenhagen has made several other surveys in Kentucky, and Willis said its employment "guarantees that the result will be thorough and constructive."

"It is important that the large sums expended for education should be wisely and efficiently administered, and the people are entitled to know where improvements and economies are possible and to have the best service we can give them. The cost of this study is reasonable, and it should result in savings far exceeding the expense of it."[1]

The governor said the survey would cover administrative and academic work at the institutions.

The governor said the program would be confined to white education. Improvements and changes are being made in Negro institutions, he continued, and he did not want to interrupt that work by a survey.

But he said he hoped to have a survey of Negro education made before he leaves office next year.

---

1. The $19,200 cost of the study was to be borne by the State Board of Education ($8,000), University of Kentucky ($4,000), and the four state teachers' colleges ($1,800 each). State Superintendent of Public Instruction John Fred Williams immediately charged that this had been "conceived in secrecy" without his consultation. He declared that his department "will not pay the amounts which we are ordered to bear." Governor Willis indicated he would use his full powers to carry out the study and issued an executive order on the matter. See *Courier-Journal*, *Kentucky Post*, and Frankfort *State Journal*, all of July 23, 1946, and Executive Order, July 22, 1946, Secretary of State's Records.

In the 1946 legislative session a bill appropriating $45,000 for such a survey had been vetoed by the governor. He indicated then that those appointed by the Democratically controlled legislature would not present an impartial, unbiased view. Ibid.

TELEGRAM REGARDING AID TO EDUCATION
Frankfort / March 13, 1947

I SENT to the *Courier-Journal* a telegram on March 11, stating that the article by Hugh Morris[1] in the *Courier-Journal* of that date did not correctly reflect my position and did not interpret accurately my conference on Monday last with the classroom teachers.[2] I further advised that no decisions were made or had been made, and that the discussion with the teachers related only to various features of the many problems involved. The importance of the subject justifies a statement correcting the false impression given to the public by that article. It was prepared by taking fragments from long conversations gathered from thirteen different people, and put together entirely apart from the context of the conversations in which the remarks were supposed to have been made. Such an article creates a totally distorted picture. Half-truths are as misleading as outright falsehood. Many of the statements, as quoted purporting to have been made, created an effect directly opposite to that intended by the speaker. The teachers emphasized the critical situation of the schools in general, and of the teachers in particular.

They referred to the large number of emergency teachers, some who are leaving the profession, others not preparing or planning to teach, and the impaired morale in the profession and among the students in their attitude toward the profession. No one is more sympathetic with the teachers' problems than I am. No one could be more anxious to find a sound solution of the difficulties. The situation is similar in practically all the states and is receiving attention from the people and the officials in those states. I am seeking to ascertain all the facts in regard to proposed action in other states. In the discussion with the teachers the different points of view on the subject were discussed without anyone deciding which was correct. Various explanations were suggested, but no one undertook to say which suggestion was the correct one. Various solutions were mentioned, and the objections to those particular proposals were discussed. But no decisions were made or attempted to be made.

The difficulties of the problem are very great, as all appreciate. I am considering it from every angle and seeking to find a solution that will meet the situation and preserve unimpaired all of the other governmental obligations and functions. It is vitally important to all the people that all the governmental functions be maintained without impairment. As I have stated before, as soon as I have completed the consideration of the subject and formulated a program to be recommended, the public will be advised and its support requested. In the meantime, the door is open for the complete consideration of all the facts and of all the proposals.

---

1. Hugh Morris (1915-   ). *Courier-Journal* reporter, 1937-69; head of paper's state capital bureau, 1952-69; assistant director, Kentucky Legislative Research Commission, 1969-80. *Courier-Journal*, May 16, 1969; information from Personnel Department, LRC, October 15, 1986.

2. On March 10, Governor Willis met with thirteen members of the Kentucky Education Association's board of directors of the Department of Classroom Teachers. No newspaper reporters were present, but Hugh Morris recreated the conference from accounts of those present. His page-one story began: "Governor Shatters Schoolteachers' Hopes." In the account, Morris told how the governor explained to the teachers that no special session would be called to aid education. See the next entry for further details.

STATEMENT REGARDING EDUCATION RECORD
Frankfort / March 13, 1947

THE diverse and contradictory opinions expressed in the *Courier-Journal* of March 13 by certain members of the group who visited the governor's office, presumably in the interest of the classroom teachers, disclose the animus and purpose of the subsequent proceedings.

The statement by Mrs. Morgan[1] that the article expressed what the governor "implied" is in itself an admission that the opinions expressed were based on inference and not on fact.

The statement of Mrs. Travelstead[2] that the teachers were "glad" they found out how the governor felt about it coupled with Miss Caldwell's[3] conclusion that "it is going to do more for Kentucky education than anything that's been done," proved that it is not a fair or just appraisement of the progress made.

The teachers of Kentucky should know how the governor feels about the teachers of Kentucky and their needs. They have not forgotten the fact that in the emergency of 1944 he advocated and approved the payment of $3 million to the teachers for the fiscal year ending June 30, 1944.

They will likewise recall that a special session was called for the sole and express purpose of adding $5 million to the per capita and equalization fund for each year of the first biennium of his administration. And at the 1946 session, after the legislature had refused to repeal the personal income tax, very large additional appropriations for education were approved by the governor. Such approval was given after the legislature had adjourned, and when the power of the governor over these additional provisions was final and conclusive.

Mary Lee Travelstead, who is now so glad about the article of Hugh Morris, on March 10, 1947, wrote to the governor as follows: "You, the governor of our commonwealth, are known as a promoter of progress and education generally. You are certainly the man of the hour in the financial economy of our state, for when did any governor ever accomplish such a saving and create such a surplus? You are acclaimed by schoolteachers throughout the state as the same friend who in May 1944 called that special session which made possible the relief they secured before."

The governor believes that every teacher in the state who is not politically biased will agree that the record of this administration proves that the governor has done more for education in Kentucky than the articles by Mr. Morris can do, as Miss Caldwell is quoted as believing.

The position of these self-appointed spokesmen for the teachers seems to be the same as that of much-favored individual who turned against his lifelong friend "because he had not done any special favors for him lately."

The governor has been informed that Mrs. Fugett,[4] who was so eager to spread propaganda that she invited Mr. Morris to luncheon, is not actually a classroom teacher but a salaried employee of a subsidiary organization of the KEA.

The Associated Press report of the conference between the governor and the school people was based on the same materials as utilized by Mr. Morris and his collaborators. When compared with the articles prepared by Morris, the proof is clear that the Morris article was obvious political propaganda and not unbiased or even correct reporting. The difficult problems presented should be solved on a professional basis, and should not be demoralized by political interference.[5]

---

1. Mrs. Eula Mae Morgan of Hazard was one of the members of the board of directors of the Department of Classroom Teachers, Kentucky Education Association (KEA). *Courier-Journal*, March 11, 1947.

2. Mrs. Mary Lee Travelstead of Franklin was another member of the KEA group (above). Ibid.

3. The newspaper accounts refer to *Mrs.* Lillian Caldwell of Williamstown, who was another of the KEA group (above). Ibid.

4. Mrs. Jessie P. Fugett of Lexington was the spokeswoman for the KEA group (above) and reportedly gave Hugh Morris of the *Courier-Journal* the details of the Willis-KEA group meeting. Ibid. and March 13, 1947.

5. The KEA had requested Governor Willis to call a special session and grant $10.5 million in state funds for further teachers' raises. No special session was called.

HEALTH AND WELFARE

SECOND ANNIVERSARY OF OPENING,
WARREN COUNTY
TUBERCULOSIS SANATORIUM
Bowling Green / October 3, 1944

"THE first responsibility of government is the health of the people. Education, so closely allied with health, is second," Governor Simeon Willis said.

The governor said he was "looking forward to the day when Kentucky's district tuberculosis hospitals are opened so that every case of tuberculosis in Kentucky may be placed in a hospital for proper care, and the remainder of the state's inhabitants may be protected from spread of the disease."[1]

---

1. In 1943 there were 1,748 deaths from tuberculosis, making it the seventh leading cause of death in Kentucky. A decade later, 642 died from the disease, while in 1973 only 77 did. See "Vital Statistics Report 1943," *Bulletin of the Department of Health* 17(August 1944): 2; *1953 Kentucky Vital Statistics Report* (Louisville, 1954), 4; and *Kentucky 1973 Vital Statistics* (Frankfort, 1974), 18.

NATIONAL FOUNDATION FOR
INFANTILE PARALYSIS
Louisville / January 14, 1945

TOMORROW hundreds of unselfish and public-spirited men and women in every county of our state start a campaign, which will extend to the end of this month, to raise funds for the relief of victims of infantile paralysis, the great majority of whom are young children.

Last summer our state suffered the worst epidemic of polio in our history. Seven hundred and fifty nine children, men, and women were stricken by this crippling disease. Fortunately we had organizations fully prepared to deal with it, and they went into action with what I am glad to say was conspicuous success.

The Kentucky Crippled Children Commission, the official agency to take care of such emergencies,[1] got in touch with every one of these 759 victims and through its nurses and doctors sent 528 of them to hospitals. There the technicians and hot packers worked with them, with the result that most of them were spared permanent deformities.

When I tell you that a total of $159,562 was spent here in our state for the relief of infantile paralysis during 1944, you will realize the necessity of responding liberally to the appeals which will be made to you during the next two weeks. When I tell you also that a careful estimate reveals that at least $125,000 will be required to rehabilitate many victims of the epidemic, some still in our hospitals and others receiving aftertreatment at the outpatient clinic recently opened at the General Hospital in Louisville, it will strengthen further your determination to help in this work.

Some of you have been under a mistaken impression of the part taken by the National Foundation for Infantile Paralysis in this work. There has been some objection to one half of the funds raised in Kentucky being sent to the National Foundation. Let me explain that the foundation uses its funds in two ways: first, to finance research into the cause and cure of polio; and second, to give aid to any community suffering from an epidemic.

As to the first, if polio is ever to be eradicated, just as smallpox, yellow fever, and other diseases have been banished, it will have to be done by an agency such as the national foundation which has the means to employ scientists and researchers. Certainly we in Kentucky could not do that work alone.

As to the second, let me tell you that last summer when the Kentucky chapter did not have enough money to control the epidemic which was raging in the state, the chapter called on the foundation for help. Promptly and without question the foundation sent $100,000 to the chapter.

I hope that we may never have another epidemic, but if we are to finish the job thrust on us by the one we have just gone through all of us must be liberal in responding to the appeal now being made to a generous-hearted people.

---

1. The Kentucky Crippled Children Commission, under the direction of Marian Williamson, was attached to the state Department of Health. *Kentucky Directory*, 112.

REMARKS REGARDING PUBLIC ASSISTANCE
Frankfort / January 17, 1945

"This is not only the biggest problem of my administration," he said, "but it is the biggest problem I ever grappled with anywhere. Sometimes I think it is insoluble. . . .

"I haven't found the answer," Governor Willis said, "and none of the other governors has either, so far as I know. There are forty-eight standards of assistance in the nation; and in some states, notably Alabama, there is a standard for each county. The old people are dissatisfied so long as one gets more than another, no matter how much each gets. But it has to be that way because the Social Security Board makes us pay according to need.

"Sometimes I think it would be best to put assistance on a flat pension basis, paying the same to all who qualify, so long as they are eligible. In fact, our Kentucky Constitution calls for just that—a pension or an annuity.[1]

"But when the old people are dissatisfied, that is just half of it. The taxpayers are dissatisfied, too. They have to put up the money, and they believe taxes are high enough now, perhaps too high. We can't pay more assistance without raising the money; that much is certain.[2]

"The only hope I can see is President Roosevelt's recommendation that the whole picture of social security and old age assistance ought to be restudied in 1945, with the view of broadening social security. I would like to interpret that as meaning social security ultimately would be broadened to cover so many sixty-five or older that it would gradu-aly eliminate the need for old age assistance."[3]

The governor said he feels it is a relatively minor thing to make a stopgap appropriation to forestall a cut for six weeks, as compared with the broad decision that must be made eventually, namely: shall Kentucky raise enough revenue by taxation to support an adequate program of public assistance or shall the state continue making payments to the needy aged and blind based on 70 percent of need, and to dependent children on 50 percent of need?

It is his purpose, the governor said, to bring that issue squarely into the open prior to the legislative campaigns this fall,[4] so the 1946 General Assembly can find out what the people want before it is called upon to determine what the public policy shall be—more taxes and more public assistance or present taxes and present assistance.

For his part, the governor said, he proposes to announce a tax revision commission shortly, and to charge it with the direct task of examining the tax structure in its relation to the best budget consistent with good government. He will expect his commission, the governor said, to name two committees—one charged with the specific task of studying the needs of public assistance, the other charged with an examination of public education.[5]

The governor said he foresees the inevitability of competition between education and assistance for the lion's share of general fund revenue, with each side seeking an advantage over the other in future budgets. He wants his tax commission to ascertain and proclaim the facts relative to both, the governor said, before the next division of money between them is enacted into law and possibly a new public policy laid down.

---

1. Section 244A has this provision and was adopted to enable Kentucky to share in federal appropriations and to pay pensions.

2. Kentucky at the time devoted 5 percent of its revenues to public assistance; the national average was 4.34 percent. *Courier-Journal*, January 18, 1945.

3. No major changes were made in the program until 1950, when more jobs were included in the coverage. "Social Security," *Encyclopedia Britannica*, 20: 763.

4. A surplus allowed the governor to call a special session in April to address this problem. See "Legislative Actions, 1943-1945" section, especially documents dated April 19 and 23, 1945.

5. The Tax Revision Commission, created by executive order on March 19, 1945, was charged with setting up committees to study "the problems of public assistance, educational institutional repairs and extension, and such other committees as many as may be deemed proper." For further details, see the document dated March 28, 1945, in "State Government Administration" section.

DEDICATION OF VENEREAL DISEASE CENTER
Louisville / February 21, 1945

A MEDICAL center for the treatment of venereal disease was dedicated by Governor Simeon Willis at the Kentucky State Fairgrounds "to the health of our people."

Governor Willis called for the uplifting of health in Kentucky and said that "one of the hardest things doctors have to fight is not the germ but the ignorance of the people." The governor said that in some of Kentucky's mountain counties "a great deal of the service to mothers in childbirth is a service of necessity and not sufficient to protect the health of mother or child."

"Our health problems will be solved by the united efforts of the citizens of Kentucky," the governor said, and he predicted that the state's "health, intelligence, and character will be lifted to a higher standard."

Governor Willis said it was his hope to help "make our people prosperous so that they can have the common necessities and conveniences of life."

DEDICATION OF RECONSTRUCTED MALE WARD
AT CENTRAL STATE HOSPITAL
Lakeland / April 18, 1945

THE governor rejoiced in the completion of the building, with its 190-bed capacity, which now makes it possible for all the white male patients to live in modern, rehabilitated wards—and his pleasure was reflected in the faces of the scores of patients, nurses, attendants, and visitors attending the ceremonies.[1]

"In this world disease and disaster overtake the individual as well as nations," Governor Willis said. "We know one problem we must deal with from the very beginning of our lives, the problem of public health. That is what we're concerned with here. The important thing in this world is the people—and institutions are for the people. There is no stigma to being mentally or physically sick—it is often unavoidable, despite the great advances in medical science."

He said Kentucky is "anxious and willing to do all it can for its sick, but we are handicapped by financial resources.

"It takes the taxpayers' money to make these improvements," he continued. "And we can spend only to the extent the taxpayers' money will permit us."

He expressed gratitude to the men and women working in the state's institutions and to Dr. Lyon,[2] "who is doing two men's jobs." There is not a person in state government who is not overworked, he said, outlining wartime difficulties in getting doctors, attendants, and material and men to complete the rehabilitation program.

"We will go forward, however, as fast and as far as we can; and finally we will win out and have what we ought to have in our state for our mentally and physically ill," he promised.

"We are doing the best we can," he said in conclusion. "It is not how much we accomplish, but how hard we try to accomplish the purposes for which we were put on this earth that counts—and you all are trying hard."

––––––––––––

1. One of the state hospitals for the mentally ill, Central State was part of program to refurbish and modernize the entire system. Some $100,000 had been spent on the three-story male ward at Lakeland, for new lighting, better drinking facilities and hospital beds, and needed fireproofing. *Courier-Journal,* April 19, 1945.

2. A.M. Lyon (1889-1971), Elliott County judge, 1923-25; bank vice president; superintendent Western State Hospital, 1939-40; director, Division of Hospitals and Mental Hygiene, 1941-44, and concurrently superintendent, Central State Hospital. *Kentucky Directory*, 115; Ogden, ed., *Papers of Keen Johnson*, 59n; Bureau of Vital Statistics, Department of Human Resources, Frankfort.

DEDICATION OF AN ADDITION
TO WESTERN STATE HOSPITAL
Hopkinsville / May 17, 1945

Governor Simeon S. Willis dedicated the new $325,000 eight-ward addition to Western State Hospital here this afternoon with the declaration that "true interpretation of dedication" of such improvements is twofold—determining how much progress has been made and what remains to be done.

The governor told the gathering that the public was "too much inclined to leave to the governor, the commissioner of welfare, and the doctors" the full responsibility of carrying out the program at state institutions. He urged taxpayers to give full support to state officials in seeing that "qualified" employees are kept on the job at state institutions and that necessary improvements are made.

The governor said that two purposes are kept in mind at hospitals for the mentally ill: the best care possible for patients and the cure and return to normal, useful life of the unfortunate inmates.

The governor told the group that citizens keep their attention fixed on their schools, where large sums of the taxpayers' money [are] spent, but often paid in taxes for the maintenance of mental hospitals and prisons and acted as if their duty was completed.

He commended the efforts of [John] Quertermous and Dr. [A.M.] Lyon, saying that Dr. Lyon was making "heroic efforts" to maintain the highest standards in state institutions.

Turning to the hospital staff group and attendants, Governor Willis said that buildings and equipment are necessary, but emphasized his view that the support of the public and hospital employees are the big factors in the mental hospital program.

DEDICATION OF NEW NEGRO WARD
AT CENTRAL STATE HOSPITAL
Lakeland / October 26, 1945

DESCRIBED by Governor Simeon Willis as "one of the finest buildings in the state," the new $500,000 Negro ward structure, with its tile walls, terrazza floors, and gleaming fixtures, glistened in the sunlight that streamed through the wide windows.

"People sometimes ask me," the governor began his speech, "why I take time out to attend dedications of buildings and institutions. I do it because I think it is the most important thing I can do that day. It is necessary for the governor to have the support of the people in everything that he does, and in order to have that support it is necessary for the people to know what we are doing and trying to do with the institutions of the state."

Referring to the new building, he said, "There is not, there never has been and never will be any discrimination as to race or color in our state institutions.[1] Our object is to care for those submitted to our custody to the best of our ability and endeavor to restore them to their families and society."

Commenting on future plans, Governor Willis warned that "you know and we all know that we can proceed only so far as the taxpayers are able to provide the money. Each taxpayer has his own obligations. The state has not one dollar except what it gathers from the taxpayers annually."

In dedicating the new ward, Governor Willis said it was the responsibility of the people to support such an institution. He added that remarkable progress had been made in view of the manpower shortage and difficulty of obtaining materials.

---

1. The governor's reference was to funding discrimination; the policy of "separate but equal" had long governed housing in state institutions and would continue into the 1960s.

DEDICATION OF NEW BUILDINGS AT GREENDALE HOUSE OF REFORM
Lexington / November 2, 1945

GOVERNOR SIMEON WILLIS dedicated new and improved buildings at the Greendale House of Reform today with the advice that better quarters would be of little benefit if cooperation between pupil and instructor is lacking.[1]

"Physical improvements which have been made and will be made at the institution will make the work more convenient and suitable," the governor stated, "but it isn't the physical equipment—it is the soul of an institution that will give it its true value.

"Those who work here give the institution its soul," he continued, urging the inmates to exercise self-discipline in the program designed to graduate them as useful members of society.

Speaking to staff members of the school, inmates, and visitors attending the exercises, Governor Willis said the "good facilities, good food, good housing, and good teachers" are essential in carrying on the rehabilitation work of the institution.

---

1. Improvements included two new dormitories for girls and a new school building for girls; modernization of the gymnasium and boys' school building; and reconstruction of the boys' hospital, the administration building, and other edifices. Fire escapes were improved or added as well. *Courier-Journal*, November 3, 1945.

CORNERSTONE FOR STATE TUBERCULOSIS HOSPITAL
Glasgow / May 15, 1946

KENTUCKY'S government is interested vitally in the health and progress of its people and cannot be maintained soundly and competently without a healthy citizenship. I am very, very happy to have had something to do with the institution and the carrying on of this program because it has been something about which I have dreamed all my life.[1] I have seen so much of tuberculosis and other diseases striking people who might have been saved if the proper hospitalization had been available. Now I think we have as good a program as could be devised. Hazelwood (at Louisville) has been enlarged very greatly, and when we get it finished—as soon as we can get it finished—it will be able to do all of the surgery for all of these hospitals, and these five hospitals will take care of as many as need be from month to month because with the turnover I think it can serve the entire population of Kentucky with these hospitals.[2]

But I want you to know that the delays have not been the fault of anybody. They have been the result of conditions. It has been impossible many times to get parts or materials or something that was needed, and even today Hazelwood is being delayed by things over which we have no control.

But we have gone along as far and as fast as we could; we have made steady progress. All of the hospitals, all five of them, are under construction, and just as soon as they are finished we will provide for them operating staffs, nurses, attendants; and in the very near future we will feel that we have all of the forces of the medical science in operation against this dread disease which has destroyed so many people and which is such a menace to the communities where it was once found.

I want you to feel that this institution is yours as a part of the people of Kentucky that they will all be happy to know that it is in a community that is alive to the needs of the time—that you will support it and maintain it; that you will do your part for the people who are here and who come here hereafter. And I'm sure that everybody who ever has to come here will be glad that it was in a community such as Glasgow—which I have known for many years to be one of the outstanding communities of all the state of Kentucky.

Let me congratulate you upon your citizenship here, upon the leadership of your doctors, upon your cooperation and all of the good things we try to do to advance the educational and the health and the welfare interests of the state of Kentucky.

I know that there are many problems to confront the people, and the people must solve them all. Government is interested in roads, in schools, in all of the activities of the people—not to take them from the people but to aid the people in carrying on successfully their activities. And back of it all is the support and the confidence and the productive capacity of the people because they cannot have more improvement, they cannot have more institutions than they themselves build and pay for, and no amount of leadership, no amount of imagination, no amount of dreaming can go any faster than the public sentiment of the state will come along and support and maintain it. I am very happy to be here again in Glasgow. I am sorry that we had this little shower,[3] but I know that it hasn't dampened your spirits any. And as we go forward hand-in-hand to accomplish things for the good old state of Kentucky, let us say those who slander Kentucky are not our friends; those who praise Kentucky and those who help Kentucky are the ones that we love and cherish and the ones whose admiration we seek.

---

1. This speech is a composite of the governor's talk from the reports in the *Courier-Journal* and the *Kentucky Post*, both of May 16, 1946, and from an almost complete recording made by WHAS radio. Portions of the newspaper accounts vary considerably from the actual address given.

2. The laying of the cornerstone for the $418,000 Glasgow hospital was the first public ceremony in connection with the five hospitals the state was building.

3. Newspaper accounts record that the 1,500 people were "drenched" by a heavy thunderstorm. The accounts also noted that the cornerstone erroneously listed Willis's middle initial as "E." *Courier-Journal*, May 16, 1946.

CORNERSTONE FOR
STATE TUBERCULOSIS HOSPITAL
Ashland / July 12, 1946

AMID solemn ceremonies, the Tuberculosis Sanatorium was dedicated here yesterday when Governor Simeon S. Willis laid the cornerstone to the structure with the warning "that the people of this vicinity face a grave responsibility."[1]

"You must cooperate with the staff here, and you must make the visitors who come here feel as though they are wanted," the governor declared.

Governor Willis said that the tuberculosis campaign was just one phase of the health program.

"The cancer situation is just as bad and we hope to do something about this as soon as it is possible," he stated.

The governor began his remarks by saying that it was always a pleasure to be back home.

"It is an especial pleasure to return this time, for the task that we are doing today will mean the alleviation of much suffering in the future," he stated.

Governor Willis said that any such action as this "depended upon the people. The people are the ones who pay the taxes—they are the ones who in the last analysis face the full responsibility of any public improvement," Willis insisted.

He warned that the people must constantly be vigilant to see that the hospital is maintained properly upon its completion, sixteen to eighteen months hence.

"We are assured by the medical profession that tuberculosis will be whipped within a few years," the governor asserted. "Then these institutions can be converted into other uses, but there always will be a need for them to protect the health of the people."

---

1. This speech is a composite of two accounts from the Ashland *Daily Independent* and the *Kentucky Enquirer,* both of July 13, 1946.

CORNERSTONE FOR
STATE TUBERCULOSIS HOSPITAL
Madisonville / August 9, 1946

"IT should be remembered," Governor Willis said in his address, "that these tuberculosis hospitals constitute but a single phase of the broader health program now under way, which includes all health services maintained by local, state, and national governments for the prevention, control, and cure of diseases."

The chief executive reminded his audience that "the field of government is constantly broadening," and warned that in such efforts, involving taxation, the "support and sympathy of the public must be maintained at all times and under all curcumstances."

He bespoke community cooperation for the new hospitals here and in Ashland, Glasgow, London, and Paris which are being built at

$400,000 each to serve, along with Hazelwood Sanatorium near Louisville, for care and treatment of tuberculosis victims, and added:

"Governments are rightly concerned about the health and stamina of the people. A great statesman has pointed out that the health of the people is the foundation of the power, progress, and prosperity of the state; and always, it must be remembered and appreciated that the field of government is constantly broadening, that the great demands on the public for education, public assistance, highways, conservation of resources, and other vital and essential services, must be met by the taxpayers; and in order that the money may be provided, the services kept in proper balance, and the vast obligations of government impartially and faithfully kept, the support and sympathy of the public must be deserved and maintained at all times and under all circumstances."

DEDICATION OF KENTUCKY STATE HOSPITAL
Danville / September 12, 1946

A CHALLENGE was offered residents of "cultured" Danville Thursday afternoon by Governor Simeon S. Willis of Kentucky when he told his audience at the ceremonies of dedication of Kentucky State Hospital, "You are the host city and people with a primary responsibility for this institution."[1]

In a three-fold charge, after he declared theirs was the burden for the continued moral advancement of the hospital, Governor Willis informed the several hundred spectators, who were almost entirely Danville and Boyle County officials and residents, it is their duty: (1) to see that the hospital atmosphere is conducive to a good institution; (2) to arrange that doctors, attendants, and other employees on the hospital's staff are made to feel welcome in this community, "where anyone would be glad to make his home"; and (3) to maintain an alertness to the needs of humanity in this "community of culture."

Citing Centre College as a place of "culture and education," Governor Willis referred to "other institutions" here which have taught us the needs of the individual and how to be good hosts to institutions.

Asserting that every individual is important, the state's chief executive declared that society is made up only of individuals who, if they are healthy, happy, intelligent, and patriotic, will make a better nation. He urged the promotion of health, strength, happiness for all.

While the people of Kentucky are awake and understanding, they must watch the direction in which we are going and be certain the tendency is upward and onward, Governor Willis explained. If progress be forward, he said, "we can be proud of what we have achieved, but there is more to do.

"Every time we redeem an afflicted person and restore him to health, we lessen the burden on the people of the state and strengthen the fabric of society," Governor Willis declared. He called for "continued faith in this institution, the state of Kentucky, and the nation" and the resolution that "we do better and better until we attain that perfection to which we all aspire."

---

1. The speech is a composite, from the Danville *Advocate-Messenger*, the *Courier-Journal*, and the Lexington *Herald*, all of September 13, 1946. For information regarding the background of this hospital, see speech of January 8, 1946, in "Legislative Actions, 1946-1947" section.

NEGRO REPUBLICAN RALLY
Louisville / December 17, 1946

THE present Republican state administration has done more for the health and education of Kentucky Negroes than any other in the state's history, Governor Simeon Willis told Louisville Negro Republicans last night.

"When you discriminate against citizens on the basis of creed or color you injure the whole fabric of society," Governor Willis said. "In this administration we have tried to build up all of Kentucky by improving the lot of all individuals in it regardless of creed or color. We've done more for the health of Kentucky than any other administration— more for the roads, more for the education, and particularly more for the education of colored citizens in proportion than for the white because the colored schools had been long neglected."

RED CROSS DRIVE
Louisville / 1947

FELLOW citizens:

While the American Red Cross moves forward to its ever-growing task (grown to great proportions through the years of war with its heritage of hunger and loss), the 136 chapters in Kentucky continue to carry their full share of the national effort.[1] This fact was made clear to me as I read concrete examples of our citizens' unwavering and unselfish devotion to their fellow countrymen in this state and in the nation which are embodied in the report just presented to me by the American National Red Cross. This report sets forth in detail the performance turned in by the citizens of Kentucky in the year 1946. And this fine performance in the name of selfless service was completed despite a weariness engendered by years of bitter war, despite pressing personal problems, and despite countless other demands upon their time, their sympathies, and their support.

During the war years the resources of the Kentucky Red Cross chapters were necessarily focused on services to the armed forces. But during the year which has just ended the focus shifted sharply to the home front. The emphasis of need shifted to the veteran and his dependents, to the hospitalized soldier still paying war's terrible price, and to civilians dazed by the sudden shocking attack of disaster or epidemic. The sons and daughters of Kentucky now abroad are not forgotten; wherever there are concentrations of American troops, there will be found the Red Cross field director and Red Cross recreational worker daily strengthening the vital link between the fighting forces and home.

But in the year just closed Kentuckians have clearly demonstrated how surely they know that the traditional peacetime services of the Red Cross were expanded in need and must be continued in fact as an obligation to the citizens of the state and of the nation. I feel that whatever demands may be upon the heart and hands of the people of Kentucky in this present year and in all the years to come will be met with the same courage and success as in the past.

In the year which ended on December 31, 1946, the members of the 136 Red Cross chapters in the state of Kentucky contributed $1,331,195 of their money and 579,040 volunteer hours of their time that the steadying influence of the Red Cross might go forward shoulder to shoulder with Kentucky citizens. Within the same twelve month period, through their home service department, Kentucky's Red Cross chapters lent a helping hand to 59,701 servicemen, 38,099 ex-servicemen and their dependents, 5,491 civilians. Whatever the request (and in many instances the requests brought into play the facilities of the Red Cross communications system between the servicemen abroad and his family at home), the chapter home service workers, both professional and volunteer, did everything in their power to fill it. In 9,620 cases of those listed above, financial assistance was required in addition to other services. This financial assistance was given on a basis of need to the amount of $233,460.35. The production record of Kentucky volunteer corps can stand beside that of any like number in accomplishment and in charity: 57,385 garments finished and 1,364,643 surgical dressings provided for use at home and for shipment abroad. Wounded men returning to the United States receive convalescent kits made by volunteers in Kentucky Red Cross sewing rooms.

In the field of health also the volunteers have made their strength felt, with 981 volunteer nurses' aids being trained by the Red Cross and 50,337 hours of their own free time given to serve in civilian and military hospitals as nonprofessional assistants to the graduate nurses.

The children of Kentucky through American Junior Red Cross played an important part in the program of service to others: 294,762 children in 2,279 schools in the state enrolled in the American Junior Red Cross in 1946 and by participating in civic and national projects learned more of the obligations they owe in a democracy and gleaned the satisfaction of serving the needs of others. The steady, eager seeking of Kentucky citizens for a better, fuller life for themselves and for those with whom they come in contact is reflected in the number of those who successfully completed the various courses offered by the American Red Cross.

With the stimulation of war ended and with the spotlight turned elsewhere, still numerous citizens contributed regularly to Red Cross chapters and many took the courses in training designed to protect the health and safety of the family and the community: 4,072 first aid certificates were issued, 1,045 life-saving certificates were issued and 2,664 home-nursing certificates were issued. And always in the forefront of the minds of Kentuckians stood their obligations (which is also a charter obligation of the Red Cross organization) to mitigate the suffering caused by pestilence, famine, fire, and flood—and to devise ways and means of preventing such damage and suffering. So when disaster struck in Kentucky, as it did eight times in the first six months of 1946, the Red Cross chapters were prepared.[2]

Fire and flood produced the need, and through that period 6,126 Kentuckians received Red Cross assistance. In all American Red Cross activities in Kentucky the people of the state have repeatedly demonstrated their desire to serve and the willingness to assume the responsibilities imposed upon them by the effort of a suffering world to secure a peace bought at a dreadful price. Through their loyalty to the Red Cross they have made important contributions to the welfare of their state and its communities as well as to their country. They have done their splendid part in keeping the Red Cross symbol of mercy alive, both at home and abroad. And because it has so capably served our sons and daughters in the armed forces, our veterans and their families, and the stricken of whatever race or color or creed, I am confident that [the] generous hearts [*sic*] of Kentucky will continue to express itself through the Red Cross this year as it has always done in the past. Congratulations to the Red Cross! Congratulations to the citizens of Kentucky! All honor to our brave men and women who serve humanity in its hour of need!

———————————

1. This speech was transcribed from a tape recording of the WHAS radio talk. Paragraph arrangement is by the editors.

2. While Governor Willis did not list the eight disasters to which he referred, they included massive flooding in eastern Kentucky in January, a blizzard the next month, a crop-damaging freeze in April, and another flood in June. See *Courier-Journal*, January 9, February 11, April 28, and June 3, 1946.

STATE GOVERNMENT ADMINISTRATION

LETTER TO MILFORD PURDY, KENTUCKY MERCHANTS ASSOCIATION
Lexington / November 27, 1943

I WISH to thank you[1] and the officers of your organization for the appeal you sent to the members of the executive and legislative branches of the new administration.

Self-government is always on trial, and the present situation presents an opportunity for all of us to work toward a demonstration of the capacity of the people to govern.

It is my fixed purpose to seek only the welfare of Kentucky, and I shall ask nothing for partisan advantage.

My appeal to the legislative branch will be for good government. I expect to obtain the services of the best men and women available, and Democrats who measure up to the standard set will be asked to serve as well as Republicans.

We are at war and our internal problems are grave. It will take the best in all of our people, united and in harmony, to achieve the best results.

I am glad to have your help, and I shall endeavor to deserve it at all times. Due credit will be given to every person and to every organization that will help us serve the needs and best interests of our commonwealth.

The same principles apply to municipal government, and I feel sure that Mayor Wyatt[2] may count on the legislative boards of Louisville for full and complete support in the manner I shall seek for the state from the General Assembly.[3]

1. Milford Purdy (1886-1965) of Owensboro. Teacher, 1905-07; insurance manager, 1907-09; bookkeeper, 1909-10; furniture company manager (1910-20), vice-president (1922), and president (since 1925). A Democrat, Purdy was president of the Kentucky Merchants Association. *Who's Who in Kentucky, 1936*, 327; Owensboro *Messenger-Inquirer*, June 25, 1965.

2. Wilson Watkins Wyatt (1905-) of Louisville. Attorney since 1927; Louisville mayor, 1941-45; administrator, National Housing Agency, 1946; director in numerous corporations, including the *Courier-Journal*, and president of several voluntary organizations; chairman of University of Louisville Board of Trustees; gave nominating speech for Alben W. Barkley at 1948 Democratic convention; personal campaign manager for Adlai E. Stevenson in 1952 presidential race and personal advisor in 1956; Kentucky lieutenant governor, 1959-63; defeated in 1962 in bid for U.S. Senate. *Who's Who in Kentucky, 1955*, 375; Tapp, *Kentucky Lives*, 611-12.

3. The letter was read at a meeting where Harry W. Schacter, vice president of the Kentucky Merchants Association, spearheaded the formation of the Committee for Kentucky. See also note 2 in document dated June 8, 1946, in this section.

LETTER TO J.S. WATKINS
Frankfort / December 8, 1943

IN his letter of appointment, Governor Willis charged Watkins[1] with the responsibility of reorganizing "the highway department along the lines and upon the general principles expressed by me in my Mount Sterling address."[2]

"This no doubt will require some legislation," the governor added, "which we will have ready to recommend to the General Assembly in January."[3]

"I want you to know," Governor Willis continued in his letter to Watkins, "that you are to have a free hand to give us the best possible administration of your department. You will have full charge of all departments under you and you will have my full support at all times. You know my views and the pledges I have made to the public. You have been in complete sympathy with my views and have helped me to formulate the principles that should control. If you need my aid at any time, you will have it.

"I know your natural reluctance to make the sacrifice required of you to render this service to the state," the governor concluded. "I deeply appreciate your public spirit which leads you to yield to my urging. Your experience in construction work of immense proportions, your education and standing in the engineering profession, and your wide acquaintance with the problems that confront us, especially qualify you for this great constructive job."

---

1. James Stephen Watkins (1892-1967) of Lexington. Laurel County road engineer, 1919; resident engineer to chief engineer, Kentucky Department of Highways, 1919-29; consulting engineer after 1933; president of Kentucky Chamber of Commerce. The appointment of Republican Watkins to succeed Democrat Richard G. Williams, Jr., as highway commissioner was Governor Willis's initial major act in his first day in office. By 1947 Watkins was said to be Willis's choice as his successor but declined to run. *Who's Who in Kentucky, 1955,* 355; *Courier-Journal,* December 9, 1943, November 3, 1967.

2. See "Preinaugural Addresses" section, first speech.

3. House Bill 15, introduced the second day of the legislative session, passed the House 95-0 on January 17 and the Senate 32-0. Approved on January 26, 1944, chapter 62 abolished the nine advisory highway commissioners. Kentucky *House Journal* (1944), 66, 341-42; Kentucky *Senate Journal* (1944), 375; Kentucky *Acts* (1944), 111.

VETO OF SENATE BILL NO. 21
Frankfort / February 28, 1944

I RETURN herewith Senate Bill No. 21, without my approval.[1]

This bill provides a different rule and a separate procedure for the discharge and tenure of employees of the state who happen to be the wife or mother of a person serving in the armed services of the nation, and others not so related. This is not a suitable basis for classification, since it has no relation to the services being classified.

The purpose of the bill to extend a special privilege to mothers and wives whose sons and husbands are serving the country overlooks the far greater number of mothers and wives to whom no such special privilege is or can be extended. Those in the service of the state need no statute to help them. And such an attempt to serve them impairs the public service and tends to create dissatisfaction and inefficiency in the departments. Moreover, our constitution forbids the grant of exclusive separate public emoluments or privileges, except in consideration of public services. Certainly no such grant could be based on the mere fact of relationship to one in the armed services.

The act runs counter to the principles of the merit system which govern all employees under the Social Security Act, and to which the state must conform in order to receive aid. A telegram from Mary E. Woods, regional director, Social Security Board, reads:

"Re conversation concerning Senate Bill No. 21, it was referred to Washington office for determination regarding its effect upon public assistance plans. Following wire received from Oscar M. Powell, executive director of [the] Social Security Board: 'It is universally recognized that every merit system for the selection of public personnel should include as an essential element selection of employees through competitive examination. Any modification of this essential element must be justified by establishing the impracticability of competitive examinations because of wartime manpower shortages, but even then noncompetitive appointments should be limited to persons meeting minimum qualifications for entrance to examination. The language of Kentucky Senate Bill No. 21 is so broad that it would give tenure to employees who have not passed the required personnel examination for state employment. It would be applicable not only to persons selected from registers duly established as the result of competitive examination, but also to provisional employees who have met only the minimum qualifications for entrance to examination and, in addition, to temporary emergency employees who may not possess even the minimum qualifications necessary to be admitted to the examinations. Moreover, the proposed tenure would extend until twelve months after discharge from the armed services of husband or son of such employee, which might be a long time after the end [of the] present war emergency has passed. The language is so broad that it even goes beyond the declared purpose in the whereas clause, lines 56 to 58, page 3, which refers only to persons who have actually passed the personnel examinations required by law for state employment. Anyone would of course favor protecting the tenure of wives and mothers who have passed the personnel examination required by law for state employment and who have been appointed in accordance with the state merit system requirements. However, to the extent that this bill gives tenure to persons who have not been so qualified and so appointed, it would be contrary to the Social Security Board's personnel standards.' "

This bill also affects the employees of the Unemployment Compensation Commission in similar fashion.

The bill is wholly unnecessary for any purpose. It does not help the class singled out for special favor and may result in injury to the rights of many others of the same class who are not now in the employ of the state.

For these reasons I have vetoed Senate Bill No. 21.[2]

---

1. Senate Bill No. 21, known as the Creasy-Cox-Smith Bill, forbade any state agency from removing an employee if that person was the wife or mother of a member of the armed forces, except in cases of gross inefficiency or criminal indictment. Kentucky *Senate Journal* (1944), 619-21.

2. The Senate passed the bill over the governor's veto by a 21-15 vote on March 1. In the House the bill went to the Committee on Rules and no further vote followed. The governor's veto was sustained. Ibid., 1842; Kentucky *House Journal* (1944), 2213.

VETO OF HOUSE BILL NO. 29
Frankfort / February 28, 1944

I REGRET that I cannot approve, in its present form, House Bill No. 29, which is returned herewith.[1]

This bill, as written, runs counter to the personnel standards of the Social Security Board to which we must conform in order to obtain aid. Miss Rhoda O'Meara, of the Social Security Board at Cleveland, Ohio, has sent a wire as follows:

"House Bill No. 29 appears to provide that persons in emergency, provisional, temporary, or probational status at time of entering military service could not upon reemployment be separated except for cause. If interpretation correct, bill not in accordance with board personnel standards. If bill revised or interpreted to provide these persons upon reemployment receive same status as they had at the time of entering military service, no question would arise. Provision for re-employment in position of equal class consistent with standards if transfer to such equal class is made in accordance with rules of Division of Personnel regarding transfer. No provision in bill for action if position abolished and there is no like position in service."

In order to conform to the requirements of the Social Security Act, and at the same time carry out the intention of the General Assembly, some slight amendments could be made and the bill repassed as amended. There is time to do so. . . .[2]

These changes would conform the act to the Social Security requirements. It is important that conflicts be avoided in order that we may get the assistance upon which so many depend. In view of this situation I have felt impelled to return this bill with the suggestion that it be corrected in order not to damage the service.

Another serious objection to this bill is the penalty imposed on the commonwealth. There is no reason or necessity for the provision that the taxpayers should be made to pay for the act of an official. The remedy against the wrongdoer affords full protection to the injured applicant. The act as written allows a double action for indemnity to the applicant, and in addition fixes a fine for the wrongdoer.

The public service is a public trust. The effort to make patriotic gestures is commendable, but the consideration of service to the public should not be overlooked. The paramount purpose in fixing rules for the public employments should be the efficiency and character of the service to the state. The preference to patriots who have served in the armed forces should not be permitted to obscure that fact. Both objectives may be obtained by reasonable care.

For these reasons, I have been constrained to veto House Bill No. 29.[3]

------

1. Introduced by J. Lee Moore, House Bill No. 29 provided that any present member of the armed forces, previously employed in state government at the outbreak of World War II, would "be forthwith reemployed in the same position" or one of equal class when that person returned from the service. Kentucky *House Journal* (1944), 127-28.

2. At this stage in the veto message, Governor Willis included several lines outlining very technical changes. Those are omitted.

3. The House passed the bill over the governor's veto by a 51-43 vote on March 2, but the Senate failed to override the veto. Kentucky *House Journal* (1944), 2307. See also the October 12, 1944, telegram in the "Republican Party Leader, 1944-1945" section.

DIRECTIVE TO DEPARTMENT HEADS
Frankfort / September 26, 1944

To the heads of all departments and divisions:

Repeating the instructions given from time to time and carrying out the recommendation of the heads of departments at a recent conference, the heads of all departments and divisions are hereby instructed:

1. Time on work. Every effort must be made to see that the employees of the state perform the work required of them and stay on the job continuously, allowing the rest periods provided by the order of the commissioner of industrial relations. Promiscuous absence from the work is not good policy, and the rest periods should be definite and steps should be taken to see that each employee renders full service at all times.

2. Expense accounts. Everyone responsible for the approval of expense accounts should be alert to see that such claims are carefully audited and that the state is not permitted to pay any item of expense not lawfully incurred and proper to be paid. When special expense accounts are authorized, careful provision should be made to see that actual expenses alone are included.

3. Nepotism. Nepotism is the employment of relatives on the basis of relationship rather than merit. The policy of this administration is against nepotism, and it will not be tolerated. Anyone having authority to employ should employ no person related to the employing authority either by blood or marriage. The degree of relationship must be so remote as to leave no inference that relationship and not merit influenced the employment. In case [a] capable and duly qualified person, available for employment, is needed in the service, the question of employment should be referred to a higher authority and in no case made by anyone bearing relationships to the applicant. No person should be allowed to work under any foreman or supervisor related to such worker.

The governor realizes the difficulty of getting help, and that many competent people in the public service have competent relatives who are sometimes available for temporary or permanent service. This situation must be met with caution and the method above outlined must be pursued.

4. Hours of service. No employee of the state should be permitted to accept any outside employment or be on two payrolls at the same time.

The heads of the departments should be on guard to prevent anything of this kind happening. If any position does not require the full time of a worker it should be combined with some other position or duties which would make full-time work for one employee. We will not tolerate any sinecurism in any department of the government, and the heads of the departments and divisions are responsible to see that this does not occur.

5. Appearance before boards. No employee of the state, whether an attorney, accountant, or otherwise, shall appear before any of the other departments or boards or represent any clients in any way before any of the departments or boards, either as a lobbyist, attorney, or otherwise.

6. Campaign contributions. Assessments for campaign purposes will not be tolerated. Every employee is free to make a voluntary contribution, but no solicitation of campaign funds by any employee or from any employee will be tolerated. No employee of the state shall be permitted to act as custodian or collector of any campaign funds.

These policies have been adopted from the beginning and will be pursued throughout this administration.

The governor is depending upon you, and each of you, to see that they are carried out without relaxation.

The constitutional officers elected by the people are requested to cooperate fully with the other members of the administration in carrying out these policies; and in order that they may be advised, a copy is being sent to each and every agency and department of the state government.

FIELD REPRESENTATIVES OF ALCOHOLIC BEVERAGE CONTROL BOARD
Frankfort / March 21, 1945

GOVERNOR SIMEON WILLIS called upon field representatives of the Alcoholic Beverage Control Board to help give the people of Kentucky an efficient, honest, and economic administration.

"With the cooperation of the various units, we will have a good administration and the kind the people want," the governor told the representatives at a session of the board's training school.

"The ability to make and enforce our own laws is the secret of success of a representative government," he continued. "A lapse in enforcement leads to corruption."

TAX REVISION COMMISSION
Frankfort / March 28, 1945

"I HAVE long thought that our tax structure, which has grown up by degrees, should be carefully considered by able and representative men from all parts of the state," Governor Willis told his commission in a brief address.[1]

"The state needs to know the facts about the present tax structure, and to have your considered recommendations for its improvement," he continued. "There must be an understanding of the limits of our ability to undertake new duties without impairment of our power to discharge existing obligations.[2]

"There is a constant demand by taxpayers for relief, and but slight reflection is required to appreciate the justice of that demand. At the same time, there is constant insistence for greater expenditures of public funds along lines of very great human appeal.

"At the very forefront, we must know how much money the state is going to expend for the various services which are required. It will be necessary to consider what is reasonable and right that the state should spend for its schools, higher education, public assistance, and for the operation of the various departments and services of government.

"After you have determined the amount that must be raised to take care of the state's obligations, it will be proper for you to consider the best methods and means, and the most appropriate sources, for raising the required amount of money.

"Naturally, there may be persons and organizations advocating a particular tax or a particular program. Sometimes these advocates become fanatical and think they have found a panacea. As practical men, it will be your task to consider many plans and various suggestions, finding the flaws, if any, and the values in all of them," the governor said.

"The *Courier-Journal*, in an editorial, has advanced two criticisms of my plan," the governor said in his speech. "One was that this commission should be tax supported, and the other was that the governor should use a part of the emergency fund for tax research.

"The answer is that we have no law for either course. We cannot wait for the enactment of a law to meet the present pressing problem. And the governor's emergency fund is restricted within designated limits, and it is not available for the purpose of tax research. The service must be rendered and paid for by patriotic people or it cannot be rendered at all.

"However, I am not convinced that better results could be obtained by the services of a paid commission. The character and type of service which you are to render cannot be purchased or hired. Probably not one of you would accept a job for pay. It is the voluntary service of patriotic men that makes self-government the best in the world," Governor Willis declared.

"Insofar as we adopt sound principles, we may confidently expect good results," he said. "If we would fall into fallacies, unfortunate results will be inevitable. I believe the good common sense of the practical people of Kentucky will be quick to perceive the difference between sound and enduring principles and fallacies that merely allure and disappoint."

The governor did not mention any specific tax to be considered by the body.

"You will find many able men and women ready and willing to serve on committees and prepared to give helpful suggestions," the governor continued.

"Your work at last will depend for its complete success on public approval. The mere passage of a bill by the legislature does not assure a permanent policy. It is public approval that maintains any tax structure.

"I believe the General Assembly will be happy to have your help in suggesting a program for the good of Kentucky. I believe the public will be prepared to approve your work, because I have confidence in your intentions and your ability to make the best solution of this problem that is possible at this time."[3]

---

1. This talk is a composite of accounts taken from the *Courier-Journal* and the *Kentucky Post*, both of March 29, 1945.

2. By executive order dated March 19, Governor Willis had created the Taxation Revision Commission of Kentucky, "to make a study of the tax structure of the state." Working with state government and the University of Kentucky, it was to ascertain needs and recommend revenue sources that were "sound, just, and equitable." Secretary of State's Records.

The thirty-eight appointed commission members included nine members of the General Assembly (five Republicans and four Democrats), six businessmen, five bankers, four attorneys, four educators, two state officials (the commissioners of revenue and finance), and eight others in various occupations. Dana E. Cross, vice-president of Belknap Hardware in Louisville, was selected chairman. *Courier-Journal*, March 20, 29, 1945, and *Kentucky Post*, March 29, 1945.

3. When the commission issued its final report on December 17, 1945, it made several recommendations, including: (1) technical assistance for local assessors, (2) discontinuation of "back tax" collection by private individuals on a fee basis, (3) simplification of tax returns, (4) revision of the composition of the Kentucky Tax Commission, (5) inclusion of the budget unit in the governor's office, and (6) possible use of other methods of raising more revenue. *Courier-Journal*, December 18, 1945.

WELFARE DEPARTMENT AND CIVIL SERVICE
Frankfort / May 16, 1945

By virtue of the authority vested in me by the General Assembly of the commonwealth of Kentucky, under the provisions of Chapter 12 of the Kentucky Revised Statutes, and on recommendation of the commissioner of welfare, I, as governor of the commonwealth of Kentucky hereby authorize and direct the establishment of a civil service system for the employment and government of all officers and employees of the Department of Welfare, including all of its institutions and divisions, which are not subject to the provisions of the joint merit system at present in operation within the Division of Personnel of the Department of Finance for the appointment and government of the employees of the social security agencies.[1]

The agencies of the Department of Welfare affected are:

Division of Corrections, which includes the Kentucky State Reformatory at LaGrange and its branches at Frankfort and Danville, and the Women's Prison at Pewee Valley; Kentucky State Penitentiary at Eddyville and Kentucky House of Reform, Greendale; and Office of Probation and Parole.

Division of Hospitals and Mental Hygiene, which includes the Eastern State Hospital, Lexington; Central State Hospital, Lakeland; Western State Hospital, Hopkinsville; and Institution for the Feeble Minded, Frankfort.

Division of Child Welfare, which includes the Kentucky Children's Home at Lyndon.

Division of Engineering and Construction.

Division of Staff Services.

1. Effective at the first of the next fiscal year, July 1, 1945, there will be established by the Division of Personnel in cooperation with the Department of Welfare a civil service system for the employment, government, and control of all officers and employees of the agencies herein set out, excepting the directors and assistant directors of divisions and the superintendents and assistant superintendents of institutions, and the deputy to the commissioner of the department; and excepting those officers and employees of the Division of Child Welfare and the Division of Staff Services who are now subject to the joint merit system for the social security agencies.[2]

2. Said civil service system shall be administered by the Division of Personnel at the advice of a board composed of the commissioner of the Department of Welfare, the chairman of the State Board of Welfare and two citizens of the commonwealth of Kentucky appointed by the governor. The governor of the commonwealth shall be an ex-officio member of said board; the membership of said board shall be equally divided between the two major political parties of the state.[3] The governor as an ex officio member shall only vote in case of a tie. The same general rules, regulations, and policies insofar as practical as apply to the joint merit system for social security agencies shall be made applicable to the civil service system established in the Department of Welfare by this order; and, in addition thereto, there shall be adopted such other rules, regulations, and policies as may be necessary to create and maintain high standards of civil service. There shall be adopted specifically, rules, regulations, and policies relating to:

a) Qualifications and experience of employees and applicants for positions, including age limits and physical fitness when desirable;

b) Open and competitive examinations to test the relative fitness of applicants for appointment;

c) The establishment of eligibility lists upon which shall be entered the names of the successful candidates in the order of their standing through examinations;

d) Filling of positions by selection from the three candidates graded highest on the appropriate eligible list;

e) A period of probation before an appointment or employment is made a regular employment;

f) Classification of positions and promotions from lower to higher grades, based on efficiency and seniority;

g) Provisions for dismissals and demotions for cause and for appeals and hearings and reinstatements;

h) Elimination of political or religious discrimination;

i) Elimination of political activities and demerits for violations;

j) Exemption from examination all persons in the employment of the said divisions and institutions as of a stated date.

It is the intent and purpose of this executive order to improve and render more efficient the operation of the divisions and institutions of the Department of Welfare by the establishment of civil service which will provide for the selection of competent and properly qualified employees, and assure such employees freedom from political interferences, permanent tenure of office for satisfactory services rendered, and promotions with appropriate increases in salaries.

---

1. The executive order affected approximately fourteen hundred workers across the state. *Courier-Journal*, May 17, 1945.

2. All divisions concerned with public assistance were already under the operation of a joint state and federal merit system. Frankfort *State Journal*, May 17, 1945.

3. The two Democratic appointees announced on May 29 were, from Shelbyville, H.B. Kinsolving, the commonwealth attorney for that district; and, from Ashland, L.J. Watson, a staff member of a federal corrections institute there. *Courier-Journal*, May 30, 1945.

KENTUCKY REPUBLICAN CLUB
DISTRICT COMMITTEE
Lexington / June 7, 1945

THE governor . . . praised the work of department heads of his administration.[1] Declaring that his philosophy of government dealt with the administration of affairs by competent officials, he said, "I have been most fortunate in the men and women who serve with me [as department heads]. The offices are held by responsible people held to these offices by a devotion to public interest. Every one of them is serving at a personal sacrifice."

Republican delegations heard Governor Simeon Willis pledge his efforts to a new philosophy of government, devoted to the public interest in the development of a statewide health program, an expanded and improved system of highways, a richer life, and justice for all people.

"More Republicans are in office now than at any time in Kentucky's history," the governor said, "and they are making good. We must build up our party by having in office men and women of character and ability, officials who will serve the interests of all the people. Today our government touches every fireside, every pocketbook. The business of the state is the business of all the people, and we have been fortunate in having the help of men and women who are devoted to the public interest," Governor Willis added.

"I have called into service more than one hundred women, Democrats and Republicans, to serve Kentucky. We are endeavoring to build highways that will reach every corner of the state; we are seeking to develop a health program that will reach into every home," he said.

"My vision of the Republican party is to see that justice prevails for all the people," the governor emphasized. "Now we are trying to regenerate the state prisons; we are going to have them safe from domination by crooks and criminals. We have finished an investigation at the LaGrange Reformatory and have replaced prison bookkeepers and recordkeepers with competent employees," he continued.[2] "We have consulted experts in prison management for recommendations for improvements at LaGrange and Eddyville. We have taken contracts for government and lend-lease war materials at both prisons and have received official commendation for the excellence of the output. We have an educational program in effect at the Greendale House of Reform; we have placed libraries in the state's mental institutions, and we believe there is a chance for redemption for many of the afflicted.

"We have made improvements in our institutions as fast as time and money will permit," Governor Willis concluded, "and the Republican party will succeed only so far as it is able to grasp the wishes of the people of the state."

---

1. This account is a composite taken from the *Courier-Journal* and Lexington *Leader*, both of June 8, 1945.

2. See messages of April 30 and May 9, 1945, in "Legislative Actions, 1943-1945" section.

STATEMENT ON FIRING OF THE
KENTUCKY AERONAUTICS COMMISSION
Frankfort / September 4, 1945

I DEEM it advisable for the good of the service to remove the appointed members of the Kentucky Aeronautics Commission.[1] An executive order has been entered accordingly.

Under date of August 1, 1945, the commission made a written request for $35,073.44 from the governor's emergency fund. In order that the public may be correctly informed as to actual use intended to be made of the money, a copy of the budget submitted is attached.

It will be noted that the money was asked for salaries for the director and chief clerk, purchase money and insurance of aircraft, a hangar for the aircraft, maintenance of the aircraft, travel expenses, and office expenses, amounting to $15,073.44. Except the items mentioned, there was nothing proposed in the way of planning. The remaining $20,000 estimated was to hire professional aid for ten progressive cities of this state.

I do not consider the purchase of an airplane to be used for the commission, nor the building of a hangar for that plane, nor any of the other items which the commission demanded, as subjects constituting an emergency or a proper claim on emergency funds. Nor is it a part of the duty or right of the governor to provide from the state emergency fund expenses which belong to municipalities. When the state provides aid to municipalities, it must be by legislative act, and the aid made available on equal terms to all municipalities similarly situated.

The aviation policy of the state must be determined by the General Assembly. The governor can only recommend a program for its consideration.

The statement made by the spokesmen for the commission that the governor failed to appreciate the need for quick action in order to secure federal funds for airports within the state and that, as a result, Kentucky will sustain a loss of federal funds, is wholly without foundation in fact.

Congress has passed no appropriation for such purposes. It is not known what action Congress may finally take. When Congress completes its program, there will be time to comply with any requirements it may prescribe.

It is my purpose now, and at all times, to meet any real emergency promptly and effectively, and to cooperate with the commissions created to promote Kentucky's welfare.

In this particular instance, I was giving earnest and constant consideration to the problems of the aeronautics commission, when the members met and aligned themselves against the governor.

In view of the nature of the requests made, the need for care and caution was apparent. The failure of the commission to get what it asked will have no effect whatever on the amount of money the state may receive from federal appropriations yet to be made or upon the construction jobs that may be developed in the future.

The action of the commission in taking a position officially on the proposed amendment to the constitution was outside the scope of its authority.[2] It showed a lack of appreciation of the duties and limitations imposed by law upon the commission.

All these facts convince me that the appointed commissioners are not suited to obtain the best results in planning for the future of aeronautics within the state, and leaves no alternative but to remove each of them and to appoint a new commission.

The new commission will be composed of able and qualified veterans of World War II who are familiar with and interested in aeronautics and who will keep abreast of developments in aviation. It is right that they have the opportunity to assist in building the aviation industry and to promote its growth in Kentucky, where many of their comrades can be employed in a field of activity in which they have become proficient.[3]

It shall be my purpose and constant effort to assist them to develop a sound, progressive, and constructive program for recommendation to the General Assembly. If and when federal funds become available for Kentucky, we shall see to it that the conditions necessary to obtain Kentucky's full share are fully met.

The unselfishness and patriotism displayed by the inspiring young men of our armed forces in the world war just ended will in the same spirit serve our country successfully in peace.

---

1. For a history of the commission and its predecessors see Marvin J. Sternberg, "Aviation," *Kentucky State Digest* 1 (March 1947): 2-3, 6.

2. The Kentucky Aeronautics Commission members opposed a proposed constitutional amendment that limited the use of highway funds to roads and bridges only. At the time much of the money went also to the general fund. *Courier-Journal*, September 5, 1945.

3. On September 25, Governor Willis appointed six World War II veterans to the commission. They were J.J. Bethurum Williams of Somerset, Phil P. Ardery of Frankfort, Stanley I. Hand of Louisville, John H. Klette, Jr. of Covington, Robert S. Griffin of Liberty, and George Ray Holbrook of Ashland. Three days later, on September 28, Lewis G. Kaye of Louisville was appointed to succeed Holbrook, who had been given a contract as special counsel for the highway department. Ibid., September 26, 1945; Lexington *Herald*, September 29, 1945; and Executive Orders, September 25, 28, October 1, 1945, Secretary of State's Records.

DENIAL OF AERONAUTICS BOARD'S CHARGES
Frankfort / November 1, 1945

THE message from Governor Willis denied categorically the testimony of Al Near,[1] Louisville, one of the commissioners ousted September 4, that the governor had timed his ouster to stifle the commission's opposition to the proposed constitutional amendment.

"In fact," he wrote, "the action of the governor was not timed at all by the governor. It was made necessary by the rash action of the spokesmen for the former commission, who selected their own time for action. They precipitated a situation which could not be tolerated, and which made their removal necessary for the best interest of aeronautics in the state.

"These men," the governor continued, "made two charges before the Legislative Council which are self-contradictory. First, they undertook to pretend that the governor was indifferent as to whether or not the good-roads amendment was voted up or down, and they sought to build a case by attributing certain statements to the governor.

"Second, and in the same breath, they charged that the governor was so determined to secure adoption of the good-roads amendment that he removed the commission to keep them from opposing it. This type of accusation made by men in a revengeful mood will deceive no one. It merely illustrates their willingness to resort to any criticism, however absurd."

Governor Willis declared minutes of a meeting June 26, attacked by Near and Carl Ulrich, former director of the commission, are "a true and permanent record of what took place June 26." He said it is incorrect that the attorney general supported the old commission's request for $35,000 from the governor's emergency fund. The attorney general did nothing more than rule the governor could pay the money "if he sees that an emergency exists," and, the governor added, no emergency existed.

Governor Willis declared in his letter that he personally favored adoption of the roads fund amendment at the coming election next week, but declared he had "not at any time sought to dominate the personal opinions of the members of the aeronautics commission, or of any other commission."

Willis also expressed hope the Legislative Council "will cooperate with the new aeronautics commission to build the aviation program for Kentucky."[2]

---

1. Albert Henry Near (1897-1951). Veteran of two wars; vice president of National Aeronautics Association; president of American Association of Airport Executives; member of president's Air Coordinating Committee and active in other organizations; original chairman of Kentucky Aeronautics Commission; director of Louisville airport. New York *Times*, May 28, 1951. Near had been appointed by Willis on January 26, 1945. Executive Orders, Secretary of State's Records.

2. This message is a composite from the Paducah *Sun-Democrat*, November 1, 1945, and the *Courier-Journal* and the Lexington *Herald*, both of November 2, 1945.

SUSPENSION OF CIVIL SERVICE
IN WELFARE DEPARTMENT
Frankfort / March 25, 1946

WHEREAS, on May 16, 1945, by executive order there was established in the Department of Welfare a civil service system in all divisions except those subject to the rules of the Social Security Administration, and

WHEREAS, the commissioner of the Department of Welfare has by letter dated March 22, 1946 (which letter is made a part hereof and set out as follows):

Dear Governor:

On May 16, 1945, pursuant to Chapter 12 of the Kentucky Revised Statutes, you issued an executive order establishing a civil service system for the appointment and government of certain officers and employees of the Department of Welfare, and creating a division of personnel in the Department of Welfare to carry out this civil service. There was no appropriation for the operation of this division, and it has been a very great strain on the department to finance its operations. We requested an appropriation of $25,000 from the 1946 General Assembly for the operation of this division during the next biennium, but in the budget bill just passed no appropriation whatever was made for the operation of the division. Furthermore, the appropriations made to the other divisions of the department were below the actual needs of those divisions.

It is obvious that there will not be money available for the Division of Personnel. We have no choice, therefore, but to call this to your attention and suggest to you that until such time as funds are made available, you suspend the civil service program in this department. We request that you make this effective April 1, 1946, because as pointed out above it is a strain on the already meager funds of the department this year; and the savings to be effected the remainder of this fiscal year will reflect in our revolving fund, which will carry over into the next fiscal year and to that extent be a cushion in view of the inadequate institutional appropriations made by the General Assembly.

You have made a great forward step and it is earnestly hoped that another legislature will see the wisdom of a proper appropriation for the reestablishment of civil service in this department. Meanwhile it is our intention to carry out the spirit of civil service in every way possible.

Sincerely yours,
s/John Quertermous
Commissioner of Welfare

has informed me that the General Assembly of 1946 failed to make any appropriation whatever for the operation of the legally constituted Division of Personnel, which division includes the civil service system for the fiscal years of 1946-47 and 1947-48, and that there are no funds available in the department or elsewhere for the operation of the said Division of Personnel and the civil service system, and

WHEREAS, the failure of the General Assembly to provide an appropriation for the Division of Personnel and the civil service system for the said fiscal years makes it impossible to continue the said Division of Personnel and the civil service system of the Department of Welfare.

NOW, I, Simeon Willis, governor of the commonwealth of Kentucky, do order that the function of the civil service system in the Department of Welfare as established by the executive order dated May 16, 1945, and by the actions of the civil service board at its several meetings held pursuant to the said executive order be suspended until such times as funds are made available by the General Assembly of the commonwealth of Kentucky.

It is further ordered that the Department of Welfare preserve all personnel records and statistical data compiled and collected by the Division of Personnel through the civil service system, and it is further ordered that the Department of Welfare maintain in the department insofar as is administratively possible all standards of employment as have been heretofore determined by the Civil Service Board.

REPUBLICAN BANQUET
Harlan / June 8, 1946

GOVERNOR WILLIS, an impromptu speaker, credited much of the success of his administration to the "able men I have been able to induce to serve the state as department heads." He praised Harlan Countian Orville M. Howard,[1] head of the Department of Revenue, as a capable and efficient administator.

Governor Willis also made reference to the publicizing of Kentucky as a backward state (which is the theme of the Committee of Kentucky's "Wake Up Kentucky" program), and countered with the declaration that "Kentucky is headed in the right direction and is making progress."[2]

"Kentucky is giving a greater percentage of its gross revenue to education than any other state in the Union, and we are raising the standards of education gradually," the governor said. "We are making progress in proportion to our ability to finance, and we should not be discouraged."

The governor said his administration, through capable leadership of the departmental heads, had been able to save millions of dollars of the taxpayers' money. He pointed out that several departments were performing greater services with fewer personnel and at lower cost than previous Democratic administrations.

"I have heard the complaint that this administration has not given enough jobs to Republicans, but I can assure you that we have had to depend on the help of Democrats because not enough Republicans were willing to serve their state at the salaries we can pay," Governor Willis said. "We invite Republicans to help us and we have taken all who have qualified for the jobs, and it must be remembered that an employee, Republican or Democrat, must be qualified. We are interested in doing a good job."

He said that one department of the state government had been operating on no greater than 235 employees, while the same department of any other administration had 750 employees. He pointed to similar savings in other departments, "and we have improved the service to the people at the same time."

Governor Willis heaped praise on Commissioner [J. Stephen] Watkins as "a man who has an understanding of his job and who is performing in a magnificent manner."

---

1. Orville M. Howard (1898-1963). Telegraph operator, L & N railroad; member of Harlan County School Board; master commissioner, Harlan Circuit Court; commissioner of revenue, 1945-47; unsuccessful Republican candidate for lieutenant governor, 1947; Kentucky director of Federal Housing Administration after 1955. *Courier-Journal*, February 10, 1963. Governor Willis had appointed Howard commissioner of revenue on April 17, 1945. Executive Orders, Secretary of State's Records.

2. The Committee *for* Kentucky grew out of a November 1943 meeting of various business groups. From that meeting, and with a great deal of support from publisher Mark F. Ethridge of the *Courier-Journal*, the organization began a public relations campaign designed to publicize Kentucky's problems, and possible solutions. Harry W. Schacter, president of Kaufman-Straus Depart-

ment Store and chairman of the board of the Kentucky Merchants Association, was chosen president, and in 1945 the group incorporated. It disbanded in 1950. See Harry W. Schacter, *Kentucky on the March* (New York, 1949), for a book-length account of the organization.

Governor Willis indicated that he disliked the negative aspects he saw in the program, preferring instead to stress the positive moves the state was making.

STATE DIVISION OF GAME AND FISH
Undated (circa 1947)

I HAVE observed with great interest the progress made by the state Division of Game and Fish since the adoption of the new civil service law effective in August of 1944. This interest had a dual foundation. First, because I enjoyed both hunting and fishing—not only for the reward, in the way of game and fish—but mainly for the restful recreation and the fine association with sportsmen. Second, the present law was an experiment of a politically free department, utilizing the talents of both parties and functioning for the good of all the people of Kentucky, unencumbered by spoils politics. I had the pleasure of approving the bill passed by the 1944 legislature and of putting it into operation.[1]

The progress made by the game and fish division speaks for itself. It became my duty at the beginning to select a bipartisan commission of nine men, one from each congressional district, to function as the policy makers of the division.[2] I was required to select these nine men from a list of forty-five. The sportsmen from each district sent in a list of five qualified and available men. This was, and ever since has been, a difficult task because of the high type of candidates picked by the sportsmen. Any of the men recommended would have made an excellent commissioner. My choice did not necessarily mean that the best was chosen but that one was chosen from the five best men of the district, and the balance was maintained over the district so as to meet the political requirements specified in the law.

In August 1944 the Division of Game and Fish had 63 employees, and during that year the gross income was $194,790.81. The present number of employees is 167, and the income for last year was

$618,000.00. We have more qualified employees of each party than either party could have had under the spoils system.

During this short period of time, the Division of Game and Fish has invested $150,000 in useful capital property. This consists of a 100-acre farm near Frankfort that has been converted into a modern game farm. This farm has been improved and equipped with the most modern and up-to-date types of incubators, breeding pens, holding pens, and brooders that it is possible to obtain. This farm, while not yet up to maximum production, is now one of the largest quail producing units in the United States. Here also are [rac]coons and various types of pheasants that are being experimented with in hopes that types can be developed for stocking in Kentucky areas where native species will not perish. A wildlife nursery where more than thirty species of trees, shrubs, and vines that will furnish food and cover for wildlife are propagated, is also located at the farm. Through a cooperative agreement with the federal Soil Conservation Service, this stock is furnished free to farmers to be planted on eroded, steep, and rocky soils, thereby improving the land, establishing wood lots, and growing into habitat and food for wildlife.

The fish hatcheries have been expanded [to] more than four times their former production for the stocking of streams. A program of stocking ponds, where the farmer will allow fishing, was started last year, and since then more than 4,000 of these ponds have been stocked.

Previous to 1944 only one project using Pittman-Robertson federal funds was ever started. More than $50,000 of federal funds had been by-passed to the disadvantage of Kentucky sportsmen. Now five projects are under way in the way of research and the stocking of deer, beaver, wild turkey, and raccoon.[3]

The education of the youth of Kentucky to a better appreciation and understanding of natural resources was begun by the Division of Game and Fish in 1945. Since that time there have been 170 Junior Clubs organized, representing over 15,000 boys. These boys receive, over a period of five years, sixty complete lessons in conservation and associated subjects: how to carry a gun, how to camp, how to cast a plug or tie a fly, the mysteries of the regeneration of wildlife, and where to find a bass.

Now almost two years old is the division's official publication, *The Happy Hunting Ground*, a magazine issued to inform the sportsmen and citizens how their money is being spent and what they are getting in return.

Conservation officers are not the old abusive wardens of a few years ago, but men who are interested in the sportsmen and help to solve their problems. They are taught to operate as a credit to their community and to educate the people to the value of obeying laws.

All this, and much more, has been accomplished in the short space of three years. Kentucky now takes a place among the other states as having a real Division of Game and Fish and is credited with having made more progress in this short time than any state in the Union.

Your present commission is sincerely trying to do the best job it can. Your director is a man with twenty years successful experience in wildlife work and is devoted to giving the sportsmen of Kentucky the best program possible.[4]

A staff of trained men administer the various departments. Some of these men have been brought from other states, simply because Kentucky had no one prepared for the service. Under the old plan there was no security offered by the Division of Game and Fish, and students could not afford to spend years in school fitting themselves for a job that offered no more than temporary political employment.

The best politics is good government. No political party or politically minded men can succeed at the sacrifice of good administration. No organization or machine is a substitute for good government.

The sportsmen are satisfied the experiment is going to be successful, and I am proud of my part in setting up the present Game and Fish Division regulations. The cooperation of the sportsmen is our guaranty of its permanence.

---

1. Senate Bill 27 passed the Kentucky House 64-15 and the Senate 32-1. The governor approved the measure on March 20, 1944. At the time of Willis's death, the official publication of the Department of Fish and Wildlife Resources declared that he "assisted the league in its first big spring from mediocrity. . . . Governor Simeon Willis signed the bill. . . , and by so doing he endeared himself to the hearts of many sportsmen!" Kentucky *House Journal* (1944), 2944; Kentucky *Senate Journal* (1944), 1150-51; Kentucky *Acts* (1944), 7-19; "Simeon Willis . . . the Helper," *Kentucky Happy Hunting Ground* 21 (July 1965): 11 (quotation).

2. Those named were George Long (R-Benton), J.B. Miller (D-Williamsburg), Erroll W. Draffen (R-Harrodsburg), all for four-year terms; O.W. Thompson (R-Pikeville), W.G. Buchannan (R-Corbin), both for three-year terms; W.H. Washburn, (D-Beaver Dam), H.M. Bertram (R-Louisville), both for two-year terms; Ed Ernst (D-Louisville), E.H. Pohn (D-Horse Cave), both for two-year terms. Frankfort *State Journal*, August 13, 1944.

3. The so-called Pittman-Robertson Act provided for an excise tax on fire-

arms and ammunition, the proceeds of which went to the states on the basis of license sales. Funded projects referred to by Governor Willis took place in the Pennyrile region, in an area between the Tennessee and Cumberland rivers, in McCreary County, in Hardin County, and elsewhere. *Your Kentucky Government, 1943-1947* ([Frankfort, 1947]), 34.

4. Stephen A. Wakefield was director. *Kentucky Directory*, 110.

REPUBLICAN PARTY LEADER, 1944-1945

KENTUCKY REPUBLICAN CONVENTION
Louisville / April 25, 1944

DR. GABBARD[1] and fellow Republicans:

For forty-five years—short years—I have been attending Republican conventions in Kentucky, but this is the best convention that we have ever had. For twelve long, long years we have seen our country mismanaged, manhandled, and outraged by a government that had no reference to the Constitution or the laws or the sentiment of sound Americanism. We have been helpless to stem that tide. But the day of our deliverance is now in sight, and this great audience certifies that the next president of the United States will be a Republican. This great audience certifies that the next Congress of the United States will be Republican. And this great audience certifies that Kentucky will have four congressmen and a senator to assist that president in carrying out the policies of the Republican party. And the reason that that is true is that the Republicans of Kentucky understand the difference between a government by executive decree and a government by constitution and law.

They talk about saving the social gains of the last twelve years. Why, certainly, we shall save the social gains of the last twelve years, but we shall also save the social gains of the 150 years under the Constitution of the United States; and we will regain the losses from the constitutional and independent gains of 150 years, and restore this government to the people and take it out of the hands of the bureaucrats.

Our fathers brought forth upon this continent a nation dedicated to liberty, and they formulated a Constitution to secure those liberties; and in 150 years under that Constitution we saw in this country thirteen little colonies along the Atlantic seaboard with a population no greater than we have in Kentucky today, spread from ocean to ocean with a population of 130 million enterprising Americans dedicated to the perpetuity of free institutions. And during that 150 years we saw more schoolhouses built on this continent; we saw more churches and hospitals and railroads and business institutions and highways. We saw more things done to raise the standard of living of the common man than was ever achieved in a like period in the entire history of this world.

It is the freedom of the people to go about their business, unhampered by government restrictions, under which accomplishment may be made. It gives wings to the imagination. It releases incentive genius. And it brings to the people comforts and conveniences that were never thought of in any country that was not dedicated to freedom of men and women everywhere.

And greater than all the material progress, greater than all the material advantages, there is something about freedom that develops the spiritual life and character of mankind to achieve and aspire until there is no limit to what may be expected of a great people united and advancing toward the ever-receding horizon. And we are eternally pledged in this country that we will remain united, that we will resist all encroachments upon the liberties of our people, that we will not defraud our sons of the future; but that we will preserve these institutions as they were handed down to us by our forefathers, and we will transmit them unimpaired to the latest generation.

We prove all things. We hold fast to that which is good. And by the Republican party forgetting any petty differences, forgetting any bitter disappointments of a day, but looking forward always to the great future, we strive to build and build and build until our fathers looking down upon us from the saintly shore will be as proud of our achievements as we are proud of theirs.

This country is dedicated to the freedom of the individual man. It is the individual that is the unit of citizenship. It is the individual that makes a country great or makes a country weak. It is the individual, average manhood of the great American people that makes them irresistible in war and unbeatable in peace. And today, while our boys and girls throughout the world are fighting for the ideals of Americanism, we pledge to them the last ounce of strength we have and the last dollar of wealth we have. We shall help them and aid them and sustain them with all that we have until the victory is won; and when that victory is won we will guarantee to them that they will come back to a country as free, as noble, as independent, and as grand as in any age in the history of the world.

We cannot discharge our duty to them merely by feeding and clothing and arming them, but we must maintain the spiritual things; we must maintain the home and the schools and the churches and all the institutions which make life convenient, which make prosperity evident to the people. And we shall march forward after this war and go forward as we have always done in the past.

The handicaps of a great debt will be met and overcome by sound government, by proper economy, by intelligent management of all of the affairs of the government, by cutting out the wasteful extravagance that has put over three hundred thousand useless officeholders on the backs of the taxpayers. We will cut out all these excrescences, and we will put in the halls of the American Congress men who will stand for the rights of the American people.

The Constitution of this country guarantees to every state a republican form of government under which they elect their representatives, and their representatives truly represent them in administering and maintaining a government of law and not a government of men.

We have seen the power and the intrusions of government into every activity of the people. We have read in the books written by Thomas Jefferson that when the people looked to Washington when to plant and when to reap, the people would go hungry. And today we have everything rationed, food rationed because there is not enough to feed our people here at home after feeding our soldiers and after dividing our surplus products with our allies. And yet the government is telling the farmer when to plant and when to sow and when to reap, and the price he is to receive for his product.

And there is no human mind wise enough to take over the control of the forces of nature and manage the entire economy of a great nation like the United States. The artificial interference of little men in big positions has caused us more suffering and more losses and more distress than any gain that could be possibly ascertained from a close calculation of what they have done.

Now we know the remedy. We know that there is but one way to salvation, and that is by us buckling on our armor and putting your arm around your brother Republican and marching straight to the polls to vote for a Republican Congress and a Republican president. And we will reverse the trend of autocracy. We will reverse the tendency toward government operation of everything because the success of government is the most costly thing in the world. And then when the people

get the government in their control, they will prosper, they will redeem
this country from mismanagement, from ill-advised leadership; and I
promise you this: that we will not have this unbuttered mush over the
radio in fireside chats, and we will not have this daily "My Day" tripe in
our papers,[2] which could not be sold to the Paintsville *Herald* if Harry
Arrowood had inherited $100,000.[3]

Now there are a few things that ought to be said. The people of this
country have a deep sense of responsibility. They have a deep aspiration to preserve all of the great things which we inherited. They know
how to achieve those blessings. They know that the history of the
Republican party is the history of success in this country. They know
that the Republican party was born in a crisis to save the nation from
disunion and disaster.[4] They know that for many, many years the
Republican party managed this country soundly and safely, and we
had prosperity. They know that when the Republican party was in
power the national debt went down every year after it was turned back
to them by the Democratic administration. There just is not the capacity
in the Democratic party to manage this country. They have just two
remedies—first, give us a blank check and give us unlimited power
over the activities of the people. And that has gone on until thoughtful
men and women everywhere, oppressed by a burden of taxation
which was never known before in this land, are now buckling on their
armor to work out during the next generation the problems that have
been forced upon us by this misfortune which came in the guise of the
New Deal.

My message to you is one of good cheer. Do not be afraid to fight this
battle. Do not be afraid of the hordes of officeholders they have. You
know they get rusty sitting around in those bureaus, and they lose interest and get dissatisfied that they haven't a better bureau and a bigger
bureau; and so it is when the American people make their charge next
November, you will see the hordes of New Deal Democrats scattering
like winter's withered leaves.

Have faith in your fellow man. Have faith in your country. Have faith
in the protection of that divine providence that has never yet deserted
us and will never desert us so long as we remain faithful and true to the
great principles upon which this country was dedicated, upon which it
has been built, and which will be perpetuated until the latest generation.

---

1. Elmer Everett Gabbard (1890-1960) of Buckhorn. Pastor of churches in
Knoxville and Chattanooga, Tenn.; president, Buckhorn Association, and pas-

tor, Buckhorn Church, 1936-56; board of trustees of Berea College; director Maryville College, 1930-40, and Louisville Presbyterian Seminary, 1930-42; defeated as Republican candidate for Congress in 1942 and 1944; moderator, Presbyterian Synod of Kentucky, 1952. *Who's Who in Kentucky, 1955,* 124; *Courier-Journal,* June 19, 1960.

2. A reference to Eleanor Roosevelt's syndicated column.

3. Probably *Henry* Arrowood (1896-1960) of Paintsville. Reporter, Louisville *Herald-Post* and *Courier-Journal;* editor of Paintsville *News* (which merged with *Herald*), 1934-41; state representative, 1941-47, 1951-53; wrote column for *Courier-Journal* during Willis years. Mitchell Hall, *Johnson County, Kentucky: A History of the County. . . ,* 2 vols. (Louisville, 1928), 2:26; *Courier-Journal,* November 14, 1960.

4. The reference, of course, is to the sectional crisis of the 1850s and the Civil War.

HAYES REPUBLICAN CLUB OF SANDUSKY COUNTY, OHIO
Fremont, Ohio / April 27, 1944

GOVERNOR SIMEON WILLIS of Kentucky tonight [said]: "The hour of destiny and the day of deliverance are at hand and the American people should not lose confidence in ridding the country of a monster who is seeking to control their destiny."

He declared the personality of President Roosevelt was disclosed in 1936 when the president informed Congress the New Deal "had created new instruments of power which in the hands of the people's government were all right but in the hands of the wrong people would shackle the liberty of America."[1]

"No man has hands white enough for such power," the Kentucky governor emphasized.

Willis observed the American people could "take heart that twenty-six Republican governors already have been elected in this country." He said that preserving ten years of social gains from the New Deal was "all right, but more important are the gains of 150 years under the Constitution."

"Wealth is created only by free enterprise in industry," Willis stated, "and is impossible under present conditions. The struggle between liberty and tyranny once again is going on."

1. In President Roosevelt's annual message to Congress on January 3, 1936, the exact quote was: "They realize in thirty-four months we have built up new instruments of power. In the hands of a people's government this power is wholesome and proper. But in the hands of political puppets of an economic autocracy such power would provide shackles for the liberties of the people." See Samuel I. Rosenman, comp., *The Public Papers and Addresses of Franklin Delano Roosevelt*, 13 vols. (New York, 1938-50), 5:16.

STATEMENT REGARDING
DREW PEARSON COLUMN
Frankfort / June 8, 1944

I KNOW of no better influence.[1] With the women doing superb work in all the war work and home work of the country, in the army and navy and defense activities of all kinds, I believe there is every reason to consult their views and to seek the counsel of as many women as possible. I recognize the women as a great moral and constructive force in the march to victory.

Insofar as Mrs. Willis[2] is concerned, her party thought well enough of her political judgment, and of her patriotic devotion, to elect her by acclamation as a member of the Republican national committee.

Officially she has a duty to perform to her party, and that, as well as her responsibility as a voter, justifies her in taking an interest in public affairs.

I consult constantly with my state chairman and chairwoman and with my national committeeman and national committeewoman. I shall continue to do so during my administration. We are in complete accord.

---

1. Washington columnist Drew Pearson had written, in reference to Mrs. Willis, that Governor Willis "is getting the reputation among Kentuckians of veering toward petticoat influence at the palace." See Lexington *Leader*, June 8, 1944, and *Courier-Journal*, June 9, 1944.

2. Ida Lee Millis Willis (1897-1978) of Ashland. Deputy court clerk until her

marriage in 1920; appointed to state welfare commission by Governor Ruby Laffoon; first director of Kentucky Heritage Commission. Mrs. Willis was a political figure in her own right. *Who's Who in Kentucky, 1955,* 366; Frankfort *State Journal,* November 12, 1978.

REPUBLICAN NATIONAL CONVENTION
Chicago, Illinois / June 28, 1944

MR. CHAIRMAN, ladies and gentlemen:

The heat is on and the heat will stay on until victory is recorded next November. Kentucky is the bellwether of the nation. In that great state where Lincoln was born the heartbeats of this country may be felt. Last November, with the aid of patriotic Democrats who put their country above partisanship, Kentucky paved the way for the nation next November.

Kentucky loves her neighboring state of Ohio. Kentucky loves John W. Bricker[1] for what he is, for what he has done, and for what he is prepared to do for the American people. The people of Kentucky, with Tennessee at our side, want the Republicans of all the other states of the Union to know that we are on the march; that we are marching to victory for Americanism, typified by those two great boys from the states of New York and Ohio, Tom[2] and John.

From the floor Governor Bricker seconded the nomination of Governor Dewey. The American people will continue the work from there on. They will bind up the nation's wounds, deliver this country from its enemies, and replace this administration; they will save this country.

I thank you.

---

1. John William Bricker (1893-1986) of Ohio. Attorney; assistant attorney general of Ohio, 1923-27; defeated for attorney general post; on Public Utilities Commission, 1929-32; elected attorney general of Ohio, 1932; lost gubernatorial race in 1936, but won post in 1938; reelected in 1940, 1942; elected U.S. senator in 1946 and served until 1959. Robert Sobel and John Raimo, eds., *Biographical Directory of the Governors of the United States, 1789-1978,* 4 vols. (Westport, Conn., 1978), 3: 1232-33; Lexington *Herald-Leader,* March 23, 1986.

2. Thomas E. Dewey (1902-1971) of New York. Attorney; special prosecutor

1934-37; district attorney of New York County, 1937-41; defeated as Republican gubernatorial candidate in 1938; won election as governor of New York, 1942, 1946, 1950; author; presidential candidate, 1944, 1948. *Biographical Directory of Governors*, 3: 1103-4; New York *Times*, March 17, 1951; *Who's Who, 1942-43*, 676.

STATEMENT REGARDING ELECTION
IN KENTUCKY
St. Louis, Missouri / August 3, 1944

SENATOR BARKLEY weakened his position in Kentucky materially when by his speech nominating Roosevelt for a fourth term in Chicago he tied himself irrevocably and more closely to Roosevelt and the New Deal.

Even more so, he became a 100 percent New Dealer. Whatever amount of prestige that he might have gained by his repudiation of Roosevelt in regard to the veto of the tax bill, whereby he may have convinced some people that he was a man of conviction, he retched up completely when he made the nominating speech at Chicago.[1]

We are stronger in Kentucky this year than we were last year because we have vanquished the ghost of defeatism. We will have a strong candidate in opposition to the senator. With the help of anti-New Deal Democrats, we will carry Kentucky for Dewey and Bricker, give them a Republican United States senator and a number of additional congressmen.

Naturally, it will be a hard fight because Barkley will struggle desperately for New Dealism and the fourth term, but the Republicans anticipate this and are already girding themselves for the battle.

---

1. The Democratic national convention took place in Chicago, July 19-21, 1944. In nominating Roosevelt, Barkley had said, "I have not always agreed with this man. . . . [But] it is quite another thing to discard . . . a leadership unsurpassed, if ever equaled, in the annals of American history." *Official Report of the Proceedings of the Democratic National Convention . . . 1944* (n.p., 1944), 72.

Earlier, Barkley had broken with the president on the tax bill question and had resigned as majority leader of the Senate. Democratic colleagues quickly and unanimously reelected him to the position. Some historians have agreed that the resignation severely damaged Barkley's chances of being FDR's vice-presidential choice in 1944. See George W. Robinson, "Alben Barkley and the 1944 Tax Veto," *Register of the Kentucky Historical Society* 67 (1969): 197-210.

DEWEY POLITICAL RALLY
Louisville / September 8, 1944

Mr. Chairman:

The governor of New York has won the hearts of Kentuckians by his battles for good government.

He was successful in his fights in New York, first as the district attorney, and then as governor of the Empire State.

Difficulties do not deter him.

Obstacles do not frighten him.

We the people of the United States now need his services. Indeed, they require them in their present crisis.

They want him to end the confusion that reigns at Washington.

They desire him to disperse the hordes of useless officeholders swarming at the capital and all over the land.

They have chosen him to [slay] the sprawling octopus that is sucking the very lifeblood of the federal government.

He is the chosen leader of the people to stop the excesses of the New Deal, to return the federal government to a rule of law, and to put the multitude of bureaucrats on the toboggan.

The people have had enough of being pushed around by petty tyrants in high positions, in which they were put without being elected and to which none of them could be elected. They have been sickened at the sight of the open alliance of the national administration with the corrupt city machines.

The people resent the use of federal patronage to feed the grasping demands of partisan political bosses.

They have made up their minds to strike down the "New instruments of power" invented by the New Dealers "to shackle the liberties of the people."

They are appalled at the ever-increasing burden of federal taxes that has been levied upon our people, and they are apprehensive at the astronomical debt that has been laid upon this and future generations of Americans.

The American people do not like the kind of government the New Dealers have fostered, and they have determined that it is time to change. They demand new blood, new vigor, and a new direction.

We are very happy tonight to have with us the gallant young leader of the Republicans of the nation, and all Kentucky is proud to acknowledge this signal honor paid to our state.

It is my privilege to introduce to you the president of the Federation of Republican Women's Clubs of America, who will introduce Governor Dewey.

The women of Kentucky have been honored by the visit of these distinguished Republicans from forty states. The women are doing great work for the party and for the country. Their influence has never been greater or more important than it is at this time.

In a very real sense, the destiny of the republic rests in their hands. And in those hands, it is secure.

The president of the federation has won her high position in the councils of the nation by hard work, superior talent, and outstanding character. The women have been wise in the selection of their leader.

I give you the president of the National Federation of Women's Clubs, Mrs. Glenn Suthers, of Chicago,[1] who will present the next president of the United States.

---

1. Marie H. Suthers (1896-1983). Leader of Republican women's clubs; teacher; Illinois state representative, 1949-51; Chicago board of elections, 1952-81. Chicago *Tribune* and Chicago *Sun Times*, both of February 11, 1983.

REPUBLICAN PARTY WORKERS LUNCHEON
Washington, D.C. / September 19, 1944

THIS is the year of crisis. Our country stands at the crossroads. The decision made this year will determine the kind of government we shall have for the next four years and the future of this generation and all succeeding generations. We know what has happened during the past twelve years. We know that the New Deal has not repented or reformed. We know that what it has done is but a forerunner of what it proposes to do.

In 1932 the Democrats were not in power. Their platform and their candidate promised the American people a reduction of taxation and expenses; a destruction of excessive government in the form of bureaus, agencies, and commissions. They promised to correct every evil which was then apparent in the life of our country and to prevent a recurrence of those evils. The people then were in a mood to accept any promise to relieve the worldwide distress of that time. They knew that Mr. Roosevelt had been a failure as governor of New York and had run the state greatly in debt, but they took him at his word and accepted his fair promises at their face value. He was elected, and very shortly after his election he forgot all his promises. He multiplied bureaus, agencies, and commissions; he increased the national debt beyond all imagination; he increased the number of federal officeholders to an extent not only unknown in history but undreamed of in the wildest flight of imagination; he created, as he himself declared, "new instruments of power" which were capable of "shackling the liberties of the people"; he fought the business interests of the country regardless of fault or merit; he created destructive prejudices in the minds of the people; he caused them to be divided; he created confusion and unrest; and one crisis followed another crisis until the people were bewildered. With borrowed money he organized the country in a way to acquire votes for a second term and then for a third term. He created wasteful projects all over the country and extended the agents of the government into every state and into almost every country; he multiplied bureaus and duplicated their functions, so that we have many agencies working at cross purposes in the same fields. He has been drunk with power and leaping forward for more power at every opportunity. The one remedy for every problem was a blank check and a blanket power. He has regulated and controlled, through executive orders, practically all the activities of the people. He devised means to strangle business by numerous agencies which made it impossible for capital to venture forth in productive enterprise. He prolonged the depression for many years beyond its natural life; and but for the war, in which we are engaged, the depression would have grown gradually worse under his leadership. And much of what he spent the nation still owes.

If he is elected for a fourth term he will take it as a mandate from the people to carry to even greater extremes the destruction of all freedom and individual initiative. He has at no time manifested the slightest regard for the Constitution or for his oath of office. In a letter to a congressman he openly flouted the sanctity of an official oath. He has followed the methods of dictatorial governments which set up agencies to promote their purposes regardless of law and without respect to the representatives of the people. When Congress has withheld an appropriation from his executive agencies, as it has done in several instances, he has simply shifted to another agency and proceeded with his purposes. He has driven from the Democratic party most of its respectable members who were Democrats by reason of their convictions and traditions. He is now surrounded by sycophants who seek his favor and is ruled by special interests, such as the corrupt city bosses of the country, the Political Action Committee under the leadership of Sidney Hillman[1] and Earl Browder,[2] and such of the bureaus and agencies he has set up as can control votes.

What could be more sinister than a president dependent for his election upon such men as Sidney Hillman and Earl Browder? Recently Mr. Hannegan[3] has denied that Mr. Roosevelt told him to "clear everything with Sidney," but Mr. Hannegan has not denied, will not deny, and cannot deny, that he did, in fact, clear everything with Sidney before it was put through the Democratic convention. The facts of the record show that Mr. Hillman vetoed the nomination of Justice Byrnes.[4] I need not dwell upon the injuries that have been inflicted upon the country. You see evidences on every hand of the devastations of the New Deal. You see the domination of the Hagues,[5] with his federal judges appointed by President Roosevelt and with all the federal patronage in his lap. There are in the state of New Jersey, where Hague resides, 65,000 federal employees; this is quite a mass of pottage for a political machine. In the state of New York, where Flynn presides as boss of Tammany,[6] there are 260,000 federal employees. In the state of Illinois, where Kelly reigns as boss of the city of Chicago, there are 117,000 federal employees. In the other states where the big city bosses prevail a similar situation exists. It bodes no good to the free American republic to have a president dominated by the corrupt city bosses, the CIO Political Action Committee headed by Hillman and supported by Browder, and the official power directed by these men.

It means a perpetual domination by destructive and alien interests. They operate on a philosophy which is at war with the principles of constitutional government and individual liberty in the United States. They believe in a government for the purpose of profit and reward to the bosses and special privileges to their favorites. They have no conception of public service honestly administered for the general welfare. It is a philosophy of government which is essentially destructive. It is set up outside of the Constitution and the laws and is operated despite the checks and balances and protections provided for by our forefathers in the Constitution. It is nothing but the old tyranny of arbitrary power.

The question is: Are the American people willing in this year of crisis for this New Deal administration to be perpetuated in power? It is clear that if every American who opposes it would do all in his power to defeat it there would be a landslide for Dewey and Bricker in November. The first question for us is this: Do we wish to win? Every man and woman who loves the country cannot help but wish that this evil thing might be destroyed and the Republic returned to sound, representative government. Do we know how to win? Everyone must do everything possible. We must not be content to leave it to the other fellow. Everyone who can speak to his neighbor, everyone who can use the telephone, everyone who can make a speech, everyone who can write a letter or article to the newspapers or magazines, everyone who can give a dollar or ten dollars or any amount, everyone who can help should do the thing he can do, and keep on doing it until the victory is won. Like the brave men in the old poem in *McGuffey's Reader:*

> Each must feel as though himself were he
> On whose sole arm hung victory.

If this spirit can be generated and organized we can win. The materials of victory are lying before us; it is our task to mold them into the finished product. Why make a weak and wasted effort? When we are fighting a dangerous enemy we do not hit lightly but with all our strength. In this battle, we have a formidable foe. We must strike with all our might. We must do the utmost in all respects, exert our strength to the limit; and when we do so the tide will turn because nothing can withstand the great flood of American public opinion. But it must be awakened and made effective. It cannot operate without leadership, without stirring, without instruction, and without inspiration. We have that leadership. We have new blood, youth, vigor; and the party is headed in the right direction. It proposes to reverse the trend of recent years and to reestablish constitutional government. We must not be frightened by New Deal propaganda or misled by its boasting arrogance that it is invincible and that its leader is indispensable. If the defeatist spirit ever conquers our country the vitality and the vigor of the people will perish. Courage is necessary at all times. It is imperative at this time.

I need not explain to you what it means to all of us and to the future for us to win this election. It will end the dynasty of the city bosses and the corrupt alliances. It will end the throttling of business by punitive measures and by antagonistic administration. It will free the people from the restraints and restrictions which have retarded progress and development and restore the country to the road which leads to prosperity and freedom. Everyone who has a part in this victory will have a feeling of being a better American, a consciousness that he has done something for his day and generation and contributed much to humanity and the future.

The hour of decision is now upon America. There must be a choice between parties, between platforms, and between men. We must choose between the New Deal party, dominated by Hillman and his cohorts, with its record of ruin and waste, and the Republican party, which is led by dynamic young men with truly American backgrounds and with records of success. We must choose between the New Deal platform which boasts of what it has done to the United States, coupled with pledges to go farther in the same direction, and the Republican platform which charts an American administration for the whole American people. And we must choose between men—Dewey and Bricker against Roosevelt and Truman.[7]

Roosevelt has been president for twelve long years. He has failed to solve a single problem. He has been a conspicuous failure as an administrator and is now tired, exhausted, and surrounded by a quarreling, contentious group of useless intimates. Truman is the product of the Pendergast machine,[8] and no one has even suggested that he was fit to be president if that responsibility should fall upon him.

Thomas E. Dewey has won the hearts of all Americans by his battles for good government. He was successful in his fights in New York, first as district attorney, and then as governor of the Empire State.

Difficulties do not deter him.

Obstacles do not frighten him.

The people of the United States now need his services. Indeed, they require them in their present crisis.

They want him to end the confusion that reigns in Washington.

They desire him to disperse the hordes of useless officeholders swarming at the capital and all over the land.

They have chosen him to slay the sprawling octopus that is sucking the very lifeblood of the federal government.

He is the chosen leader of the people to stop the excesses of the New Deal, to return the federal government to a rule of law, and to put the multitude of bureaucrats on the toboggan.

The people have had enough of being pushed around by petty tyrants in high positions, in which they were put without being elected and to which not one of them could be elected. They have been sickened at the sight of the open alliance of the national administration with the corrupt city machines. The people resent the use of federal patronage to feed the grasping demands of partisan political bosses. They have made up their minds to strike down the "new instruments of power" invented by the New Dealers "to shackle the liberties of the people."

They are appalled at the ever-increasing burden of federal taxes that has been levied upon our people, and they are apprehensive at the astronomical debt that has been laid upon this and future generations of Americans.

The American people do not like the kind of government the New Dealers have fostered, and they have determined that it is time to change. They demand new blood, new vigor, and a new direction.

Governor John W. Bricker has proven his fitness to be vice-president or president. His record as governor of Ohio, like that of Governor Dewey in New York, commands the confidence of the people. We have the men to lead. We have the right on our side. Our country has suffered enough at the hands of the New Deal. The moment to decide is now, and that decision must be that Dewey and Bricker will be triumphantly elected next November.

With that election, this country will enter upon a new era of progress and prosperity.

----

1. Sidney Hillman (1887-1946). Lithuanian-born, imprisoned for labor activities there, moved to the United States; leader in clothing strike in Chicago; president of Amalgamated Clothing Workers, 1914-46; member NRA and NIRA labor advisory boards; helped establish CIO and became vice-president; associate director general of Office of Production Management, 1940-42; helped form World Federation of Trade Unions in 1945. *DAB, Supplement 4:* 375-77.

2. Earl Browder (1891-1973). Accountant; lawyer; manager of farm cooperative store; in prison during World War I for opposition to draft; edited pro-Communist paper in Kansas in 1919; jailed sixteen months on conspiracy charge; head of U.S. Communist party, 1930-46; author of *Marx and America.* New York *Times,* June 28, 1973.

3. Robert Emmet Hannegan (1903-1949). Attorney; chairman of St. Louis Democratic Central Committee, 1934-35; Truman-supported collector of internal revenue for eastern district of Missouri, 1942; U.S. commissioner of internal revenue, 1943; chairman of Democratic National Committee, 1944; postmaster general, 1945-47; owner of St. Louis baseball team, 1948-49. *DAB, Supplement 4:* 356.

4. James Francis Byrnes (1879-1972). South Carolina attorney; solicitor, sec-

ond circuit court, 1908-10; U.S. House of Representatives, 1911-25; U.S. Senate, 1931-41; Supreme Court, 1941-42; director of economic stabilization, 1942-43; director of U.S. War Mobilization Board, 1943-45; U.S. secretary of state, 1945-47; governor of South Carolina, 1951-55. *Biographical Directory of Governors*, 4: 1438-39.

5. Frank Hague. See document dated September 29, 1943, in "Preinaugural Addresses" section.

6. Edward Joseph Flynn (1891-1953). Attorney; New York state assemblyman, 1917-21; sheriff of Bronx County, 1921; as chairman of Democratic executive committee after 1922, he controlled party affairs in the Bronx for thirty years; New York secretary of state, 1929-39; national chairman of Democratic party, 1940-43. *DAB, Supplement 5:* 227- 28.

Tammany Hall, a term derived from the meeting place, was the name given the powerful New York City Democratic organization.

7. Harry S Truman (1884-1972). Judge of Jackson County, Missouri, court, 1922-24, and presiding judge 1926-34; U.S. senator, 1934-45; vice-president of U.S., 1945; president of U.S., 1945-53. *Who Was Who in America . . . 1969-1973,* 5: 732.

8. Thomas Joseph Pendergast (1872-1945). Deputy county marshal of Kansas City, 1896-1900; city superintendent of streets, 1900-02; county marshal, 1902-04; city council, 1910-14; operated a wholesale liquor business, concrete factory, and hotel; as Democratic city boss, he endorsed Harry Truman's successful bid for county judge and became important in New Deal patronage; convicted of income tax evasion in 1939. *DAB, Supplement 3:* 596-97.

REPUBLICAN RALLY FOR BRICKER
Bowling Green / October 2, 1944

SIXTEEN years is too long for any one man to be president. Three million, one hundred and thirteen thousand federal employees is too great a load for the people to carry. The countless bureaus, agencies, authorities, and commissions set up by this administration are too much for any government to support or any people to bear.[1]

The people of the United States realize this fact and they are going to end the New Deal next November 7. This is a year of crisis. We stand at the crossroads and must choose now the type of government we shall have at Washington for the next four years. We have to choose between parties, between platforms, and between men.

In the choice between parties, we are limited to the New Deal party and the Republican party. There is no longer a Democratic party as it was once known to the people of this country. The New Deal excesses have driven out of the old Democratic party all the men with convictions and traditional principles who believe in a government of the people, by the people, and for the people. The New Deal party is dominated by the big city bosses, Sidney Hillman, with his Political Action Committee and his recruits from the Browder Communists, with the New Deal excess baggage headed by their candidate for a fourth term.

The Republican party has demonstrated in twenty-six states its fitness and capacity to govern. In three-fourths of the population of the nation Republican governors and Republican administrations are giving the people good government and restoring confidence and faith in our institutions. Between this motley crew masquerading under the name of New Dealers, and the Republican party as represented by Governors Dewey and Bricker, the people must make their decision.

The platform of the New Deal party is composed of two things: first, a reliance upon what it has done to the people in twelve years, and a promise for the next four years that it will not repent or reform. Hillman has solemnly stated: "We know what we want," and since everything is to be "cleared through Sidney,"[2] it is very plain that if the New Deal succeeds Hillman and Browder will get what they want.

The platform of the Republican party is based on the philosophy that the people are the government and that it should be administered according to the Constitution and laws enacted by their chosen representatives. They do not want to be pushed around by petty tyrants in big places to which they were not elected and to which not one of them could be elected.

And, finally, there must be a choice between men. On the one hand we have worn out, tired, and quarrelsome men, each suspicious of the others. These men, grown tired in the offices they held, are not anything like as tired as the people are of having them in the offices. On the other hand the Republican party gives you men with vigor, ability, and harmony among themselves, with perfect faith in our country.

We have with us today the Republican candidate for vice-president, who typifies the best there is in American life. He has had experience in difficult times. When he became governor he found the state of Ohio, like the nation is now, overloaded with debt, overcrowded with parasites, and confused with conflicting clamor for place and power. He has paid off the debts, he has accumulated a surplus, and he has demonstrated to the satisfaction of the people of Ohio what good government means for their state. He has the courage to face any issue, and he has the character and intelligence to solve the problems of the future. He has a firm and unyielding grasp of the principles of government, and he has faith in the American people. He is not discouraged by difficulties, and he is not afraid of obstacles. Being governor of our neighboring state of Ohio, the people of Kentucky have watched his progress with admiration and affection. They rejoiced in his nomination for vice-president, as the unanimous choice of a great Republican convention. His opponent was selected under circumstances which have put him on the defensive. Nobody has ever claimed Senator Truman was selected because of any public service he ever rendered or because of any peculiar fitness for the office. He was selected by the city bosses because he is one of the favorite products of the city machine. The difference between the parties and the difference between the men presented to the American people is sharply illustrated by the two men selected for vice-president. Senator Truman had to be "cleared with Sidney," but Governor Bricker was the choice of the Republican party.

The philosophy of government which dominates the New Deal has outraged the American people, and they will have no more of it. It is time to restore integrity to the White House and all along the line. Governor Bricker for vice-president and Governor Dewey for president have won the hearts of all Americans by what they are, by what they have done, and by what they are prepared to do for the good of the American people. It is my privilege and my very great pleasure to present to you the governor of Ohio, the Republican nominee for vice-president, the Honorable John W. Bricker.

---

1. Governor Willis gave virtually the same speech at Columbus, Ohio, on October 13; at Providence, Rhode Island, on October 17; and at Evansville, Indiana, on November 4, 1944. These are not included.

2. President Roosevelt's remark concerning his choice of a running mate—"Clear it with Sidney [Hillman]"—became a Republican rallying point.

TELEGRAM TO SENATOR BARKLEY
Frankfort / October 9, 1944

"IT has been brought to my attention that you stated in a public speech that I did not sign the bill giving soldiers away from home the right to vote," Willis said in a telegram to Senator Barkley.

"This is an error which I hope you will correct immediately. I signed the bill for absentee soldier ballots as soon as it was presented to me.[1]

"An insinuation that the Republican administration at Frankfort has not cooperated fully in all movements to benefit returning soldiers is without basis in fact. Every bill for the benefit of soldiers and sailors was approved and signed by me.

"I further recommended a constitutional amendment for the permanent benefit of soldiers.[2] This recommendation was partially followed, but the legislature failed to adopt that part of my recommendation to the effect that soldiers in the service would be exempted from taxation and that their property be exempted from seizure while they are in the service of their country."[3]

---

1. Chapter 134 (House Bill 255), "an act relating to elections . . . declaring who is an absent voter," more readily enabled soldiers to vote. It was passed March 10, 1944, enrolled March 13, and approved four days later. That was roughly the average amount of time between enrollment and approval. Kentucky *Acts* (1944), 282-91.

2. See "State of the Commonwealth" message of January 10, 1944, in the "Legislative Actions, 1943-1945" section for Governor Willis's recommendations.

3. The only constitutional amendment concerning soldiers focused on their voting rights. See Kentucky *Acts*, 6-7.

RALLY OF INDIANA REPUBLICANS
Boswell, Indiana / October 10, 1944

KENTUCKY'S GOP governor made a fighting, partisan speech which covered the whole range of his party's attack from "end regimentation" to "clear everything with Sidney [Hillman]."

He explained how he won his race for governor of Kentucky last year with the aid of the votes of Democrats when some Republicans in the Bluegrass State said there was no hope for victory.

"Now the Republicans in Kentucky are not afraid," he continued. "We have a fine candidate running against Senator Barkley, and I can give you my very good promise that there will be a new Republican vote in the Senate after November."[1]

In addition, Willis said, the GOP would have some new Republican congressmen. All this will happen, Willis declared, because Democrats themselves, everywhere, are tired of the present Democratic national administration, and in Kentucky, "Almost as many Democrats as Republicans are contributing to our campaign. . . .

"If anything has sickened our Kentuckians it was that the president should offer to clear everything with Sidney."

With this as a springboard, Willis impeached President Roosevelt's denial of support from Communists, saying Earl Browder proved by his own words that the Communists were supporting Roosevelt.

Other points of attack emphasized by Willis were:

On regimentation—"There never was a government agent who had enough sense to run a farm. If he did he would be running a farm instead of being a government agent."

On wartime controls—"It never was necessary to ration anything in this war. All that was needed was to tell the people what to do. It was all done to make jobs for Democrats—not the kind that voted for me over in Kentucky and will vote for Dewey—but Democrats who follow the New Deal."

On bureaucracy—"Executive orders that create agents to reach their hands into the pockets of the people."

Democratic ticket—"Truman is a product of the Pendergast machine, picked by big city bosses and 'cleared with Sidney.' The people should never vote for a man for vice-president who would not be fit to be president in event a tragic event should make it necessary for him to serve."

President Roosevelt—"A tired and worn-out man who never worked a day himself and who never has met a payroll."

The president's administration—"The administration is not half as tired and worn-out as the people are with them."

Summing up the case for the Republicans, Governor Willis recalled the story of the man who received a telegram from an undertaker saying that the man's mother-in-law was dead and asking whether the body should be embalmed, cremated, or buried.

"The man answered without hesitation, 'Take no chances. Embalm, cremate, and bury,' " Willis said, amid gales of laughter. "And I say to you take no chances with the New Deal. Embalm it, cremate it, and bury it."

---

1. That vote would not be from Kentucky. Barkley defeated Republican James Park by a count of 464,053 (54.8 percent) to 380,425 (44.9 percent), a margin of over 83,000 votes. Jewell, *Kentucky Votes*, 1:49.

INTERVIEW REGARDING ELECTION
Indianapolis, Indiana / October 10, 1944

A PREDICTION that the Bluegrass State would join with Indiana in giving Republican presidential nominee Thomas E. Dewey its electoral vote was made in an interview here last night by Governor Simeon Willis of Kentucky.[1]

The Kentuckian declared "this issue of communism is a very important one in this campaign. This issue is driving many old-line Democrats away from their party. They don't like the association with Earl Browder and Sidney Hillman."

Willis asserted that Majority Leader Alben W. Barkley, who is seeking his fourth term as senator from Kentucky, faced an uphill fight and that it was common talk in Kentucky that Barkley "kicked Roosevelt in the pants and then grabbed his coattails."[2]

He said it is the objective of Republicans in his state to defeat Senator Alben Barkley and, with that, to score a complete Republican victory. Asked by what margin the GOP would carry Kentucky, Governor Willis said, "I'm a warrior and not a prophet."

He added that the Democratic organization in the Bluegrass State is claiming victory by a small majority.

The swing against the New Deal, he said, is coming from old, red-blooded Jeffersonian Democrats who don't like the thought of associating with the Hillmans and Browders.

One of the best harbingers of a Republican victory in Kentucky, he said, was "the general upsurge all over the state." The Republican gains there in 1943, he said, were uniform in all sections and with all occupations. "This brought a definite improvement in Republican morale," he commented.

Speaking of Senator Barkley, who broke with the president several months ago and then joined the New Deal fold, Governor Willis said, "People always take Barkley's latest position on any subject to be his real one. His position, therefore, has to be redefined frequently."[3]

---

1. Franklin D. Roosevelt carried Kentucky by a vote of 472,589 (54.5 percent) to 392,448 (45.2 percent); Dewey, however, did win Indiana's electoral vote by a 94,488 margin. Congressional Quarterly, *Presidential Elections Since 1789* (Washington, D.C., 1975), 92.

2. A reference to the tax veto controversy discussed in the note to the document dated August 3, 1944, in this section.

3. This is a composite account drawn from the Lexington *Leader,* October 11, 1944, and the Indianapolis *News,* October 12, 1944.

TELEGRAM TO SENATOR BARKLEY
Enroute to New Castle, Indiana / October 11, 1944

THANKS for your telegram correcting your earlier misstatement.[1] Your further questions to me indicate that your source of information is still unreliable.

The bills and my action on them are of record in secretary of state's office and you need not rely on misinformation.

I vetoed a ripper bill that took the administration of the disabled veterans service out of the hands of the lieutenant governor, the adjutant general, and the state commander of the American Legion and placed it in unofficial hands, excluding the veterans of the present war and many veterans of previous wars from any representation at all.[2]

I also vetoed two acts which were protested against by representatives of the Social Security Board as destructive of the merit system, thereby endangering federal assistance. I recommended corrections of the acts to make them conform to federal laws, but my recommendations were not accepted by the legislature and my vetoes were not overridden.[3]

Do you favor any one of the acts which I vetoed?

The attorney general of Kentucky obtained a declaratory judgment sustaining the validity of the absent voters law.

This proceeding was necessary to meet questions raised as to the validity of the law and which had to be met to enable the secretary of state to carry out its terms.

Are you accepting support in your race for a fourth term from Hillman and Browder, or will you do so?

Last February you stated that the president made a calculated and deliberate assault upon the legislative integrity of every member of Congress.

Have you changed your view on that statement? If not, how can you support the president for reelection in the light of that assault?

As you are a candidate, the voters are entitled to know your latest views and to be advised of your changes of position.

---

1. Senator Barkley had sent a telegram the day before, admitting his error in declaring that Willis had failed to sign the soldiers' vote bill. He addressed two further questions to the governor, however, and this document is Willis's response to those queries. *Courier-Journal*, October 12, 1944.

2. House Bill 170 gave the governor power to appoint five members to the Disabled Ex-Servicemen's Board. The appointees were to come from a list of three names for each position, the list to be approved and submitted by the American Legion's executive committee. It was adopted February 17, 1944, by the House and March 10 by the Senate; Governor Willis vetoed it on March 25, 1944. See Kentucky *House Journal* (1944), 1592-1600, and *Courier-Journal*, March 26, 1944.

3. For Governor Willis's veto of Senate Bills 21 and 29, see the "State Government Administration" section.

REPUBLICAN RALLY
Portsmouth, Ohio / October 12, 1944

"PRESIDENT ROOSEVELT has been in office too long, and the liberties we have known are in grave peril," Governor Simeon S. Willis of Kentucky declared.

Asserting that "you must choose in November between a New Deal party and a Republican party whose governors in twenty-six states have returned their government to the people," Willis urged that you "feel the vast importance of this election to yourselves, your children, and your children's children and vote for the trend back to liberty."

"The Democratic party of old basically no longer exists," Willis said, "and it has been replaced by a New Deal party. The New Deal party is a three-legged stool—one leg, useless office holders; the second, Sidney Hillman, with whom he clears; and the third, Earl Browder and his four hundred thousand Labor party votes in New York State."

Charging that President Roosevelt has "made common cause with this nation's enemies, including Communist Earl Browder, who is fighting to reelect him for a fourth term," Willis declared that the "defeat of any man who unites with Browder is essential to America's liberty."

"They are trying to elect him for a fourth term; that would be an aggregate of sixteen years. Sixteen minutes is too long for a president who makes common cause with the country's enemies to serve."

"The New Deal administration," Willis said, "exercises arbitrary powers over the rights of the American people through its bureaus. There is not a bureaucratic agency operating successfully. They quarrel over power and they are failures."

Referring to Senator Alben W. Barkley's fight with Roosevelt last February, Willis declared Barkley "got mad at the president and attacked him openly. But that didn't last long," he said, "and now Barkley is supporting Roosevelt for a fourth term. We want to see that neither of them gets a fourth term."

Discussing the bureaucratic control of agriculture and industry, Willis asserted that "people are not wise enough to supplant the laws and nature, and the farmer will plant what he knows his land will produce. Industry will produce what it can sell. The administration has throttled business with antagonistic laws."

Referring to the staggering national debt, Governor Willis declared that the only way it could be mastered was by "the industry and thrift of the American people."

TELEGRAM TO SENATOR BARKLEY
Youngstown, Ohio / October 16, 1944

YOUR wire of October 13 has just reached me here.[1]

There is a lack of candor or a failure of comprehension in your references to the bills vetoed by me and to the suit conducted by the attorney general. I have allotted $35,000 from the governor's emergency fund to pay the expense of soldiers' voting and will spare no effort in my power to give the opportunity to vote to every Kentucky voter in the service of our country.

You distort my written words and you misrepresent my official acts. You dared not answer my questions, but resorted to evasion and subterfuge.

Your deliberate misstatements regarding my campaign last year, and respecting the orderly accomplishment of my constructive program this year, prove that you were trying to create confusion to conceal your own record.

Your telegram discloses that you are so far out of touch with Kentucky that you do not know what documents are filed in the secretary of state's office.

The program advocated by me last year, and opposed by you, has been largely accomplished despite your opposition and the obstruction of your present campaign manager. My whole program will be achieved during my term of office. The second report to the people on August 31[2] contains a statement of the facts, both as to things already accomplished and plans for final completion of the entire program.

Last year you tried to divert attention from the record of your gang at Frankfort, and this year you seek to dodge your own record at Washington.

You will not be allowed to run away from your own words, or to escape from your own alliances and antics. Hillman and Browder may not vote in Kentucky, but they have agents in the state and are spending money to elect you and their other friends on the New Deal ticket. If you do not repudiate their support, the public will expect and demand that you explain what you have given for that aid.

You say that Hillman contributed to the campaign fund to elect District Attorney Dewey several years ago. If that is true, it is now plain that Hillman could not clear with the district attorney because he sent the gangsters and crooks to prison and in some instances to the electric chair. Hillman did not like that and now chooses to spend millions to elect a New Deal crowd that will "clear everything with Sidney."

Your shuddering at the mention of embalming, cremating, and burying shows your fright and explains your desperation as you contemplate your approaching political fate on November 7.

----

1. Answering Governor Willis's telegrams of October 12 (in this section), Senator Barkley had attacked the state's chief executive for his stands on the income tax question and on state expenses. He then dismissed Willis's previous reference to Sidney Hillman, saying that Hillman had contributed to Dewey's campaign when Dewey was a candidate for district attorney. See *Kentucky Post*, October 13, 1944.

2. In the "Legislative Actions, 1943-1945" section.

REMARKS REGARDING ELECTION
Frankfort / October 23, 1944

GOVERNOR SIMEON WILLIS returned to his office today after a six-state speaking tour in behalf of Governor Thomas E. Dewey, convinced that Dewey's organization of the twenty-six Republican governors at St. Louis has been the most productive single factor in the Republican nominee's campaign for president.

Asked how he thinks Kentucky will go November 7, the governor replied, "Well, the experts and some of the polls seem to give Roosevelt a small advantage, but I sense a definite trend to Dewey. You might say my own barber poll shows Dewey will carry the state."

Willis expressed belief Dewey would carry Kentucky and the nation and said that at all the meetings he addressed in Indiana, Ohio, Rhode Island, New York, New Jersey, and West Virignia on his trip standing room was at a premium except in one instance.[1]

----

1. As earlier noted, Kentucky gave its electoral votes to Roosevelt; Dewey carried twelve states with 99 votes, while Roosevelt won thirty-six states and 432 electoral votes. *Presidential Elections*, 35.

REPUBLICAN RALLY
Lexington / October 27, 1944

LAST night over the radio a more or less famous editor of this city, Tom Underwood, is reported in the role of a critic of the state administration.[1] He first apologized for his folly, but went through with it at the demand of somebody. But you should not be too hard on Tom, for he is suffering a lot these days. You know last year he lost his reputation as a prophet when he predicted a majority of twenty thousand for my opponent.

Then he lost his job with the State Racing Commission. He also lost to Lyter [Donaldson] his position as chairman of the Democratic State [Central] Executive Committee, which deflated his ego and damaged his political prestige. Now he is about to lose the confidence and respect of the people, and his pretense of being a gallant and chivalrous gentleman is no longer regarded seriously by the good people of central Kentucky.

He supports the bumbling Barkley against Lexington's favorite son, James Park, whom Underwood admits is the finest man he ever knew. He goes out of his way to make cheap flings at a lady with whom he has no more than a speaking acquaintance,[2] and he talks about subjects with which he has not even a bowing acquaintance.

His desperate struggle to swallow the Hillman-Browder-Barkley fourth term mess has left him cynical and sad, and I ask you to forgive him and forget his mistakes.

---

1. Thomas Rust Underwood (1898-1956). Newspaper editor, Lexington *Herald*, 1935-56; secretary of Kentucky State Racing Commission, 1934-49; U.S. congressman, 1949-51; appointed to fill vacancy in U.S. Senate, 1951, defeated for that office in 1952. *Who's Who, 1956-57*, 2625; Thomas Rust Underwood Papers, Special Collections, University of Kentucky Library.

2. The reference is to Governor Willis's wife, Ida.

REPUBLICAN RALLY
Paintsville / October 28, 1944

IT was particularly pleasing to see the final link in the Paintsville-Louisa-Ashland road under construction. For twenty-five years many people have struggled to get this road completed. It is a vitally important road and was recently released by the War Labor Board for immediate construction. The road to Inez badly needs completion, and it will be attended to as soon as the after-the-war pool is opened. The people realize that the whole power of the state is supporting the war effort, and construction projects must await the release of men and materials. The obvious trend in the campaign is to the Republicans. It is noted by all the observers and has been fully reported in the papers. The time to change has arrived. Great enthusiasm for Dewey and Bricker, Park, and Gabbard is apparent wherever you go; and it seems to me that the rising tide points to Republican victory on November 7.

I have been made very happy by the warm greetings of my friends in the Sandy Valley, and I thank them one and all.

REPUBLICAN RALLY
Lexington / October 31, 1944

EVERYONE must appreciate the serious concern of the people about the issues of the pending contest. They rightly appraise it as one of deep and lasting effect on this and future generations of Americans.

The candidate for a fourth term in the presidency first promised that he would not campaign in the usual way. He soon forgot this promise, and at the teamsters meeting in Washington he resorted to ridicule and cheap comedy, followed by the rowdy assault on some convalescent naval men at the Statler Hotel.[1] This proceeding shocked all thoughtful people and alarmed the New Dealers. Immediately the candidate abandoned his first plan, as promised, and since then has been carrying on a regular barnstorming campaign in his usual, familiar style. He is concentrating his attention on the big cities where the city bosses have machines that control large blocs of votes. The strategy is perfectly apparent. It is to muster enough votes in the boss-controlled big centers of population to overcome the Republican majorities in the portion of the states outside the big cities. That is true in New York, where the fourth termers are counting on Tammany Hall, the Hat, Hillman, and Browder, to amass enough votes in the city to exceed the Republican majority in upstate New York. It is the same plan they successfully used in 1940. They are doing the same thing in New Jersey, where Hague reigns; in Chicago, where Kelly rules; and in other states where the big city vote is concentrated and controlled. If he could carry the electoral votes of these states it would be enough, when added to the Solid South, to secure another lease of life of four years for the New Deal.

It is clear now that the voters are ready to make their decision. They are fed up on the New Deal record of blundering, incompetence, and confusion. They are tired of hearing the fourth-term candidate make promises already discredited by his official conduct contrary to such promises. They resent the endless repetition of his egotistic "I", which the candidate used forty-one times in his Chicago speech last week.[2] He has used it countless times during his twelve years in office. In tone, in spirit, and in arrogant expression, the speeches of the fourth-term candidate are self-revealing. They show him as the personification of one-man government. From his long time in office, and the patient endurance of the public, the man who wants sixteen years of power thinks of himself as the be-all and the know-all in government. It is the unconscious arrogance of conscious power long enjoyed. One-man government at home and abroad has become an obsession with the New Dealers, and intolerance of dissent has led to an insolent assumption of invincible power in one indispensable candidate. It is necessary but to recall his condescending to grant to the people of the nation a "breathing spell" from the New Deal depredations on business, large, small, and medium sized. Likewise his boastful desire to be the master of the people, and at last his proud and sinister declaration that he had created "new instruments of power" capable of "shackling the liberties of the people."

The philosophy of the New Deal has spread throughout the government, both at home and abroad. The same excess of officials and of expense is observed. The foreign field is in the same mess as is the administration at home. Senator Butler's report on South America,[3] and such fragments of information as have been obtained from other nations, show the confusion wrought by New Deal bungling. The shipping of scrap iron to Japan, while that nation was preparing to make war on us, was carried on until shortly before Pearl Harbor.[4] The deal with Browder and the Communists has sickened the whole American people. I do not know what you think about it, but I can never believe that the citizens of Kentucky desire to vote with Earl Browder and his Communist associates. When Browder declared that the election of the fourth-term candidate was necessary for the aims of the Communists, he proved to the people of the United States that the defeat of that candidate was necessary for the safety of America. He has driven all of the Democrats of conviction and by tradition out of the New Deal party. He has no real Democrats as his close advisers. No, not one.

In a message to Congress on January 12, 1937, the fourth-term candidate made this declaration: "If we have faith in our republican form of government, and in the ideals upon which it has rested for 150 years, we must devote ourselves energetically and courageously to the task of making that government efficient. The great stake in efficient democracy is the stake of the common man . . . . In striving together to make our government more efficient, you and I are taking up in our generation the battle to preserve that freedom of self-government which our forefathers fought to establish and hand down to us. . . . Our struggle now is against confusion, against ineffectiveness, against waste, against inefficiency. This battle, too, must be won, unless it is to be said that in our generation national self-government broke down and was frittered away in bad management." In the face of this noble declaration that candidate has given the most extravagant, the most wasteful, and the most inefficient administration of government known to history. Characteristic of the whole New Deal program, they have held forth bright promises and fine objectives, only to betray the people into confusion, waste, and bewilderment. It has grown worse from day to day and from year to year and will continue to grow worse until the whole New Deal outfit is defeated.

It is time to change senators, too. In defeating the fourth term in Kentucky the people should also defeat the bumbling Barkley. He himself declared, in his speech on February 23, 1944, that for twelve years he had carried the flag of Franklin D. Roosevelt. Since Franklin D. Roosevelt is to be defeated on November 7, Barkley will have no flag to carry, and there will be no use for him in the Senate. In that same speech Senator Barkley made the statement that the president had "made a calculated and deliberate assault upon the legislative integrity of every member of Congress. Other members of Congress may do as they please, but as for me, I do not propose to take this unjustifiable assault lying down." The senator achieved a momentary glory by his show of spunk, but he laid back down, and has been taking it ever since and liking it. Senator Barkley referred to the president's unjustifiable methods and inferred that the president was using material cooked up for him by others. He said, in so many words, "the president has resorted to one of the most unjustifiable methods of calculation it is possible to conjure up, which obviously was handed to him by a mind more clever than honest."

A few days ago the president referred to Governor Dewey's campaign as a "Me Too" campaign, indicating that the governor was imitating the tactics of the fourth-term candidate. On the same page of the newspaper Senator Barkley was quoted as stating that Governor Dewey's campaign was "low grade." It was probably what Mr. Barkley regarded as "low grade" that made the fourth-term candidate mistake it for an imitation of his own practices. The fourth-term candidate has made and disregarded so many promises, and Senator Barkley has been on so many sides of so many questions, that it is no longer possible for them to get together on anything. Both have served entirely too long. Both have become arrogant and careless of the rights of the people.

Finally, Senator Barkley, in that same speech, said spectacularly: "But, Mr. President, there is something more precious to me than any honor that can be conferred upon me by the Senate of the United States or by the people of Kentucky, or by the president of the Republic, and that is the approval of my own conscience and my own self-respect." Alas, he has forgotten his self-proclaimed conscience and self-respect, and is now exerting all his powers of endurance to aid the man he denounced in an effort to get for him what no man should have, and in trying to inflict upon this great country a degradation it does not deserve, by lining up with Browder and his crowd.

Fortunately we have the right leaders to take over in Governor Dewey and James Park.[5] They are young men of high character, fine records, and sound philosophies of government. They possess the confidence of the people. They understand the necessity of government according to the Constitution. They understand the need of returning this nation to a government of law. They realize the peril of going in debt year after year until today we have a national debt that exceeds the assessed value of all the real estate in all the forty-eight states of the Union.

A new day will dawn with the election of Governor Dewey as president, with a Congress to support him. James Park is the man to represent Kentucky in the Senate. He knows Kentucky and her people; he knows her institutions and her industries and her interests, and he will represent them faithfully.

The day of one-man government in a great country like the United States is at an end. The day of rubber stamp senators has passed away. The greatest waster and spender of all time, the greatest creator of bureaucracy in all the world, must retire to private life in order that the country may revive and go forward to production and development in order to pay the great debt that has been fastened upon us.

The voters are ready to change from the kind of government that they have been having to the kind of government ordained by the forefathers, which is the only government worthy of Kentuckians and Americans.

It is time to change the president and it is time to change the senator, too.[6]

---

1. The reference is to Roosevelt's famous "Fala" speech on September 23, 1944, during which he was interrupted some fifty-six times by "cheers, laughter, and table-thumping" from the crowd of one thousand, according to the Washington *Post*, September 24, 1944.

2. On October 28, 1944, President Roosevelt had delivered a forty-five-minute address to a crowd of eighty-four thousand at Chicago's Soldier Field. As printed, the address contained the words "I, me, my," some thirty-seven times. FDR, however, used "we, our, us" some ninety-four times. See Chicago *Tribune*, October 29, 1944.

3. Hugh Butler, Republican senator from Nebraska, reported to the Senate on November 26, 1943, and January 20, 1944, that, based on his recent trip to Latin America, the American Good Neighbor policy there had failed. He estimated that over the last three years the policy had cost the United States more than $6 billion. Democrats denounced both his conclusions and his estimates. See *Congressional Record*, 78th Congress, 2nd Session, 441-48; appendix A, 2733-35.

4. The United States declared a full embargo on all iron and steel cargo shipments to Japan on September 26, 1940. See Robert Dallek, *Franklin D. Roosevelt and American Foreign Policy, 1932-1945* (New York, 1979), 241.

5. James Park (1892-1970). Attorney; professional baseball player, 1915-20; coach and athletic director at Transylvania College and coach at the University of Kentucky, 1915-16, 1919-22; member, Kentucky legislature, 1922; county attorney for Fayette, 1926-27; elected commonwealth attorney, 1927, 1933, 1939, 1945; delegate to Republican national conventions; board of trustees, University of Kentucky; defeated for U.S. senator in 1944. Lexington *Herald*, December 18, 1970; *Who's Who in Kentucky, 1936*, 310.

6. His address was delivered over the radio in Lexington.

REPUBLICAN RALLY
Owensboro / November 3, 1944

SIMEON WILLIS, speaking here Friday night in the courthouse to one of the largest crowds of the campaign, likened the New Deal to a three-legged stool.[1] One leg, he said, consisted of 313,000 officeholders under the New Deal, to which he alleged 96,000 have been added within the past three months of the national campaign. Another, he said, was the Roosevelt alliance with the Hillman-Browder element that he claimed is heading the government toward communism; and the third leg he named for the big city bosses, the nucleus about which, Governor Willis said, the New Deal was built.

Governor Willis, who was a judge of the Court of Appeals, and one of the state's leading lawyers before his election to the governorship last November, used the pleading tactics of a skilled attorney in presenting his arguments, submitting to the audience a series of charges against the Roosevelt administration's New Deal, which he asserted bordered on the surrender of individual liberty and the assumption of authority by the government. And this, the governor said, is contrary to the American way.

After a severe denunciation of "the rapid encroachments of communistic influences of America," citing the surrender of initiative by the farmers, bankers, and businessmen generally under "the lashing demands of the New Deal," he dealt at length with rationing. The governor said:

"No one objects to rationing where there is a shortage of something and rationing is necessary to secure fair and equal distribution of such supply as there may be. What the people resent is the excesses committed in the name of rationing.

"Everyone appreciates the patriotic service rendered by many good citizens in seeking to carry on a sensible, sound and equitable rationing of essential things which are not sufficient to supply the demand. Yet no one doubts that great abuses have been perpetrated in the salaried positions and in the administration of the whole rationing setup. The people willingly submit to any sacrifice that is necessary to make the war effort a success and to enforce a fair distribution of necessary things. That spirit of patriotism and cooperation should be protected against the confusion, injustice, and bungling that has been allowed.

"No restrictions on the rights and liberties of the people should be made unless necessary, and even then the restrictions should cease when the necessity ends.

"The simple truth about the whole matter should be given to the people so that they might judge for themselves the quality of service and be prepared to meet the actual requirements.

"The abuses of the old WPA should not be carried over into the rationing of necessities. Rationing should not be made a dumping ground for New Deal politicians. It is the way it has been mishandled that Governor Dewey described in his speech at Buffalo.[2] Governor Dewey said: 'The world trembles in the greatest war of the ages and bureaucracy puts out the following ruling: Mashed potatoes offered a la carte for weekday lunches would be in the same class of food items as potatoes au gratin offered a la carte for weekday lunches, but would be in a different class than mashed potatoes offered a la carte for weekday dinners or Sunday suppers.'

"Well, that's the New Deal way of being mindful of the problems of small business. It's the same from restaurants to beauty shops to the insurance business.

"And that's why it's time for a change—before it's too late."

---

1. This is a composite of an account in the Owensboro *Messenger*, November 4, 1944, and speech portions located in the Willis Papers.

2. Dewey's speech, delivered October 31, 1944, was printed in the New York *Times*, November 1, 1944.

STATEMENT REGARDING WATERFIELD CAMPAIGN SPEECH
Owensboro / November 3, 1944

I LEARNED from the papers this morning that former Speaker of the House Harry Lee Waterfield, and present campaign manager for Senator Barkley, made a speech on the radio last night.

He referred to the election of the Republican ticket last year as a mistake. I have had some experience with Mr. Waterfield. He was Speaker of the House in the last General Assembly. He endeavored to defeat the common school bill. He was largely responsible for the necessity of an extra session. He was an obstructionist and played petty partisan politics with his office as speaker. He cost the taxpayers a large sum of money for an extra session, by refusing to permit the General Assembly to pass the budget bill at the regular session. He wasted many weeks of time in a drive to pass an unconstitutional bill which was correctly described as "The Snooper Bill."[1] He was a complete failure as the Speaker of the House. He refers to my speech at Mt. Sterling, Kentucky, opening my campaign for governor.[2] He mistakes that speech in every reference to it. That speech does not contain anything that Mr. Waterfield attributes to it. The speech was written and was printed in the newspapers and is available to the public at all times. It constitutes a constructive program for Kentucky. All of which will be carried out during my administration. Much of it has been carried into effect already. The school program has been completely fulfilled. If Mr. Waterfield does not think so, let him ask the school leaders and the school children of the state—they know.

The road program is being developed and fully carried out exactly in accordance with the program outlined. The fish and game department has been placed in the hands of sportsmen.[3] Let him ask any sportsman of the state what he thinks of the performance of the program for the sportsman. The welfare department was placed in the hands of the most able, capable, and conscientious men; and they are performing to the eminent satisfaction of the people.

Mr. Waterfield has just discovered that his candidate for the Senate is facing defeat and that his fourth-term campaign is a failure. He turns from the task which he had undertaken and jumps into the campaign of next year, when the people of Kentucky will select a new House of Representatives and one-half of the Senate.

The representatives from this section—Mr. Taylor of Hancock County, Mr. Riley and Mr. Bolling of Daviess County—rendered complete cooperation in all of the constructive programs before the General Assembly.[4] This is the type of men that should be sent to the legislature instead of men like Waterfield, who seek to delay, obstruct, and defeat progressive legislation.

Mr. Waterfield also refers in his speech to the money spent for the maintenance of the mansion. He calls it being spent for window shades and wallpaper.[5] The General Assembly appropriates money for the maintenance of the mansion and other public buildings, and it is being properly expended for that purpose by the engineering department. The money could not be used for any other purpose except maintenance of public buildings. As a matter of fact the amount appropriated for the maintenance of the public buildings was reduced fifty thousand dollars below previous appropriation, and this was done at the direction of the governor. It is absolutely necessary to maintain the public property, and politicians who try to make capital out of ordinary maintenance will find themselves mistrusted by the people.

He also intimated that I was not taking any active part in the current campaign. Evidently, he has not been reading the papers. It is the part I am taking in the campaign which makes him so angry; and it is the success of my meetings everywhere which makes him so bitter.

---

1. House Bill 241, which would create a joint legislative commission to investigate state financial matters, was opposed by the governor. Defeated in the House, the idea was then introduced in the Senate, where it passed 21-15. The House, on a tie vote, again rejected the concept. Representative Claude Hammonds attacked the proposal as "some kind of machine to always be snooping into the affairs of government." See *Courier-Journal*, January 13, February 3, 6, 16, 18, 29, March 2, 3, 1944.

2. See "Preinaugural Addresses" section.

3. See undated letter at end of "State Government Administration" section.

4. C. Waitman Taylor (1898-   ). Car dealer; undertaker; farmer; mayor of Lewisport, 1937-38; elected state representative 1941, 1943. Republican.

Wade D. Riley (1877- ?). Farmer; elected state representative 1935, 1939, 1941, 1943. Democrat.

Douglas T. Bolling (1893-1961). Oil operator; elected state representative 1935, 1939, 1941, 1943; Owensboro Democrat. *Kentucky Directory*, 186, 184, 172; *Courier-Journal*, April 6, 1961.

5. Waterfield, in a November 2, 1944 speech at Louisville, asked what answer Willis could give "if someone asked him how the state can find $15,000 to buy window shades and wallpaper for the governor's mansion he lives in when money is scarce to pay the needy enough to keep body and soul together." *Courier-Journal*, November 3, 1944.

APPOINTMENT OF U.S. SENATOR
Frankfort / November 19, 1945

WHEREAS, there is now a vacancy in the office of the United States Senate from the commonwealth of Kentucky created by the resignation of the Honorable A.B. Chandler, senator from Kentucky, whose written resignation is herewith filed in the office of the secretary of state of Kentucky—[1]

Now, THEREFORE, I, Simeon Willis, governor of the commonwealth of Kentucky, by virtue of the authority vested in me by the Constitution of the United States and the constitution of the commonwealth of Kentucky, do hereby appoint Honorable William A. Stanfill,[2] Hazard, Kentucky, to the office of United States senator to fill the unexpired term of the said A.B. Chandler, and to serve until his successor for the unexpired term shall have been duly elected at the next regular election, as provided by law; and it is ordered that the said William A. Stanfill, of Hazard, Kentucky, be forthwith issued a commission in the manner and form provided by law, as United States senator from the commonwealth of Kentucky.

---

1. In a letter dated October 30, 1945, Senator Chandler resigned his office, effective November 1, in order to serve as commissioner of baseball, a position he had held, without salary, since April of that year. See Chandler to Willis, October 30, 1945, in Executive Order folder dated November 19, 1945, Secretary of State's Records; and William J. Marshall, "A.B. Chandler as Baseball Commissioner, 1945-51: An Overview," *Register of the Kentucky Historical Society* 82 (1984): 360-66.

2. William Abner Stanfill (1892-1971). Attorney; member of board of regents of what is now Morehead State University, 1927-31; chairman of Republican State Central Committee, 1944-48; served as U.S. senator from November 19, 1945 to November 5, 1946. *Biographical Directory, 1949*, 1853; Tapp, *Kentucky Lives*, 518; Lexington *Herald*, June 13, 1971.

WORLD WAR II

STATEMENT REGARDING KENTUCKY MEN
TRAINING AT ST. PETERSBURG, FLORIDA
Undated

SALUTE to Kentucky men in training at St. Petersburg in the United States Maritime Service Training Station, and to all Kentuckians in the armed services stationed in the state of Florida:

The people of Kentucky are justly proud of the present generation of Kentuckians serving in the cause of our country in all the fields of usefulness. Kentucky is a typical pioneer state with traditions of courage, adventure, sacrifice, and achievement. The early settlers conquered a wilderness and constructed a commonwealth. In every stage of history this state has played a part worthy of the heritage given by our fathers.

In every field of service today the Kentuckians are maintaining the highest ideals of service.

In the training stations wherever established, the young Kentuckians are preparing to take the places of those now serving, and to provide the manpower to carry the banner of freedom triumphantly to every battleground.

It is my privilege as governor to extend the greetings and best wishes of the people of Kentucky to Kentuckians throughout the world now serving in the armed services; and in particular, I am happy to greet our boys in training at St. Petersburg in maritime service; and to those stationed in Florida.

Let all be assured that wherever duty may call them in the service of the country, the love and loyalty and prayers of the people of Kentucky will follow them and abide with them in all trials and triumphs.

BOYD COUNTY
LINCOLN DAY DINNER
Ashland / February 12, 1944

"IT is not true that Lincoln lived in a state of poverty.

"He lived in a house as good as his neighbor's. He left Kentucky at the age of eight[1] and lived in Indiana—lived to accomplish many things. The greatest of these was the fact that he was not afraid of work, and that early in his life he pledged himself to destroy slavery," Willis told his fellow townsmen.

"He studied the life of Washington, Henry Clay, and Thomas Jefferson, and thus he studied the works of freedom," Governor Willis declared.

"Through his studies he learned the value of service. Lincoln faced many serious problems in his day, but we face a more serious situation than Lincoln," the speaker said.

"War involves all great dangers, liberties of government, control of government, and justice of government. The greatest danger we face in all three is control of government, and unless we halt this change, God only knows what will happen.

"We lived for 150 years under one rule. During that time we suffered privations, destruction of property rights; and our very existence was threatened at all times. That was a lesson we should never forget. We fought to erase it, and Lincoln struggled to save it.

"Lincoln's spirit is the spirit that made this nation grow from 130,000 to 130,000,000 people," Governor Willis said. "He carved the opportunity for the barefoot boy of yesterday. We must not close the path of opportunity to the barefoot boy of today."

---

1. Actually, Lincoln left Kentucky at age seven.

RED CROSS CAMPAIGN
Frankfort / February 27, 1944

I AM very happy to participate in the opening of the Red Cross campaign. The quota this year for [the] Franklin County chapter is increased 75 percent above last year. The amount required for the present campaign is $38,500. This is rendered necessary by the increased demands made for the services which the Red Cross renders. The goal for the whole nation is $200 million. The drive continues throughout the month of March. The money raised locally is spent for the benefit of the members from this county, except the part sent to the national organization for the men in the service in this country and abroad. The services to the armed forces comprise the greater part of the Red Cross work. In order that you may appreciate the extent of the work, let me give you a few figures.

In Franklin County during the past year 1,644 pints of blood were collected. In the entire field of Red Cross work 5 million pints of blood were collected. This is the greatest lifesaver that has been discovered in many years, and has lowered very greatly the fatalities from casualties. The number of surgical dressings shipped during 1943, from this chapter, was more than a million. In the entire organization 925 million surgical dressings were prepared. The kit bags supplied the soldiers totaled 1,408. Each of these bags contains useful things to make the life of the soldier more comfortable and convenient. There have been many home service cases in this county. Mrs. Lang[1] and her staff handled 1,999 such cases. Loans have been made to servicemen and their families, and medical care and emergency needs have been provided. Assistance has been given soldiers in regard to their furloughs, claims for family allowances, and many other necessary services. The camp and hospital service last year sent 5,864 articles to Fort Knox Station Hospital, Bowman Field Station Hospital, and Nicholas General Hospital. The chairman of this service, Mrs. R.D. Medley,[2] has been elected a member of the Kentuckiana Camp and Hospital Council, which directs the Red Cross work for the hospitals just mentioned.

The Junior Red Cross, employing the younger people, has sent 5,406 articles to the hospitals and to children abroad and to soldiers in hospitals overseas.

In the recruitment of nurses for the service the Franklin County chapter has reached its quota, as has the whole state of Kentucky. They added a program for the recruitment of cadet nurses from high school graduates, and each high school in this county has had speakers on this subject.

The work of the Red Cross is done largely by volunteers. The volunteer special service, of which Mrs. William H. Reese,[3] is chairman, covers a variety of projects. In the past year these volunteers have prepared over a million surgical dressings; knitted 503 garments and sewed an unspecified number. Others have contributed hours of service in the canteen and motor corps units. Forty-six who were trained as nurses' aides in 1943 are pledged to service 150 hours a year in the local hospital, where they assist the trained nurses and are of value to the sick in the community. Many serve beyond the time pledged. Many have taken the staff assistants course and put in hours at the chapter house, typing, filing, working at the switchboard, and doing other office work. Three volunteers assist the chairman of the home service, and Mrs. Julia Buckner[4] is rendering a splendid service with the colored people.

Thus you will see what one county does through the Red Cross. The amount required is $38,500 from this county. I am sure that neither [the] Franklin County chapter nor any chapter in the state will fail to reach its quota. The increasing burden on the Red Cross reflects the increasing war effort and the terrible tragedy of suffering, because it is the sick, wounded, and disabled men that increase the Red Cross services everywhere. So long as there is human suffering and human need the work of the Red Cross will be uppermost in the minds of the merciful and helpful. The American Red Cross has stood shoulder to shoulder with our fighting forces on all the battle grounds. It has extended the hand of help to more than can ever be counted. These helping hands lift loads of care from the hearts of men and women in our military and naval hospitals on land and sea. Red Cross workers with understanding, skill, and devotion carry to the uttermost parts of the earth the Christian spirit which at last must redeem the world. Let us not falter in meeting the needs not only of the local but of the national Red Cross.

---

1. Probably Madeline S. Lang, wife of Gerald J. Lang, auditor of the Social Security Board. *Polk's Frankfort City Directory, 1942* (Cincinnati, 1942), 133; and ibid., *1945-46* (Cincinnati, 1946), 107.

2. Lucile S. Medley, spouse of Reuben D. Medley, a design engineer in the Department of Highways. *Frankfort Directory, 1942*, 151; ibid., *1945-46*, 121.

3. Henrietta M. *Rees* was married to William H. Rees, associate justice of the Court of Appeals. *Frankfort Directory, 1942*, 180; ibid., *1945-46*, 145.

4. Julia S. Buckner was listed as a teacher in the Frankfort Nursery School in the 1945-46 *Frankfort Directory*, 39.

100th ANNIVERSARY OF YMCA
Russell / April 19, 1944

"No nation can be stronger than its citizenship, and the type of each generation is stamped upon each succeeding generation," Governor Simeon Willis said.

Declaring that the only way to have good government is through good citizenship, Governor S.S. Willis last night before more than two hundred guests at a banquet at Russell in observance of the 100th anniversary of the YMCA, added, "The American people have a rich heritage. It is one that is precious and should have the full protection of people with good, Christian character and ideals.

"We are in the midst of a serious war, one with the same background as that in which we won our freedom. We must sacrifice everything for the same ideals and principles for which our forefathers gave their lives in order to keep the paths of opportunity open for the barefoot boy of the future."

Governor Willis told his listeners: "It is up to us today to preserve our rich heritage, to raise people of good Christian character and forethought. No nation can be stronger than its citizenship."[1]

---

1. This address is a composite of accounts in the Lexington *Leader* and the Ashland *Daily Independent*, both of April 20, 1944.

RED CROSS DRIVE
Anco / April 21, 1944

I CONGRATULATE the Knott Coal Corporation and its 138 employees on the record they have made. I congratulate the Red Cross on the inspiration it has given these men.

The employees have contributed to the 1944 Red Cross War Fund an average sum in excess of twenty dollars. A number have contributed the entire pay for three shifts. This is probably the highest per capita contribution of any mine in the nation.

This mine is located in Knott County, a few miles from Hazard and approximately 150 miles from Lexington. The mine works two shifts day and night, six days per week. The average production of coal per man is more than eleven tons.[1] The average for the whole industry is about five and a half tons per man. The miners here are permanently employed. Eighty percent have never worked in any other mine. In some instances three generations of one family work here. They are familiar with the traditions of the Cumberland Mountains, and several of them are skilled in the making of music with the fiddle and the banjo, the guitar, and other instruments that accompany the singing of old ballads. All the workers in the mine are third and fourth generation Americans. All of them are descendants of early settlers from North Carolina and Virginia. All of them are devoted to independence and thrift, and patriotic in the highest degree.

Of the entire quota for Knott County for the Red Cross, more than one-third has been given by this company and its employees at this mine. Largely more than half of the workers live in their own homes on their own land. Many men from here are in the armed services of the nation, in all ranks, from private to lieutenant colonel. The average length of service of the 138 employees is twelve years. Such a record challenges the attention of the nation and inspires the pride of the state.

The Red Cross serves humanity all over the world. It receives gifts from the people according to their ability and gives service to humanity according to its needs. Wherever there is suffering and disaster you will find the Red Cross ministering to the stricken and comforting the heartbroken. It appeals to the best in human nature and commands the gratitude and respect of all the races of men. No one can calculate the good it does, the suffering it lessens, or the comfort it carries to the afflicted.

While man's inhumanity to man still makes countless thousands mourn, the mercy and greatness of the Red Cross spreads over the world and restores faith in human kindness and in man's capacity to rise above the meanness and the cruelty of the wicked and the arrogant.

The record made here is a tribute to the genius of our institutions, under which men and women can work together for their mutual advantage and for the general welfare of all our people. It proves the worth of cooperative effort and demonstrates the capacity of people to pull together for peace and justice.

In this terrible war, which engages all the energies of the nation and engrosses the attention of the whole world, we have an abiding faith in the righteousness of our cause and in the final triumph of American ideals. Our hearts and our prayers are with our brave ones on all the battle fronts of the world. No sacrifice we can make to support them is anything compared to the sacrifice they are making in fighting the battles of our country.

We know, as Senator Ben Hill[2] said, that, "He who saves his country, saves himself, saves all things, and all things saved *do* bless him. He who lets his country die, lets all things die, dies himself ignobly, and all things dying curse him."

Let us here rededicate ourselves to our great task, and with increased devotion to the eternal principles of liberty and justice, again highly resolve to carry on to the end, proving us to be worthy of our heritage, and determined at all costs to preserve for our generation and all future generations of Americans, the last, best hope of earth.

---

1. According to the *Annual Report of the Department of Mines and Minerals . . . for the Year Ended December 31, 1944* (Lexington, [1945]), by that date the Knott Coal Corporation employed 162 men, who worked 295 days a year on the 72-inch seam, producing 396,316 tons of coal. The superintendent was C.A. Combs; the foreman, Kanawha Sloan.

2. Benjamin Harvey Hill (1823-1882). Member, Georgia House of Representatives, 1851; state senator, 1859-60; originally Unionist but later senator in Confederate Congress, 1861-65; U.S. congressman, 1875-77; senator from Georgia, 1877-82. *Biographical Directory, 1949*, 1309.

LEXINGTON OPTIMIST CLUB LUNCHEON
Lexington / June 9, 1944

GOVERNOR SIMEON S. WILLIS declared at the luncheon meeting of the Lexington Optimist Club today that the American people "must resolve that we shall be worthy of the heritage of our forefathers."

Asserting that "these are times of solemn responsibility," the governor said "we must maintain our faith, we must maintain our optimism, we must not fail.

"These are fateful days," the governor continued, "when the creed of the Optimist Club is just as important as the day of the organization's founding. . . . The creed of the Optimist is that thing called morale. . . . It is that thing which ministers call faith. . . . It is that which carries us heroically through times of great sacrifice."

In opening his address, the chief executive said that he was an optimist, literally. "I was an optimist," he said, "or I never would have called the legislature into special session."[1]

---

1. The first special session opened on May 19, 1944. Only three days after this speech, on June 12, 1944, a second special session was called and the budget was approved. See "Legislative Actions, 1943-1945" section.

OPENING OF FIFTH WAR LOAN CAMPAIGN
Louisville / June 12, 1944

"THE brave men at the front who are making heroic sacrifices and thrilling every true American with gratitude and admiration expect those at home to back them to the limit," Governor Willis said.

"They have a right to expect it, and I am confident our people will not disappoint them," he added.

Kentucky's quota of the $16 billion national goal is $118 million, and Jefferson County's is $50 million, the governor pointed out.

A sales plan has been perfected providing for fifteen thousand workers in the field, most of whom are house-to-house canvassers, who are promoting the sale of the "E" bonds, the governor said.

"Such a bond is a practical investment and at least $31 million of that type should be sold," he continued. "It is necessary that these bonds be sold now and regularly each month. They should be held until maturity, making a splendid annuity for each investor. Government bonds are the best investment in the world.

"It is essential for each and all to give the utmost aid. These are fateful days involving the destiny of the United Nations. We are the trustees of a priceless heritage from our heroic forefathers. Let no one falter in preserving that heritage for this generation and for future generations of Americans. May we so perform that our children can truthfully say of us that we proved worthy of our traditions. I bid you Godspeed and triumphant success."

FLAG DAY
Ashland / June 15, 1944

"The flag is the symbol of our country—it represents all of our achievements, all of our people, all of the aspirations of today and of the future," Governor Simeon S. Willis, chief executive of Kentucky, declared before a large audience composed of members of the Daughters of the American Revolution and their friends at the annual Flag Day ceremony in Central Park last night.

"It represents all of our tears, the blood that is shed in battle, the sacrifices of our mothers, wives, and sweethearts, and the hope of mankind. Because of what it represents we love it so," the governor said.

"In fateful days such as this we realize its significance. Each generation must make its own history and because of this we shall not fail," he added.

"Our flag represents the best in human nature, the best in human aspirations, [and] reveals our greatest ambitions," Governor Willis explained.

The governor upheld the present generation and stated that he would take issue with anyone who said that the younger generation had "grown soft." He declared that anyone could see that the young men of today were meeting the responsibilities "like men." "Yesterday," he said, "they were boys, and we thought of them as boys. Today they are men and doing the deeds of great men. The record will show no greater or braver soldiers than our American boys on all of the warfronts," he emphasized.

The governor urged support of the Fifth War Loan drive now being conducted throughout the nation. He explained that it cost money to conduct a war and said that it should not be necessary to be solicited for funds. He declared that it was a privilege for every American to "loan money" to his government in this hour of crisis.

"Don't wait for someone to ask you to buy a bond," the governor appealed, "but go down to a bond booth tomorrow and buy all you can and then go down next week and do the same thing and keep on doing it until the war is brought to a successful close," Willis urged.

The governor closed his address with a stirring appeal for cooperation in all war work. "It is not enough to 'love' the flag," he said, and added, "We must work for it. The individual at home must bear the burden, because liberty is the greatest thing in the world. We are the trustees of the most precious gift. We must keep it for our boys who come home," he concluded.

KENTUCKY LEGION CONVENTION
Lexington / July 26, 1944

VETERANS of both World War I and World War II at the Kentucky Legion convention at the Phoenix Hotel today heard Governor Simeon Willis laud the fighters for great courage and diligence and warn them that they must see to it that no letdowns occur at home to prevent surer, speedier victory abroad.

"The American Legion has been the great stabilizing force for patriotism and justice," Governor Willis said in addressing the legion meeting.

"In this meeting," he added, "a solemn note characterizes all sessions as our hearts are with our comrades on all battlefronts. They are conducting themselves valiantly, and we must see to it that no battles are lost because of our failures; we must not fail them."[1]

---

1. The account is a composite drawn from the Lexington *Leader*, July 26, 1944, and Lexington *Herald*, July 27, 1944.

KENTUCKY STATE FEDERATION OF LABOR
Lexington / September 12, 1944

IN this country, the greatest country in the world in human resources, material resources, and organizing genius, nothing has equalled the performance of the American people in producing the things necessary to carry on the war effort, Governor S.S. Willis yesterday told the delegates to the fortieth annual convention of the Kentucky State Federation of Labor, meeting this week at the Lafayette Hotel.

"This is a tribute to the loyal working men, farmers, and others who are striving to provide the means and facilities which will make victory possible," Governor Willis asserted.

The wisest union is the one that works the hardest for the general welfare, since we know that by union, by reason, and by justice we are tied together as one in confronting our enemy, the governor asserted, urging close cooperation among the various labor organizations and warning that many sacrifices must be made before the end of the war.

COMMISSION ON NEGRO AFFAIRS
Frankfort / September 21, 1944

BY authority vested in the executive office, a Commission on Negro Affairs is hereby created to obtain and to study all the facts and conditions relating to the economic, educational, housing, health, and other needs for the betterment of the Negro citizens of Kentucky.

The commission shall provide the means for its own necessary expenses and shall make its own organization. For the purpose of calling the first meeting of the commission, J.M. Tydings,[1] one of the members, is hereby designated and authorized to make such a call. The commission shall further appoint such committees and subcommittees as may be needed from time to time to perform such duties as may be assigned to them, and upon recommendation of the commission the governor will approve and commission such committees and subcommittees.[2]

The jurisdiction of the commission shall extend throughout the commonwealth. All departments of the government are requested to cooperate fully with the commission in facilitating its study, including the Department of Research of the University of Kentucky.

When the commission shall have completed its studies it shall make a report to the governor, with its recommendations. It will make preliminary reports if deemed necessary, but the final report should be made to the governor not less than ninety days before the next session of the General Assembly of Kentucky.[3]

---

1. J. Mansir Tydings (1905-1974). Architect; business manager of Lincoln Institute; founder in 1945 of Kentucky Council for Inter-Racial Cooperation; executive director of Jefferson County Human Relations Committee, 1962-67; editor of *Journal of Intergroup Relations*. J. Griffin Crump, "J. Mansir Tydings, 1905-1974," *Journal of Intergroup Relations* 4 (1975): 3-6.

2. The committee consisted of Charles W. Anderson, W.K. Belknap, Tarlton Collier, William H. Ballow, J.J. Kavanaugh, Robert E. Black, William H. Perry, all of Louisville; Maurice K. Rabb of Shelbyville; Christine Bradley South of Frankfort; William H. Vaughan of Morehead; J.M. Tydings of Anchorage; and Mrs. W.H. Fouse of Lexington.

Subcommittees were formed on economic affairs, education, health, civil affairs, and housing. The full report was completed on November 1, 1945, and was submitted by Governor Willis to the legislature on February 4, 1946. It was printed in the Kentucky *Senate Journal* (1946): 880-942, and Kentucky *House Journal* (1946): 2974-3032.

3. Among the recommendations of the commission was that it should be made a permanent body, a move that failed to receive strong legislative support.

Other comments by the commission included references to the "second rate services" provided blacks and the "twofold economic burden" brought about by segregation. They suggested repealing the state's "Jim Crow" laws; modifying the Day Law, which forbade integrated schools; and eliminating salary differences for educators. The commission also requested that blacks be appointed to the State Board of Education and other boards, that blacks should be hired in more professional positions, and that "the state and city administrations should take the lead in nondiscrimination employment practices." See Kentucky *Senate Journal* (1946): 87-95.

LINCOLN DAY DINNER
Louisville / February 12, 1945

GOVERNOR WILLIS told the crowd that "in Kentucky, we have no reason to be discouraged at the result of the presidential election." He said the Republican candidates got more votes in Kentucky than Republicans ever got before; that the trouble was "the other fellow got more votes than we did." He also said that Republicans should be encouraged by the fact Republicans throughout the United States carried more counties than they had since 1928.

Willis said that "all restrictions necessitated by the war should be removed as soon as the war is ended." Whoever impairs any of the liberties that have been handed down from Lincoln, he said, "is an enemy of the people."

Approximately nine hundred persons who attended the dinner heard Governor Simeon Willis of Kentucky urge the people of the state to rededicate themselves to the principles of liberty enunciated by the Declaration of Independence, by the Constitution of the United States, and by Abraham Lincoln.

Governor Willis declared that "we in America today have a generation of young men and women who believe in the principles of liberty, who will live for, fight for, and die for the principles in which Lincoln believed."[1]

---

1. The account is a composite drawn from the *Courier-Journal* and Lexington *Leader*, both of February 13, 1945.

V-E DAY
Frankfort / May 8, 1945

THE defeat of Germany is now an accomplished fact. Unconditional surrender of all forces of the German army has been announced.

The work in Germany proper will be a rebuilding and reorganization which will proceed under the direction of the allied armies. Law and order will have to be carved out of chaos. This will be a difficult task and will require the patient cooperation of the people while it is being accomplished.

It is natural for us to rejoice, as we should, in this great victory which has attended the efforts of our armed forces. But in our rejoicing we must not forget the sacrifices that have been made that this victory might be achieved. Young men and women from Kentucky, and from every part of our great country, have given their best to the achievement of this great victory. Many have made the supreme sacrifice for their country. Many more have been wounded and disabled in this terrible ordeal. The "blood and sweat and tears" required have affected every fireside.

Wars are not won without great sacrifice of flesh and blood, powered by stout hearts, on the battlefields where destiny takes its toll. The news is wonderful, but nothing can restore the broken hearts. All we can do is to honor our heroes so long as we live, and see that our country shall forever honor them by preserving the ideals for which they served and suffered and died.

In our rejoicing, we must not forget that God rules the lives and destinies of men and nations. All Americans accept the victory with humble hearts and with thanksgiving that the great task is thus far advanced. This day should be one of dedication, devotion, and prayer. We must continue our work because we still have a desperate and dangerous enemy to conquer. The resolution of the people must not be relaxed until the complete success of our armed forces on all battlefields and against all foes. Then the great problems of peace and reconstruction of the civilized world will require the best heart and brain to make secure the fruits of victory. All essential work should go on without the loss of momentum. In the home or church or working place let each American rededicate his life to the cause of humanity and righteousness. Let us highly resolve to make the American ideals of peace and justice real and enduring. The unity of men and women of good will must not be broken. The best thought of our country must be concentrated on finding ways and means for the preservation of liberty and the security of world peace founded on justice. No one man has all the answers, but the whole people must unite to accomplish the ideals for which so much sacrifice has been made. Our faith must not fail; our courage must not falter; and our high purposes must not be diminished.

LETTER CONCERNING WENNER-GREN AERONAUTICAL RESEARCH LABORATORY
Frankfort / July 24, 1945

Mr. Harry M. Caudill[1]
University of Kentucky
Lexington, Kentucky

Dear Mr. Caudill:

Some weeks ago you gave me a petition bearing seventeen signatures and dated April 2, 1945. At the same time you gave me a letter stating the reasons for delivering the petition to me.

Immediately after that I obtained from the university a complete statement from the records in regard to the aeronautical research laboratory. I am handing you a copy of that report. It states the facts, which should be sufficient to remove all grounds of complaint.

This matter has been investigated several times, and on April 28, 1944, the special assistant to the secretary of war[2] wrote a letter to Senator [A.B.] Chandler in which he stated that the War Department was fully advised of the operation of the Wenner-Gren Aeronautical Research Laboratory on the campus of the University of Kentucky by Mawen Corporation, and that the arrangement was entirely satisfactory to the War Department. You will find the letter in full on pages 27 and 28 of the report.

In view of that letter I see no reason to pursue this subject further.

I certainly hope the university may find a way to print this report as a public document and make it available to everyone interested.[3]

1. Harry Monroe Caudill (1922-   ). Graduate of University of Kentucky Law School, 1948; Whitesburg attorney; elected to Kentucky House of Representatives, 1954, 1956, 1960; author of *Night Comes to the Cumberlands* (1963) and other works; University of Kentucky history department, 1977-85. Faculty/Staff Biographical Files, University Archives, University of Kentucky Library.

2. Julius H. Amberg.

3. In *The Facts: A Report on the Aeronautical Research Laboratory, University of Kentucky* (n.p., [1945]), a full summation was given of the rather complex affair. Basically, engineering Professor Andre J. Meyer was asked by Mawen Motor Corporation to give advice on an aircraft engine. They later sought to enlarge his role and place him in charge of a new laboratory. James H. Graham, dean of the College of Engineering, in an effort to keep Meyer, suggested the building be placed at the university, which was done. Axel L. Wenner-Gren, a Swedish national, financed the $150,000 cost through the Viking Foundation. The only stipulation was that the building be named for him. That was done on the final acceptance on July 12, 1940.

In February 1942, Wenner-Gren was placed on the proclaimed list of blocked nationals for his connections with Germany. In the Amberg letter to Chandler the War Department found the university's arrangement concerning the laboratory "entirely satisfactory." The Kentucky attorney general on June 2, 1944, said it was permissible to remove Wenner-Gren's name from the building until he was cleared from the "black list."

The controversy focused on the January 1943 letter of Richard C. Stoll, chairman of the board of trustees, to Cordell Hull. The seventeen students attacked the letter, suggesting that it had advocated removing Wenner-Gren's name from the list; they called for a public hearing on the matter. As reprinted in *The Facts*, the letter simply reiterated the events to that time and made no such suggestion. The Kentucky House investigated the matter in 1946, issued a two-hundred-page report, and resolved that it had "complete confidence" in the university's handling of the affair. See *The Facts*, 8-54; Lexington *Leader* and *Courier-Journal*, both of July 25, 1945; and Kentucky *House Journal* (1946), 4400-4600.

STATE HOLIDAY—VICTORY OVER JAPAN
Frankfort / August 14, 1945

WHEREAS, God in his infinite wisdom has so bountifully blessed the peace-loving nations of the world by granting to them the wisdom and power through which victory has been won; and

WHEREAS, the United States of America and her allies have, through their courageous armed might, defeated the aggressor nations who sought to destroy civilization and to drive Christianity, liberty, and freedom from the face of the earth; and

WHEREAS, the president of the United States has declared Wednesday, August 15, and Thursday, August 16, as holidays; and

WHEREAS, it is fitting and proper that we spend these days in thanksgiving and prayer for these blessings—

NOW, THEREFORE, I, Simeon Willis, governor of the commonwealth of Kentucky, by virtue of the authority vested in me, do hereby declare Wednesday, August 15, and Thursday, August 16, as holidays in the commonwealth of Kentucky and urge that all persons go to their places of worship and offer up thanks to Almighty God.

V-J DAY
Frankfort / August 14, 1945

THE surrender of Japan marks the end of the war and brings rejoicing to all Americans and to the allies who joined in the war against Japan.

In our rejoicing, let us not forget the sacrifices and suffering of the men and women of our armed forces to whom our country owes so much.

With humble hearts, let all of our people join in thanksgiving and prayer and dedicate themselves with increased fervor and resolution to the rebuilding of a torn world and to the reestablishing of peace and justice among all peoples.

Americans must do everything possible to promote unity and understanding at home and abroad.

The days ahead will be difficult, and all the genius of free institutions will be needed to carry the nation safely through the storms.

With firm reliance on Him who has guided and sustained us in all trials and struggles, let us go forward with manly hearts and unabated faith to achieve the destiny our fathers dreamed for this favored land.

KENTUCKY AND THE
POSTWAR ERA

POSTWAR PLANNING COMMISSION
Frankfort / October 6, 1944

By virtue of the authority vested in the chief executive, it is hereby ordered that a commission to be known as Postwar Advisory Planning Commission be created to study and investigate the physical and human resources of the state and to formulate plans and make recommendations for the full development of such resources for the aid of agriculture, labor, manufacture, mining, transportation, conservation, and all other interests of the state. The commission will consider and coordinate the plans and recommendations of all other planning bodies, including private and governmental bodies, as related particularly to the opportunities and problems of Kentucky.

The commission will provide its own organization, plans of work, and financing; and it may create such committees and subcommittees as may be necessary to facilitate its work. Such committees may include any suitable persons, whether members of the commission or otherwise.

The research department of the University of Kentucky and all departments and agencies of the state government are requested to aid and cooperate in the work of the commission.

Committees appropriate for consultation with other bodies created by statute or executive order concerning any pertinent subject matter should be formed. The executive will approve and commission any committees requested by the commission.

The commission will make reports to the governor from time to time with its recommendations, and a final report prior to the next session of the General Assembly.[1]

---

1. Initial members of the commission were Rufus B. Atwood (Frankfort), Paul G. Blazer (Ashland), John N. Browning (Maysville), Roy Burlew (Owensboro), Herman L. Donovan (Lexington), E.J. Evans (Paintsville), Robert S. Gruver (Ashland), Thomas Graham (Louisville), William B. Harrison (Louisville), J.B. Hill (Louisville), J.E. Johnson, Jr. (Hazard), John Wesley Marr (Lexington), James B. O'Rear (Frankfort), W.P. Offutt (Louisville), O.K. Pemberton (Louisville), Fred L. Seale (Middlesboro), E.E. Stokes (Covington), James C. Stone (Lexington), George E. Tomlinson (Winchester), J.S. Watkins (Frankfort), Tom Wallace (Louisville), H. Frederick Wilkie (Louisville), Carl B. Wachs (Lexington), Freeman Webb (Olive Hill), and J.R. Weyler (Louisville). Later, Harold W. Cain (Somerset), Fred Mutchler (Bowling Green), Louis Igert (Paducah), and John E. Ramsey (Hopkinsville) were added. Executive Orders, October 6, 1944, January 29, 1945, Secretary of State's Records.

Chaired by Wilkie, the commission issued a 318-page final report in 1945. Nine committees presented plans for veterans, agriculture, education, industrial relations, industrial plants and opportunities, coordination of government activities, natural resources, laws, and transportation. This involved what they called "a three-fold program of action"—private enterprise, legislation, and financial programs. The commission also prepared a 28-page pamphlet entitled *A Program of Action for Kentucky* for widespread distribution.

Among the recommendations were: improved conservation, better adult education, a new constitution, "just" social legislation, more state parks, increased teacher education, and a higher minimum wage. The group also called for establishment of a state chamber of commerce, a housing commission, and an area zoning commission. See Postwar Advisory Planning Commission of Kentucky, *Final Report* (Frankfort, 1945).

LOUISVILLE PHILHARMONIC ORCHESTRA
Louisville / November 10, 1944

LADIES and gentlemen, it is, perhaps, the persuasive spell of the world's great music, so brilliantly performed, that leads one into speculating on the design of the future, the design of "things to come." But there seems almost no boundary to the imagination when we think of what a magnificent contribution to the cultural life of Kentucky these symphonic broadcasts and concerts are now making, and will continue to make. Throughout our commonwealth there are young musicians (composers, conductors, gifted young artists) who seek an outlet for their talents. They have it in this organization.

When the war has been completely won Kentucky boys and girls are coming home again to pick up their violins and trumpets and cellos, as well as their plows and scythes and law books. They will want a medium through which to express their musical talent. They will have it in this organization.

And this it is that I say: this philharmonic orchestra is the proud possession of the entire Kentucky community—and that it belongs more fully now to all of us through the generous sponsorship of Stewart's. It is with certain pride that I congratulate Mr. Robert Whitney,[1] the members of the orchestra, the Stewart Dry Goods Company, and all of the people whose work has brought us to this evening and to the threshold of great musical accomplishments. Thank you, and congratulations for many Friday evenings to come, when Kentucky's noble tradition will be more greatly enhanced—through music.

---

1. Robert Sutton Whitney (1904-1986). Native of England; conductor of Louisville Orchestra, 1937-67; dean, School of Music, University of Louisville, 1956-71; composer. *Who's Who, 1970-71*, 2444; Debbie Skaggs, University of Louisville, to editor, July 11, 1985; Lexington *Herald-Leader*, November 23, 1986.

TWENTY-FIFTH ANNIVERSARY DINNER— OWENSBORO CHAMBER OF COMMERCE
Owensboro / November 16, 1944

GOVERNOR WILLIS listed three things he hoped to accomplish for Kentucky: (1) education of the children of the state; (2) hospitalization of victims of tuberculosis; and (3) construction of highways. "But," he said, "we must let nothing stop our winning of the war. We must work hard to end the war as soon as we can, so that these postwar plans may be made realities the quicker."

The governor discussed his administration's postwar program, which he said included extensive road construction. He stated that the state highway department is planning a great road building pool to be started after the war when men and materials are available.

Among other plans for the future of Kentucky, Governor Willis listed the Youth Guidance Commission,[1] which, he said, is already working to organize the moral power of Kentucky to restrict and halt the delinquency of young people; the Postwar Planning Advisory Commission,[2] which, the governor stated, will solve problems caused by the war, such as changing instruments of war to instruments of peace—"that is, helping returning soldiers, war workers, and others whose lives have been disrupted by the war to find security" in a world at peace. "Although the government can do little toward this end, since industry will have to take up these returning citizens, all that can be done will be done," he [added]. "Twenty-five able men have been selected to study this problem."

The governor said a commission had been appointed to study the question of taxes.[3] First, he added, this commission will learn how much money will be needed to meet the financial demands of postwar Kentucky and then will endeavor to learn the most equitable way to raise the needed money through taxes. "This," said the governor, "will do more to advance Kentucky than any other single factor."

Kentucky has not kept pace with surrounding states in industrial development partly because of rate inequality, he stated. "At a meeting with other southern governors on Thanksgiving this will be the topic of discussion, and plans will, no doubt, be formulated to combat it."[4]

Touching on the subject of the education of the children of the state, the governor said that was a perpetual problem because of the perpetual need for it.

His advice to the people of Owensboro was to "stand by the chamber of commerce and help in every way you can—try to help build Owensboro."

---

1. See document dated June 23, 1944 in "Legislative Actions, 1943-1945" section, especially note 2.

2. See first document in this section.

3. See document dated March 28, 1945, in "State Government Administration" section.

4. See next document.

STATEMENT REGARDING ICC RATE QUESTION
Biloxi, Mississippi / November [24 or 25], 1944

GOVERNOR KERR:[1]

Your question is an important one, and its understanding is fundamental to a correction of the discriminations that have vexed the nation.

I recognize that rate questions are technical and require the services of experts. But, at the same time, it must be recognized that discrimination against one necessarily results in favoritism to another section, and that rate experts must approach the question with a purpose to achieve equality and to avoid discrimination.

Injustice always results in injury. The federal Constitution was framed for the purpose of establishing justice and equality of opportunity among all the states of the Union. That policy to a large extent has been frustrated by artificial devices that have advanced regional and sectional conflicts among economic interests.

The nation is served as a whole by the complete and equal development of every portion of its territory. Just as a state is benefited by the equal development of all of its potential capacities, so the nation is benefited by the complete development of all of its latent possibilities. The equality of transportation charges will result in equal opportunity for every portion of the nation to participate in the markets and commercial opportunities of the country.

Unity and good will are essential to the welfare of the nation, and equality of treatment in a national freight rate structure will promote that objective. Recent experience has proven the value of complete cooperation among all of our people. The future of the nation depends on the genius and enterprise of Americans, and every portion of the nation is benefited by the progress and advancement of the social and economic interests of every other portion thereof. Such development broadens and encourages the genius and enterprise of the whole nation.

In these crucial days when the combined talent of the United Nations is being organized to promote peace and good will among nations, we must see to it that the internal economy of the nation is cleared of all obstructions and obstacles, and that the full power and genius of America be free to fulfill the fondest hopes of our people for the welfare of our country as one nation indivisible and indestructible.

---

1. Robert Samuel Kerr (1896-1963). School teacher, 1916-17; attorney; involved in oil business; member, Democratic National Committee, 1940, 1944, 1948; Democratic governor of Oklahoma, 1943-47; U.S. senator, 1948-63. *Biographical Directory of Governors*, 3: 1250.

STATEMENT REGARDING FEDERAL AID
TO EDUCATION
Frankfort / March 16, 1945

WILLIS declared his stand had been known since his campaign for governor in 1943, but that as far as he knew the commission did not know he had authorized state Superintendent of Public Instruction John Fred Williams to send the telegrams and he did not know the commission was going to discuss the question.[1]

"I'm not trying to dictate to the commission," the governor declared in commenting on his written statement, which accused the newspaper of "petty faultfinding."

"If I had wanted to dictate to the commission, I would have appointed a different type of men," he continued.

"Whether intentional or inadvertent, the headlines in the *Courier-Journal* article this morning stating that 'Willis Indorses U.S. School Aid Despite Board,' was calculated to mislead the reader. It was very unfair to me. The word 'despite' had no proper place in the recital of the actual facts. There was no connection whatever between my prior statements and the discussion of the education committee's report to the Postwar Advisory Planning Commission.

"My position on the question of federal aid for education was publicly stated at Mount Sterling on September 29, 1943,[2] as correctly quoted at the end of the *Courier-Journal* article. Many times thereafter that position was repeated in various parts of the state. Federal aid was acceptable only with complete state control. At St. Louis in August 1944, the Republican governors took a similar position.

"On January 27, 1945, Governor Robert S. Kerr of Oklahoma, chairman of the Southern Governors' Conference, wired me a copy of his telegram to the president, indorsing the proposal and requesting me to take such action as I felt would serve the best interests of my state.

"This telegram was referred to the educational department, and on March 9, John Fred Williams, with my approval, sent a message to Senator Murray and Chairman Graham[3] which was quoted in the *Courier-Journal*. At that time I was not aware that the subject would be discussed at the meeting of the Postwar Advisory Planning Commission on March 13. So far as I know, the commission members were not aware of my messages.

"The action of the Postwar Advisory Planning Commission was so badly reported in the *Courier-Journal* that Mr. Wallace,[4] editor of the Louisville *Times*, who is a member of the commission, felt it necessary to set the record straight in an editorial.

"The Postwar Advisory Planning Commission is an able, independent, and patriotic body of men who are rendering a great service at considerable sacrifice. They are striving to build a constructive program for the good of Kentucky. It is unfortunate that the *Courier-Journal* does not lend its powerful aid to the high purposes of this commission instead of seeking to create controversy and confusion.

"I heartily commend the Postwar Advisory Planning Commission and each member thereof for the earnest, conscientious, and vigorous investigation and discussion of all subjects of vital interest to the state. The subject of education, in which my interest is very great, deserves the best thought of all good citizens.

"It is [doing] exactly as I would have them do because it is their judgment that the state desires, and it is their help that will lift the state to a higher level of prosperity and progress. The earnest discussion in the body is a wholesome sign, and I am sure that its work will bring good results.

"I wish we could have the wholehearted support of the *Courier-Journal* instead of petty faultfinding. I believe its persistent effort to divert the public mind from the great issues involved should cease.

"My position toward the centralization of power in the federal government is well known. I regret the tendency toward increasing centralization of power over the activities of the people. I wish that trend could be reversed, and I shall do all in my power to accomplish that objective. But that does not alter the realities of the existing situation. At the present time the federal government is taking more than $600 million per year from the taxpayers of Kentucky.

"When the states are restored to their full potential capacity to meet their obligation, they will gladly do so. Until that time the government should return to the states at least some of the money to help with our fundamental problems, such as education, welfare, and the like. On all wartime measures we expect to do our full part, as we have done. By the exemption of industrial alcohol from the production tax, Kentucky has contributed several million dollars to the war effort over and above all of its other efforts. Kentucky should not be the victim of discrimination.

"This educational bill is not a wartime measure. It has been before Congress for many years and has received much discussion. It will continue to receive discussion until the question is finally settled. So long as the federal government absorbs the major portion of the tax-paying capacity of the people it is but just [that] a fair share of the money be returned to help the state meet its burdens.

"I congratulate the Postwar Advisory Planning Commission on its course of intelligence, independence, and patriotism. I hope it will continue its discussions on the same high plane, and when its work is completed I desire to aid in bringing before the people a constructive program which will be of great and permanent value to the state of Kentucky and the nation."

---

1. In a telegram, Governor Willis's administration had urged passage of a congressional bill that would grant $300 million to the states for aid to public schools. The Postwar Advisory Planning Commission later voted eight to six against endorsing this method. Louisville *Courier-Journal* headlines suggested one action had been taken "despite" the other; Governor Willis in his statement stressed the independence of the actions. See *Courier-Journal*, March 14-17, 1945.

2. See "Preinaugural Addresses" section.

3. James Edward Murray (1876-1961). Canadian born; attorney; banker; county attorney, 1906-08; delegate to six Democratic national conventions; U.S. senator from Montana, 1934-61. *Biographical Directory, 1961*, 1375.

Frank Porter Graham (1886-1972). Attorney since 1910; high school teacher, 1910-12; history professor, 1915-30, and president, 1930-49, University of North Carolina; member of numerous government committees, including President's Committee on Education; appointed as Democrat to U.S. Senate to fill vacancy and served 1949-50; served with the United Nations, 1951-67. Ibid., 963-64; New York *Times*, February 17, 1972.

The *Courier-Journal* of March 16, 1945, indicated that the telegram had been sent to Graham A. Borden, a representative from North Carolina. Governor Willis's reference to "Chairman Graham" more likely applies to Frank P. Graham (above).

4. Tom Wallace (1874-1961). Editorial writer and drama critic, 1905-19, associate editor, 1919-23, Louisville *Courier-Journal*; chief of editorial staff, 1923-30; editor, 1930-48, Louisville *Times*; involved in conservation; president, American Society of Newspaper Editors, 1940-41. *Who's Who in Kentucky, 1936*, 419; *Who's Who in America, 1961-1968*, 979.

CITIZENS LEAGUE OF BELL COUNTY
Middlesboro / April 21, 1945

GOVERNOR SIMEON S. WILLIS of Kentucky, speaking at Baraca Hall Saturday night, said that the success of the San Francisco Conference[1] for the establishment of a world peace plan depended on the people of America and the world to carry out the plan after it was formulated.

The governor also said the strength of our society and of our nation depended on individual strength. "If the people are corrupt, immoral, weak, or dishonest, then the nation cannot endure," he said.

"Ever since the beginning of man two forces, liberty and arbitrary power, had fought for dominion; and we cannot keep our glorious country free unless we foster good citizenship and elevate and improve our people by education," the governor said.

---

1. The United Nations Conference on International Organization met at San Francisco from April 25 to June 26, 1945, and drafted the charter for the United Nations. The U.S. delegation consisted of Secretary of State Edward R. Stettinius, Senator Tom Connally (D-Texas), and Senator Arthur Vandenberg (R-Michigan). See John E. Findling, *Dictionary of American Diplomatic History* (Westport, Conn., 1980), 429-30.

INTERVIEW REGARDING POSTWAR KENTUCKY
Frankfort / May 8, 1945

RESPONSIBILITY for industrial and civic development in the postwar era is basically that of the individual communities, with the officials of Kentucky offering what assistance is found possible under existing laws and the constitution.

Governor Willis explained carefully that in general about all the commonwealth would be able to do would be to serve in an advisory and assisting capacity in aiding communities to develop and carry out programs designed to create the maximum municipal development.

Existing law in Kentucky does not provide the necessary vehicle for providing direct financial assistance to communities within the commonwealth, the governor continued, although a comprehensive program developed by the state highway department will be of great value to the municipalities in every section of the state.

The chief executive of the commonwealth, in discussing the situation, expressed great reliance upon his postwar planning commission, saying that such an organization of leaders in virtually every field of endeavor [was] much better qualified to judge the needs and offer the assistance in planning statewide and [in] community development than any single person.

There will be specific problems that will confront every individual community that cannot be solved by an overall statewide plan, the governor declared, and suggested that the citizens of each municipality or county provide a strong framework to work closely with the general state planning board.

Everything that can be done will be done by the state agencies, the governor declared, but [he] returned to the thesis [that] in the final analysis it will be the work of the local agencies and local governments that will return the most desirable results.

Thumbing through reports of states and cities which already have virtually completed tentative plans, the governor pointed out that no single agency, be it state, local, or national, can hope to solve all of the problems that will confront the citizens.

He suggested, by inference, that community leaders in Kentucky study what has been done in other places and adopt suggestions in those plans that will conform to their particular requirements.

The governor expressed considerable interest in the announced plan of State Highway Commissioner J. Stephen Watkins for the establishment of an aviation section in the state highway department and ventured the statement that possibly in the field of aeronautical development the commonwealth would find the opportunity for greatest and most successful assistance to municipalities.

HEALTH TRAINING SCHOOL
OF KENTUCKY FEDERATION
OF WOMEN'S CLUBS AND
STATE DEPARTMENT OF HEALTH
Lexington / September 18, 1945

AMERICA'S new responsibility as custodian of the greatest implements of destruction known to man requires "us to raise up the best generation of Americans in history," Governor Simeon Willis said here tonight.

Discussing the atomic bomb, air power, and other forces of war, the governor said "there exist today powers looking to a new era. If they are left in the hands of wicked people they will be used wickedly.

"Perpetuity of our race depends on building generations of good people, not wicked people, and it is the responsibility of every individual. The stronger the individual, the stronger the nation."

CHRISTMAS GREETINGS
Frankfort / December 22, 1945

"THE citizens of Kentucky deserve thanks and congratulations for the contributions made to the war effort and for devotion to the cause of liberty, peace, and justice.

"The problems of peace require unity and understanding and the cooperation of the whole people.

"I am sure that Kentuckians appreciate the true spirit of the Christmas season, and out of that appreciation will be derived the determination to carry forward the principles of Christian unity.

"The times demand the best of all of us to promote peace on earth and good will toward men."

To officers and employees, the governor sent these greetings:

"The war is ended, but consequences of war remain. Its tragedies and devastation will leave indelible marks that will require many years to efface.

"With gratitude for the victory, let us resolutely dedicate ourselves to the great tasks of reconversion to the ways of peace and the reconstruction of our own country and a war-torn world.

"It requires unity of purpose and community of effort to maintain the prosperity and happiness of the people.

"I thank each of you for loyal, devoted, and competent service and trust you to keep your record high in the future."

KENTUCKY SELECTIVE SERVICE
OFFICIALS MEETING
Lexington / February 18, 1946

A "GRATEFUL nation's tribute—for a job well done" was paid by Governor Simeon S. Willis to 723 Kentucky Selective Service officials whose "loyalty and untiring efforts built the greatest force that this country ever mobilized."

Governor Willis and Colonel Frank D. Rash,[1] state Selective Service director, reminded the uncompensated members of local boards and boards of appeal of "a still greater job ahead of us"—that of helping returned veterans readjust themselves.

"The boys that you called up are now returning home to take again their respective places in their own communities," Governor Willis said. "It is up to all of us to help them in their problems of readjustment to civil life.

"Many agencies and organizations have been set up to assist them, but Selective Service is charged with providing adequate facilities to render aid in the replacement in their former positions or securing new positions for the veterans."

The governor outlined the federal and state aid programs set up for veterans, stressing particularly the GI Bill of Rights, which he said would give the veteran the greatest comfort in later life because of the educational opportunities offered.

"We should make the young veteran realize that in education lies the cornerstone of his future," Willis said. "These young men during the past four years have been taught to destroy. Now we must teach them to build, create, and prepare for the job that lies ahead of them as citizens and civilians. This can be accomplished by education and instruction.

"If these young veterans will go back to school, it will give the older veterans who feel they are a little too old to go to school a better opportunity to obtain a job in industry."

The governor paid tribute to Colonel Rash for his "diligence, his discretion, his tact, and his glowing patriotism" as state director of Selective Service and for his "foresight" in establishing guidance committees in each local board to assist veterans.

"It should be noted," he said, "that not one case of a Kentucky registrant was ever presented to the courts in which it was found that any registrant was erroneously inducted, or that agriculture was apparently injured by the orderly withdrawal of men from the agricultural areas. The deferment policies left sufficient men on the farms for remarkable achievements in steadily increased agricultural production from year to year."

Governor Willis also extolled Major General Lewis B. Hershey as national director.[2]

---

1. Frank Dillman Rash (1878-1946). Engineer, manager, vice-president, and president of Earlington, Ky., mining company, 1901-24; city councilman and mayor of Earlington; president of Federal Land Bank of Louisville; state director of Selective Service, 1940-45; headed Kentucky American Legion and Masonic Lodge; Democrat. Hambleton Tapp, *A Sesqui-Centennial History of Kentucky*, Frederick A. Wallis, ed., 4 vols. (Hopkinsville and Louisville, 1945), 3: 1281-82; Ogden, ed., *Papers of Keen Johnson*, 163n.

2. Lewis Blaine Hershey (1893-1977). School teacher, Steuben, Ind., 1910; principal, Flint, Ind., 1914-16; military service, 1916-40; appointed general in 1940; deputy director, Selective Service System, 1940-41; director, 1941-70; Republican; presidential advisor on manpower mobilization, 1970-73. *Who's Who, 1942-43*, 1059; New York *Times*, May 21, 1977.

This speech is a composite drawn from the *Courier-Journal* and the Lexington *Herald*, both of February 19, 1946.

LIFTING OPA CONTROLS
Louisville / July 1, 1946

"WITH these OPA restrictions now removed, the responsibility is squarely upon the people themselves to act soundly, justly, and with reason," the governor said.[1]

"If they do so, there will be no need for further legislation, and there will be no danger of inflation. The time has come when the people must assert their ability to handle their affairs, and just to the extent that they fail, they invite the intrusion of public authority."

The governor said the U.S. and state governments have the power to deal with any "unlawful combinations to control prices or restrain trade." This power, plus the good sense of the great majority of the people, will serve to avoid a dangerous inflation, he said.

The conflict of opinion in Washington over the extension of OPA controls indicates, he said, the uncertainty that surrounds "any attempt to regulate by law the general conduct of many people."

"The state of Kentucky has not undertaken to control the economy of the people. They are free to fix their own prices so long as they are not the result of unlawful combinations.

"There is no power in any state official or state authority to manage the economy of the people.

"There has been widespread belief among vast numbers of people that the patriotism and wisdom of the people alone was the best safeguard against runaway prices and inflationary transactions."

Referring to President Truman's veto of the bill to extend the life of OPA with its powers drastically cut, Governor Willis declared:

"The inability of the Congress and the president to agree upon the form and extent of authority that we are to exercise to prevent inflation and to promote reconversion to peacetime production has left the whole matter in the control of the people themselves.

Willis urged buyers not to contribute to a "runaway market," not to pay more for an article than it "is reasonably worth," and continued: "On the other hand, if you have something to sell, do not attempt to extort excessive prices for the article. Any such attempt may create a spiral that will react to destroy the very profits that were extorted."

"Let us not permit our sound judgment to be warped by propaganda or our fears to be generated by the selfish greed of others," he said.

"The moral stamina of the people requires that trade and commerce shall be fair—that not more than a fair price shall be exacted—and that the needs of the people be supplied without oppression or extortion.

"The people of Kentucky never run away from their responsibilities," he said. "They will meet it without fear and with the same patriotism and resolution they have shown in every emergency.

"The fear of inflation has a tendency to bring about inflation. It creates a feeling of panic and disregard of actual values. It has a tendency to stampede people into action they would not take deliberately."

But he asked in closing, "Why shouldn't Kentucky be trusted to handle her own business affairs?" and added: "Her record in production and on the battle line is one that will fill our histories forever, and today she should turn her thoughts to what her sons have done. And remember that you can do it because self-confidence is one of the great things that brings even greater accomplishments."[2]

---

1. The Office of Price Administration had been headed by Chester Bowles until his resignation in early 1946. Kentuckian Paul A. Porter succeeded him. In late June 1946, Congress extended OPA with restricted authority for a year. President Truman vetoed the measure, in Robert Donovan's words, "in the hope that public opinion would force Congress to pass a stronger law. After a wrangle Congress passed a new OPA extension bill that was at best somewhat tougher, which Truman signed 'with reluctance.' " Later actions rendered it largely ineffective, however. See Robert J. Donovan, *Conflict and Crisis: The Presidency of Harry S. Truman, 1945-48* (New York, 1977), 167, 235-36.

2. This address is a composite drawn from the *Courier-Journal*, the Lexington *Herald-Leader*, the *Kentucky Post*, the Owensboro *Messenger*, and the Frankfort *State Journal*, all of July 2, 1946.

PROCLAMATION REGARDING COAL SHORTAGE
Frankfort / November 25, 1946

Whereas, a national and state emergency does exist by reason of the coal shortage in the nation and in Kentucky; and

Whereas, a survey indicates that local stocks of coal now held by consumers in retail dealers' yards and elsewhere contain for emergency distribution only a few days' supply of bituminous coal;[1] and

Whereas, it is important that every means available be made to conserve such fuel as is now at hand and which may not soon be re-supplied;

Now, therefore, I, Simeon Willis, in the interest of the public health and welfare, do hereby proclaim a state of emergency to exist; and Honorable Charles E. Whittle, chairman of the Kentucky Public Service Commission,[2] is hereby designated to cooperate fully with the federal officials and local officials in coordinating all efforts to determine the needs with reference to the stocks of fuel now available.

The mayors of cities, city managers, county judges, and all local officials are hereby called upon to determine what activities should be given preference and what activities should be curtailed so that the health and general welfare of each community may be best maintained. The authorities in each community should determine whether available fuel stock should be conserved by dimout, restricting amusement places, closure of schools, curtailment of power for industrial purposes or whether such stocks are sufficient to justify continued operation of these various activities.

The chairman of the Public Service Commission will cooperate fully with all local authorities in conservation of those means necessary for preservation of the health and general welfare of each community and will coordinate such local efforts with the federal agencies involved.

All citizens of Kentucky are hereby requested to assist patriotically in this important measure. Each knows how he can best conserve.

---

1. On April 1, 1946, some four hundred thousand soft-coal miners had gone on strike. By May 13, with rail service and electrical power disrupted, United Mine Workers President John L. Lewis had sent miners back for a truce period. When negotiations stalled, President Truman had ordered the mines seized; eight days later a coal pact had been signed. But in October Lewis declared the agreement void; the government cut the mileage of coal-burning trains and

ordered "dimouts" in twenty-one states in order to conserve electricity. A court order directed Lewis to cancel his strike plans on the grounds that strikes against government facilities were illegal. The strike began, however, on November 20—five days before this address by Willis. It ended December 7. In March 1947 the U.S. Supreme Court by a 7-2 vote upheld Lewis's conviction for contempt of court and ordered the UMW to pay a fine of $700,000. See Donovan, *Conflict and Crisis*, 209-10, 218, 239-42; Lexington *Herald*, November 26, 1946.

2. Charles Edward Whittle (1900-1973). Attorney in Brownsville; president of Ogden College, 1923-25; defeated for congressional seat, 1926; county attorney of Edmonson County, Ky., 1926-30; state associate commissioner of revenue, 1943-44; member of Kentucky Alcoholic Board of Control, 1944-45; member of Kentucky Public Service Commission, 1945-48; delegate to Republican National Convention, 1940; author. Tapp, *Kentucky Lives*, 589; Executive Order, June 13, 20, 1944, Secretary of State's Records; Bureau of Vital Statistics; Nancy Kaul, Brownsville, Ky., to C. David Dalton, February 19, 1986.

Governor Willis named Whittle state coal conservator to coordinate conservation efforts. *Courier-Journal*, November 26, 1946.

KENTUCKY CHAMBER OF COMMERCE DINNER
Frankfort / July 10, 1947

MR. MUIR,[1] members of the board of directors of the Kentucky Chamber of Commerce, gentlemen:

I am very happy to be with you on this occasion and to have the encouraging report just made by the president of your organization. The Kentucky Chamber of Commerce fills a long-felt need in the industrial life of this commonwealth. I am glad to have played some small part—along with a number of Kentucky's public-spirited leaders from all parts of the state—in giving impetus to a movement which culminated in the formation of this effective development agency.

By executive order—issued October 6, 1944—I authorized the creation of a Postwar Advisory Planning Commission to study and advise on matters vitally affecting the economic future of the commonwealth. The purpose and function of that commission was twofold: first, to study and investigate the physical and human resources of the state; and second, to formulate plans and to make recommendations for the full development of such resources—as an aid to agriculture, labor, mining, transportation, conservation, and all other activities of the state. The Postwar Advisory Planning Commission was empowered to consider and coordinate the plans and recommendations of all other planning bodies—both private and governmental—as related especially to the opportunities and problems of Kentucky as a state. Like the state chamber of commerce, its membership was nonpolitical and nonpartisan and was composed of men and women of real capacity and sincerely and deeply interested in the solution of our most pressing problems. It provided its own organization, planned its own work, and financed its own activities. It was not in any sense a government agency. Businessmen, farmers, representatives of organized labor, education leaders, and other professional men and women, were appointed to the commission or served as advisors to its members.

By the time their final report was made, it was clear from their findings that the establishment of an industrial development agency within the state government itself was not the best solution for the state's development problems. The commission did recommend, however, the establishment of an *independent* Kentucky Chamber of Commerce, sponsored by local, private support.[2] In making this recommendation, the report pointed out the urgent need for such a body, because of, first, the lack of any existing agency to meet requests of out-of-state business interests for information regarding suitable plant locations and facilities; second, the lack of coordination between existing local chambers of commerce, civic groups, and local governments; and third, the obvious fact that a state chamber would have ready acceptance and wide support.

It is a source of pride to me—and I am sure to all my fellow Kentuckians—to know that today we have a state chamber of commerce, functioning in the best interests of the state, and dedicated to the vital task of building Kentucky's industrial future.[3] What we have just heard has convinced me that this commonwealth—with the full support of all its citizens—is embarked on a program of development in which all Kentuckians will share.

Kentucky has much to offer the rest of the nation, much that those outside our borders could profit from and enjoy, and through this profit and enjoyment serve to enrich the lives of our own citizens. In the language of the day, Kentucky "has what it takes." We are rich in raw materials and natural resources, and they are just beginning to be tapped. The great majority of them await development and exploitation. We have, for example, one-fifth of the nation's coal supply and one of the greatest hardwood timber reserves east of the Mississippi

River. Our limestone deposits are tremendous, and our reserves of basic materials—such as oil, fluorite, lead, and zinc—are more than sufficient to support industry on a profitable basis.

Kentucky's transportation system is adequate to meet our needs and is constantly being improved and broadened in scope. Our highways, airways, railways, and waterways are the broad arteries through which flow the industrial lifeblood of the commonwealth. The state's low tax rates and licensing fees in this field help to speed this flow.

Kentucky offers a plentiful supply of natural power, with abounding fuel sources close at hand for quick delivery, to any part of the state, at low transportation cost.

Thanks to the thrift and conservative nature of our people, we can offer to outside industry a surplus of private capital for investment in new plants and enterprises within our own borders. An intelligent fiscal policy in state government affairs—adhered to by successive administrations here in Frankfort—is another indication of Kentucky's sound financial structure.

Our central geographic location and our nearness to heavily populated centers and ready markets place Kentucky in a strategic crossroads position in relation to all other sections of the nation.

In addition, we offer a friendly atmosphere for private enterprise—agreeable labor-management relations and the willing effort and cooperation of all Kentucky's people—her greatest pride.

Mr. Muir has touched on Kentucky's tax structure and need for intelligent revision in our tax laws. We must have the cooperation of the public and of the Kentucky Chamber of Commerce in that respect. It is obvious, as Mr. Muir has pointed out, that the state inheritance tax and the tax on intangible property, under changed conditions, are both deterring factors in our competition with other states for new industrial enterprises. In the final report made last year by the Tax Revision Commission of Kentucky—a commission of outstanding private citizens who made an exhaustive study of our tax structure—it was noted that Kentucky's inheritance tax rate is relatively high and that the tax on intangibles is considered by many to be excessive.[4] Some of you gentlemen here tonight were members of that commission and of course are thoroughly familiar with our tax problems. I thank the members of that body for having made available a copy of the commission's report to each member of your board of directors. It is worthy of your careful consideration and analysis. I recommended its study to the members of the last state legislature, and the next legislature this coming January in Frankfort should continue to give consideration to the facts assembled and the information furnished. The tax modifications embodied in the resolution adopted by you at your business meeting earlier today should be placed in the hands of every member of the next General Assembly.

One of Kentucky's great potential sources of revenue which I have not touched on so far—and one with which the Kentucky Chamber of Commerce must be increasingly concerned—is the proper development of our tourist trade. No other state in the Union has more natural wonders, greater scenic beauty, or more inspiring points of historical interest than our own state. We who live among them are sometimes prone to take them for granted. To some of us they may be just the familiar landmarks of home. But the visitor from beyond our borders will tell you that Kentucky is a great treasure-house that all the world should see. We must open wider the gates to this land, which has always been famous for its gracious hospitality to the stranger.

To make our attractions fully available to the traveler, and to assure that his visit among us may be as pleasant as possible, we must do three things: first, our hotel accommodations must be measurably increased and made more attractive. At present they are far from adequate. The hotels and inns at some of our major points of interest often have many more requests for reservations, both from visitors and from our own people, than they can possibly fill; second, our program of road building must be greatly expanded and our present plans for the highway system carried into execution; and third, we must let the outside world know, in no uncertain terms, what Kentucky has to offer the prospective traveler. This latter task will rest more and more heavily upon the shoulders of the Kentucky Chamber of Commerce, but it is up to all of us to help you "spread the good word."

And now a few words about Kentucky's future as I see it. In reviewing the commonwealth's advantages as a place in which to live and enjoy the fruits of our labors, there is one great, intangible factor that must be considered: the will of the people of Kentucky to forge their own future. Only a full realization by our people of our state's problems—and a strong determination to *work together* toward their solution—can give Kentucky her rightful place in the sun. The combined efforts of the Kentucky Chamber of Commerce, the state government agencies, and all other public and private organizations will be futile unless they are fully supported by all of our people.

Kentucky's problems are many and varied. Some of them present great difficulties, but none of them are insoluble. By your very presence here this evening you give evidence—as private citizens as well as members of this organization—of your deep interest in these problems and of your belief that they *can* be properly solved. That is the spirit which must animate all Kentuckians, if we are to go forward to a brighter, happier, more prosperous future. It is your determination to work in harmony with each other that must inspire all of us to go forward together as a team. I sincerely hope and trust that such a spirit will be contagious.

I have said that Kentucky's future must be *forged* by her own people. I used the word "forge" advisedly. Webster defines it as meaning "to impel forward or to shape." Such a movement forward—with its implication of intelligent guidance—cannot be effected unless we are all determined to unite our efforts toward that end. A people divided among themselves—or indifferent to their future—cannot function effectively or achieve anything but chaos. Kentucky's motto—United We Stand, Divided We Fall—states our case perfectly.

I have enumerated our great wealth of resources—human, cultural, and material—which must serve as the raw materials from which to build Kentucky's future. The use we make of these materials will determine what that future shall be. The manner in which we apply their use to the solution of our problems will decide whether or not the people of Kentucky deserve to wear the distinguished mantle of their hardy pioneer fathers.

Just what are the immediate problems that face us? They are not difficult to name because they touch the lives of all of us, and the need for their solution is constantly with us. They involve our educational system, our industrial and agricultural status, and the general health and welfare of all our citizens. These problems, and others of lesser importance, are elemental, easily understood, and possible of solution, if we really try to solve them.

With 70 percent of our people living on farms or in small rural communities, we are primarily an agricultural state and will be for some time to come. Our steady growth toward industrialization is evident in the fact, however, that not so many years ago only 10 percent of our population was urban.[5] With so many of our people living on farms, the prosperity of rural Kentucky is of the utmost importance to all of us. The fundamental problem in agriculture is that of gaining a good living from the land in such a way that its resources will be protected and built up for the future. The production record of our soil speaks for itself. Through many years of dependence upon its yield, we know what a rich storehouse of natural wealth it is. Along with such natural resources as coal, lumber, and minerals, it forms the basis for the wealth of the entire state itself.

Our great resources afford us now, and in the immediate future, the finest opportunity we have had in our history to supply the raw products for manufacture. With proper use and conservation of these materials, and without burdensome taxation, we are in a position to build a prosperous industrial and agricultural structure that will support an educational system of the first rank, a greatly improved and enlarged transportation system, necessary public development institutions, and other greatly needed benefits.

Slowly but surely, we are learning to use our own raw materials to provide, for our own use, the finished products necessary for a richer material life. By fortifying our predominantly rural economy with a solid industrial structure, we will someday have the balanced economy we desire and need. It is important that we expand our efforts toward the building of that industrial structure. It is, of course, the primary goal of your organization, the Kentucky Chamber of Commerce.

I call upon all my fellow Kentuckians to help you achieve that goal. With their full support, and with God's help, I know we will go forward together and make tomorrow Kentucky's greatest day.

---

1. Earl Robert Muir (1896-1980). First involved in railroad, automotive business; officer of Louisville branch, Federal Reserve Bank, 1917-31; vice president, president, and chairman of the board, Louisville Trust Company, 1931-65; president, Kentucky Bankers Association, 1936-37; president, Kentucky Chamber of Commerce. *Who's Who in Kentucky, 1936*, 295; enclosure, E. Robert Muir, Jr. to the editor, June 30, 1986.

2. See document of October 6, 1944, in this section, and Postwar Advisory Planning Commission Report.

3. On November 22, 1944, the Kentucky Development Association was incorporated, and in December Earl Muir (above) was chosen as president. From that organization came the Kentucky Chamber of Commerce, incorporated June 29, 1946. The chamber, with a contributed treasury of $128,000, immediately began its work. Like Governor Willis and his Postwar Advisory Planning Commission the group gave little cooperation to Harry Schacter's Committee for Kentucky. Earl R. Muir to Ida L. Willis, January 5, 1965, in editor's possession.

4. See notes 2 and 3 in document dated March 28, 1945, in "State Government Administration" section.

5. In 1860 the state's population was 10.4 percent urban. See *1970 Census of Population: Kentucky*, 1: part 19 (Washington, D.C., 1973), 19-7.

GROUND-BREAKING FOR VETVILLAGE
Cold Spring / July 13, 1947

TERMING the veteran "the backbone of our country and the stabilizing influence for the American way of life," Governor Simeon Willis lauded the enterprises of Campbell County former servicemen at ground-breaking ceremonies of the Vetvillage Home Builders Association, Dodsworth Lane, Cold Spring, Sunday.

"The starting of this project today signalizes the intense interest of American veterans in American enterprise," Governor Willis said, "for whenever the American people will to solve a problem they always accomplish their purpose.

"The primary things needed in life are food, raiment, and shelter," he said, "and during the war as well as thereafter we have been short of building materials and the cost has been prohibitive.

"However, you veterans started to study early and grapple with this all-important problem and you are to be honored for promoting such a project and accomplishing such an achievement, for it is the spirit that solves our problems here in America.

"This same spirit has placed America in the forefront in many fields, and especially is this true in inventions. It is the way that such things inspire us and gird us to fight on for enterprises and the development of our state and nation.

"In the light of long-range programs the housing project you have today started is to be solved. We live in the greatest country in the world, but we are living in a world of great stress today, for all the world is looking to us for the further development of our inventive genius, for the establishment and preservation of peace throughout the world, and not these accomplishments by government alone, but by the will of the American people.

"As we grapple with these problems we must show to the world our way of solving problems and obstacles which at times seem almost insurmountable."

DEDICATION OF WORLD WAR II MEMORIAL
Owensboro / August 14, 1947

"WE can best show our appreciation for what these dead have done by preserving those things for which they gave all," the commonwealth's chief executive declared.

In delivering the dedicatory address, Governor Willis said he felt grateful to the Davets[1] for inviting him to serve on this occasion, "one filled with patriotism and inspiration."

"This dedication is significant not only locally, but statewide, nation-wide, and worldwide," the governor continued, "because the sacrifice made by these 228 young heroes was for a country that is a key to the preservation of civilization."

He felt that it might properly be interpreted to the people whose hearts were closest to the object at the meeting, the governor said, with reference to the Gold Star parents present.[2] To do this he recalled that in ancient Athens there was a law that people assemble annually to pay tribute to the sons of Athens who had lost their lives in battle. "On one of these occasions," said Governor Willis, "the great Greek orator Pericles delivered an address which has become a model for all time to express what is involved in occasions of this kind. In it he extolled the values and virtues of his country, reminding his hearers of the freedom of the people, their liberty to employ their minds in whatever pursuits they chose and to express themselves freely, to use their talents as they chose and enjoy the institutions and fruitful way of life that their forefathers had built for them under their system of government. Then turning to speak of those who had made the supreme sacrifice for the glory and perpetuation of Athens, Pericles pointed out the futility of trying to pay tribute to them because he felt that all he could say would seem wholly inadequate to the loved ones of the fallen warriors, and appear exaggeration to those who did not know them.

"The thought I would leave with you is that the country for which these men died was worth dying for. Though their years were short, they have lived fuller lives than most men who live to a full four score and ten years. They have accomplished for world progress more than most men do in a long lifetime. And as for what people do for their country, these men have contributed to it all they could, all they had.

"So as we dedicate this monument in Owensboro in these beautiful surroundings today, let us appreciate the effort that brought it about. Let us realize and accept our responsibility to carry forward the princi-

ples for which they died, whose memory we now honor. As did the
people of Athens, let us take stock of the blessings of our country and
strive to advance civilization to a higher level. Let us remember that we
are the living comrades of those who have made the supreme sacrifice
and that it is our duty to perpetuate the cause for which they fought.
Let us prepare to preserve and perpetuate our country, knowing that
the future belongs to those who prepare. In no other way can we show
our appreciation than by preserving that which men have been willing
to die throughout the ages to preserve—the right to be free. Let us
rededicate our lives to right thinking and right living and resolve that
these men shall not have died in vain. In their heroic spirit let us go
forward as militant Americans, 'that this government of the people, by
the people, and for the people shall not perish from the earth.' "

---

1. Formed eleven months before this address, the Davets (from Daviess
County Veterans) was an organization of World War II veterans. Their president was Victor W. Topmiller. Owensboro *Messenger*, August 15, 1947.

2. On October 21, 1946, Governor Willis had proclaimed December 1 of that
year as "Gold Star Remembrance Day" and asked citizens to join him "in thus
paying tribute to these great heroes who have given the fullest measure for
their country and their home." Executive Orders, Secretary of State's Records.

TRANSPORTATION AND TOURISM

THE problem of America is the development of the character and strength of our people, and nothing is more helpful than travel and recreation in creating the atmosphere and conditions for growth and progress, Kentucky's Governor Simeon S. Willis told a special conference of governors and officials of the Upper Great Lakes region here today.

"Kentucky," Governor Willis said, "is vitally interested in your plans and similarly in the development of greater interest in the facilities for recreation and vacationists in my home state of Kentucky, really the center of America.

"Kentucky," Governor Willis told the conference, "hopes to be able to bring to all America the attractions and the history of Kentucky so that no American will be content until he has seen and enjoyed the hospitality of the state which is the very heart of America. The state . . . has hundreds of miles of beautiful rivers, parks, and recreation facilities throughout its length and breadth. Kentucky has the famous Bluegrass country, the birthplaces of Abraham Lincoln and Jefferson Davis, and the universally known Old Kentucky Home.

"Boys from Michigan and Kentucky," he said, discussing kinship among the states, "have been comrades in foxholes on the fighting fronts. For years to come they will desire to visit and revisit each other, and all of the people will be of a mind to travel and to know their country better.

"For this reason this has been a constructive conference. It has emphasized the spirit of good will with our neighbor at the north and brings sharply into view the unity of the people who think alike. Out of this conference will come factors which will enable us to know each other better, and the better we know each other the better we shall appreciate the greatness of our heritage."

REMARKS REGARDING TOURISM
Frankfort / August 2, 1945

ADVOCACY of a state organization similar to boards of trade in other states whose principal function would be to foster and promote tourist travel in Kentucky was announced by Governor Simeon Willis. The governor said he had not yet arrived at a definite plan for such an organization but that it would be allied with similar organizations in the Great Lakes area and southern Canada in a concerted action toward a common goal.

While some of the states, the governor said, already had organizations in one form or another it was agreed state organizations among all of them should be perfected without delay and allied as a Great Lakes association.

Governor Willis said the conference took the view that its movement was one of national scope and benefit. He pointed out that during the meeting a message was received from Governor Earl Warren of California[1] congratulating the meeting on its efforts and stating that he felt certain all promotional work done by the state of California and by every state accrued to the benefit of the nation at large.

"The value of money to our people," Governor Willis said, "depends upon the rate at which it circulates. No other dollar flows more quickly through channels of commerce or is spread more evenly among the people than the tourist's dollar. Tourist money," he continued, "is new money—cash money—from out of state that leaves a profit with every individual through whose hands it passes."

Development of Kentucky Lake State Park, near Eggner's Ferry, at an estimated initial expenditure of $250,000 is just one of Kentucky's potential attractions that might be fostered by a state board of trade or similar organization associated with a Great Lakes association to its maximum advantage, the governor added.

---

1. Earl Warren (1891-1974). Attorney; deputy city attorney, Oakland, 1919-20; deputy, chief deputy, and district attorney, Alameda County, 1920-29; California attorney general, 1939-43; governor of California, 1943-53; defeated as U.S. candidate for vice-president on Republican ticket, 1948; chief justice of the United States, 1953-69. *Biographical Directory of Governors*, 1: 123-24.

GREATER PADUCAH ASSOCIATION DINNER
Paducah / August 24, 1945

GOVERNOR WILLIS and J. Stephen Watkins made short talks at the dinner, and both spoke of their recognition of the importance of removing the tolls from bridges and of the possibilities for the future development of Kentucky which arise from free bridges.

"The people of America are going to rediscover America after all travel restrictions have been removed," Governor Willis said. "Americans won't be fenced in. Men who have served in the armed forces will want to visit their buddies all over the land, and others will want to get out and see the country. No place in this nation is more attractive than Kentucky. But it will take a lot of effort, thought, and cooperation to develop its resources to attract tourists."

FREE BRIDGE CELEBRATION
Eggner's Ferry / August 25, 1945

TODAY every American is thrilled with the happy knowledge of victory in the greatest war of all times. Every patriot rejoices that our soldiers are now coming home to rebuild their own careers and to help maintain free institutions. To those who gave the last full measure of devotion and who will not return, we owe an undying debt of gratitude, and to them we pay the tribute of our tears and praise.[1] In all honor, we give to them the pledge of America that the institutions for which they suffered and sacrificed will be preserved and maintained. To those who were disabled and maimed in the war, the people stand ready to make every provision that is possible to be made for their security and happiness. With appreciation and gratitude for the great accomplishments during the war, we turn our faces to the future without fear, but with a clear comprehension of the difficulties of the task. It will not be easy to rebuild a war-torn world. Unanticipated difficulties will necessarily arise, but the same resolution and genius that won the war will conquer the difficulties that follow the war. From the drama and suffering of battle, we turn to the less dramatic problems of peace.

Our primary duty and first responsibility is at home. There must be cooperation and unity among all the people and by their representatives occupying places of public responsibility. The task requires the best thought of all the people and the best efforts of all the leaders. There must be unity and understanding; there must be tolerance and good will. The patriotism of peace must be equal to the patriotism of war. Management, labor, government, are each and all responsible to the people. They must recognize that responsibility and endeavor by every means that genius can devise to work together for a better world. We must have statesmen, not only in high office, but in every branch of our activities and in every walk of life. Here at home there is much to do. Neglect can no longer be endured or tolerated. There are many programs to be carried to completion.

Eight toll bridges in various parts of the state were freed a week ago when sufficient funds were collected to discharge the debts incurred to build them. This action became necessary because the money was on hand to pay the bonds, and the law requires that collections of tolls shall cease when sufficient funds are realized to meet the obligations. The users of the bridges were entitled to free passage at the earliest possible moment. The formal celebration of the great event could wait a week to serve the convenience of the public. The keynote of administrative policy in this state now is strict adherence to the law and diligent action for the convenience and service of the public.

The highways, with free bridges, tie in with every program of progress. Every plan and pattern of the administration is connected directly or indirectly with the building and maintenance of a first-class road system. The roads carry trade and commerce, the products of the farm, factory, and mines; they serve military, police, patrol, and other enforcement officers; they help to advance the health program, the conservation plans, the educational and welfare work of the state. Good roads and free bridges are an essential part of every constructive activity in the development and upbuilding of the commonwealth.

Kentucky is a natural field for the tourist trade of the United States. Here the heartbeat of the nation can be felt, and here we have not only natural attractions, but historic shrines which appeal to every American. By good roads and free bridges, this business will be attracted to Kentucky. The people of the whole country have been taught by the war the great need of greater knowledge of our resources and opportunities. Other states and regions are preparing for this particular type of development, and Kentucky must keep abreast of the times. I am happy to know that our park, publicity, and conservation officials are awake to this opportunity.

The public health is ever a primary concern of government. Good health of the individuals is the basis of a strong nation. The health department is operating with efficiency and is advancing on every front. We are preparing to build five new tuberculosis hospitals, located in various parts of the state. These structures must be pushed to a rapid completion and placed in service as soon as possible.

The welfare department, with responsibility for public assistance as well as the custodial care of the wards of the state, is performing a difficult task with outstanding ability. The buildings and farms under that department are being improved, personnel is being enlarged, and the standard elevated. We have every reason to expect the complete success of the new program now in process of completion. Much is being done, but a great deal remains to be done.

Many of the ablest men in the state are making studies for postwar planning and for rebuilding of the tax structure along lines to provide for the essential needs of the government, with the greatest encouragement to the development of the state's potential resources.

Every activity of the state—agriculture, mining, banking, manufacture, trade, transportation, commerce—must be encouraged and stimulated to the limit of our capacity. The common schools, colleges, and the university are the peculiar care of the people of Kentucky, where education is recognized as a primary responsibility for the future welfare of the nation.

The military department, which is the sheet anchor of law and order and the first line of defense for the safety of the people in all times of peril, is being reconstituted and will continue to occupy the best attention of the men best fitted for the task. We should have more armories properly located to take care of the materials and equipment and for the training of men who will be enlisted for the necessary advancement and perfection of the National Guard.

We are not unmindful of the importance of aviation in the transportation of the future, and intensive study is being given to the matter of airports, landings, and roadways, as well as to the legislation pending in Congress and contemplated for the state. The highway department and the Aeronautics Commission have kept in touch with the progress of aviation, especially as it relates to our own situation in Kentucky. Trade and commerce, culture and progress, are promoted by every means of transportation, and good roads and free bridges are vital to every form and means of travel. As pointed out by other speakers on this program, the freeing of the bridges constitutes a milestone of progress affecting advantageously all of the plans for the future. There need be no conflict among the various agencies when coordination and cooperation is the watchword and the keynote.

It is proper, on this occasion, to say that Mr. J. Stephen Watkins, commissioner of highways, has earned the thanks of every Kentuckian by his outstanding administration of the highway department. It is a happy coincidence that he was chief engineer of the department when the program was initiated[2] and is now commissioner of highways when the crowning act of the venture has been accomplished. I congratulate the people of Kentucky that they have a highway commissioner of the character, capacity, and devotion to duty of Steve Watkins.

We have sought, and are still seeking, and shall continue to seek, the best talent available for the management of all the agencies. Administrative expenses have been cut to the bone, and the savings already accomplished have reached a record surpassing all previous experience in this state. Much has been accomplished under very great difficulties, and we are planning to accomplish even more in the coming months as opportunity widens.

We ask the cooperation and support of the people and of their representatives in the General Assembly. It is our purpose to carry forward these programs, affecting every governmental activity and agency, and set a standard for our successors in obtaining and maintaining good government. Every part and parcel of the state is embraced within the pattern of future development, and every resource within our reach and within the limit of our finances will be used to improve the standard of living and to promote the capacity and usefulness of the individual men and women of Kentucky. In carrying on these many related programs, it is essential that proper balance be maintained so that the orderly progress of the state will be assured.

Let us resolve to maintain in peace and reconstruction the same ability, devotion, and energy that was displayed in conducting the war against tyranny and oppression. It will achieve like results and bring the same rewards. Kentuckians once more will demonstrate to the world that "Peace hath her victories no less renowned than war."[3]

---

1. V-E Day was May 8, 1945. On August 6 and 9 atomic bombs had been dropped on Japan. The official surrender date was September 2, 1945. Kentucky, with 2.1 percent of the nation's population, had furnished 2.0 percent of the members in the armed forces and had suffered 2.2 percent of the dead and missing. See *World War II Honor List of Dead and Missing: State of Kentucky* (Washington, D.C., 1946), i.

2. Under Governor Flem Sampson.

3. The quote is from John Milton (1608-1674) to Oliver Cromwell in 1652. See John Bartlett, *Familiar Quotations,* 13th ed. (Boston, 1955), 251.

FREEING MAYSVILLE BRIDGE CEREMONY
Maysville / October 1, 1945

FELLOW citizens:

This celebration marks the fulfillment of well-laid plans. For more than a century this spot has afforded the crossing place from the South to the North and East. Tradition has kept alive historic incidents of the early travel of famous men to the national capital, and even yet along the route the stopping places of those travelers are remembered. New conditions bring new methods, and in 1931 the need for a bridge at this point could not longer be postponed. Looking forward to this day, the farseeing men of that day planned wisely for the achievement of this modern improvement. To the foresight of those men who planned this bridge we owe a debt of gratitude and praise.

Highways, with free bridges, are basic in a complete system of transportation. They are essential to all other forms of travel and transport. Those who use rail, river, or air for the carriage of passengers and cargo must first use the highways. Good roads tie in with every program of progress. Whether relating to education, health, welfare, or public safety, every plan and pattern devised for the promotion of such objectives must rest primarily upon good roads and must depend at last upon the maintenance of highways and bridges for safe and convenient communication. The many services which modern government undertakes to render to the people would not be possible without highway connections. It opens the market to the products of the farm, factory, and mine. It provides means of travel to the schools, churches, hospitals, and to all the institutions maintained for the public welfare.

The future belongs to those who prepare for it. In a competitive world, economic law will always rule. As new methods are found, adjustments must be made to meet them. In this modern age our people must be the masters of the making and management of machines. As America leads the world today in the field, that leadership must be maintained by preparation for the future. The world has been brought closer together than ever before. The inventions of genius and the advances of science have brought all nations and all peoples closer together. There must be a unity and understanding among all nations and peoples in order that peace may be maintained. The art of living together must be learned anew by all peoples. The experience in the great war which has just ended has proven the value of unity, understanding, and cooperation.

The same principles that brought success in armed conflict must be applied to bring success in the days of peace. Above all, and over all, there must be unity and understanding among our own people. Such unity and understanding comes from knowledge and tolerance and good will. The development of new ideas and the progress of invention will constitute a continuing challenge to the sufficiency and soundness of our systems of government and education. We must see to it that our people know and understand the history of our country and its accomplishments and the unexampled success of free institutions. By such understanding, we may be sure of the acceptance of the principles and practices of a people's government. Nothing succeeds like success.

The great problem is to establish and maintain justice among our own people and with all the nations of the earth. This can be done only by developing a generation of just people. Every activity of the state, as well as new activities that may be developed in the future, must be coordinated with the fundamental principles of free institutions. Management, labor, and government are each and all responsible to the people as a whole. They must recognize that responsibility and endeavor by every means that genius can devise to work together for a better day and a better world. We must have statesmen, not only in high office, but in every branch of our activity and in every walk of life.

As we grapple with problems, we must realize the inescapable limitations inherent in a government of restricted powers. We must avoid the falsehood of extremes. We must "prove all things and hold fast to that which is good." The significance of an occasion like this, when a great public improvement has been completed, is that it marks a milestone in the progress of a people and a stepping stone toward further advancement. Locally, where the benefits of this free bridge will be most immediately realized, the people are to be congratulated. It will add much to the future welfare and prosperity of this thriving community. But beyond the local significance of this occasion we may envision the broader, indirect benefits to the whole state. It is by the development of local communities that the state is enabled to advance. With due local pride in every community, the fact must not be over-looked that the rights and interests of the whole people must be carefully safeguarded. It is easy to see the advantage of a particular improvement, but it is the combination of all local improvements that builds up the greatness of the state and the nation.

As we go forward in the work of building let us seek cooperation and support for the things that make for the general welfare of the state. Building, not only for today, but for tomorrow as well, let us resolve to maintain in peace and reconstruction the same high qualities that characterized our efforts in the war. The motto of Kentucky is "United We Stand." Forgetting all petty differences, and bravely facing diffi-culties, let us strive to maintain unity from day to day. The achieve-ments of the past are but a prelude to greater achievements for the future.

KENTUCKY GOOD ROADS FEDERATION
Lexington / October 15, 1945

FRIENDS and lovers of Kentucky:

The good roads amendment was passed by the General Assembly in 1944 by a unanimous Senate and with but one dissenting vote in the House. It was approved by the governor and will be on the ballot for the action of the voters on November 6.[1] Opposition has since developed, and I have carefully considered the objections made by the opponents of the measure. Some of these objections are so flimsy and unfounded as to impugn the good faith or good judgment of those who interpose them. Yet there are some sincere and genuine friends of good roads who do not understand the true situation, and they are being misled by two fallacies: first, that it is not necessary to have a constitutional amendment to protect the road funds from diversion to other purposes; and, second, that the proposed amendment is not clear enough as to its purpose and effect. Sixteen other states have found it necessary to adopt such amendments, and several states are proceeding in the same manner to protect their road funds. We have learned from our own experience that such a provision is necessary, because at every session of the legislature weeks are spent in combatting efforts to make inroads on the road fund. Mere statutory protection is not enough. It is too easily overturned. Already, since 1935, more than $10 million of highway users' taxes have been diverted to nonhighway purposes. Certainly protection is necessary when so much money is being diverted from the road funds to other purposes. This is especially rough treatment of the road users because they pay all the taxes for the roads and a very large proportion of all other taxes which make up the general fund. The assumption that the amendment is not necessary is contrary to the facts and does not convince anyone who has been in close contact with the subject during the last decade. The amendment is absolutely necessary to secure the road fund, now and in the future.

The second objection that the proposed amendment is not clear, but vague and ambiguous, is not tenable. Any such argument is derived from commentators on the amendment and disregards the words of the amendment itself. Its language is perfectly clear and simple. It provides in unequivocal terms that no money derived from excise or license taxation relating to gasoline and other motor fuels shall be expended for other than the highway purposes specified. It provides further, in terms equally clear, that no monies derived from fees, excise, or license taxation relating to regulation, operation, or use of vehicles on public highways shall be used for other than the highway purposes specified. There is nothing else covered or touched by the proposed amendment. It is limited strictly to the type of taxation specified, which is nothing more than the direct taxes paid by the road users of the state.

The highway purposes specified for which the funds may be used, if the amendment is adopted, include: (1) cost of administration; (2) statutory refunds and adjustments; (3) payment of highway obligations; (4) cost for construction, reconstruction, rights of way, maintenance, and repair of public highways and bridges; and (5) expense of enforcing state traffic and motor vehicle laws. These are the obligations and expenses directly and incidentally resulting from the construction, maintenance, and patrol of the state highway system. It does not touch in any way, directly or indirectly, any ad valorem tax or any other taxes than those specified by name and description in the amendment proposed. It does not affect the truck license taxes now returned, in part, to the various counties, because such money can now be used only for roads and bridges, and that specific use is within the terms of the proposed amendment. There is no confusion about the amendment, but there is an effort to create confusion by those who do not desire to promote the good roads program. The only confusion is in the minds of those who wish to be confused, to create confusion, or who do not understand the true situation. The opponents of the good roads amendment resort to groundless excuses. The public cannot afford to follow those who resort to phony arguments. The power of the legislature is not improperly curtailed. It remains perfectly free to levy the taxes for the roads and all other taxes. The only limitation is that taxes levied on these particular sources cannot be diverted from highway purposes. It secures to the road funds all taxes of the nature, type, and character specified. The greatest need in Kentucky today is the completion of our highway system and the construction of our rural roads. We have 130,000 farm units desperately in need of good roads. The cost of such work is very great, and in order to build these roads the money must be provided. The rural road program stands at the forefront because it affords access to the schools, churches, and markets. It will reduce the unfortunate record of absence from the schools which is too great to be endured. The money is needed now for more construction, and as construction is completed the need for maintenance will require more money and more revenue.

Aviation is tied in with good roads. The highways will always do more for aviation than any possible gas tax can compensate. The development of our aeronautics program will be promoted by the development of our road program. Those who seek to create confusion and division among our people retard the progress of the state. If all the roads we need were built today it would yet require all of the fund derived from these sources mentioned by the amendment for perpetual maintenance and proper upkeep. We know it will require many years to build the roads needed in Kentucky. We must be prepared to match federal funds for the highway program, and we must have sufficient funds for the immediate development of the rural road program which has been planned. It is strictly a nonpartisan, progressive step, which sixteen other states have already taken. All parties should support it because it will benefit all. I believe the adoption of this amendment will advance the welfare of Kentucky and of all Kentuckians. I heartily and unreservedly support it. I regard the objections interposed to it as frivolous and fallacious. I ask all voters to support the amendment, which will advance the greatest road program ever planned for Kentucky.[2]

---

1. The amendment (Senate Bill 37, Chapter 9) provided that money derived from gasoline taxes and other highway-connected sources must be used only on road-related expenditures. See Kentucky *Acts* (1944), 22-23. See also document dated September 4, 1945, in "State Government Administration" section.

2. Voters overwhelmingly approved the amendment by a 160,533 to 42,458 vote margin, and it was declared in force on December 11, 1946. See Executive Orders, Secretary of State's Records.

STATEMENT REGARDING OPENING
OF CLAY'S FERRY BRIDGE
Clay's Ferry / August 17, 1946

To all Kentuckians and Visitors to Kentucky:

Today marks another forward step in Kentucky's highway system. Today we are opening Clay's Ferry Bridge spanning the beautiful Kentucky River from one palisade to another, the highest traffic bridge in America east of the Mississippi River. This essential span will secure the safety of the traveling public and eliminate the small iron bridge that has connected the two great counties of Fayette and Madison on this much-traveled route.

Inestimable commercial value will result over the years to come from this improved transportation facility. The scenic beauty in this surrounding community is not surpassed in the world. Tourists will come from far and wide, and we shall welcome them and greet them with true Kentucky hospitality.

This is but another small link in the chain of progress that is intended for Kentucky, Kentuckians, and all who come within her borders.

DEDICATION OF CLAY'S FERRY BRIDGE
Clay's Ferry / August 17, 1946

AFTER Mr. [J. Stephen] Watkins had recited the history of the bridge and its predecessor and had given various measurements, statistics, and cost figures, Governor Willis said his purpose was to "interpret what it means to us." He said he was "proud of the people of Kentucky for their resolution to press forward," and [he] expressed confidence that Kentuckians, in addition to acquiring improved bridges, highways, and airports, also would insist upon further educational progress and improvements in cultural and spiritual conditions of the commonwealth.

The governor asserted transportation was "basic in every human activity," adding, "You cannot have adequate business activities or advancements in human society without it. Increased transportation facilities will result in increased prosperity and happiness of all the people."

Governor Willis called attention to the fact that Clay's Ferry always had been the scene of progress in transportation, saying a ferry established there in 1792, the year Kentucky achieved statehood, might appear crude when compared to 1946 standards, [but] it sufficed in those days.

He pointed to Kentucky's now having a population as great as that of the original thirteen colonies prior to the establishment of the old ferry and said the old iron bridge of 1869, considering the state's population and the amount of travel then, was an advancement comparable to the erection of the new bridge being duplicated.[1]

---

1. Kentucky's population in 1940 was 2,845,627; the United States' population in 1790 had been 3,929,214. *Sixteenth Census* (1940), 1: 6, 19.

FREEING LIVERMORE BRIDGE CEREMONY
Livermore / August 30, 1946

THE governor warned that in this age of science and invention the people should be cautious about permitting the government to engage in too many projects affecting the welfare of citizenry.

"We should permit nothing to be done by the government that we can do ourselves," said Governor Willis. "It has been our experience that government work costs us more."

He explained, however, that "there are some things which affect the welfare of all which we have to permit the government to undertake—education and the building of hospitals and other public institutions."

Then he gave another admonition, this time that "the extent and caliber of service rendered by the state to the people depends largely on the degree of their intelligence and alertness."

"The significance of an occasion such as this lies in the fact that it marks the progress of our people," Governor Willis said. "The progress we are making in Kentucky is important."

He pointed out that transportation is "the great and important" element in the nation's commerce and that transportation depends on highways and bridges.

"The highway department deserves your gratitude and thanks for a job well done," the governor declared. "It doesn't matter which political party did it. The important thing is that it has been done."[1]

---

1. This account is a composite drawn from the *Courier-Journal*, August 31, 1946, and the Owensboro *Messenger*, September 1, 1946.

DEDICATION OF "MISSING LINK" OF U.S. 23
Lowmansville / September 14, 1946

MR. FORGEY,[1] distinguished guests, ladies and gentlemen:

I know you will permit me a few personal words on this occasion. Colonel Forgey regrets that his picture was not put in the program. It was wholly unnecessary. Anybody who ever saw Mr. Forgey's face never forgets it. Senator See[2] has been very gracious in his remarks, and it is due him to say that night or day at his own expense he helped in bringing about this great day.

Any day is good to dedicate a road, but this day is perfect for the purpose. I must think of those who have helped and are no longer with us. And so it seems to me that in dedicating this road we dedicate it to the memory of those who are gone. We dedicate it to the honor of those who are still with us helping. And we dedicate it to the future use of all Kentuckians and Americans everywhere.

I am exceedingly proud of this occasion. You have heard something of the difficulties even more than you realize. This road has been only one of the countless problems with which the people of Kentucky have had to grapple. They have faced their problems resolutely. They have faced them with good will. They have faced them with an ardor that never dies. It is easy to criticize; it is lovely to praise. But it is the things accomplished that give us a stepping stone to ever greater things.

Transportation is essential in every activity of our lives. You cannot build a home without involving transportation. You cannot build or attend or maintain a school or church without transportation. You cannot conduct a business without transportation. And transportation is impossible without the facilities of transportation.

Our great forefathers could get along on horseback. But as population increased, as the machine age came upon us, transportation had to be advanced to keep step with the progress of humanity. The people of Kentucky are keeping step. They try to compare us unfavorably with the accomplishments of some other states, but in the character and courage and the stamina and the stability of our people we have no superiors anywhere on the face of the earth.

And the important fact is not how tall are your buildings or how big the things you have made, but how great is the character and the capacity and the aspirations of your people. That is the test. And Kentucky is moving in the right direction and will not be diverted from her path.

You are interested in roads, of course; you are interested in many, many other things. You are interested in your construction work; you are interested in your school work; you are interested in your military reorganization; you are interested in all of these activities which are being carried on for you and with your support and at your expense to make our security greater, to make our national defense more certain. We are going into an age of the greatest competition ever known in the world. The transportation facilities involve roads; they involve waterways; they involve rails; and they involve the air. And all forms of transportation must be used and will be used rapidly as we advance in the future.

Balance your programs; permit no excess in any direction but keep going forward all the time. I think the spirit of Kentucky and the spirit of America was expressed by that old admiral who said, "Damn the torpedoes! Move on!"[3]

The Latins had a maxim about difficulties which must be overcome to reach the stars: The greater the difficulties, the greater the achievements. And those difficulties are overcome. Just as an individual is a greater individual if he overcomes difficulties, so a people are greater as they overcome difficulties. And when you overcome one difficulty you will find others in your path. And you will observe when a great road is finished—like this one—which means so much to the people of this part of the state and to all the people of the state, it involved the construction of other roads immediately. Roads leading to this road; roads connecting this road with those across the counties.

So that your problem is to think clearly; decide wisely and go forward as far and as fast as common sense and your ability will permit you. Listen not to promises or listen not to those who try to tell you they will do the impossible, but look at the problem yourself and see how much we can do to advance the interests of Kentucky. And those interests involve the health of the people of Kentucky, and we have in progress and advancing day by day a great program for the health of the people of Kentucky. We have made advancements in the educational field, and we are planning ever greater advancements. Because a free people must educate its youth, we must preserve and protect and develop every individual in our society. With such a program we will learn to know each other better, build good will, maintain faith in God and faith in each other.[4]

---

1. Benjamin F. Forgey (1866-1960). Teacher and superintendent in Ohio schools in late 1880s and 1890s; editor of newspapers in Ironton, Ohio, and Catlettsburg, Kentucky, before becoming editor, then president, publisher, and chairman of the board of the Ashland *Independent;* president of Kentucky Press Association. Robert A. McCullough, Jr., to the editor, August 6, 1986, and enclosures; Lexington *Herald-Leader,* September 15, 1946.

2. Ira See (1887-1975). Attorney; editor of Louisa paper; postmaster of Louisa for thirteen years; elected senator 1935, 1939, 1943. *Kentucky Directory,* 170; Bureau of Vital Statistics.

3. Loyall Farragut, in his *Life of David Glasgow Farragut* (New York, 1879), 416-17, indicated that Admiral David Glasgow Farragut (1801-1870) had uttered

the words, "Damn the torpedoes. . . . Go ahead. . . . Full speed," on August 5, 1864, at the Battle of Mobile Bay, Alabama.

4. The last paragraph of the talk is a composite taken from the Ashland *Daily Independent*, September 15, 1946, and the Paintsville *Herald*, September 19, 1946. The bulk of the address is transcribed from a recording made from the governor's talk as given over WHAS radio. Paragraph arrangement is by the editor.

DEDICATION OF MAMMOTH CAVE
AS NATIONAL PARK
Mammoth Cave / September 18, 1946

Mr. Chairman, Secretary Krug,[1] ladies and gentlemen:

On behalf of the people of Kentucky it is my privilege to present to the nation the park area known as Mammoth Cave. Irvin Cobb[2] described it as an open mouth to proclaim the glories of Kentucky and an open door to her hospitality. Here the beauty, the mystery, and the magnificence of nature's handiwork is [*sic*] richly displayed for the contemplation and enjoyment of mankind.

It was long apparent to farseeing Kentuckians that here was a perfect setting for a great national park. Leading men set about to accomplish a dream. Generous-hearted people gave of their means, their time, and their talents to bring reality to that dream. Many who helped are no longer with us. We dedicate this day to honor the memory of those who did not live to enjoy this day's triumph; to congratulate those still with us who struggled for the ideal; and to the millions who will come here from all over the world we hope to provide entertainment, instruction, and inspiration.[3]

The facts of this long struggle are well known and have been related in the press. It remains for me, Mr. Secretary, only to present to you as the representative of all people of the United States this great natural asset to be preserved and used for the welfare and happiness of the people of today and for generations yet unborn.

Kentucky does not part with Mammoth Cave; it merely transfers to the custody of the nation a great national asset for the perpetual use of a great and generous people.[4]

1. Julius Albert Krug (1907-1970). Involved with various utilities in Wisconsin, 1930-35; public utility expert, Federal Communications Commission, 1935-37; reorganized Kentucky Public Service Commission, 1937; chief power engineer, Tennessee Valley Authority, 1938; head of power branch of Office of War Utilities and chairman of a War Production Board committee, 1943-44; chairman of War Production Board, 1944-45; U.S. secretary of the interior, 1946-49; president of a Tennessee asphalt company. Robert Sobel, ed., *Biographical Directory of the United States Executive Branch, 1774-1977* (Westport, Conn., 1977), 211.

2. Irvin Shrewsbury Cobb (1876-1944). Reporter and managing editor, Paducah *Daily News,* and later *Daily Democrat;* reporter, New York *Evening Sun,* 1904-05, and *Evening World,* 1905-11; staff contributor, *Saturday Evening Post,* 1911-22, and *Cosmopolitan,* 1922-32; author of "Judge Priest" series of stories, numerous books of humor, and an autobiography; scriptwriter and actor after 1934. *DAB, Supplement 3:* 170-71.

3. In 1924 the Mammoth Cave National Park Association was formed to create a national park in the area; two years later President Calvin Coolidge signed a bill permitting federal acceptance when minimum land requirements were met.

A decade later, in 1936, those requirements had been realized; and on July 1, 1941, the park received its first federal appropriations. The war delayed formal acceptance until 1946. See *Courier-Journal Magazine,* September 15, 1946.

4. This account is a transcription of a WHAS radio recording of the talk. Paragraph arrangement is by the editor.

NORTH-SOUTH HIGHWAY EXPOSITION
Owensboro / October 11, 1947

GOVERNOR SIMEON WILLIS told an audience at a dinner in his honor here tonight that the theme of the North-South Highway Exposition— to free the Owensboro bridge and build an improved highway through Indiana, Kentucky, and Tennessee—is a commendable one and that the people who are backing the project are to be encouraged and congratulated for their endeavors.

"Nothing gives me more pleasure than freeing bridges," Governor Willis said, "since it is a sign of progress. Transportation is the lifeblood of the growth of a community, and the fewer barriers to that facility, the greater the progress of the community. The use of tolls is not the best way to build bridges, but in many instances that has been the only means at our disposal in constructing them. Many things must be considered in a program to eliminate the toll charges, and we must be careful to go about such business in a businesslike manner so that we may do the best thing for the community and state at large."

FREEING MILTON-MADISON BRIDGE CEREMONY
Milton / November 1, 1947

EARLIER, in the formal speeches, Willis hailed the event as opening wide the road for ever-increasing cultural and economic intercourse between the people on the opposite sides of the river.

"The people of Kentucky and Indiana are more than just neighbors," Willis said. "They are, in fact, kinfolks—that is what makes Indiana great."

LEGISLATIVE ACTIONS,
1946-1947

STATE OF THE COMMONWEALTH
Frankfort / January 8, 1946

THE constitution of Kentucky directs the governor, from time to time, to give to the General Assembly information of the state of the commonwealth and recommend to their consideration such measures as he may deem expedient.

The statute is more specific. It requires the governor to submit a budget message, giving a summary description of his proposed financial policies and plans, and explaining the more important features of the proposed financial and operating programs and their anticipated effects on the finances and welfare of the state.

The duties thus imposed I shall now proceed to discharge in a spirit of complete dedication to the welfare of our state, and with the desire to give fullest cooperation with you in your legislative work.

The first problem confronting us is the determination of the amount of money to be expended during the two fiscal years beginning July 1, 1946. We must first explore the available resources and then adjust the expenditures to be made for all purposes to those resources.

We start with the proposition that the budget must be kept in balance. We can expend only the amount of money that we have or can reasonably anticipate. This is a sound requirement of the law. It is good sense and good housekeeping.

The requests of the various agencies, or so-called budget units, which spend money far exceed the estimated revenues and the accumulated savings known as the surplus. This is not intended as a criticism of the agencies asking money. It is natural for them to seek expansion of their services, and to desire an extension of their operations. It is the usual experience here and elsewhere, and you need not be surprised when you see the many requests for a doubling of the appropriations to certain units. But they know, and you know, that such a thing is not possible. We can only distribute fairly among the many deserving objectives the money that the people are able to supply. An appropriation bill has been carefully prepared, based on my considered recommendations. It is ready for your consideration. The complete budget report has been prepared and is in the hands of the printer. It will be on your desks in a very short time. It will contain the vital facts essential for your study in reaching conclusions.

The total amount proposed to be appropriated by this act for the fiscal year 1946-1947 is $34,212,215. This does not include the provision made for $2 million for the institutional improvements to be carried on from time to time as needed and as the money is available. It excludes county fees because they are merely cleared through the state treasury without any addition to the revenue or any reduction of expenses. For the second year, 1947-1948, the total amount to be appropriated is $34,402,215 on the same basis as for the first year and subject to the same explanation. This will maintain the current level of expenditures for all the departments of government, with some necessary increases to meet new obligations and proven needs. There is an increase over last year for the welfare department in order to meet the ever-increasing responsibility to the wards of the state. This does not include any provision for the operation of Darnall Hospital, which is expected to be turned over to the state very soon. That subject is being studied thoroughly, and a special bill will be offered in due time at this session to take care of the operation of Darnall.[1] Such information as we have has been given to the Legislative Council and to the public. It will require an appropriation for the remainder of this fiscal year and for the next biennium. The proposed act contains an amendment to the appropriation act of the special session of 1944 to make the balance of the special institutional improvement fund applicable also to Darnall and the Kentucky Children's Home at Lyndon. Certain additional information will be necessary in order to make the necessary provisions for Darnall, which will be given to you later in the session. But we know that Darnall will render necessary a substantial addition to the Department of Welfare appropriation for ordinary and recurring expenses of operation.

In view of the conditions following the end of the war, it is deemed wise to keep within the present limits of expenditures. We are returning to normal conditions from an economy of war, and during the transition period there will be many adjustments to be made. We are faced with dangers both in this state and in the nation. It is prudent to await developments before any attempt is made to enlarge the demands upon the state treasury.

The educational department is carried on the same level as it was in the last appropriation act. You will recall that there was a substantial advance in the provisions made for the common schools. A special appropriation of $3 million to the Department of Education was made for the fiscal year ending June 30, 1944, and the school fund was advanced $5 million over the prior years for each of the last two fiscal years. It was the provision made for the schools and for welfare that prevented a reduction of the appropriations in 1944. The crisis in which the schools were then engulfed is passing, and the shortage of teachers which was critical in 1944 will soon be over. In returning to normal conditions, the present provision will undoubtedly enable the schools to perform their tasks. As to the institutions of higher learning, the amounts needed have to be determined from past experience, and with consideration of probable future needs. During the past two years all these institutions of higher learning have been occupied in war work. The budget, however, was maintained on the assumption that normal conditions would soon return, and the provisions made for them should be ample for economical administration under present conditions, and with the existing or expected enrollment. The Kentucky State College for Negroes has been given an increased appropriation. This was necessary because its enrollment and the work it is expected to accomplish could not be done without it. A capital outlay of $200,000 for the two years has been authorized to meet the pressing needs of that institution. In view of the importance of that school, it must be more strongly supported to enable it to meet the demands the state is putting upon it.

We are proceeding with the construction of the five tuberculosis hospitals, as directed by the act of 1944. Advertisements for bids on two of them are now out, and the others will be issued as fast as the architects and engineers can prepare for them. The contracts for the five buildings will be let at the same time. Provision is made for completing and equipping them in the emergency fund of $2 million if that becomes necessary. The present appropriation of $1,500,000 is expected to construct the five tuberculosis main buildings, and when they are completed, it will be necessary to equip them and to build the subsidiary structures. Various suggestions have been made as to the cost, but no definite estimate has been made. It is not possible to estimate now what costs may be a year or so ahead. It is not practical to make provisions for the equipment until the buildings are completed and the equipment to be installed is determined. If it is necessary to purchase a portion of the equipment or do additional work before the next session of the General Assembly, it can be paid for out of the emergency fund of $2 million set up in the appropriation act. It may be possible that the Public Health Service of the United States will be prepared by that time to provide funds equal to what the state expends in the tuberculosis institutions. That is the expectation of the public health officials, and legislation to that end is pending in Congress. If this materializes, it will be a great assistance to the tubercular hospitals and will simplify our problem when it arises. If it does not become available, the provision made by the present bill will carry them to the next session in 1948.

Other capital outlays will consist mostly of repairs. By reason of the acquisition of Darnall Hospital, the welfare department will be able to cancel the construction of two or more buildings that were contemplated in the institutional program. The work provided for in this act will be as extensive as the capacity of the department can carry on economically because when work is being done at an institution, operation must go on, and only a limited amount of work at each institution can be done at one time.

The state departments are operating efficiently and economically. They will continue to do so, and in my opinion they can carry on their work within the appropriations recommended without impairment of efficiency. This is not the time for the expansion of expenditures. That should be determined after conditions have become stabilized and after the questions have been discussed before, determined upon, and decided by the people. The present policy, in the middle of a term, is and should be economy and curtailment of expenses in every way, consistent with competent performance of governmental duties. It would be a fine thing if the state was able to meet all the meritorious requests that come before the General Assembly, but the estimates of possible revenue admonish us to be realistic in determining what can be done with what we have or can reasonably expect.

It is not deemed prudent at this time to make further reductions of the departmental appropriations. There are a large number of appropriations that are fixed and unchangeable, and it is not necessary to discuss them. They must be paid in any event. The ordinary emergency fund of $250,000, which has proven sufficient in the past, has been retained. No doubt it will be sufficient in the future to meet all administrative emergencies. I have steadfastly refused to expend any of that money except for the most pressing needs, and that shall continue to be my policy. It is necessary, however, to have it available in case of actual necessity for carrying on administrative functions.

During the past two years a great deal of work has been done in the face of endless difficulties. Improvement has been marked at all of the institutional buildings. I hope you may visit them and see for yourselves. As before mentioned, the welfare department has the increased responsibilities which require that its former appropriation of $2,760,000 be increased to $3,125,000. Moreover, a supplemental appropriation for the operation of Darnall will be necessary. In addition to that amount, there is provision for public assistance in cooperation with the federal government under the Social Security Act. The former appropriation was insufficient, and a special session was necessary in order to avoid missing a payment for the month of June, 1945. It is necessary to raise this appropriation to $5,050,000 in order to maintain the present level of assistance, which we trust will carry us through the next two years. The commissioner of welfare may need a deficiency appropriation to carry the public assistance at the present level to June 30, 1946. If so, you will be advised about that in due time.

The appropriations for the highway department have been changed somewhat in order to meet the alterations in the allocation of federal grants. The highway department will explain fully all the details of the changes that have been made necessary. The most drastic and important change is with reference to rural roads, which are vital to the upbuilding of Kentucky. The appropriation heretofore of $2 million annually for rural roads has been increased to $4 million as a minimum or to 20 percent of the state road income, if that amount is greater than $4 million. The expenditure of this money must be safeguarded so as to secure the best results. Care must be exercised in order to keep a proper balance among the classes of roads which receive federal aid in order that we may match all federal funds. The federal department has made its rules and fixed the relative amounts to be allocated on the several classes of roads. The highway department has carefully planned to meet this situation and to comply with all requirements. There will be some requests for legislation in order to facilitate the highway program, and I recommend that you give most careful consideration to these requests. Road building has been at a standstill because of the war, and there [are] now on hand available funds, perfected plans, and a determined purpose to carry on a road building program of the greatest magnitude ever known in this state. It must be encouraged and aided. Your cooperation will be greatly appreciated by the people of Kentucky, who desire this program to be advanced and facilitated. Nothing is more important in this state today than the building of rural roads.

The highway patrol is rendering excellent service. It is being improved in efficiency, in personnel, and in public esteem. It is recommended that it remain at its present limit in numbers. By the use of proper radio equipment, it is believed that its efficiency will be multiplied much more than would be possible by an increase of personnel. It is difficult to obtain and retain good personnel in the lower brackets at the salaries now paid. We have asked for an additional appropriation in order that these salaries in the lower brackets might be raised slightly and to pay the expense of operating the radio system. The former appropriation of $500,000 has been increased to $750,000. One half, or $125,000, is to complete the radio station and equipment. The other half [is] to provide the increased pay for the patrolmen and for the expense of operation of the radio system.

I believe the expenditures proposed by the act are reasonable and necessary. I believe that they are as economical as it is safe to attempt at this time. I believe they meet the expectations of the people and that they will maintain the present level of governmental service in the state. The general welfare of the people of Kentucky will be prompted by your approval of this program.

The next subject of vital importance for your consideration is the revenue which may be expected to meet the expenditures called for by the appropriation act. As I have said, only the amount of money actually realized can be expended. If the appropriations should exceed the revenues, it would be necessary to reduce the sums appropriated so as to be within the income, regardless of the amount of the appropriations. Such a result was avoided in the appropriation bill of 1944 by creating an emergency expenditure fund from the surplus. This was a wise provision, and it has been carried forward in the proposed appropriation bill. This will prevent a reduction of appropriations in case the revenue should fall off; and if the revenues equal the appropriations, then the emergency expenditure fund will revert to the general fund for appropriation again by the General Assembly. A word of caution is necessary in dealing with estimates. They are based on the assumption that present conditions and trends of income will remain constant. A number of things could occur that would reduce the actual below the estimated revenues. Allowances must be made for fluctuations, which frequently occur in times of economic readjustment. The commissioner of revenue emphasizes this factor in explaining the estimates, and it must be kept constantly in mind in order to avoid a disastrous mistake.

The estimate of total income by the Department of Revenue for the first fiscal year, 1946-47, including the additions by the finance department of revenues that are not collected by the revenue department, is $36,738,152, excluding county fees which clear through the state treasury but add nothing to the income. For the second year of the biennium the estimate is $36,695,052, likewise excluding the county fees. These estimates have been verified by both the finance and revenue departments. If the amount of these estimates is realized, the appropriations will be within the estimated revenue. For the first fiscal year the expenditures proposed would be $2,525,937 less than the estimated revenue, and for the second fiscal year the expenditures would be $2,292,837 less than the estimated revenue. As noted before, this does not include the $2 million for institutional repairs and equipment, which can be included without exceeding the estimated revenue. The $2 million for improvement of the institutional buildings is to be made from surplus and is not included in this calculation. If the personal income tax, which is estimated to produce $4 million for the last year of the biennium should be repealed, the estimate for the second year of the biennium, 1947-1948, would be reduced to $32,695,052, which would be $1,707,163 less than the appropriations proposed for that year. That deficit would be protected completely by the "emergency expenditure fund" which has been set up. It is clear, therefore, that you can now repeal the personal income tax and maintain the present level of governmental services without any new or additional taxes. The surplus fund is a cushion against declining revenues and should be used wisely for the financial management of the operations of government. The estimates vary as to the probable amount of the surplus that will exist on June 30, 1946. It will depend on the collection trends holding up and upon the deficiency appropriations which you may make at this session. It will undoubtedly be sufficient to meet the requirements of this bill, and for that reason I do not try to supply you with a definite estimate. A substantial amount should be kept free to meet any contingencies that may arise. It is not only unwise but dangerous to dissipate the whole surplus. It is derived from taxes and belongs to the people to be devoted to their service. The proposed act would devote not to exceed $2 million of it to capital outlay and institutional improvements. The sum of $4 million for each year of the next biennium is placed in an "emergency expenditure fund" for protection against a possible failure of the revenues to equal the appropriations proposed. A similar fund was created by the Appropriation Act of 1944 and proved its wisdom. It is likely that some deficiency appropriations will be made by you which will reduce the amount of it.

But the provision made will still leave a safe cushion to carry the state through the period of reconversion.

As I explained to the General Assembly in 1944, I favor the reduction of taxes for the relief of the taxpayers of Kentucky. As we pass from the economy of war to normal conditions the burden on the taxpayers will be more and more difficult to bear. The federal government and other states have recognized this fact and have made substantial reductions in taxes beginning this year. A repeal of the personal income tax will benefit all taxpayers because the income of the people of the state is the basis and source of all tax payments. Heroic efforts are being made by the business, educational, and professional men of the state to promote and develop the economic interests of the commonwealth. We all realize that the way to reach the higher level of governmental service which we desire ultimately to attain in Kentucky is to build up our productive capacity and increase the per capita income of our people. On a per capita income of less than $700 per year we can never make expenditures equal to those states which have a per capita income of twice that sum. By building up the income of our people as a whole we can obtain a higher level of service to the public, as well as a higher standard of living. That is the long-range objective. As a matter of prudence and safety we should retain, for the present, the corporate income tax. The taxpayers not only pay large sums to the state of Kentucky, but they pay even larger sums to the local governments and to the federal government. We know that one of the most difficult problems of the people of Kentucky is to meet their financial responsibilities to governments. The people have a right to expect, as we return to normal conditions, a reversal of the trend toward ever-increasing governmental expenditures. Just as we do not maintain in peace the high level of production which we maintain in war, we cannot maintain in a reconversion period the high level of expenditure which war entails. The primary purpose of government is to promote the safety, welfare, and happiness of the people. This cannot be done unless due regard is given to all the people, and consideration for the taxpayers is of paramount importance. Taxes are paid in the sweat of everyone who works and affect every person, directly or indirectly. A benefit to the taxpayers redounds to the good of all.

The repeal of the personal income tax will place the state in a sound competitive position to attract new business enterprises and to retain that which we now have. Along the borderline it will give special impetus to enterprise. It will stimulate the expansion of industrial and manufacturing concerns, both large and small, already engaged in business in this state, resulting in increased employment and enlarged incomes. It will build up the faith of the people in the friendly attitude of our lawmakers toward industrial development, and reflect the sense of justice of the lawmakers of Kentucky. It will retard the tendency toward inflation. It will free a substantial sum to aid in maintaining a high standard of living among our people of all occupations.

I am very glad that the time has arrived when it is possible to repeal the personal income tax. Two years ago I advised the General Assembly that just as soon as the revenues and savings produced sufficient funds to balance the budget and maintain the essential services of the government, I would recommend repeal. It is now clear that we can maintain the present level of service and expenditures, finance the new obligations that have arisen, and repeal the personal income tax. That would reduce the estimated income for the second fiscal year to the extent of $4 million. That would require resort to the emergency expenditure fund to the extent of only $1,707,163, if the estimates were exactly realized. If so, there would be left a safe surplus at the end of the last fiscal year.

The years of war from which we have just emerged have disrupted the ordinary lives of the people, and the look ahead is obscured by uncertainty and constant change. The menace of inflation and the long delays attending reconversion call upon us to proceed with caution. There is deep concern in Washington and throughout the country about immediate prospects for the employment of our workers and of our returning veterans. The aftermath of war brings new and difficult problems of readjustment and resettlement. No one can certainly predict the conditions that will confront us in the next two years or even in the next six months.

It is no time for a spending spree, which would certainly be unwise and might prove disastrous. It is no time to make radical changes in our obligations and commitments. Kentuckians should be given every possible encouragement through this difficult and uncertain period of reconversion. The solvency of the state government should be scrupulously safeguarded.

There are some revisions of certain taxation statutes that should be considered.

I recommend consideration of a tax on pari-mutuel betting. The racing states very generally place a tax on the money that is bet, and it produces substantial revenue without any adverse effect on the breeding industry.[2]

The estate and inheritance tax law should be revised so as to give more protection to surviving wives and infant heirs.[3]

The insurance tax laws, the reciprocity law, the beer and retail liquor tax laws, all need revision to remove inequalities, and such laws will be offered by the departments having to do specially with those subjects. The recent decision of the Court of Appeals that annuities and other rights to receive income were subject to ad valorem taxation, upon a valuation based on the life insurance mortality tables, calls for careful consideration by you. A more just formula for valuation of such rights should be enacted by you, and a classification carrying a lower rate is recommended.[4]

During the past year I have asked many able and patriotic citizens to render service to the state on various commissions. They have accepted the task with a spirit that is very heartening to all persons who are interested in good government and in improved services. The work done by these able and busy men should be appreciated and every effort made to carry their recommendations into effect insofar as possible. There was no partisanship in their appointment or in their work. Their reports are here, and I recommend that you cause them to be printed and made available to each member of the General Assembly and to the public generally. I will refer to the other reports later in the session, but one of them merits a discussion now.

On October 6, 1944, an executive order was issued which created the Postwar Advisory Planning Commission of Kentucky. That commission was composed of leading citizens of the state representing both political parties, men from all walks of life and from both races. The group included educators, businessmen, industrialists, manufacturers, bankers, brokers, lawyers, labor people, ministers, and farmers.

The commission was charged with the study and investigation of the physical and human resources of the state and with the formulation of plans and recommendations for the full development of such resources for the aid of agriculture, manufacture, mining, transportation, conservation, and all other interests of the state. It was further charged with the task of considering and coordinating the plans and recommendations of all other planning boards, including private and governmental bodies, as related particularly to the opportunities and problems of Kentucky.

The Research Department of the University of Kentucky and all departments and agencies of the state government were requested to aid and cooperate in the work of the commission, and they did so.

I am happy to say that the commissioners have worked diligently during the past year. The full commission met monthly, and its various committees were in almost continuous session. The entire work was conducted on a voluntary basis, and the best brains of the commonwealth were consulted.

The commissioners have now placed in my hands their final report, a copy of which is available to each member. The commission has met my request to complete its findings and recommendations for presentation at this session. I have examined these reports, and I desire to thank the commission for the excellent job which it has accomplished. Men may honestly differ with some of the recommendations, but the commission should be congratulated on furnishing the people of the commonwealth with a starting point for discussion.

I have been kept in very close contact with the commission and have received frequent progress reports from them. The commission was charged with disseminating their recommendations and findings as widely as possible throughout the state, and this request has been answered with the preparation of a work kit, a copy of which is also on your desk. I urge each of you to go through the kit carefully and to notice the material that has been designed to bring the problems of Kentucky to the attention of the people.

I take this opportunity also to point out that the commission was the first group in Kentucky to develop up-to-date reports on agriculture, coordination of governmental affairs, education, industrial plants and opportunities, industrial relations, military affairs and returned veterans, natural resources, organic laws and legislation, and transportation.

All of the work of the commission has been done without cost to the commonwealth. The commission has financed itself and has financed the publication and dissemination of its material. I consider its work an outstanding example of what a truly representative citizen group can accomplish. The report is now in your hands for your study, your consideration, and your action.[5]

1. The Postwar Advisory Planning Commission has made a recommendation that a permanent body be created to continue the study of economic, financial, and governmental problems, with a regular staff and a financial budget sufficient to make its work effective.

2. The Taxation Revision Commission, in its comprehensive, factual report assembled for your consideration, also recommends that a permanent body be available for continuous study of tax questions in the light of changing conditions.

3. The Negro Affairs Commission made a very exhaustive study of conditions affecting racial relations and economic conditions of our Negro population. Its report is a most constructive one and has at-

tracted attention all over the country, and particularly in the South. One of its recommendations is that some similar body be continued permanently and financed and staffed to keep up the study and to keep the legislature and the public advised of progress and of remedial measures.

4. The Recreation Commission has appeared before the Legislative Council and requested a body to represent and carry on programs for the recreation and health of the people.

5. The Youth Guidance Commission was created by statute to study conditions affecting youthful delinquency and report results to you. The report is complete and constitutes a real contribution to the knowledge of conditions in our state affecting the moral and spiritual welfare of the youth of our state. One of the recommendations is for a continued paid staff to keep up the study.

The parks and conservation require constant study and improvement, and the plans of the park director and conservation commissioner have a strong appeal. In the nature of things, it is not economical or advisable to create numerous commissions with scattered and divided authority and duplicate staffs. I recommend that one overall body, with ample funds, be created and be given authority to create divisions or committees to carry on studies of all of the various subjects of public interest, including industrial development, tourist travel, tax structures, Negro affairs, recreation, parks, forests, soil conservation, youth guidance, and all other subjects of vital interest to the people. Such a commission should consist of the heads of the departments particularly concerned in the subjects embraced and of representative men and women from all parts of the state who could carry on this work. Committees could be appointed by the commission from the public generally with special reference to qualifications and talents. A single staff, with a reasonably ample budget, could be maintained to serve all of these needs; and it could obtain the service of experts and specially qualified persons, without the duplication of numerous bodies working from different angles. This commission should have authority by concession to private persons on some reasonable basis to provide facilities that render service to the state. It should also have power to finance by revenue bonds all necessary improvements of public property; such bonds, payable over a period of years out of the revenues derived from the facility, would provide every sound enterprise with a means of accomplishment. Definite power could be delegated, and by exercising it private industry could be enlisted in carrying forward these public enterprises, which would serve the needs of the state without a drain on the public treasury. In fact, it could be made a source of revenue to the public treasury and materially assist, if not completely pay, the expense of the various departments directly affected. This body could work with private organizations to promote industrial developments and desirable public improvements and facilities of all kinds. It would save us from wasteful and discouraging ventures. It would meet the needs of this day with a modern instrumentality and undoubtedly would achieve results valuable to the commonwealth.[6]

The shocking and distressing tragedy in the coal mine in Bell County has emphasized the need for immediate revision of our mining laws and for a more adequate provision for the Department of Mines and Minerals.[7] These laws have grown up over the years and have not been kept abreast of developments in modern mining, particularly in mines electrically equipped. Such revisions and additions as may be necessary to keep the laws abreast of modern developments in mining should be immediately enacted. The aid of the mining institute, the miners' organizations, the operators of mines, and other qualified [persons] could be called in to help.

The present Department of Mines and Minerals is not sufficiently equipped with men or means to carry out the obligations of the law, even as it is at present. The salaries of inspectors are certainly inadequate when compared with similar salaries paid by other governments for similar service, and when compared with salaries in the mining industry. The problem arises from the industry itself, and it is but fair that the industry should bear the cost of a completely equipped mining department. There should be a sufficient number of inspectors capable of carrying out the mandate of the law for quarterly inspections and for follow-up supervision. This is impossible with an inadequate force. They should be compensated commensurately with the work, skill, and responsibility of their positions. There should be a force sufficient to keep in contact with each mine where improvements are necessary until the improvements are actually completed. In order to provide a force suitable and sufficient for competent inspection and rigid enforcement of the rules adopted, the Department of Mines and Minerals should have both power and money to discharge the duty to provide for the safety of the workers in the mines. But a small sum from each mine, collected on some fair and equitable basis, would provide the money necessary to employ sufficient personnel and to maintain rescue stations in strategic locations, adequate personnel to ascertain and correct dangerous practices, and to maintain regular safety schools. There are probably 1,700 mines in Kentucky, and the expense of securing and maintaining safety in so many mines is substantial. But the very operation of the business creates the necessity for safeguarding the men in an employment so hazardous, and it would not be too great a burden on the producers of coal, or affect them adversely in a competitive market, to provide every possible means of safety that experience and engineering ability can devise. And regardless of the extent of the burden, the duty is mandatory and should be discharged. I recommend that this be done. When a shocking tragedy occurs it is easy to see the faults of a system. The state cannot afford to delay the correction of dangerous conditions, insofar as [it is] humanly possible to correct them. When we have more particulars, further recommendations may be necessary, and these recommendations do not exclude other means of attaining the objective.[8]

The budget report will give you the details upon the subjects upon which you may desire information and which I have not mentioned specifically.

It is likely there will be other matters to submit to you from time to time during the session.

The recommendations I have outlined are practical, safe, and sound, as I believe. The adoption of all of them by you will be an assurance to the people that you have their interests at heart and are awake to the aspirations of the people. Let each of us here and now rededicate to our beloved commonwealth the best thought, the most diligent effort, and the wisest judgment of which we are capable. Let us here resolve that we shall never forget, even for one moment, the common welfare of the great people of Kentucky, who look to us for a faithful discharge of the sacred trust they have placed in our hands.

---

1. Originally conceived as a mental institution, Darnall Hospital sat on 1,301 acres near the Mercer-Boyle County line between Danville and Burgin. In the summer of 1941 the U.S. Army had leased the 250-bed unit for one dollar a year. On February 10, 1946, the hospital, valued at $6 million, was returned to the state for one dollar. The sum of $250,000 was appropriated to cover additional expenses incurred in the transfer and operation up to June 30, 1946. Owensboro *Messenger*, February 2, 1946; *Courier-Journal*, February 10, 1946; Kentucky *Acts* (1946), 511. See also document dated September 12, 1946, in "Health and Welfare" section.

2. A Senate bill placing a 5 percent tax on pari-mutuel receipts was introduced but died in committee. Kentucky *Senate Journal* (1946), 629, 662. In the House four similar but separate bills were introduced and all received a second reading; none came up for a vote. See Kentucky *House Journal* (1946), 21, 375, 1077, 2008, 2488, 2620, 2625, 2630.

3. All three attempts (House Bills 38, 62, and 308) at inheritance tax revisions

failed, receiving only a second reading. Kentucky *House Journal* (1946), 2621, 2626.

4. Chapter 39 (House Bill 128) related to ad valorem taxation of the right to receive income. It regulated the assessment value and prescribed the rate of taxation. Both houses passed the bill unanimously, and it was approved by the governor on March 14. Kentucky *Acts* (1946), 104-5; Kentucky *House Journal* (1946), 2194-95; Kentucky *Senate Journal* (1946), 2772.

5. The report was published on December 15, 1945. The 318-page study focused on returning veterans, agriculture, education, industrial relations, industrial opportunities, intergovernmental cooperation, natural resources, and transportation. For a brief summary see *Courier-Journal*, December 16, 1945.

6. Governor Willis's plan for a single, unified commission did not receive legislative support.

7. The December 26, 1945, Straight Creek disaster claimed the lives of twenty-four miners. The coal company involved had made no provision for compensation for the 23 widows and 123 orphans. Since the Court of Appeals had, in 1914, ruled mandatory workmen's compensation unconstitutional, attempts were under discussion to circumvent the ruling. Sam Caddy, president of District 30, United Mine Workers, threatened to bolt the Democrats if safety laws were not enacted. *Courier-Journal*, March 24, 1946.

8. The mine bill passed both houses of the legislature without a dissenting vote. The main Senate bill required that the employer of three or more persons in a "hazardous" occupation must operate under state law. Another bill, originating in the House, provided for the filing of a bond with the commissioner of industrial relations for those firms rejecting the state plan. *Courier-Journal*, March 24, 1946; Kentucky *Acts* (1946), 320-27 (Chapter 120, H.B. 440, approved March 22), and 656-57 (Chapter 124, S.B. 243, approved March 23).

PUBLIC ASSISTANCE
Frankfort / February 28, 1946

I THANK the senators for granting this hearing. It is my responsibility to recommend and yours to determine what is to be expended during the next two years for the various purposes of government.

I have heretofore explained to you the financial policies that I deem wise. You are now considering a bill to put into effect your final determination of your will. It is not my desire or purpose to reargue the issues which you have been considering.

It is my desire and purpose to carry out in good faith and to the best of my ability the laws that you enact. But the consequences of the proposed changes in the appropriation bill before you upon the public assistance program of the state are so serious that I have asked Mr. Oscar M. Powell,[1] executive director of the Social Security Board, to come here to explain to you the minimum requirements to conform our law to the social security laws with which we must conform to maintain the program. In all matters which are controlled by the state alone, the administration must be adjusted to allotments you make. But the public assistance program is a joint program of the state and nation, and if we fail to meet the requirements of that federal law, we will lose the help of the federal contributions which we must have to maintain the level of aid to which our old people, dependent children, and needy blind have become accustomed. It would be a tragedy indeed if that program was frustrated.

The policy of this administration has been to hold administrative expenses as low as possible consistent with efficiency, and the record shows that we have accomplished much along that line. But the time has come when the expense of administering public assistance must be increased. This necessity arises from three principal sources:

1. The mechanical equipment must be repaired, and obsolete machines must be replaced.

2. The raises in salaries which had to be made and the increased personnel, which must be promptly recruited, require some substantial additional operating costs.

3. During the war certain waivers have been obtained from the Social Security Board which cannot be continued, and we are faced with the necessity of compliance with the standards of the Social Security Board in order to obtain assistance from that source.[2]

I wish to thank Mr. Oscar M. Powell, executive director of the Social Security Board, for accepting my invitation, and I ask him to give you the benefit of his experience and knowledge of this very large and very difficult problem which confronts us.

---

1. Oscar Morgan Powell (1899-   ). Texas attorney, 1922-36; regional director, Social Security Board, 1936-38; executive director, Social Security Board, 1938-46; regional director, Social Security Administration, 1946-48; advisor on social insurance to Greek government, 1948-50. *Who's Who, 1950-51,* 2206.

2. An act (Chapter 188, S.B. 115) passed on March 13 appropriated $321,809

for the fiscal year ending June 30 in order to meet costs in the child welfare, aid to dependent children, and aid to the blind programs. Kentucky *Acts* (1946), 516-17.

VETO OF HOUSE BILL NO. 397
Frankfort / March 14, 1946

I CANNOT approve House Bill No. 397, which disrupts the classified service in the city of Louisville. The act of 1942 placed in the classified service under the merit system certain offices, positions, and places of employment in several departments of the city government and provided authority and methods for the extension of classified service to other offices, positions, and employments.[1] Administration of the act was placed in a Civil Service Board composed of three persons "in sympathy with the merit principle of public personnel administration."

It is a sound principle that any governmental policy should be administered by those who believe in that policy. You should never trust a child with a nurse that does not love it. This bill takes out that provision of the law and substitutes a bipartisan board that need not be in sympathy with the merit principle. Indeed, it will not only encourage partisanship in the selection of personnel, but it will inevitably promote factionalism in both parties. Factionalism is destructive of party responsibility and damaging to good government.

The extension of the classified service as provided by Section 9 of the original act is forbidden by the present act, which says that "no office, position or place of employment which is placed in the classified service after February 15, 1946, by action of the legislative body of the city shall be in the classified service."

The act does not correct or improve any defects or insufficiencies that may have been found in the present system, but removes the very provisions that have been proven of real value to good service.

The administration of city government becomes more difficult and complicated as the services to the public are enlarged and extended. The merit principle must be observed in good faith if good service is to be realized.

This session of the General Assembly has given careful study to the improvement of the civil service in other cities of the state, and it is unfortunate that a backward step should be taken in our largest city. The present bill was put through in a relatively short time without hearings or any extended debate. I am sending it back promptly so that you may have as much time as possible for a further consideration of the subject matter involved.

It is clear that the present bill emasculates the present system of classified service and is a first step toward total destruction of the merit system. Such an important step should be carefully considered, and the wishes of the people concerned should be consulted. The alternative to the merit system of city government is the kind of city government that has afflicted so many of our great cities and which [has] become a menace to self-government in large centers of population.

For these reasons I have vetoed House Bill No. 397 and return it herewith to the House, where it originated.[2]

---

1. Chapter 16 (Senate Bill 30) had been approved February 11, 1942, and went into effect July 1. Kentucky *Acts* (1942), 122-40.

2. On March 18, 1946, the House overrode the governor's veto by a 54-28 count; two days later the Senate did so as well, by a 21-16 margin. See Kentucky *House Journal* (1946), 3699; Kentucky *Senate Journal* (1946), 3932; and Kentucky *Acts* (1946), 270-74.

VETO OF HOUSE BILL NO. 416
Frankfort / March 18, 1946

I RETURN herewith House Bill No. 416 without my approval.

The bill is an anomalous one. It sets up in the Department of Industrial Relations an Employment Service Commission composed of a director of employment service and two other persons to represent labor and management.

There is no provision for the appointment of the director. The two members representing labor and management are to be appointed by the commissioner of industrial relations, with the approval of the governor, from lists of names submitted to him by representatives of labor and management. There is no restriction on the number of names or on the number of persons that may assume to represent labor and management. This is the only duty or power vested in the Department of Industrial Relations.

The director is made chairman of the commission. Only one man in the state, it has been stated, is eligible to the office of director.[1] He must have had at least four years full-time paid experience in the administration and supervision of the statewide system of public employment service offices, and shall have been a citizen of Kentucky for at least two successive years immediately prior to his appointment. The appointing power would have no choice but to commission the man described, but not named, in the act.

The director is given power to determine and establish his own organization, employ such personnel as he deems necessary, and fix their duties and compensation. This places it outside the law so far as compliance with the statutes that govern the other departments, agencies, and employees of the state [is] concerned. The wholesome requirements of K.R.S. 42.120 are completely nullified.

By Section 8 of the act, it is provided that when and if the employment service returns to state control, a transfer shall be made to employment in the statewide system of public employment offices, without adverse adjustment in their classification or compensation status of all officers and employees of the federal government who had been employed in the performance of employment service functions in Kentucky on the day preceding the effective date of such transfer. And further, not later than thirty days after the date of return of [the] employment service to the state, all properties, including equipment now in possession of the Unemployment Compensation Commission, purchased by the Kentucky State Employment Service under the Unemployment Compensation Act of 1938, shall be transferred to the Employment Service Commission created by this act.

K.R.S. 340.080 is repealed. That is the statute under which the employment service was set up and operated before it was lent to the federal government for the duration of the war.

It seems obvious that the legislature has no power to create this unlimited number of offices and positions and automatically to fill them with federal officers and employees as of a certain date. The legislature may create offices, but the executive or administrative officers must fill them.

In *Pratt* v. *Breckenridge* [sic], 112 Ky. 1, (at page 10)[2] the Court of

Appeals thus explained the distinction between legislative and executive power in respect to the creation and filling of offices:

> Each house may perform the executive act of electing its own officers (Secs. 34, 249), and the judicial act of judging of the qualifications, elections, and returns of its members (Sec. 38), punishing disorderly behavior and expelling members (Sec. 39). The framers of the constitution having deemed it necessary expressly to permit the legislature to exercise the executive power of appointment in specified cases, this permission, by implication, forbids the legislature to exercise such powers in any other case.
>
> The creation of an office is accomplished by the exercise of legislative power. It is done by the enactment of a law. The filling of it, when not exercised by the people, or in some manner directed or permitted by the constitution, is executive, and must be performed by an executive officer.

This has been reaffirmed in many cases, such as *Silbert* v. *Garrett*, 197 Ky. 17; *Rouse* v. *Johnson*, 234 Ky. 473, and cases cited in those opinions.

The salaries paid in the federal setup are much greater than is permitted under the state organization act, and the number of employees is far beyond what the state would or could employ. It would be demoralizing and damaging to all the other departments of government to import into our service a large number of high-salaried employees not required to qualify under Kentucky laws.

Moreover, the plan set up by this act would make it impossible to carry on the employment service if and when it is returned to the state.

The employment service was set up in 1932. In 1933, Congress passed the Wagner-Peyser Act, which provided certain benefits to states that accepted it.[3] Kentucky complied with the act and operated successfully until the service was lent to the United States on January 1, 1942, with the understanding that it would be returned after the termination of the war. It is now expected to be returned to the state on July 1, 1946, although there is some controversy in Congress about the date of return.[4]

The employment service is an essential part in the operation of the unemployment service. It could not be operated conveniently or successfully apart from the unemployment compensation setup.

I am advised that the larger portion of the expense of administering the employment service through the unemployment commission was provided by the Social Security Board. It could not supply any funds to the proposed commission because it is not placed on a merit basis. The Social Security Board may make allotments for the purpose stated but is forbidden to do so unless it "finds that the law of the state provides such methods of administration (including after January 1, 1940, methods relating to the establishment and maintenance of personnel standards on a merit basis) as are found by the board to be reasonably calculated to insure full payment of unemployment compensation when due."

The Kentucky Employment Service, when it was a part of the Unemployment Compensation Commission, was entitled to grants under the Social Security Act because—(1) the grants were being made to the Unemployment Compensation Commission for the administration of an Unemployment Compensation law; and—(2) the unemployment compensation law provides for the maintenance of personnel standards on a merit basis.

No money is provided or available under either state or federal law to operate the anomalous plan set up by House Bill No. 416.

In view of these facts, it is plain that the bill is unworkable and can do no possible good. For these reasons I have vetoed House Bill No. 416 and return it herewith to the House, where it originated.[5]

---

1. The reference is to William H. Fraysure, a Democrat and head of the U.S. Employment Service in the state. See Frankfort *State Journal*, March 8, 1946.

2. *Pratt* v. *Breckinridge*, decided in 1901 by a 4-3 vote, concerned the office of attorney general and the contested election of 1899. Democrat Robert J. Breckinridge was removed in favor of Republican Clifton J. Pratt. *Pratt* v. *Breckinridge*, 112 Kentucky Reports 1-69.

3. Named for Theodore A. Peyser and Robert F. Wagner, both of New York, the bill set up federal employment agencies to work in cooperation with state ones. Signed into law on June 6, 1933, it initially provided $1,500,000 for 1933-34 and $4 million thereafter, to 1938, with the money distributed as to population. See *Congressional Record*, 73d Congress, 1st Sess., 4468.

4. After extended discussion, Congress returned joint operation of the U.S. Employment Services (USES) to the states, effective November 15, 1946. In 1948 Congress sought to move the federal part of USES from the Department of Labor to the Federal Security Agency; President Truman's veto of that bill was overridden. See *Congressional Record*, 79th Congress, 2d Sess., *Index*, 612; *United States Statutes at Large . . . 1946* (Washington, D.C., 1947), Part 1, 684; *Public Papers of the Presidents of the United States: Harry S. Truman . . . 1948* (Washington, D.C., 1964), 103, 135-36.

5. House Bill 416 had passed on March 7. On March 19, the House, by a 64-24 vote, and on March 20, the Senate by a 20-16 margin, overrode the governor's veto. Kentucky *Acts* (1946), 280-84; Kentucky *House Journal* (1946), 3736; and Kentucky *Senate Journal* (1946), 3942.

VETO OF HOUSE BILL NO. 187
Frankfort / March 18, 1946

I RETURN herewith House Bill No. 187, without approval.

House Bill No. 187 is a ripper bill, removing from the Department of Military Affairs the Veterans Division and transferring to the Kentucky Disabled Ex-Service Men's Board the entire appropriation heretofore made to the Veterans' Division in the Department of Military Affairs.

The present setup is satisfactory and renders efficient service to the veterans without partiality or discrimination. It is required to perform the following duties:

a) Prepare in proper form, present, and prosecute the claims of disabled ex-servicemen and women and their dependents with the United States Veterans' Administration and other federal agencies;

b) Secure and expedite action on the claims;

c) Keep in contact with the United States Veterans' Administration so that the status of any claim may be known at any time;

d) Continue to survey the state to make certain that no disabled veteran or his dependents are neglected; and

e) Perform such other duties as the adjutant general directs. The veterans to be served are defined to include any individual who served on active duty in the army, navy, or Marine Corps of the United States and who has received an honorable discharge from such service.

The adjutant general is required to exercise general administration of the work of the division and to direct the work in the light of advice from the Kentucky Disabled Ex-Service Men's Board.

The current appropriation of $60,500 to the division for each year has been increased in the new appropriation bill to $100,000 for each of the next two fiscal years.

This tried and proven plan is completely destroyed by House Bill No. 187. The Division for Veterans' Affairs is abolished. Its appropriation is transferred to the new board provided for by the act. The duties placed on the adjutant general are withdrawn.

A new administrative personnel will have to be set up at an increased cost and without any added benefits to the veterans. The work of the division has been satisfactory, and the service to the veterans has been excellent.

The new board created by this bill is made an independent agency. It is changed from a mere advisory body to one with full responsibility and control. It is composed of five men, three of whom must be chosen from a list of five names submitted by the commander of the American Legion, with the approval of the executive committee of the legion. The lieutenant governor and the adjutant general are ex-officio members.

Thus one organization of veterans is given complete control of an agency designed to serve all veterans of all wars. No representation whatever is given to the veterans of World War II who are not members of the legion, although constituting the most numerous group. No other organization of veterans is represented at all.

The appointment of governmental officers should not be placed in private hands, no matter how public spirited they may be. This will not make for harmony and unity among the various organizations of veterans, but will tend to engender jealousies and resentments.

It is my hope that the Division of Veterans' Affairs can be preserved and allowed to carry on its noble objectives with the full benefit of its past experience and with the additional money provided for the service of the veterans.

For these reasons I am constrained to veto House Bill No. 187, and it is returned herewith to the House, where it originated.[1]

---

1. One day after the veto message, the House overrode the governor by a 75-3 margin; on March 20, the Senate voted 28-5 to take the same action. See Kentucky *House Journal* (1946), 3731; Kentucky *Senate Journal* (1946), 3940; and Kentucky *Acts* (1946), 143-44.

SPECIAL SESSION
Frankfort / July 10, 1947

FELLOW citizens of Kentucky:

Last February the officers and directors of the Kentucky Education Association [KEA] presented a formal request for an extraordinary session of the General Assembly for the sole purpose of appropriating $10,500,000 for increasing the salaries of teachers, both in the common schools and in the institutions of higher education.

They were advised that consideration would be given to the request and when a decision was reached the public would be informed. The facilities of this radio station [WHAS] were placed at my disposal to make this announcement. I have given the subject most careful and thorough consideration from all angles. This was necessary because of the effect of any action on the other departments of the state government and by reason of my requests for the inclusion of other meritorious subjects. The constitution empowers the governor to convene a special session on extraordinary occasions, and only such subjects as may be specified in the proclamation can be the subject of valid legislation at such a session. Clearly, this is a limitation on the governor, and special sessions should be called only when the necessity is urgent and immediate and the occasion extraordinary.

The subject of education at all levels is of profound concern to the people of Kentucky, and from the very beginning of this administration every effort has been exerted to advance the standard and to meet the requirements of the times. At the regular session of the General Assembly in 1944 a special appropriation of $3 million was made to supplement teachers' salaries for the fiscal year then current, 1943-44. At the special session in 1944 the appropriation for the next biennium was increased $10 million—$5 million for each fiscal year—and for the first time the full 10 percent allowed by the amendment to the constitution was placed in the equalization fund for the aid of the districts entitled to share in it.

At the regular session in 1946 long and careful consideration was given to the balancing of the needs of all the governmental services, with the greatest effort ever made in Kentucky to provide as much money as possible for education at all levels. The result was another large increase for the common schools, [for] the university, and for all the colleges. The progress upward of the per capita will illustrate the extraordinary efforts made.

For the fiscal year 1942-43 the per capita was $12.88. The next fiscal year, 1943-44, by reason of the $3 million special appropriation, the per capita was raised, and in the first full fiscal year of the present administration, 1944-45, the per capita was $19.16. For the second year of that biennium it was $19.77. These extraordinary efforts were believed at the time to be sufficient to solve the problems. However, at the 1946 session of the General Assembly the cost of living and the high level of compensation afforded by other vocations had neutralized to a great extent the benefits expected from the increased appropriations. At that session the per capita was raised to $24.40 for the fiscal year ending June 30, 1947, and to $25.56 for the year beginning July 1, 1947, and ending June 30, 1948. This was an all-time high for the state of Kentucky's contribution to the common school funds. Substantial increases were made in the provisions for all other educational services.

Equal consideration and support was given to the University of Kentucky, the four teachers colleges, and the educational institutions for Negroes.

The increases for the university in 1946-47 over 1943-44 were $1,130,050.

The total increase in 1946-47 over 1943-44 for the four teachers colleges was $818,000.

The grand total of increases for capital outlay and recurring expenses for the Department of Education, University of Kentucky, and the four teachers colleges was $11,759,123.44. In addition to that, the Negro educational institutions in 1946-47 were given an increase of $438,006.00, which was more than double their appropriations for 1943-44.

In the face of all this effort, we are met with the insistent fact that the critical situation of the schools continues to disturb thoughtful people. A nationwide crisis has developed, and every state in the Union has been seeking to find ways and means to solve the problem. During the period referred to the necessity for the use of emergency teachers has grown. The Department of Education has furnished the following table of the increase annually in the number of emergency certificates:

School Year	Emergency Teachers
1942-43	2,600
1943-44	4,100
1944-45	4,500
1945-46	5,200
1946-47	5,300

These emergency teachers are those who have only high school training or less.

Moreover, the reports indicate that students in the colleges preparing to enter the teaching profession are decreasing at a rapid rate. The decrease for elementary schools is said to exceed 66 percent, while those preparing for high school teaching [have] decreased approximately 50 percent. These facts admonish us that every effort possible should be made to reverse these trends.

At the 1946 session of the General Assembly the permissible levy for school purposes in each school district was raised to $1.50 on each $100.00 of property subject to local taxation, and a poll tax not exceeding $2.00 on each male inhabitant over twenty-one years of age, not exempted by law, was authorized.[1] Some of the districts have exercised all or part of this authority, and as a result the teachers' salaries have been substantially increased since the request of the KEA was made. The exact figures have not been made available to me, but very great progress along this line is manifest. It is obvious that the local districts should be encouraged to exercise the power of self-help thus given.

The same living costs that have affected the schools have fallen heavily on the old persons, dependent children, and needy blind who participate in public assistance. The appropriation for this program for the fiscal year which began on July 1, 1947, was $4,750,000 plus the sum of $445,000 added by the so-called escalator clause in the Budget Act of 1946. Beginning last October, the federal government increased the available funds so that the average grant for July 1947 for old age assistance was $17.50, for aid to dependent children was $13.80, and for aid to the needy blind was $18.40. The number of aged receiving aid for July 1947 was 48,505, the number of dependent children was 25,666, and the number of needy blind was 1,760. The total number of each is gradually increasing, and that of the dependent children is increasing very rapidly. In order to add $5.00 per month aid to each of the three classes of recipients, considering the probable increases in recipients, would require an appropriation of about $3,300,000, which would be matched by the federal government.

If the case load remained constant at the present number, it would not require quite so much, but it is certain, from pending applications and from past experience, that the case load will increase each month. The estimate of $3,300,000 is regarded as conservative, allowing only a very small margin of safety. It appears to me that a raise of $5.00 per month to these old, needy, and dependent people is desperately needed to help meet the increased cost of bare necessities.

Misapprehension is general respecting the surplus fund and the services for which it has been employed. The surplus fund is the combined result of savings and increased collections of revenue over and above the total amount of the appropriations by the legislature and the expenditures imposed by law. It is not wise, as a rule, to pay recurring expenses from nonrecurring funds.

On July 1, 1946, the so-called surplus fund was $17,977,906.60. Wild estimates were widely published as to the probable surplus on July 1, 1947, and based on these unofficial estimates some people were eager to find ways to spend more money than we had.

As a matter of fact, the amount of revenue for the fiscal year which ended June 30, 1947, over and above the expenditures imposed by law, and the appropriations yet to be paid from it, was only $3,523,821.50, which is the amount left of the $5,748,821.50 by which total revenue exceeded total expenditures after payment of the sum of $2,225,000.00 appropriated by the so-called escalator clause of the Budget Act of 1946.[2] So that the actual surplus available for consideration is not $24 million, as has been published in the papers, but only $21,501,728.10.

Of the $2,225,000 appropriated by the escalator clause, 20 percent, or $445,000, goes to the Division of Public Assistance for payment of Old Age Assistance, Aid to the Needy Blind, and Aid to Dependent Children.

The common school per capita fund gets 40.5 percent, or $901,125, and the equalization fund, 4.5 percent, or $100,125. That adds up to 45 percent, or a total of $1,001,250, for addition to the funds for the common schools.

Sound business in operations of the magnitude of the state government requires approximately $5 million to assure the payment of the current expenses of the government. This is so because the collections come in over an annual period and in some months do not provide sufficient ready cash to meet the monthly obligations. Reserving that amount of what might appropriately be called operating or working capital, the surplus available for actual expenditure is reduced to $16,501,728.10.

It has been the fixed policy to devote the surplus to capital investment, insofar as possible, and to avoid resort to it for recurring expenses. This wise policy has enabled the state to proceed with the rehabilitation of its institutional, educational, and essential buildings, which means so much to the mentally sick and other wards of the state.

Those of you who have visited these institutions will appreciate the progress that has been made and the pressing need for its continuance without interruption or delay. Not less than $5 million should be reserved from the present surplus for this purpose, and to carry on that program. That would leave only $11,501,728.10.

It would be folly to dissipate the surplus for recurring expenses when so many of the wards of the state are dependent upon it as the sole source for completion of the rehabilitation program thus far so successfully advanced.

It is apparent that the recurring expenses will be increased next January by the addition of the five tuberculosis sanatoria and the necessity of increased operating expenses for the institutions in the welfare department. If the present level of expenditures is maintained, it will likely take all the revenues. The total income for the last fiscal year was augmented almost $4 million by the nonrecurring tax collections from the Southern Pacific Railroad.[3]

It is estimated that to operate the five tuberculosis hospitals will require an annual expenditure of $750,000; and Hazelwood, when completed, will require an estimated $425,000. In order to assure their prompt and full operation next January, it is imperative that $1,125,000 be saved from the present surplus, which would leave $10,376,728.10.

The welfare department estimates that $971,275 [in] additional funds for operations will be required this year. That would leave $9,405,453.10, which is the utmost that could be delivered to recurring expenses for education and public assistance, even in the present emergencies.

If the public assistance is given an additional $3,300,000 there would be left the total of $6,105,453.10 for the further aid of schools and other emergencies. If given $5,500,000 now, with the added funds of the escalator clause and the raises given the teachers by the local units or districts, the approximate amounts deemed necessary by the KEA to solve the problem would have been provided.

The presidents of the four teachers colleges have requested the amendment of KRS 164.320, so as to give a fixed tenure to the regents. General agreement seems to prevail that the power of removal of regents should be restricted to removal for cause. This is urgent because of the attitude of the accrediting association and should be done. I have long favored this action.

The Kentucky School for the Deaf at Danville is confronted with an emergency, as represented to me by the superintendent and the board, together with the teachers and employees. The appropriation for the present fiscal year for ordinary and recurring expenses of operation is $150,000 for the white and $10,000 for the colored. Teachers reaching retirement age are required to retire or forfeit their retirement benefits. Replacement of teachers at present salaries is practically impossible, and the sum of $25,000 additional is requested by them. I am convinced that this request is meritorious and urgently needed.

Many other worthy requests have been addressed to me, but I have concluded that they can await consideration at the regular session.

The people are complaining about the prevalence of open gambling in many parts of the state, and particularly in populous centers. It is reported that the operators of gambling machines and gaming houses are brazen, and rumors are rife that they corrupt the law-enforcing officials, either directly or indirectly, and in some cases are actually protected for pay.[4] Such conditions are causing unrest and creating distrust of government. It is a dangerous symptom of the arrogance of lawlessness and calls for action. A law should be adopted giving power to the governor to employ nonpartisan, able, and high-standing lawyers, investigators, auditors, and accountants to investigate and ascertain the facts in regard to this and to report to the next General Assembly a comprehensive remedy to root out the evil. It should investigate the alleged alliance of gambling and other lawbreaking groups with public officials and party leaders. These investigators should be given full investigating authority to require evidence on oath touching any matter involved and to have lawful access to all books, records, accounts, or other sources of evidence. Obedience to process should be enforced by circuit courts and the Court of Appeals. An appropriation of $100,000 should be ample to obtain the services of competent men and women and a comprehensive and complete report of the facts so that the ax could be laid at the root of the evil. This would be but a small outlay to correct a condition that tends to undermine the whole fabric of law and order. The people are calling for such correction.

If these additional items amounting to $125,000 be allowed, then the fund remaining would be $5,980,453.10.

If acceptable to the members of the General Assembly, I would approve the following appropriations:

1. For the school program, including the per capita fund, equalization fund, and for the institutions of higher learning, $5,500,000 divided $500,000 for the university and colleges and $5 million for the two common school funds;

2. $3,300,000 for public assistance, including Old Age Assistance, Aid to the Needy Blind, and Aid to Dependent Children;

3. $25,000 for the School for the Deaf, to be used as needed for the white and Negro schools;

4. $100,000 for the employment of the investigators of the gambling conditions in Kentucky.

If the program outlined be adopted, the immediate needs will be met, and other meritorious claims can be postponed to the regular session next January.

If the program I have indicated meets with the approval of the members of the House and Senate, and they will so advise me within six days, I will call a special session with the understanding and agreement:

1. That the session will continue only long enough to enact the bills, not to exceed ten days;

2. That no other subjects will be brought up for discussion or consideration at the session or requests made by either house for an enlargement of the call;

3. That the appropriations will not exceed the limits I have stated, and the program will be accepted in its entirety.

The state Aeronautics Commission and its staff are giving thorough study to a state airport plan which contemplates legislation and appropriation. It will require more consideration and discussion than is possible at a brief special session. Hence I have decided it is best to postpone it to the regular session.

I realize that a political campaign is in progress and every candidate will desire to promote his interests.[5] So far as I am advised, no candidate is opposed to the proposals I have stated. I trust that everyone will appreciate that these subjects are not political and relate only to the proper spending of the taxpayers' money to achieve constructive results in matters of vital public concern. KEA directors in one of their resolutions stated: "That it respectfully requests all factions of all political parties to declare a moratorium on politics during such proposed special session to the end that the funds may be appropriated and the benefit of the increased funds may be secured for the school children of Kentucky."

The members of the House and Senate are requested to wire or write me their decisions at once in order that I may determine without delay whether this proposed program can be enacted. Unless the assurance and agreement requested is given to me by the individual members of the House and Senate within six days, no call can be issued. I ask your most careful and earnest consideration of these important subjects.[6]

---

1. Chapter 36 (House Bill 121) authorized "not less than twenty-five cents annually . . . or more than one dollar fifty cents," plus a two dollar poll tax. Passed February 14, it became law without the governor's signature. Kentucky *Acts* (1946), 58-59.

2. The 1946 legislature, in order to restrict Governor Willis's control of any surplus funds, had decreed that $2,225,000 over the appropriated amount would be divided among seven state groups. In the next paragraph Governor Willis gives that breakdown and the percentages involved. See ibid., 100-101.

3. Sixty-three years before, the General Assembly granted a charter to the Southern Pacific Railroad, which subsequently made its legal—but not active—headquarters first in Anchorage, Kentucky, then in Spring Station. With no tracks and very little tangible property in the state, the company received a favorable tax situation. In December 1944 a suit was filed, claiming the company owed $5 million for taxes on bonds over an eight-year period. Attorneys John E. Tarrant and Earl S. Wilson of Louisville agreed to prosecute the case. While the suit was dropped, the Southern Pacific eventually paid $4,001,693.90 to Kentucky. It then declared it would move its headquarters elsewhere. See *Kentucky Post*, April 4, 1947, and Executive Order, April 24, 1946, Secretary of State's Records.

4. In the previous months newspapers contained numerous stories detail-

ing gambling across Kentucky, but particularly in Jefferson, Fayette, and Kenton counties. In April, for instance, Louisville police made 143 arrests on gambling charges and in mid-June 25 people were arrested on the same basis in Covington. See, for example, *Courier-Journal*, May 3, June 7, 11, 17, 21, 25, 1947.

5. The primary election would be held August 2, 1947.

6. Recalling his problems with the special sessions of 1944, the governor sought to limit such actions in 1947; thus this specific limiting appeal.

SPECIAL SESSION
Louisville / July 24, 1947

My fellow citizens:

On July 10, over this station, I submitted a proposal for a special session of the General Assembly, provided the program was acceptable to the individual members of the House and Senate. The address set forth the actual financial condition of the state, and the offer went as far to supplement the state aid to education, the aged, and needy blind, and dependent children as could be done safely at the present time.

The plan proposed carefully safeguarded the financial stability of the state government, assured continuance of the rehabilitation program for the buildings at the various state institutions, anticipated the operation of the five tuberculosis sanatoria, together with completed Hazelwood, saved sufficient sums for the increased obligations and burdens of the Department of Welfare, and took care of other pressing demands of the state without injury to the operations or functions of any agency or department of the government.

A copy of the address was sent to each member of the House and Senate, with a request that I be advised in six days of his or her decision. Favorable replies were being received when suddenly the Speaker of the House, Mr. [Harry Lee] Waterfield, summoned a caucus of the Democrat members of the House to meet him at Louisville on Sunday, July 13. I received a telegram that same Sunday evening bearing the names of forty-five Democrat members of the House wholly rejecting the offer for a special session, on the ground that I had no right to ask in advance the opinion of the members or to seek an agreement to limit their action once they were called in session.[1]

It is to be noted that no attempt was made to question any of the facts stated in my address, or to answer the logic of my conclusions, or to deny the needs I had designated.

The position taken by the House Democrats was obviously political because it was a self-serving defense of the signers, without committing them to any program. The alleged reasons assigned for rejection of the plan were purely fictitious. Ample time was given for decision, as proven by their rejection in half of the six days allowed. The cry of dictation by the governor was a mere evasion. Plainly, a proposal for an agreement is not dictation. The members were to decide on the proposal and were free to accept or reject it. They chose to reject it as a result of a political caucus and not of their own free will. When the caucus telegram was received, I wired Mr. Waterfield for himself and his associates as follows:

TELEGRAM

July 13, 1947
To Harry Lee Waterfield
Louisville, Kentucky

Your [Democratic] caucus group evidently is not as greatly interested in helping the school teachers, the aged, the needy blind, and dependent children as they professed to be when urging a special session of the legislature.

I have presented an opportunity for you and have made the way clear and simple and easy, and at a minimum loss of time and expense to the state.

I have intentionally barred the way to a political session of the legislature, which would result in injury to the state and in unnecessary expense to the taxpayers.

If your group is acting in good faith and for the best interest of Kentucky, the terms I have outlined should have strong appeal to you.

For you to say "No" to the efforts to help education, the aged, and the needy blind in the present emergency is a plain admission that your group is more concerned with politics than with the welfare of those in question.

I have acted under my constitutional rights, and with no thought but the good of Kentucky. It is now up to the members of the legislature to adjourn politics and keep faith with the people. It is not a problem for a Democrat caucus, but for each individual member to determine for himself. The responsibility is his, and his alone.

Simeon Willis
Governor.

Some unthinking criticism was made that the proposal had not been submitted before July 1. It was absolutely necessary to wait until after

July 1 in order to know exactly the amount of surplus money available for present appropriation. So many wild and exaggerated estimates had been made that it was necessary to prevent any attempts to spend money the state did not possess. The exact amount could not be known earlier. The political campaign was in progress but no more so than it was during all the previous months, when the matter was pressed on my attention. It was merely closer to the date of the primary election.

But the whole program outlined required only five days to enact into law, and if it was acceptable to the members no debate or extended discussion was appropriate. The time necessary to pass the bills was actually doubled and allowed ample margin for unexpected developments. Since the House Democrats decided against the proposal in three days, it is clear the time given was not merely liberal, but generous.

The precautions taken by me were necessary to prevent a political session with its resulting damage and expense to the state. A free-for-all political session at this time at the expense of the taxpayers would have done untold harm. The assurances given me from many sources that a business session could be agreed upon and held were proven to be groundless by the action and reactions of the Democrat members of the House.

The efforts of candidates to promote themselves by baseless criticism of the governor [are] sufficient proof of the wisdom of restricting them within reasonable bounds. If doubt existed in any sane mind as to the wisdom and necessity of prior agreement, it was completely dissipated by the action of the House Democrats. My own experience on previous occasions, and the general knowledge of the experience of other governors, convinced me that the precautions I had to take were necessary to the welfare of the state. If anyone desires still further proof, the attitude and statements of the hostile partisans of both parties [supply] it in abundance.

In a telegram to me on May 19 the Speaker, Mr. Waterfield, said: "But the importance of solving the present critical situation which affects the lives and well-being of Kentucky youth transcends political consideration. Am urging you to issue the call to convene the legislature for the specific purpose of providing adequate financial support to education. I wish to pledge my support and cooperation in attending to the legislation without fanfare and delay. I have had opportunity to contact many Democratic members of the House of Representatives. I am in position to commit the cooperation of the majority."

That telegram was released to the press before I received it. When put to the test, Mr. Waterfield did just the opposite to what he had promised. He rushed in to prevent a special sesson, and the responsibility for his action rests upon him and those who aided him.

I have offered a program of constructive action, meeting the problems of today, while protecting, preserving, and safeguarding the financial stability of the state for the future. That program has been flatly rejected by the House Democrats, at the instance and with the aid of the Speaker. It is proper to state, however, that a number of high-minded, uncontrolled Democrat members of both the House and Senate were ready and willing to join in carrying out the proposals as outlined. All honor to them. Some members of the House and several senators failed to answer, probably because the action of the House Democrats on Sunday rendered further efforts futile.

I proposed a short and simple program to be carried out in a short, businesslike session. It was met with immediate political maneuvering, and the House Democrats hastily rejected the whole plan. Those who desired to help the causes included in the proposals promptly offered to cooperate fully in the whole procedure. But they were not enough. The responsibility for the present situation rests squarely on the shoulders of the House Democrats who joined Mr. Waterfield to prevent a special session. In view of these facts, there can be no extra session.[2]

The people will select a new legislature this year. When it assembles at Frankfort next January it will find the state in sound financial position. The services of the state government to the people in every department and function are at the highest level ever attained in Kentucky. It will require sound judgment and firm resolution to maintain the standard that has been set and to meet the new obligations that will arise from the additional responsibilities the state has assumed. That responsibility is in the hands of the people, who will elect all the members of the House and a majority of the Senate at the election this year. May we indulge the hope that the people will elect representatives and senators responsive to the people's will.[3]

---

1. Forty-six of the sixty-nine Democratic members of the House met at the Seelbach Hotel in Louisville and refused to agree to the governor's proposal. Nine others agreed by phone to that stand—a majority of the House. The telegram mentioned read, in part, "When you act under your constitutional right and call the legislature into session, the Democratic members of the House will provide for needs to education and welfare under their constitutional rights." *Courier-Journal*, July 14, 1947.

2. It should also be noted that if not appropriated in a special session, the funds, in large part, would be carried over to the next administration, which was expected to be Democratic.

3. The 1948 legislature would be Democratic by 75-25 (House) and 29-9 (Senate) margins. *Courier-Journal*, January 4, 1948.

REPUBLICAN PARTY LEADER,
1946-1947

FIRST DISTRICT REPUBLICAN RALLY
Kentucky Lake / September 2, 1946

GOVERNOR WILLIS cited the fact that in his victory for the governorship by a margin of around eight thousand votes, he polled eighteen thousand votes in the First District. This demonstrates the importance of getting out a large Republican vote in this section, even if the Democrats poll a larger vote in the district. Republican margins elsewhere can offset the First District's Democratic majority, he declared.

It is possible through coordinated efforts to bring out a vote of twenty-five thousand Republicans in this district, the governor added, and declared that if this is done it will mean a sweeping victory for Cooper.[1]

Commenting on a recent allegation by Brown[2] that all the Democrats and two-thirds of the Republicans "are mad at the Republican state administration," Willis said that neither the Democrats nor the Republicans "are mad at the record which has been made in the highway department of freeing the bridges and building roads; they are not mad at the progress which has been made to control tuberculosis through the building of new hospitals; they are not mad at the work which is being done in the conservation department to promote Kentucky, such as that here at Kentucky Lake State Park.

"I find there are far more Democrats who are mad at Brown than there are who are displeased with the state administration," he continued. "If Brown wants to attack the state administration, that is all right, for what we have done will answer him."

The voters will make the issue for themselves, the governor declared, and that issue will be the fitness of Brown for the senatorship as compared with that of Cooper.[3] He praised the record and qualifications of the Republican nominee for the post.

"If Brown wants to attack my administration, let him start where he will. We will be there to show the people of Kentucky we have given them the kind of government they wanted."

The state's chief executive predicted that if First District Republicans "cash in your twenty-five thousand votes" Cooper will win over Brown by a fifty thousand majority.[4]

----

1. Republican John Sherman Cooper, after overwhelming Roscoe C. Douglas in the party primary, faced John Y. Brown, Sr., for the right to fill the rest of the term of A.B. Chandler, who had resigned to become commissioner of baseball. Governor Willis's appointee until the election, William A. Stanfill, declined to run. Brown, in a closer primary race, had defeated Philip P. Ardery of Paris by 55,297 (43.6 percent) to 42,423 (33.5 percent). Other candidates had polled 29,978 votes. In the general election the district gave the Republicans 14,566 votes. Jewell, *Kentucky Votes*, 1:51-55.

2. John Young Brown, Sr. (1900-85) of Lexington. State representative, 1930, 1932, 1946, 1954, 1962, 1966; Speaker of the Kentucky House, 1932; U.S. representative, 1933-35; unsuccessful candidate for U.S. senator and governor in several primary and general election races; attorney. *Biographical Directory, 1949*, 900; Lexington *Herald-Leader*, June 17, 1985.

3. John Sherman Cooper (1901-   ) of Somerset. Kentucky House, 1928-30; Pulaski County judge, 1930-38; Board of Trustees, University of Kentucky, 1935-46; U.S. Army, 1942-46; U.S. senator, 1946-49; 1952-55; 1956-73; U.S. ambassador to India, 1955-56, and to East Germany, 1974-76. *Biographical Directory, 1949*, 1018; *Who's Who in American Politics*, 9th ed. (New York, 1983), 526.

4. Cooper won the election with 327,652 votes to Brown's 285,829—a margin of nearly 42,000. Jewell, *Kentucky Votes*, 1:55.

EIGHTH DISTRICT REPUBLICAN RALLY
Morehead / October 12, 1946

WE have just twenty-four more meatless days until election. This year we hold a national election. The entire House of Representatives and one-third of the members of the United States Senate are to be selected to represent the people of America in their aspirations for sound and honest government at home and a foreign policy which will be an assurance of lasting peace and friendship among the nations of the world.

As the president said in January of this year: *"1946 is our year of decision.* This year we lay the foundations of our economic structure which will have to serve for generations. This year we shall have to make the decisions which will determine whether or not we gain the future at home and abroad which we fought so valiantly to achieve."[1]

It was never more important than at this time that we elect a Congress composed of honest, intelligent, and trustworthy men. Here in Kentucky the opportunity presents itself to the people, regardless of their political affiliation, to make the choice between two men, one of whom will represent Kentucky in the United States Senate after November of this year. We believe this contest in Kentucky not to be a contest between the Republican and Democrat parties, as we have known them in the past, but between two distinct philosophies of government; between two candidates who so clearly and unquestionably represent those two philosophies of government.

Our opponents seek to prevent a change and to continue the present policies. The present administration acts upon the philosophy that the government belongs to their party and is to be used for their benefit and the benefit of their supporters. The first necessity is to reverse that policy and return the government to the people to be administered in accordance with the Constitution and fair play to all. The confusion, frustration, and internal strife within the administration [are] the cause of the unrest, uncertainty, and dissatisfaction in the nation.

This campaign is a crusade to rescue the government from the control of those who have caused the evils from which the people are suffering. Excessive power over the activities of the people cannot be endured. The administration in Washington has interfered with practically every activity in the factory, on the farm, and even with the contractual relations of individuals and organizations. The condition in which our nation finds itself today is the logical and inevitable result of the policies of the present national administration.

A start must be made to restore the confidence of the people in their government and to end the feeling of unrest which is prevalent everywhere throughout this land of ours and to bring back faith in the integrity and solvency of our government. These corrections can be obtained only by the election of a Republican Congress, because the Democrat party has been taken over by the radical element of the New Deal and cannot help themselves out of their own dilemma.

We are all dissatisfied with the domestic policies of the present administration at Washington, and *the only possible way to remedy the situation is to defeat every candidate for office who is pledged to continue it.*

The foreign policies of Secretary Byrnes, Senator Vandenberg,[2] and other statesmen proceeding on patriotic and nonpartisan lines [have] the unqualified support of the Republican leadership and will be sustained by a Republican Congress. The United Nations is the product of the joint efforts of both Republicans and Democrats, working with statesmen of other nations to establish and secure the peace of the world. It may well be described as "the last, best hope of earth." In order to sustain it, a Republican Congress is necessary because of the grave danger of sabotage by the supporters of the present administration, as typified by Henry Wallace and his group of Communistic followers.[3]

The inconsistent, confused, and self-contradictory work of the present administration renders it incapable of correcting the evils of this time, which it has largely created. A Republican Congress will clarify the air. It will clean house at Washington, which has grown foul by housing contradictory and conflicting elements, and by pursuing policies by expediency designed only to perpetuate in power the unsavory combination that has so shocked and injured the nation. The sole remedy in the hands of the people is the election of a Republican Congress. The opportunity of the people to employ that remedy is now at hand. It is apparent that the people are ready to embrace that opportunity.

Here in Kentucky for the past three years I have attempted to give the people the kind of government which they want and which they are entitled to. It has not been my aim or intention to give you a government for the sole benefit of politicians, but a government for the benefit of the people. I am well satisfied with the attitude of the electorate in regard to the aims and accomplishments of this administration, and when the proper time arrives I will gladly and freely debate the issues of this administration with anyone who questions them. Let it be sufficient to say at this time that every policy which I advocated has been put into effect, with the exception of the repeal of the income tax.

In 1946, I asked the General Assembly to repeal the personal income tax. I recommended a budget, at the same time, which would have maintained the educational system at the high level already established. At the same time I recommended an appropriation for the administration of the hospitals and the welfare institutions of the state which was adequate. But the legislature, dominated by a Democrat majority, cut it down. This cutting down on the appropriations for

Darnall and the hospitals and institutions housing the helpless wards of the state was done against the urgent insistence of the state administration that it was insufficient. The state institutions are now reaping the consequences of that slash made by the Democrats in the budget recommendations made by the administration. If anyone doubts this let him read the budget bill which was offered by the Republican leaders at the beginning of the 1946 General Assembly, and compare its figures with the budget bill finally passed as a compromise.

I was against freeing the toll bridges by the diversion of highway funds. Well, I am proud of that record, and I think the great majority of the people of Kentucky are proud of it, too. This is proven by the fact that one year following the attempt made to divert the road funds to the freeing of toll bridges, the people of Kentucky, by a majority of more than one hundred thousand, adopted a constitutional amendment to prevent such diversion of road funds for any purpose whatever. However, it is wholly true that the freeing of the toll bridges was hastened by this administration because of good management. And we did not lose the matching money from the federal government for roadbuilding, which we would have lost if we had freed the bridges by diversion of road funds. The federal government will not match road funds spent for any purpose other than roadbuilding, and that is another good reason why all the Republicans in the state Senate voted against that bill. You owe them a debt of gratitude for doing so, and, in all fairness, let it be added that most of the Democrats voted the same way.

Everybody in the whole state of Kentucky, I believe, must be familiar by now with my opening speech at Mt. Sterling, which proclaimed sound policies of government which have been pursued. In that speech, as you well know, I advocated a raise of $5 million for the common schools for the two fiscal years following my election to the office of governor, and an added $3 million for the fiscal year ending June 30, 1944.

When the General Assembly convened in January 1944, I asked them to pass this legislation. They passed the $3 million for the then current fiscal year but failed to agree on a budget bill. The General Assembly left the school teachers of Kentucky just where they had been for many long, weary, underpaid years under numerous Democrat administrations. I called a special session of the legislature for the sole purpose of passing the legislation I had recommended for the aid and benefit of the schools and school teachers. That record is there for all to see, and I point with pride to these four facts:

1) During the first year of my term as governor the school fund was increased $3 million for the fiscal year ending on June 30, 1944.

2) At the special session the schools were given an increase of $5 million for each year of the biennium, 1944-1946.

3) At the beginning of the second session of the legislature in 1946, I advocated a budget which would have maintained the all-high level already attained and still repeal the income tax.

4) When the legislature declined to repeal the income tax, I agreed with the leaders in the legislature that a large portion of the money which had been set aside for repeal should be used for the benefit of education. I signed the bill which gave this additional increase to the schools and colleges, though I could have vetoed it in whole or in part. It could not have been passed over my veto because the legal time for doing that had passed while the Democrats in the House were disagreeing among themselves. *I have fought for education;* I advocate continuous advancement through both increased pay and increased efficiency, but the two must go hand in hand.

As I said before, these issues will be debated when the proper time arrives. They will be debated by me and by others, fully and gladly. I think there are some good Democrats in Kentucky who will debate them on our side because they have been helpful in bringing the light of progress to Kentucky and have supported this administration in its effort to operate the state government for the benefit of all its citizens.

But this year we are engaged in the important task of electing a senator and additional congressmen to go to Washington and clean house there; we intend to leave no stone unturned to elect John Sherman Cooper.

We need also in the Congress of the United States, to back up John Cooper in his leadership, another man of character, ability, and respectability who has also served his country faithfully and well. Let the workers and the voters and the free and independent men and women of the Eighth District give their best and most devoted effort to sending these two outstanding young fighters for freedom to Washington on November 5.[4] *It can be done; you can do it,* and with the help of those free citizens who believe this country of ours needs a change, I believe it will be done. Let us all buckle on our armor and from this day forward devote all our time and effort to win this election in the Eighth District, while others like you are doing the same thing in the other parts of the state.

In this year of decision, if the people of America exercise with care and intelligence their constitutional right of the free ballot, there will begin a new era of progress and improvement; we can (when we select the men with the greatest care who represent us in all phases of our government) see better days for this generation and those coming after us. Or we can delay or even destroy the hopes of our people for the fulfillment of the American dream and American right. Great dark clouds of dissension and incompetency are hovering over Washington, and many evil men are in places of power.

This election on November 5 pretty well tells the tale of whether those clouds portend a great and destructive storm or whether they will sail away in due time, leaving an America aglow with light and courage.

Let us not be satisfied until we go back to our communities from this meeting, with a pledge to ourselves that we will strive untiringly to elect these two fine young men who have offered their lives and their services to their country, both in war and in peace. *Remember there is no ceiling on votes for Cooper and Schmauch.*

---

1. As reported in the New York *Times,* January 4, 1946, Truman's State of the Union speech of the third varied slightly from the way it was reported that Governor Willis quoted him. Truman said: "This year we must decide whether or not we shall devote our strength to reaching the goal of full production and full employment. This year we shall have to make our decisions which will determine whether or not we gain that great future at home and abroad which we fought so valiantly to achieve."

2. Arthur Hendrick Vandenberg (1884-1951), from Michigan. Editor of Grand Rapids newspaper, 1906-28; member Republican State Central Committee, 1912-18; appointed to U.S. Senate 1928, reelected and served, 1928-51; president pro tem of Senate, 1947-49. *Biographical Directory, 1961,* 1746.

3. Henry Agard Wallace (1888-1965), of Iowa. Editorial writer and editor of Des Moines *Wallace's Farmer,* 1910-33; U.S. secretary of agriculture, 1933-40; U.S. vice-president, 1941-45; U.S. secretary of commerce, 1945-46; editor of *New Republic,* 1946; author of several works; candidate for president in 1948 on Progressive party ticket. *DAB, Supplement 7:* 750-63.

Wallace's calls for increased Russian-American understanding in a time of rising tensions, his liberal policies, and later his endorsement by the American Communist party in his 1948 race led to charges by many that Wallace sympathized with the Communists. Ibid., 763.

4. The reference is to Ray Schmauch, the Republican nominee for congressman. Opposing Democrat Joe B. Bates, he lost in the general election 33,408 (52.6 percent) to 30,127 (47.4 percent). Jewell, *Kentucky Votes,* 3:70.

Schmauch (1889- ?) worked in steel mills, then, for twenty-three years, in the wholesale grocery business. After service in World War II, he returned to be state property officer for the adjutant general's office. *Courier-Journal,* November 3, 1946.

RADIO ADDRESS ON THE ELECTION
Louisville / October 29, 1946

As November 5 draws near our minds are turned to the senatorial and congressional election in Kentucky and in the nation. It is in the newspapers, on the air, in every conversation.

In America we have grown to take our elections as a matter of course. We can scarcely comprehend how truly phenomenal it is that, sure as death and taxes, the American people will have an opportunity every two years to reelect or replace the whole of the House of Representatives and one-third of the Senate.

In most countries the government goes along until it hits a snag and loses control. But in America the process of affirmation or replacement occurs every two years in orderly, organized fashion. Although we all agree that our system is the best, we find that our people become so used to elections that the very frequency with which they occur has a tendency to make them seem monotonous; and unless very compelling personalities are involved, we show our apathy by just not voting.

This is our first peacetime election in eight years; if we fail because of apathy to cast our votes to change the congressional majority, we shall be labeled as being well on the way to a complete totalitarian state. This is one of the serious challenges of the November election. This is a challenge which you personally cannot afford to thrust aside. It is a challenge demanding vigorous activity every day between now and the election, to bring about a change in leadership in our national seat of government.

By putting a Republican majority in Congress this November the American people will show faith in themselves, show they still believe in what they fought for, and indicate they still believe in changing administrations when administrations turn "sour."

So it is obviously the duty of every public-spirited citizen to participate in the election, to make his voice heard in the election of a Republican United States senator and congressman in Kentucky. Nothing is gained by standing on the sidelines and criticizing. If the citizen doesn't like the way things are run he should get busy and do his part to change them. This is representative government in action. This and this alone is *effective citizenship.*

This is a year of important decisions for all those sorely concerned with their own future and that of their country. I do not need to remind you of the critical nature of these decisions or your responsibilities in molding public opinion toward the right decisions. The predominant issues cover many fields; and because the ground has already been pretty thoroughly covered on the issues of OPA [Office of Price Administration], domestic and foreign policy, etc., I would like to deviate from those subjects and talk to you about two issues which have not been so freely discussed, but which have an overpowering influence in the coming November election, and our obligation to bring about the election of a Republican senator and Republican congressmen.

Far too long we have been hearing the boastful claims of the New Deal administration in regard to their so-called liberal policies, their self-described liberal planning. It has made many of us wonder, stop and think, and analyze what *the liberalism of the New Deal party* means, what it has brought to these United States of ours, what it augurs for the future. I should like to point out how important a part *"true liberalism"* has played in evolving a great America, a producing, progressive country, as it sped along for many years under the Republican concept of liberalism. *The kind of liberalism we want* is one of the first decisions to be made by the voters on November 5.

We know all through history *liberalism has been the honest fight to protect the rights of the individual against infringements by government.* Hundreds of years ago the liberals concentrated on freeing the people from the clutches of kings and emperors. Today, *true liberalism* is the fight against any form of government—monarchy, totalitarianism, or bureaucracy—working to limit the freedom of the individual needlessly.

Before you invest your vote you should take stock, look over the records of the two major political parties. The New Deal party has, of late years, been trying to show itself as the exponent of liberalism. How has it done it—by printing millions of questionnaires and forms? By creating constricting alphabet agencies in wholesale lots? By disunity within itself, the exact opposite of liberalism; setting up one class against another; having outright Communistic alliances; condoning the operation of political machines? This is the kind of so-called liberalism the New Deal party extends to the citizens of the nation.

Some ninety-two years ago the Republican party was founded to fight and end slavery. This was coincident with the beginning of the greatest era in our history. In *one* century, our country progressed from obscurity to the leading position in the world today, and more than three-fourths of that time was under a Republican administration. Ninety years ago the Republican concept of liberalism meant the end of slavery; today it means a "go signal" to production, the death of bureaucracy, *again a chance,* an opportunity for every man and woman. The specific goals may have changed with the times. The principle has not.

In the record of the Republican party, you have a record of *true liberalism.* It is predicated on the belief that individual freedom must be conserved, must be protected against an all-powerful government. It is patterned so as to provide wider economic opportunity for all; to eliminate the abuses of bureaucracy; to put an end to the loose, wild-eyed spending schemes; to make the wheels of government proceed on a safe and sound basis.

The record of liberalism, as evidenced by the true philosophy of the Republican party, offers you an investment for your vote that is substantial in background, unfaltering in principle, and sincere in its promise to endorse the ideals of our founding fathers. Your government is not your ruler. It is your servant. This is the kind of liberal government the Republican party proposes to produce for you, your families, your children, and the public welfare.

The first big step toward that realization will be the election of a Republican senator and Republican congressmen on November 5 who will begin our establishment of *true liberal programs* and restore honesty in government in this country.

And now, how about the moral issue? This is a second issue which is going to have a great influence in bringing about a change in Washington.

The New Deal party has built up contempt for our courts. The law of the land is no longer held in high respect. It is no longer a shameful thing to break it in spirit or in letter. Some think they are clever when they "get around" the law. The New Deal has placed order upon order, decree upon decree, regulation upon rule, until the sincere and honest citizen wouldn't have to read—much less obey—all of them. The New Deal has set up the executive branch of the government as the almighty agency—the executive branch with its bureaus and offices, its appointees and minions. The youth of our nation has seen the sorry spectacle of the rewards going to those who "knew the ropes"—those who could reach the "right people" to obtain favors in the form of contracts or jobs. Many young people see these things and conclude that it is "smart" to be "sharp"; to break the law and not be caught.

What is the answer? What can we do to reinspire our young men and women with faith in our government? Time was when we learned at home and in school that our government was good—that it was an honor and a solemn privilege to be elected to public office. The men and women we respected and admired were those whose wisdom and experience, coupled with unshakable integrity, kept them in positions of public trust.

The New Deal party today is a goulash of radicals—both the domestic variety and the well-meaning Utopia seekers and the imported variety of bloodless revolutionists; those who fondly seek Utopia in America and those who believe that Utopia is another name for Moscow. Add a generous number of race-baiting bigots and some of the more bewildered types of long-time Democrats who can't bring themselves to accept the fact that their party is a political captive; sprinkle generously with big city bosses; and you have a tasty dish of political poison called the New Deal.

I firmly and devoutly believe that the present regime is incapable of reform; nothing short of a change of administration will sweep the sycophants from the halls of government. Within its structure it lacks the elements of traditional Americanism—those elements which are basic to justice in all times and in all conditions—integrity, independence, self-respect, and a sense of responsibility.

I believe with equal fervor that these elements are present and vital in the Republican party today; I believe they are present and vital in our effort to offer you the best in bringing about a change from the New Deal majority to a Republican majority. You can look at our candidate for senator and you will find him defending his point of view honestly and publicly, willing to take the consequence of his own candor. There is no attempt to deceive, to avoid issues, or to avoid a frank and sincere discussion of the issues at stake.

Vote for John Sherman Cooper and the Republican ticket, and give the deserving people of our country an administration of true liberalism, and again encourage our youth to believe again that instead of the false philosophy of government which has successfully implanted fear in their hearts and made them seek security through dependence on their government, that if they build a better mousetrap than anyone else, the world will make a beaten path to their door.

Our candidate for the United States Senate from Kentucky, who heads the Republican ticket for which you will cast your vote on November 5, is an example of just such a philosophy of greatness. When he, at a very young age, had barely finished his college, his father passed away suddenly and left upon his young shoulders the responsibilities of a home, consisting of his mother and four younger brothers and sisters. John Cooper shouldered this responsibility; and although the income-producing member of the family was gone, he took charge of his father's business and stepped into his shoes as the head of the family, the breadwinner for his sisters and brothers, and his mother's solace and protector. Through hard struggle, but with never an idea of turning anywhere else for help, he brought his father's business to a successful state and educated, as he has been educated, his four sisters and brothers. He earned the love and respect of his fellow man; they paid him the highest compliment that free Americans can pay: they elected him to the office of county judge at a very young age; in 1939, his friends urged him to become a candidate for governor of Kentucky. He did so, and the fact that he was unsuccessful in that race did not in any way spoil his chances for the future, for he made friends wherever he went during the campaign.

When the war broke out he enlisted in the army as a private; he was sent overseas and did not return to his native land for a period of three years; near the end of the three years he was elected without opposition to the office of circuit judge of the 28th District; in May of 1946, he was the unquestioned and unanimous choice of all Kentucky Republicans for the still higher office of United States senator.

John Sherman Cooper will be elected to that office on November 5, 1946. He will make Kentuckians proud because he will give to this state a sample of the *true liberalism*, the freedom of the individual, the opportunity for every man and woman, for a productive and progressive country, under the Republican concept of liberalism. He will restore to the American youth the faith and confidence in the virtues of honesty, integrity, and self-respect.

REPUBLICAN RALLY
Carlisle / October 31, 1946

GOVERNOR SIMEON WILLIS, speaking here Thursday in behalf of John S. Cooper, senatorial nominee, and other Republican office seekers, said the war was "only partly the cause" of current high prices and shortages.

Shortcomings of the Democratic administration were blamed by the governor for much of the nation's "economic headache."

"Since the Democratic party has been in control for the last sixteen years, the government's payroll has increased to three million men and women," he stated. "They have increased every kind of taxes, taken meat off the tables, shirts off of men's backs, and blame it all on the war.

"The production of food was so great they cut down the production and killed the pig.

"Self-government is what we need. Government ruling always increases costs and expenses. We should never look to the government for anything we can do ourselves, and the philosophy of the Republican party is not to seek control."

He expressed a satisfaction the Republicans would carry normally Democratic Nicholas County[1] and said the party would carry the state "if all the Republicans and dissatisfied Democrats will go to the polls."

---

1. Nicholas County supported the Democratic party in the congressional vote (63.8 to 36.2 percent) and the senatorial vote (61.5 to 38.3 percent) by approximately the same margin it had in 1942 and 1944. Jewell, *Kentucky Votes,* 3:70; 1:55.

FAYETTE COUNTY REPUBLICAN CLUB
Lexington / December 4, 1946

THE governor pointed out that the Sixth Congressional District produces more Republican votes than any district in Kentucky except the third (Jefferson County) and the ninth (in eastern Kentucky), and declared that Republican voters were increasing in number in all sections of the state.

The people realized, he said, that the New Deal type of government was leading them to a bad end. "There was too much government at Washington and not enough self-government at home. The true political philosophy is to let the people do for themselves all that they are capable of doing, and to let the government do only what the people in their collective capacity can do better than they can as individuals. The New Deal philosophy is to let the government do everything."

As evidence that the Republicans would be able to solve the problems facing the nation, Governor Willis cited the records made by Republican governors of twenty-three states in which, he said, the budgets are balanced, expenses cut, and the people given good government.

STATEMENT REGARDING CANDIDACY
OF THRUSTON MORTON
Frankfort / March 30, 1947

MR. MORTON[1] came to Frankfort last evening and we had a conference. Naturally, we discussed his candidacy for governor. We agreed that an early canvass of the districts should begin and that the campaign should be built up from the precincts in every district.

I consider Mr. Morton a splendid candidate and believe he will make a fine governor. Mr. Morton has strong support in every district from which to build his organization.

Of course, I am for Mr. Morton. My previous statement should leave no question about that fact.

In view of Mr. [Allan] Trout's article in today's *Courier-Journal*, when he was compelled to rely upon inference from assumed facts that did not exist,[2] I would like to state further that I am for Mr. Morton because I consider him the strongest candidate that the Republicans have available this year.[3] His fine character, his outstanding ability, and his record of service to his state and country give assurance that he will lead Kentucky forward.

The *Courier-Journal* has in the past three years predicted curious things in regards to me and my motives and ambitions. First, it predicted that I would not be elected governor, then that I could not survive the Democratic legislature, and again that I would resign and go to the U.S. Senate. Now they are predicting that I have aspirations on a national level and that my acts are shaped to further my ambitions, all of which was . . . pure speculative rubbish.

I repeat that I am for Mr. Morton because I believe he measures up to the requirements of the occasion. If Mr. Trout can find nothing more damaging to say against Mr. Morton than that he is a back-slapping politician, such as Mr. Trout says his two Democratic opponents are, I am fortified in my belief in the outstanding fitness of Mr. Morton for the governorship of the state.

Many ambitions have been ascribed to me by my press critics. My greatest ambition, the one which rises above all others, is the election to succeed me of a Republican governor of character and ability to carry on good government for Kentucky. I believe Mr. Morton can do it. My reason for being for him is just that simple.[4]

----

1. Thruston Ballard Morton (1907-1982) of Louisville. Involved in family business since 1931; U.S. Navy, 1941-46; on boards of numerous companies; Republican congressman, 1947-53; assistant secretary of state, 1953-56; U.S. senator, 1957-68; chairman of Republican national committee, 1959-61. *Who's Who, 1982-83*, 2385; Frankfort *State Journal*, August 16, 1982.

2. Trout's article, entitled "Patronage and Willis' Ambitions Figure Strongly in Morton's Candidacy," said that the governor entertained ambitions for national office in 1948 or, at the least, a cabinet or judicial appointment should the Republicans win the presidency. His support of Morton, according to Trout, resulted from his desire to have the backing of Louisville Republicans in later races. *Courier-Journal*, March 30, 1947.

3. On April 19, Governor Willis added, in reference to this part of his statement: "That statement certainly is no reflection whatsoever upon any man who might aspire to be governor of Kentucky." He then reiterated Morton's strengths, concluding of the candidates: "I commend all of them unstintingly and take great pride in their accomplishments." See ibid., April 20, 1947.

4. As it turned out, Morton later withdrew from the race. Originally, both Governor Willis and Jouett Ross Todd, national committeeman from Louisville, supported Morton, while Congressman John M. Robsion went for Attorney General Eldon S. Dummit. The old urban-mountain Republican split seemed evident.

Earlier, Governor Willis appeared to be backing highway commissioner J. Stephen Watkins as his successor, but six days before Morton withdrew, Watkins stated he was not running for the office. Thus, on Morton's withdrawal, Governor Willis was without a candidate. He eventually supported state Superintendent of Public Instruction John Fred Williams, who had earlier opposed the governor on several educational matters. Meanwhile, Todd and Robsion joined forces behind Dummit and another factional battle developed. See ibid., May 11, 1947, and passim.

PRIMARY ELECTION
Louisville / July 31, 1947

FOUR years ago the people turned away from the domination of machine politics and elected a governor to carry out a program which they approved.

That program related to the schools, the highways, public assistance, public welfare, and to every department and function of the state government. It involved the application of business principles and of common honesty to the administration of the powers of government. The governor called to his aid the best and ablest men in the Republican party, practically every one of whom accepted public responsibility at considerable personal sacrifice.

In the highway department the nine political commissioners were abolished, and the management of the department placed in the hands of an experienced and competent engineer. The result is that today Kentucky is near the top of the list of states in highway construction, all of the toll bridges but two have been freed, the money provided by the taxpayers of Kentucky and the United States has been applied to the business of building and maintaining highways, and Kentucky has the greatest and most carefully planned highway program in its whole history. No candidate for office has dared to favor, at least in public, a return of the highway department to the old system of political favoritism and machine domination.

In 1942-43, the per capita for the common schools was $12.88. In my campaign in 1943, I advocated, and as governor in 1944 I approved, a special appropriation of $3 million to supplement the per capita fund for the common schools for the fiscal year ending June 30, 1944. In 1944, when the regular session of the General Assembly refused to meet my recommendations for education, I called a special session limited and restricted to the sole purpose of making the appropriations for schools at the figures I had advocated in my campaign. I was successful, and the equalization fund of $400,000 for the 1942-43 fiscal year was increased to $1,500,000, which was the maximum 10 percent allowed by the constitution. For the fiscal year 1944-1945 the per capita was $19.16, and for the next fiscal year it was $19.77. At the 1946 session the provision for schools was again increased so that the per capita last year was $24.40, and for the current year it is $25.56—an all-time high in Kentucky. I approved the 1946 bill at a time when the legislature had adjourned and when I had complete control. I approved many other bills for the improvement of education. Since I became governor, I have approved every step taken for the advancement of education, and many of them were taken only after hard and long drawn-out battles. Not a single step forward has been made in that time without my approval. Certainly every intelligent man and woman in Kentucky must know these facts. Proportionate increases have been provided for the University of Kentucky and for the four teachers' colleges, as well as for the Negro educational institutions. I have gone as far to help our state educationally as it is possible to go at this time without disastrous effect on other essential and indispensable functions of the state government. The advances made in expenditures for education during this administration are greater than were the total expenditures for the same purpose in any one year of any previous administration, and with it the financial soundness of the state government has been maintained.

The public assistance program has been broadened and the Aid to Dependent Children has been developed. What was formerly one program is now three programs: Old Age Assistance, Aid to the Needy Blind, and Aid to Dependent Children. The average for Old Age Assistance has been increased from about $11.00 to $17.50, per month. The average Aid to Dependent Children is $13.80 per month, and for the needy blind, $18.40. The federal government increased its contribution beginning last October, which enabled the Division of Public Assistance to reach and maintain these averages.

The building program at the state institutions has been carried on successfully and the well-planned rehabilitation is so far advanced that completion will be realized in a few more years of uninterrupted progress.

There has been rigid economy and skillful management in every department of the state government. Equal credit is due the many other departments where like efficiency and success has been attained, but which cannot be explained separately in the time allowed. It is sufficient to say, that the services of the state government in every department and function are now at the highest level ever attained in this state. No taint of graft or favoritism has marred the vast volume of business conducted. We are told that the establishment and maintenance of these policies in the last 3½ years has made some enemies to this administration. Knowing the honest heart of Kentucky, I have no doubt that for every single enemy it has made, thousands of friends have been gained. In any event, I have no apology to make to the enemies I may have made in excluding grafters from the public treasury or in preventing unfit and unworthy men from holding public office.

Because of the record of this administration the Republican party deserves the support and confidence of the people of Kentucky. That the people fully appreciate this record is manifest by the gains registered by the Republicans in the elections. The Republicans have added a United States senator, two congressmen, two judges of the Court of Appeals, and many circuit judges. The representation in the state Senate has been increased. At this very hour, there are many thousand more Republicans in responsible public office than ever before in the history of the state. And this very year, by reason of this record, and the prospect of success it affords, great desire is exhibited for places on the Republican ticket.

The question before the people in the primary next Saturday is whether we shall continue to elect Republicans and serve the people, or shall we sacrifice the opportunity to the selfishness and greed of a few who seek to control the party solely for their own purposes. In every battle this administration has fought to carry out its great program for the betterment of conditions the same opposition which is so noisy now has vainly sought to prevent our success. The type of campaign which has been carried on in this primary is proof enough that no hope of victory in November is being entertained by its sponsors. Compare the personalities you have heard from the opposition[1] with the position of John Fred Williams, who has said, and said repeatedly: "My purpose as your candidate for nomination is to be elected in November on a constructive program with other Republican candidates. I shall not criticize in a destructive manner public officials or leaders of my own party because I know that in doing so I would be performing an act of sabotage, and damaging the chances of my party to win in November."

That type of campaign makes for good will and good feeling among Kentuckians and helps to build up the morale and the strength of the Republican party. The opposite type of seeking office does not augment the standing of the party or foster good will among our people.

I will give you now some of the reasons why I am going to vote next Saturday for John Fred Williams for governor, and for the other state offices, for those men and women who support him.

I would like to see the great programs of this administration continued and carried to full fruition. I would like to see the progress and advancement which the state has made serve as a stepping stone to still greater progress and advancement. This can be done only by those who believe in the philosophy and policies which have brought about success, notwithstanding adverse conditions. Those who believe in a policy will fight to see it through.

John Fred Williams is one of Kentucky's own. He is a product of the best pioneer stock of the Big Sandy [River], with a background knowledge of the conditions, traditions, and ambitions that animate our Kentucky people. He has convictions and he has the courage to fight for them. He is a vote getter, as shown by his successive elections to office in his home county, and by his obtaining in 1943 the largest majority of any candidate on the ticket except the governor. His career has been carved out of hardship and pushed through obstacles which fit him for the great task he has set for himself.

I would like for our party to be successful in November in order that it may continue to serve Kentucky and in order that its path to victory may be smoothed for the great battle of 1948.

Kentucky is the only state where the election this year will be watched by the whole nation. This is so because Kentucky and Mississippi are the only states where the governor is to be elected. This state alone will provide evidence of the trend of public opinion.

A Republican victory here will encourage the party everywhere, and go far to assure the state to our candidate for president in 1948.

It is because I love Kentucky that I hope to see her government in clean, competent, and trustworthy hands. I want to see a governor who will put in office able, patriotic, and public-spirited men and women.

As the poet laureate, Jesse Stuart,[2] from my old home county of Greenup has written:

> Kentucky is my land
> It is a place beneath the wind and sun
> In the heart of America.
> Kentucky is neither southern, northern, eastern nor western
> It is the core of America.
> If these United States can be called a body,
> Kentucky can be called its heart.

Four years ago, the Republican party made its decision. That decision has resulted in a record of achievement for the welfare of the state, and a record of success for the Republican party.

There can be no retreat without disaster to the party and to the state. Kentuckians never retreat. In the primary next Saturday, let every loyal Republican endorse the record of his party, nominate John Fred Williams for governor, give him loyal nominees for the minor offices, and carry on to victory next November. In that way, and in that way alone, can be preserved the progress the party has made, with the assurance of continued progress in the years to come. Victory now and victory in the future can be expected only when it is deserved. It can be deserved only by loyalty to the philosophy and policies that have been tried and tested and found good for the people of Kentucky.

For the good of Kentucky, and for the salvation of the Republican party, I urge all registered Republicans to vote and work for the success of John Fred Williams and his associates on the primary ballot next Saturday. You will then have crossed the first hurdle in your march to victory.[3]

---

1. The reference is chiefly to Eldon Dummit's campaign speeches.

2. Jesse Hilton Stuart (1906-1984) of W-Hollow. School teacher; superintendent, city schools, Greenup, 1941-43; lecturer at several colleges and universities; author of numerous prize-winning short stories, poems, and books. *Who's Who, 1982-83*, 3247; Lexington *Herald-Leader*, February 18, 1984.

3. Dummit defeated Williams with 68,755 votes (52.0 percent) to 60,345 (45.6 percent). Jewell, *Kentucky Votes*, 2:33.

MEMORANDUM TO ELDON DUMMIT
Frankfort / August 1947

1. I would plant the fight squarely on state government, pledging in no uncertain terms the continuance of the policies of the Willis administration and the application of its philosophy to each new problem that arises.[1]

2. I would clearly proclaim my devotion to the objectives thus far advanced and set my face against any retreat toward machine government. I would emphasize my determination to treat all Republicans with absolute fairness and impartiality, and to all supporters of good government, regardless of party, I would give like assurance.

3. I would not be drawn into a discussion of collateral issues, but reject them with a clear explanation of their irrelevancy in this state election.

4. I would emphasize in the opening a program of progress and achievement along the lines now clearly defined by this administration

and reserve criticism or debate on our opponents for the speeches to be made in the campaign. The opening address should be in the nature of a platform defining objectives and principles of administration. In your campaign from day to day you can discuss the incidental issues, and meet the events that may shape or influence your action.

5. In the short time I have had to examine your address, it has not been practicable to make specific suggestions, or to recommend any definite commitments that could be safely made beyond these general principles. The financial problem overshadows all proposed action, and every objective should be conditioned on the ability of the state to carry out successfully any program developed.

I am convinced that some of the commitments contained in this proposed address will run you into great difficulties, and I regret to see you put yourself out on a limb.

If all proposals involving expense are conditioned on the ability of the state and the availability of funds, you would have an anchor to windward.

The balance in sustaining the numerous services and expenditures on a safe administrative and financial basis is not touched. This is fundamental in meeting all the responsibilities.

The omission of any rule as to new taxes or the repeal of particularly oppressive taxes may hurt. Also the new services that must be financed, such as Darnall and the TB hospitals, should not be overlooked. You may have meant to include these in your plan for future discussion, but there should be at least an indication of awareness that such problems are in the program.

---

1. Dummit, apparently in an attempt to heal the factional breach in the party, had asked the governor to comment on his opening address draft. Willis, whose administration Dummit had attacked in the primary, responded with this memorandum. Willis Papers.

RADIO ADDRESS REGARDING THE ELECTION
Louisville / September 26, 1947

BECAUSE of the record of this administration the Republican party deserves the support and confidence of the people of Kentucky.[1] That the people fully appreciate this record is manifest by the gains registered by the Republicans in the elections. The Republicans have added a United States senator, two congressmen, two judges of the Court of Appeals, and many circuit judges. The representation in the state Senate has been increased. At this very hour there are many thousand more Republicans in responsible public office than ever before in the history of the state. And this very year, by reason of the men we have been able to obtain, the public service is at the highest level of efficiency ever known in Kentucky. Because of this record we ask, and have a right to expect, the continued support of the people of Kentucky.

On August 6, 1896, a son was born in Missouri to Kentucky parents who had emigrated to that state. That son attended Drury College and the University of Kentucky, graduating from the College of Law at the university in 1920, his education having been interrupted during the First World War when he served as private in the United States Army. After teaching law for a few months at Lincoln Memorial University, he returned to Lexington in 1921 to practice. He has been engaged in the legal profession of that city ever since, and his first race for office took place in 1943, when he was the successful candidate for attorney general. He is the first Kentuckian to be chosen as president of the Southern Conference of Attorneys General, and he is now a member of the executive committee of the National Association of Attorneys General. In the course of his term as attorney general he has rendered over five thousand opinions. He was elected state commander of the American Legion in 1931 and president of the Optimists International in 1941.

He is now the nominee of the Republican party for the office of governor of Kentucky.

I present your nominee, General Eldon S. Dummit.

---

1. The previous seven paragraphs of this address correspond exactly with those in a talk given July 31, 1947 (and printed herein). Governor Willis simply changed the last paragraphs from a summary of Williams's life and career to Dummit's.

WHAS ROUNDTABLE
Louisville / October 2, 1947

GOVERNOR WILLIS mentioned several possibilities for the Republican presidential nominee. But he was careful to mention them by office, not by name.

"Whether the Republicans turn to the states and nominate a governor or pick a senator or representative for the post or adopt a military leader, the material available is abundant," he said.

Governor Willis . . . did not believe foreign policy would play too great a part in the 1948 election because it would be one of "unity backed by the leaders of both parties.

"The American people," he said, "are interested in their own firesides. Their interest in foreign nations is limited to what is for the best interest of the United States. They are more interested in what they pay in taxes and for food. They are beginning to realize how much has been put on the backs of the American people."

Governor Willis declared that a "complete change will have to be made" in 1948 because the people "demand a reduction in the cost of government, in federal taxation, and in the national debt."

TWENTY-FIFTH ANNIVERSARY OF WHAS
Louisville / October 2, 1947

I. I congratulate this radio station, WHAS, on its silver jubilee. It has maintained the ideals on which it was founded by Judge Robert Worth Bingham "to carry religious consolation, entertainment, and a wide knowledge of world affairs to the listeners in this area."[1] And our best wishes attend the rededication of the station by the present owner—a worthy son of a worthy father, determined to carry on in the same high spirit.[2] Since tonight's program seems to be dipping into prophecy, we may be permitted to predict that the future of the station will surpass its successful past. This is assured because of the purpose to keep abreast with the latest developments in radio, and to render to all the people the highest service possible.

II. It is my very real pleasure to extend a Kentucky welcome to the governors of three sister states who are with us tonight. In character, in ability, and in achievement, they deserve our admiration and our praise. Governor Caldwell of Florida has served in his state legislature, in Congress, and is an outstanding governor.[3] Governor Thurmond of South Carolina has served in his state in educational and judicial capacities, and during his first year as governor has commanded the respect and confidence of his colleagues.[4] Governor Gates of Indiana has rendered great service to his state as a lawyer and executive of political organizations and is giving Indiana an administration of which that fine state is justly proud.[5] He has endeared himself to all the governors. These distinguished men are lawyers; each has served worthily in the armed services during the world wars; and each of them is a top representative of his political party and an asset to his state and nation.

III. We come now to our topic. The director gave the title, "Let's Look at '48" and explained his plan in these words: "We want to analyze the forthcoming presidential election from the standpoint of the issues both international and domestic which will be involved, and the personalities of the candidates for the nominations at the conventions next summer." The situation at present is that the Democrats have the presidency and the executive offices; while the Republicans have a majority in both branches of Congress. The problem of each is simple: to hold what he has and to take over what the other party has. From the standpoint of the Republicans, we find a serene confidence in the ability of their party to hold Congress and to win the presidency next year. There are many reasons for this confidence. In the first place, the Republicans have twenty-four governors, and the states where they are in power furnish a big majority of the electoral votes. These governors have given excellent service, and are in position to give their party the benefit of their power and popularity. In the next place, the Republicans have a majority in both branches of the Congress, and the record of work already done commends the party to the favorable consideration of the country. The special elections held this year to fill vacancies have been won by the Republicans, with an increased percentage of the total vote over the elections in 1946. This trend in favor of the Republicans has been apparent for a long time, and there is nothing to indicate any sudden reversal of it. Finally, the Republicans have confidence because they have all the best of the arguments. The long siege of the party in power has had the inevitable effect of loading the party with burdens and handicaps too great to bear. The people demand a reduction in the cost of government, in federal taxation, and in the national debt. In order to obtain these results, a complete change will have to be made.

The Governors' Conference at Salt Lake City, in July of this year, discussed foreign policy and fixed the policy for the governors in these words: "The Governors' Conference hereby asserts its conviction that the foreign policy of this country transcends in importance all partisan, personal, or political considerations and should be at all times an American foreign policy, representative of the best in America and representing the United States to the nations of the world as a country that seeks peace and is united in its determination to protect the inalienable rights and privileges that our citizens now enjoy."[6] Foreign policy in 1948 will, in my judgment, be one of unity backed by the leaders in both parties, and will play small part in the campaign, unless nonpartisan action should be denied or defeated, or some happening across the sea should change the present attitude. The issues will relate to the domestic problems and the discussion will revolve around the large national debt; government controls; the excessive number of civil employees on the federal payroll; the veto by the president of tax-reduction bills; the high cost of living, inflation; the fair adjustment of management and working men's relations; and the countless forms in which issues have a way of coming up out of the events of the day. The personalities of the candidates have an abiding human interest and often play a greater part in the decisions of elections than the issues involved. The conventions will be seeking the nominees believed to be the best vote getters; and that field is wide open insofar as the Republicans are concerned. They have a large field of able men of proven worth. Whether they turn to the states and nominate a governor, or pick a senator or representative for the post, or adopt a military leader,[7] the material available is abundant. The choice is in the laps of the gods and there it may be safely left.

---

1. Robert Worth Bingham (1871-1937) of Louisville. Born in North Carolina; county attorney of Jefferson County, 1903-07; appointed mayor of Louisville, 1907; appointed chancellor of Jefferson County Circuit Court, 1911; owner of Louisville *Courier-Journal*, 1918-37; ambassador to Great Britain, 1933-37. *DAB, Supplement 2:* 38-40.

On Bingham's influence on the radio station's early years, see Terry Birdwhistell, "WHAS Radio and the Development of Broadcasting in Kentucky, 1922-1932," *Register of the Kentucky Historical Society* 79 (1981): 333-53.

2. The reference is to Barry Bingham, Sr. (1906-   ), son of Robert Worth Bingham (above) and owner of WHAS radio. *Who's Who, 1942-43*, 323.

3. Millard Fillmore Caldwell (1897-1984) of Florida. County attorney in Milton, Florida; state House of Representatives, 1929-31; U.S. Congress, 1933-41; governor of Florida, 1945-49; chairman, Southern Regional Education Board, 1948-51; justice of Florida Supreme Court, 1962-69. *Biographical Directory of Governors*, 1: 270; and Samuel Proctor, University of Florida, to editor, July 19, 1985.

4. James Strom Thurmond (1902-   ) of South Carolina. School teacher, 1923-29; superintendent of education, 1930-38; city and county attorney of Edgefield, 1930-38; state senator, 1933-38; circuit judge, 1938-42, 1946; U.S. Army, 1942-46; governor of South Carolina, 1947-51; presidential candidate on States Rights ticket, 1948; defeated for U.S. Senate, 1950; appointed, then elected, senator, 1955 to the present. *Biographical Directory of Governors*, 4: 1437-38.

5. Ralph F. Gates (1893-1978) of Indiana. U.S. Navy, 1917-19; attorney; state chairman of Republican party, 1941-44; governor of Indiana, 1945-49. Ibid., 1: 420; New York *Times*, July 30, 1978.

6. The resolution, presented by New Jersey governor Alfred Driscoll, passed by unanimous vote on July 16, 1947. See New York *Times*, July 17, 1947.

7. Dwight Eisenhower was already being mentioned for the office he would gain in 1952.

RADIO ADDRESS REGARDING ELECTION
Louisville / October 14, 1947

FELLOW Kentuckians:

We are called upon once more to determine the kind of government we shall have for the next four years. In the last state campaign in 1943 the Republican nominee for governor[1] stated the problem before the people in these words: "The central issue in this campaign is a conflict between two ideas of government. My own idea is that the people should rule and that this should be a government by the people and for the people. The concept of machine rule is that the people are to be exploited for the benefit of the machine." The people made their decision, and for four years they have been rewarded with the greatest advances in all levels of public service ever attained in any like period in the history of the state.

In its issue of October 9, the *Courier-Journal*, in an editorial article by Mr. Allan Trout, referred to the great battle of 1943 as "a reckless campaign" and one of "irresponsible promises." In view of the fact, admitted on all sides, that every policy advocated and every pledge made in that campaign has been put into effect with great benefit to the people of Kentucky, it need be said only that such a charge by a newspaper writer is a very good example of reckless statement and irresponsible reporting. If Mr. Trout would adopt for his partisan political writing the same philosophy he employs in his barnyard science, he would "embrace the truth where he finds it," and not predicate an argument on false assumptions of historical facts or upon direct misstatements of the written record.

Since some may have forgotten, and many may not have known the facts of the campaign of 1943, let us take a look at what was advocated by the Republican candidate in that year and what has been accomplished by him as governor in pursuance of that platform. Here is the record.

I. The very foundation of the 1943 platform was the prosecution of the war to a conclusive victory. It must be remembered that in 1943 we were in the midst of the greatest war of all times. The Republican candidate advocated the effective prosecution of the war and, insofar as possible, the negotiation of a permanent peace. The war work was carried on with such skill and devotion that the commander-in-chief and the leaders of the army and navy issued medals and citations to the executive officials who handled the Selective Service in Kentucky. Not a word of criticism has ever been spoken respecting the prosecution of the war work by this administration.

II. The second proposition, and one that constituted the very basis of cleaning up the government, was the destruction of machine control, the elimination of assessments of the state employees, and stopping the shakedown of businessmen who had transactions with the state. That program has been completely accomplished, and every man or woman who works for the state, or who does business with the state, will gladly testify that the policy advocated by the Republican candidate for governor in 1943 has been fully and completely vindicated. It has resulted in great savings for the state and in an improved efficiency and morale in all parts of the government.

III. The philosophy of taxation was stated and the repeal of the income tax was advocated. The article referred to stated that there was a promise to repeal the income tax and intimated that the promise was not kept. Nothing could be farther from the truth. The governor earnestly and consistently advocated the repeal of the income tax by the General Assembly at the earliest possible time it could be done without impairment of the solvency of the government. It was not safe at the first session of the legislature to repeal any tax and still meet the financial requirements then confronting the state. But at the second session of the legislature in 1946 the governor strongly recommended the repeal of the personal income tax and demonstrated conclusively that it could be done safely, without impairment of the levels of government which had been attained. Experience now has established that the income tax could have been repealed in 1946, without lowering the standard in any branch or department of the government, and still have left in the treasury a sufficient surplus for sound financial management of the business of the state. But that effort of the governor was frustrated, and it was defeated in the House of Representatives by more than fifty-one Democrat votes. A few of the Republicans deserted and failed to back up the governor, but a large majority of the Republicans, and a substantial minority of the Democrat members, did back up his recommendation. The responsibility for the failure to repeal the income tax rests squarely on the shoulders of the Democrat members of the House of Representatives in 1946. There are those who should be estopped from nagging the governor about the repeal of the income tax because they violently opposed all efforts of the governor to accomplish this objective. Their inconsistency will not escape the observation of the people, who know perfectly well that the governor was sincere in his purpose to repeal the income tax and was prevented from getting it done solely by the opposition of the Democrats in the House.

Moreover, the governor appointed a tax commission composed of outstanding businessmen from all walks of life to make a complete study of the tax structure. These men made an exhaustive study and constructive report, but the legislature was controlled by the opposition and took no action about it. So far as the governor is concerned, he did everything in his power to carry out an improvement in the tax situation, and that work has not ceased. It is being carried on through organizations of able men, and ultimately some action will have to be taken in order that a fair and equitable tax structure may be devised. The inequalities and injustices that have developed in the present tax structure ought to be eliminated for the good of Kentucky and her people.

IV. The power of the machine was centered in the highway department, which under the previous administration was in factional politics up to its neck. It was run by nine commissioners coming from nine districts in the state who operated as political bosses in their respective districts and in the state as a whole.

The governor advocated and accomplished the destruction of this advisory commission and placed the management of the highways in the hands of a competent engineer. This was a constructive achievement and has resulted in placing the highway department in the strongest position with the people it has ever occupied. It is now devoted exclusively to planning and executing a great road program.

Rural roads were neglected and the appropriation for them under the previous administration was barely sufficient to maintain the rural roads without any provision for extending the system. The Republican nominee in 1943 stated that "under a proper reorganization the rural road fund can be materially increased, and probably doubled." Was that statement reckless or irresponsible? The fact is, that fund has been more than doubled and the rural roads are now receiving the consideration due them. They will be advanced in a well-balanced system along with the other roads. No one has ever questioned that the plan of the governor with respect to the highways was a sound and progressive one, and no one can deny that it has been carefully and fully carried out. The result is that today Kentucky stands near the top in the construction and maintenance of highways. We are better off even than could have been anticipated three years ago. There has been improvement in the highway patrol by the addition of the radio and teletype system, and in many ways. A new spirit has been infused into the work of that great department, and people now come before the department with facts and arguments showing their need rather than to rely on political pressure. I congratulate the people of Kentucky on what has been done in the highway department.

V. Education was pointed out as a fundamental necessity for progress in a free country. The condition of the educational system in 1943 was serious, and there was a crying necessity for something to be done to rescue it. The article referred to a deficiency appropriation of $3 million as "a bag of money" and as "a bold proposition." It treated that as the whole program and the sole proposal. Such attitude shows an utter misconception of the educational program advocated in 1943. The deficiency appropriation was to relieve the immediate crisis, and was but a detail of the long-range program contemplated. That program called for $15 million for each of the fiscal years of 1944-1945 and of 1945-1946 with the full 10 percent authorized by the constitution to go into the equalization fund. Furthermore, it contemplated greater progress in the institutions of higher learning and in the Negro schools and colleges. That school program was regarded as the minimum required at the time, and it was carried out to the very letter. Not a single item of it failed of success. But conditions that developed later in the aftermath of war proved that still further aid was needed for education, and this problem is one that requires the most thoughtful, continuous, and patriotic consideration. This administration has done all that was possible to be done within the limitations of available revenues to help out and advance the educational system. It has done, not less, but vastly more than that which was advocated in the campaign of 1943.

VI. In the welfare department there were many problems. The Republican candidate for governor in 1943 stated that the administration of that trust should be removed from politics, placed in the hands of able administrators, and the purposes of the law fully carried out. That policy has been consummated. It has been practiced in the prisons, in the mental institutions, and in every branch of the service rendered by the welfare department, including, of course, the program for public assistance. You hear on all sides that never before has the work of the welfare department reached such a high plane. Not only did the administration carry on the work of the welfare department, but it has improved it in every detail, rebuilt the buildings that were falling into decay, and successfully administered the whole program to put these institutions into sound condition. No one with any candor or conscience would say that there has been any failure to carry forward every pledge or promise in respect to the welfare department and all of its varied duties and obligations in full, heaped, and rounded measure.

VII. The finance department contains the Division of Purchases where scandals developed under the previous administration.[2] It then was the object of criticism for favoritism and waste. The department has been placed in the hands of able, capable, and diligent men, and they have carried on a program of efficiency and honesty. Their administration has resulted in great savings in the administrative expenses of government. I congratulate the people of Kentucky upon the outstanding work done by the finance department and its divisions. The successful management of the finance department is proven by the fact that, although we have done more work than was ever done in any similar period and have met more obligations than ever before, yet we have accumulated the largest surplus ever known in this state. The soundness of financial management of all the state's business has brought constant praise to the splendid citizens in the department who have rendered such a magnificent service to the people. It should be remembered that every policy and plan in the governor's whole program was conditioned upon a balanced budget, and the state's ability to carry it forward within available means.

VIII. The Republican nominee for governor in 1943 often stated that he would call to the service of the state the best and ablest men he could find. This has been done, and many men and women now render public service who would not be attracted by the meager compensation allowed by the state. Moreover, hundreds of private citizens have accepted the call of the governor to render public service, and the state has had the benefit of the contribution made by outstanding men to the promotion of the general welfare. The standard of public service is at its highest level. The governor, from the beginning of his campaign, advocated peace and good will among all our people by fair dealing and justice to all, and in pursuance of this plan he has not spared himself in going to all parts of the state to aid the material advancement and moral progress of the state.

As to every other department, division, or function of the state government, the same philosophy was applied, and equal praise is due them all for important tasks competently performed. Indeed, I have never failed in all my reports to the people to give complete credit to the many fine Democrats in the legislature, in other positions, and in private life, who have helped this administration to carry out its objectives and to improve conditions in Kentucky. The significant accomplishments in improving the educational and other needs of our Negro citizens surpass all previous records.

These specifically were the policies advocated in the campaign. I submit to the people whether any of these policies were reckless or whether any of these plans were irresponsible. The complete answer is that all of them were successfully accomplished. It is proper to say that beyond the matters that were advocated in the campaign, or were promised, if anybody prefers to call what is being advocated a promise, there are many things that have been done that were not discussed in the campaign or anticipated four years ago.

A. Early in the administration the program was started for the building of five new tuberculosis hospitals, and the complete rehabilitation and enlargement of Hazelwood. This program has been carried forward and is nearing completion.

B. The Postwar Planning Commission was created by executive order, and able men were called from all walks of life to give an intensive study to everything that was possible and practicable for the good of Kentucky. Its work is bearing fruit.

C. The Tax Revision Commission, already mentioned, initiated a study that will be developed in future years and will be turned to for guidance and information in finding a solution fo the vexing problem of taxation.

D. In addition to the educational program announced and successfully completed, the governor, under authority vested in him by law, employed Griffenhagen and Associates to make a study of our educational system. This work is being followed up and implemented. It has met with the approval of forward-looking men and women of the state.

E. The administration has worked constantly on the problem of juvenile delinquency, on improving the administration of the probation and parole of prisoners, and for the general improvement of the corrective and rehabilitation services rendered to the prisoners and wards of the state. One of the new steps was the creation of a recreation division. In the health department much time and effort has been expended to advance the conditions of good health among our people.

F. The Game and Fish Commission has been taken out of politics and placed in the hands of sportsmen. This improvement has created good will and enthusiasm among the sportsmen for the conservation of our wildlife and natural resources. It is only one of many important improvements in the conservation of our human and natural resources.

A new spirit was instilled in all of the arms and branches of the public service, and all of the employees of the state felt the impetus of that spirit. It is the record of this administration that is now before the people for consideration and judgment. It is too late for a captious critic to belittle it because the people know and enjoy the results of good government. There should be no retreat from the high levels we have attained. Such a retreat would damage Kentucky and retard her progress.

In order that the policies and principles of this administration may be preserved and advanced, the Republican party deserves to be continued in power. The Republican nominee for governor, and his associates on the ticket, have pledged themselves to carry on the policies and principles of this administration. Pending programs are to be completed and the same philosophy of government is to be applied.

In making this record, the Republican party has redeemed its pledges. It has kept the faith, and it has established the fact that a good government is the best policy. This administration has conducted a large volume of business without waste, and it has advanced a great improvement program without debt. It has practiced economy without denying any service to the public. What has been accomplished is a source of satisfaction, but we must not forget that much remains to be done. In order to assure still further progress, the people must manifest their appreciation of progress already made. Nothing succeeds like success.

The government belongs to the people of Kentucky. They make it as they wish it. In their hands is the power to determine the kind of administration they desire for the next four years. The greater the interest and attention the people give to the problems of government, and to the performance of their servants, the greater will be the achievements for the public good. As the powers of government expand, and the services to the people become more comprehensive, the necessity of constant and intelligent attention to public affairs becomes clearer to the people. It is upon their judgment that all must rely, and upon their justice all may depend. Upon this record, we make our appeal to the people of Kentucky to elect the Republican ticket next November.

---

1. This is an unusual speech for Governor Willis in that he seldom spoke in the third person form, as he chiefly did here.
2. See Odgen, ed., *Papers of Keen Johnson*, 94n.

RADIO ADDRESS REGARDING ELECTION
Louisville / October 31, 1947

THANK you, Mrs. Joplin,[1] for your very gracious introduction. It is a splendid thing for Kentucky that the women of the state are taking an interest in politics and public affairs. They bring to the consideration and determination of issues and men a wise intuition, a quick judgment, and a moral exactness that men sometimes overlook. I am grateful that during my term of service the women have multiplied their activities in political life and that today they exert more influence on our public affairs than at any previous period in our history. By the same token, I am grateful for the increased interest and participation in politics of our best and ablest men. It has been my purpose to elevate the standard of political management, as well as of the public service, and I rejoice that so many fine men and women have participated in my administration and have accepted responsibility in party management. Politics will be no cleaner than the men and women who engage in it. The gains the Republican party has made since 1943 attest the value to the party of recognizing and enlisting its best talent, its ablest men, and its most sterling advocates, in the service of the people.

In this campaign the Republican party has the great advantage derived from four years of successful management of the state's business, and the development and advancement of constructive programs to satisfy the reasonable expectations of a progressive people. The Democrat nominee for governor [Earle Clements] is reported in the press to have made five statements which show a lack of familiarity with some well-known facts.

1. On October 18, referring to the rural road fund, he said, "It is $5 million now, thanks to a Democratic legislature, that doubled it over the objections of the Republican administration at Frankfort." If the Democrat legislature had adopted the recommendation of the governor, the rural road fund would have been over $6 million this year. The governor wrote into the budget bill proposed by the administration a provision to allot to the rural highways 20 percent of all state revenues credited to the state road fund during each fiscal year. Since the revenues so credited during the fiscal year were in excess of $30 million, the governor's proposal would have yielded to the rural road fund a total in excess of $6 million per year. The Democrat nominee now thanks the Democrat legislature for denying to the rural road fund an extra million dollars a year, as recommended by the governor.

2. Again, on October 20, the Democratic nominee for governor is reported to have said, "that the state of Kentucky has stagnated for four years." That was said in the face of the fact, admitted on all sides, that the state has advanced on all levels, and made more progress in all directions, than was ever made in a like period in the whole history of the state. Does the Democrat nominee for governor believe that there has been stagnation in the common school program when the per capita fund has been advanced from $12.88 in 1942 to $25.66 in 1947? Does he believe that there has been stagnation at the university, where the enrollment is more than twice what it was in 1942 and the provision made for the university both in operating expenses and in capital improvement is the greatest made in any previous four years? Does he believe that there was stagnation in the tubercular hospital program, which was started immediately after the inauguration of the governor and has been carried forward in the face of the greatest difficulties? Does he believe that the millions of dollars of improvement made at the

five mental hospitals has been stagnant? The Democrat candidate must have had in mind the conditions found at the mental hospitals when the present governor was inaugurated. Does he know of the improvements and advances made at the children's home, and at the reform school, and in the state prisons? Does he know or care about the progress made in the conservation department in the Divisions of Parks, Forestry, and Recreation, and in the Negro schools? Has he heard from the sportsmen about the great work done by the Game and Fish Division? Instead of the stagnation bequeathed to us by the previous administration, the present administration has advanced all along the lines of public service, and has put a new breath of life into every service and every department of the state government. Not stagnation, but progress has been the watchword of the present administration.

3. The Democrat candidate is quoted in the press as follows: "Not only have they brought no new industry into the state, but they have driven out some we had. The Southern Pacific Railroad just paid up everything they asked and moved out. The company said it would not do business in Kentucky, where it was harassed by this administration." Insofar as the Southern Pacific was concerned, it left the state because the laws of Kentucky required it to pay more taxes than would be exacted of it in the state of Delaware. The present administration enforced the law as it was written, and the officers of the state could do nothing less and be faithful to the oath of office. Does the Democrat nominee mean to imply that he would have let the Southern Pacific remain in the state without discharging its legal obligations to the state?[2] The constitution, Section 174, requires that all property, whether owned by natural persons or corporation[s], shall be taxed in proportion to its value. The law of the state is so framed. This administration did not make the law. It was required to enforce it, and that was all it did. The Democrat nominee was a senator for four years and did nothing to change the law. His campaign remarks would indicate that he does not approve of administration officers enforcing impartially the tax laws of the state. Does he propose a return to the favoritism of the Johnson administration? The people should know now if they have a candidate for governor who would not follow the law or respect the oath of office. As to his further statement that this administration has done nothing to bring new factories and industries into the state, he is equally wrong. If he would consult those who know the facts, he would find that there has been more new industry located in the state during this administration than ever before in a like period of time. The Kentucky Chamber of Commerce is doing a great work. It was created

as a result of the recommendations of the governor's Postwar Advisory Planning Commission, and the governor and this administration have cooperated, and are every day cooperating, with the chamber of commerce, and local interests, in bringing new industries to Kentucky. If the Democrat nominee reads the newspapers he will see announcements from day to day about new industries being established in every part of the state. A full list can be obtained from the Kentucky Chamber of Commerce. The governor's office has given all the aid possible with the facilities provided, and has received letters of thanks for effective aid given to those who are working for new industries in Kentucky. The Democrat nominee talks of tourist trade in the future, which he promises to encourage, but he overlooks the work already done and in course of completion by this administration to build up the tourist trade of the state and to care for it when it comes. Certainly the hundreds of people interested in, and the thousands of men employed by, the new industries now operating in the state, will be aroused by such efforts of a candidate to injure those who are helping the enterprises of the state.

4. At Covington on October 27, the Democrat nominee was quoted as saying: "As a member of the state Senate I supported the legislation creating the present tuberculosis hospital program, with the understanding that one of the five hospitals was to be constructed in northern Kentucky. A Republican-appointed commission took that hospital from you." As a leader of the state Senate, the Democrat nominee caused an appropriation of $1,500,000 to be stricken from the tuberculosis sanatoria bill, and as the bill was passed at the regular session in 1944, it carried no funds to put it into effect. At a special session later we were able to get the appropriation included in the special building fund. The act directed the governor to appoint a Tuberculosis Sanatoria Commission, consisting of the commissioner of health, three other doctors who were members of the state medical association, and eight members engaged in different trades, occupations, and professions. I appointed two members from the House and one from the Senate, being the sponsors of the bill in those bodies. I appointed also four men and one woman, and all the appointees were outstanding citizens. They proceeded to select sites in five districts created and defined by the law itself. The Northern Kentucky District was number 2 and contains twenty counties. The commission selected Paris, in Bourbon County, as the proper place for the hospital in that district. Does the Democrat nominee approve of the hospital at Paris? The legislature approved the work of the commission and has given complete support

to the program. What do the people of Paris and Bourbon County, and of the other nineteen counties in that District, think of the hostile attitude of the Democrat candidate? Does he propose to stop work being done at Paris in the Northern Kentucky District, and in other districts?

5. The Democrat nominee also repeated in that speech at Covington a statement that he had made before to the effect that the present governor in his campaign of 1943 promised everything and then promptly repudiated every promise he made. That statement was made in the face of the admitted fact that every promise made by the Republican nominee in the campaign of 1943 was kept and performed, with the result that there has been more progress made during the last four years, more advances in educational work, and more improvements in the state institutions, than ever before. It should be noted also that, by good management and strict economy, the state has the largest surplus in its history to carry on the program thus far advanced.[3] It seems that the Democrat candidate does not want to discuss the work of this administration, but he and the fragments of the old and shattered machine, which he has reassembled, desire to discuss the campaign of 1943. They fail, however, to discuss the actual campaign of 1943, but build up a straw man and strike at their own fictitious creation. In the actual campaign of 1943 the administration of former governor Keen Johnson was under review. Mr. Johnson, himself, is seeking to advise the people this year and dares to compare his administration with the present administration. Johnson was the one under whose administration stagnation of the whole building program occurred; and when this administration came into power, all building was at a standstill, and much of it under injunctions obtained by Attorney General Meredith. Johnson was the man who was enjoined by the courts from violating the laws he was sworn to enforce. He is the man whose administration collected bridge tolls to the extent of $400,000 or more after the bridges were entitled to be freed. He talks about the additional cost of government and undertakes to deceive the people by including the capital investment, the increased money for education, and the advances in the welfare program, as though these items were a part of the administrative expense. As a matter of record, the administrative expenses of the government have been greatly decreased, and the money saved and the additional moneys collected under the same tax structure have been applied to capital investment, increasing the assets of the state, in the educational, conservation, welfare, and other fields. The fact is that more money has been col-

lected by this administration, and it has been applied as directed by the General Assembly. The people have received full value for every dollar spent.

Your state government is in sound financial position. The state properties as a whole are in the best condition ever known at the end of a term of office. The vast assembly of equipment in your institutions and in your various agencies is in good working condition. There are now complete inventories of state-owned properties, materials, machines, and tools. The past four years have proven how valuable it is to the people to have a program of service and progress. Men of principle and good will can work together for the good of the state. This was proven conclusively in 1944 and again in 1946. Party unity may be the sole object of self-seeking politicians, but the unity the people cherish is for all the representatives of the people, regardless of party, to work together for the general welfare. Too much power in the hands of one party is not good for the state. It tends to arrogance and exploitation and leads to contempt for good government.

Good government and faithful service in every department or agency designed to meet a public need is good politics. This administration has shown how good government can be attained, and it has proven how good government makes for good will and sound progress in public and private relations. It will require sound judgment and firm resolution to maintain the standard that has been set. It will demand constant diligence and devotion to complete the great programs now under way. You may not safely entrust a program of good government to those who do not believe in it with all their hearts.

The course of wisdom is to retain in power the Republican party, which has proven its desire and its competence to establish and to maintain the high levels which a progressive people demand and deserve.

The Republican party, by its record in office, deserves your confidence and support. With the approval of the people, we may look ahead with faith and courage to even greater progress in the next four years. Let there be no retreat to the evils which you corrected four years ago. Let our watchword be onward and forward, with a firm reliance on the wisdom and justice of the people of Kentucky![4]

---

1. Unidentified. Possibly Alice E. Joplin, wife of Dr. Robertson O. Joplin and one of two Mrs. Joplins cited in *Caron's Louisville City Directory, 1949* (Cincinnati, 1949), 495.

2. See note 2 in document dated July 10, 1947, "Legislative Actions, 1946-1947" section.

3. The governor left a surplus of some $26 million. See *Annual Report, Commission of Finance for Fiscal Year Ending June 30, 1947* (n.p., 1947), 148.

4. Democrat Earle Clements defeated the Republican nominee, Eldon Dummit, 387,795 (57.2 percent) to 287,756 (42.5 percent). Jewell, *Kentucky Votes*, 2:35.

VALEDICTORY

VALEDICTORY ADDRESS
Frankfort / December 9, 1947

MY fellow Kentuckians:

It is a great honor to have served the people of Kentucky as chief magistrate. In the circumstances of a world war and the aftermath of war many difficulties have had to be met. The task has been made easier by the loyal service of faithful officials and employees who have carried on the endless details of the executive work.

It is my pleasure on this occasion to offer my grateful thanks to the heads of departments; to the directors of divisions; to the many employees who have worked so ardently to advance the welfare of the people and to increase the efficiency of government. The hundreds of patriotic private citizens who have responded to my call to render high public service without pay are equally entitled to the highest praise and the deepest gratitude.

The record of the past four years speaks for itself. It will stand as a tribute to the many fine men and women who have endeavored at all times to advance the material, educational, cultural, and spiritual welfare of our state. If there be any who have failed to help, we can only say that they lost a golden opportunity to distinguish themselves.

To our successors, we extend our congratulations and best wishes for a happy and successful administration. We pledge our earnest and constant cooperation in all efforts to promote good government, to build a greater and better Kentucky, and to advance the interests of all of our people. Your state government is in sound financial position. The state properties as a whole are in good repair, and the vast assembly of equipment in your various agencies is in good working order.

There are now complete inventories of state-owned properties, materials, machines, and tools. Your farms at the several institutions are in a high state of production. Every department and branch of the government is operating smoothly and functioning effectively. The foundation for further progress has been firmly laid, and plans for it have been wisely patterned.

There are grave and difficult days for our state and nation, and those charged with official responsibility are entitled to every help that can be given to them by a loyal and generous people.

In every crisis in our history our people have risen to the responsibilities of the hour. I have an abiding faith that whatever difficulties may come, the same courage, fortitude, and competence which has characterized our people in the past will carry us triumphantly and safely over the rocky roads of the future.

With firm resolve, with high hope, and with reliance on divine guidance, we must go forward confident that the nation will ride out the storm and that Kentucky will contribute her share in full measure to the solution of every problem.

APPENDIX
Public Speeches, Statements, and Extended Remarks

*Included in this volume.

100TH ANNIVERSARY OF YMCA, Russell, April 19, 1944*

RED CROSS DRIVE, Anco, April 21, 1944*

KENTUCKY REPUBLICAN CONVENTION, Louisville, April 25, 1944*

HAYES REPUBLICAN CLUB OF SANDUSKY COUNTY, OHIO, Fremont, Ohio, April 27, 1944*

SPEECH TO REPUBLICAN STATE CENTRAL COMMITTEE, Louisville, May 5, 1944

REDEDICATION OF MT. ZION CHURCH, Perry Park, May 7, 1944*

STATEMENT CONCERNING THE VICE PRESIDENCY, Frankfort, May 10, 1944

PROCLAMATION FOR SPECIAL SESSION, Frankfort, May 15, 1944*

STATEMENT REGARDING SPECIAL SESSION, Frankfort, May 15, 1944*

SPEECH TO KENTUCKY WOMEN'S CLUB GOLDEN JUBILEE DINNER, Lexington, May 18, 1944

SPECIAL SESSION, Frankfort, May 19, 1944*

STATEMENT IN RESPONSE TO CLEMENTS' LETTER IN *COURIER-JOURNAL*, Frankfort, May 22, 1944

SPEECH TO KIWANIS CLUB, Barbourville, May 22, 1944

SPEECH AT UNION COLLEGE COMMENCEMENT, Barbourville, May 23, 1944

EDUCATION BILL, Frankfort, May 31, 1944*

MEMORANDUM TO SENATOR MOSS, Frankfort, June 1, 1944*

STATEMENT URGING SUPPORT FOR EDUCATION BILL, Frankfort, June 3, 1944*

KENTUCKY WESLEYAN COMMENCEMENT, Winchester, June 5, 1944*

REMARKS PAYING TRIBUTE TO BISHOP DARLINGTON, Graefenburg, June 6, 1944

STATEMENT REGARDING DREW PEARSON COLUMN, Frankfort, June 8, 1944*

LEXINGTON OPTIMIST CLUB LUNCHEON, Lexington, June 9, 1944*

PROCLAMATION FOR SECOND SPECIAL SESSION, Frankfort, June 12, 1944*

OPENING OF FIFTH WAR LOAN CAMPAIGN, Louisville, June 12, 1944*

FLAG DAY, Ashland, June 15, 1944*

REMARKS CONCERNING MEETING OF GOP DELEGATES, Frankfort, June 15, 1944

REMARKS TO "YOUNG VOTERS FOR DEWEY" CLUBS, Park City, October 2, 1944

SECOND ANNIVERSARY OF OPENING, WARREN COUNTY TUBERCULOSIS SANATORIUM, Bowling Green, October 3, 1944*

POSTWAR PLANNING COMMISSION, Frankfort, October 6, 1944*

TELEGRAM TO SENATOR BARKLEY, Frankfort, October 9, 1944*

RALLY OF INDIANA REPUBLICANS, Boswell, Indiana, October 10, 1944*

INTERVIEW REGARDING ELECTION, Indianapolis, Indiana, October 10, 1944*

POLITICAL SPEECH, Indianapolis, Indiana, October 11, 1944

TELEGRAM TO SENATOR BARKLEY, En route to New Castle, Indiana, October 11, 1944*

SPEECH FOR DEWEY-BRICKER TICKET, New Castle, Indiana, October 11, 1944

REPUBLICAN RALLY, Portsmouth, Ohio, October 12, 1944*

SPEECH TO NORTHSIDE REPUBLICAN CLUB, Columbus, Ohio, October 13, 1944

TELEGRAM TO SENATOR BARKLEY, Youngstown, Ohio, October 16, 1944*

POLITICAL SPEECH, Providence, Rhode Island, October 17, 1944

POLITICAL SPEECH, Bergen, New Jersey, October 18, 1944

POLITICAL SPEECH, Elizabeth, New Jersey, October 19, 1944

POLITICAL SPEECH, Beckley, West Virginia, October 21, 1944

POLITICAL SPEECH, Logan, West Virginia, October 21, 1944

REMARKS REGARDING ELECTION, Frankfort, October 23, 1944*

SPEECH AT ANNUAL CONVENTION OF THE ORDER OF THE EASTERN STAR, Lexington, October 23, 1944

SPEECH AT DEDICATION OF REHABILITATION ADMINISTRATION BUILDING, CENTRAL STATE HOSPITAL, Lakeland, October 25, 1944

SPEECH AT KENTUCKY REPUBLICAN FUND DINNER, Louisville, October 26, 1944

SPEECH AT DEDICATION OF THREE NEW WOMEN'S WARDS, EASTERN STATE HOSPITAL, Lexington, October 27, 1944

REPUBLICAN RALLY, Lexington, October 27, 1944*

REPUBLICAN RALLY, Paintsville, October 28, 1944*

Republican Rally, Lexington, October 31, 1944*

Remarks to Opening Session of Postwar Advisory Planning Commission, Frankfort, November 1, 1944

Republican Rally, Owensboro, November 3, 1944*

Statement Regarding Waterfield Campaign Speech, Owensboro, November 3, 1944*

Speech for Dewey-Bricker, Evansville, Indiana, November 4, 1944

Statement on Election Results, Ashland, November 8, 1944

Eastern Kentucky Education Association, Ashland, November 9, 1944*

Louisville Philharmonic Orchestra, Louisville, November 10, 1944*

Remarks on Requests for Special Session to Avoid Reductions in Old Age Pensions, Frankfort, November 14, 1944

Speech on International Relations to the Frankfort Chapter of the AAUW, Frankfort, November 15, 1944

Remarks at the Annual Thoroughbred Club of America Dinner, Lexington, November 15, 1944

Twenty-fifth Anniversary Dinner—Owensboro Chamber of Commerce, Owensboro, November 16, 1944*

Statement Regarding ICC Rate Question, Biloxi, Mississippi, November [24 or 25], 1944*

Remarks on Need for Special Session, Frankfort, November 28, 1944

Speech to the Judicial Council, Frankfort, November 30, 1944

Statement Regarding Public Assistance, November 1944*

Interview Regarding First Year in Office, Frankfort, December 2, 1944*

Speech to Civic Club, London, December 8, 1944

Statement Denying Charge of Dictation to Legislature, Frankfort, December 8, 1944*

Speech to State Mining Institute, Lexington, December 9, 1944

Speech to Kentucky Sheriffs Association, Louisville, December 15, 1944

Speech to State Farm Bureau, Louisville, January 11, 1945

National Foundation for Infantile Paralysis, Louisville, January 14, 1945*

Remarks Regarding Public Assistance, Frankfort, January 17, 1945*

Speech to Junior Chamber of Commerce, Lexington, January 17, 1945

Statement Encouraging the United Mine Workers to Work Two Sundays to Help Replenish the Nation's Coal Supply, Frankfort, January 18, 1945

Speech at Boyd County Lincoln Day Dinner, Ashland, February 10, 1945

Lincoln Day Dinner, Louisville, February 12, 1945*

Dedication of Venereal Disease Center, Louisville, February 21, 1945*

Speech to Lexington Rotary Club, Lexington, February 22, 1945

Founders' Day, Lexington, February 22, 1945*

Speech at Nichols General Hospital, Louisville, February 23, 1945

Statement Dismissing the Charges against the Sheriffs of Campbell and Kenton Counties, Frankfort, March 1, 1945

Statement Regarding Federal Aid to Education, Frankfort, March 16, 1945*

Field Representatives of Alcoholic Beverage Control Board, Frankfort, March 21, 1945*

Tax Revision Commission, Frankfort, March 28, 1945*

Speech Honoring Major Kadel, Mammoth Cave, April 12, 1945

Speech Honoring Circuit Judge William B. Ardery, Frankfort, April 16, 1945

Remarks on Special Session, Frankfort, April 17, 1945

Dedication of Reconstructed Male Ward at Central State Hospital, Lakeland, April 18, 1945*

Proclamation for Special Session, Frankfort, April 19, 1945*

Citizens League of Bell County, Middlesboro, April 21, 1945*

Speech at Henderson Settlement School Commencement, Bell County, April 22, 1945

REMARKS REGARDING TOURISM, Frankfort, August 2, 1945*

STATE HOLIDAY—VICTORY OVER JAPAN, Frankfort, August 14, 1945*

V-J DAY, Frankfort, August 14, 1945*

GREATER PADUCAH ASSOCIATION DINNER, Paducah, August 24, 1945*

FREE BRIDGE CELEBRATION, Eggner's Ferry, August 25, 1945*

SPEECH AT WESTERN KENTUCKY'S LABOR DAY COAL FESTIVAL, Central City, September 3, 1945

STATEMENT ON FIRING OF THE KENTUCKY AERONAUTICS COMMISSION, Frankfort, September 4, 1945*

REMARKS TO OPENING SESSION OF LEGISLATIVE COUNCIL, Frankfort, September 10, 1945

DEDICATORY SERVICE, BROADWAY METHODIST CHURCH, Paducah, September 15, 1945*

HEALTH TRAINING SCHOOL OF KENTUCKY FEDERATION OF WOMEN'S CLUBS AND STATE DEPARTMENT OF HEALTH, Lexington, September 18, 1945*

SPEECH AT LESLIE COUNTY FAIR, Hyden, September 22, 1945

REMARKS PRESENTING EAGLE SCOUT BADGES, Paris, September 23, 1945

FREEING MAYSVILLE BRIDGE CEREMONY, Maysville, October 1, 1945*

KENTUCKY GOOD ROADS FEDERATION, Lexington, October 15, 1945*

SPEECH HONORING THE FRANKFORT HIGH SCHOOL FOOTBALL TEAM, Frankfort, October 17, 1945

SPEECH DEDICATING NEW BUILDING AT KENTUCKY CHILDREN'S HOME, Lyndon, October 19, 1945

SPEECH TO THE ORDER OF THE EASTERN STAR OF KENTUCKY, Louisville, October 22, 1945

STATEMENT TO LEGISLATIVE COUNCIL: BUDGET, Frankfort, October 23, 1945*

STATEMENT REGARDING TAX POLICY, Frankfort, October 25, 1945*

DEDICATION OF NEW NEGRO WARD AT CENTRAL STATE HOSPITAL, Lakeland, October 26, 1945*

DENIAL OF AERONAUTICS BOARD'S CHARGES, Frankfort, November 1, 1945*

DEDICATION OF NEW BUILDINGS AT GREENDALE HOUSE OF REFORM, Lexington, November 2, 1945*

Speech at Army Day Celebration, Frankfort, April 6, 1946

Statement Read to Federal Power Commission Hearings, Charleston, West Virginia, April 11, 1946*

Speech Welcoming the College Publicity Association, Lexington, May 7, 1946

Kentucky Rural Church Council, Dinner Meeting, Lexington, May 7, 1946*

Speech to YMCA's Boy Model Legislature, Frankfort, May 10, 1946

Labor Day Program, Berea, May 14, 1946*

Cornerstone for State Tuberculosis Hospital, Glasgow, May 15, 1946*

Speech at Commencement—Clay High School, Webster County, May 17, 1946

Statement Regarding Dr. W.H. Vaughan, Frankfort, May 22, 1946*

Statement Regarding Possible Inquiry at Morehead, Frankfort, May 23, 1946*

Republican Banquet, Harlan, June 8, 1946*

Speech to Conference Called to Promote Industry in State, June 21, 1946

Speech to Kentucky Press Association Convention, Lexington, June 28, 1946

Lifting OPA Controls, Louisville, July 1, 1946*

Cornerstone for State Tuberculosis Hospital, Ashland, July 12, 1946*

Speech at Ceremony Laying the Cornerstone for London Tuberculosis Hospital, London, July 19, 1946

Remarks Regarding Griffenhagen and Associates' Survey of Education, Frankfort, July 22, 1946*

Speech at Ceremony Laying the Cornerstone for Paris Tuberculosis Hospital, Paris, July 25, 1946

Cornerstone for State Tuberculosis Hospital, Madisonville, August 9, 1946*

Statement Regarding Opening of Clay's Ferry Bridge, Clay's Ferry, August 17, 1946*

Dedication of Clay's Ferry Bridge, Clay's Ferry, August 17, 1946*

REMARKS TO REPUBLICAN 221 AND LINCOLN CLUB, Louisville, August 21, 1946

SPEECH HONORING CHIEF JUSTICE VINSON AT BOYD COUNTY BAR ASSOCIATION MEETING, Ashland, August 23, 1946

FREEING LIVERMORE BRIDGE CEREMONY, Livermore, August 30, 1946*

FIRST DISTRICT REPUBLICAN RALLY, Kentucky Lake, September 2, 1946*

SPEECH AT DEDICATION OF KENTUCKY HOUSE OF REFORM, GREENDALE, Lexington, September 5, 1946

SPEECH TO STATEWIDE COUNTY AND DISTRICT CHAIRMEN OF GOP WOMEN'S CLUBS, Frankfort, September 11, 1946

DEDICATION OF KENTUCKY STATE HOSPITAL, Danville, September 12, 1946*

DEDICATION OF "MISSING LINK" OF U.S. 23, Lowmansville, September 14, 1946*

DEDICATION OF MAMMOTH CAVE AS NATIONAL PARK, Mammoth Cave, September 18, 1946*

SPEECH TO THE SOUTH END OPTIMIST CLUB, Louisville, September 20, 1946

SPEECH AT THE DEDICATION OF BUILDINGS AT KENTUCKY CHILDREN'S HOME, Lyndon, September 20, 1946

SPEECH TO FIELD AGENTS OF ALCOHOLIC BEVERAGE CONTROL BOARD, Frankfort, September 25, 1946

SPEECH AT DEDICATION OF EASTERN STATE HOSPITAL, Lexington, September 26, 1946

SPEECH TO THE KENTUCKY ARMY ADVISORY COMMITTEE, Frankfort, October 2, 1946

REMARKS ON THE ACQUISITION OF THE LOUISVILLE MUNICIPAL BRIDGE, Frankfort, October 9, 1946

SPEECH AT THE OPENING OF THE BOURBON COUNTY FALL FESTIVAL, Paris, October 9, 1946

EIGHTH DISTRICT REPUBLICAN RALLY, Morehead, October 12, 1946*

SPEECH AT THE FOURTH ANNUAL TOBACCO FESTIVAL, Shelbyville, October 18, 1946

SPEECH IN SUPPORT OF REPUBLICAN TICKET, Stanton, October 25, 1946

SPEECH SUPPORTING REPUBLICAN TICKET, Greenville, October 29, 1946

Radio Address on the Election, Louisville, October 29, 1946*

Republican Rally, Carlisle, October 31, 1946*

Speech Turning Louisville Municipal Bridge over to the State of Kentucky, Louisville, October 31, 1946

Speeches on Behalf of the Republican Ticket, Olive Hill and Grayson, November 2, 1946

Statement on the Republican Victory in State and Nation, Frankfort, November 6, 1946

Speech at Dedication of the Blue Grass Airport, Lexington, November 10, 1946

Speech at Armistice Day Ceremonies, Frankfort, November 11, 1946

Speech to the First Annual Trade Dinner of Manufacturing Representatives, Louisville, November 13, 1946

Speech at a Republican Victory Dinner, Louisville, November 22, 1946

Proclamation Regarding Coal Shortage, Frankfort, November 25, 1946*

Fayette County Republican Club, Lexington, December 4, 1946*

Speech to the Kentucky Chapter of the National Foundation for Infantile Paralysis, Louisville, December 16, 1946

Negro Republican Rally, Louisville, December 17, 1946*

Speech to the Louisville Board of Trade Sales Managers Council, Louisville, December 30, 1946

Red Cross Drive, Louisville, 1947*

State Division of Game and Fish, 1947*

Joint Convention, American Association of Schools and Departments of Journalism and American Association of Teachers of Journalism, Lexington, January 10, 1947*

Speech at Swarthmoor Community Club, Louisville, January 13, 1947

Speech to the Kentucky Press Association, Louisville, January 17, 1947

Speech to the Boy Scouts, Frankfort, January 23, 1947

Remarks to a Delegation from the Kentucky Education Association Requesting a Special Session, Frankfort, February 5, 1947

An Appeal to Kentuckians to Conserve Natural Gas, Frankfort, February 7, 1947

Boyd County Lincoln Day Banquet, Ashland, February 8, 1947*

Speech at Lincoln Day Dinner, Cold Springs, February 10, 1947

Lincoln Club, Louisville, February 12, 1947*

Remarks Concerning the Calling of a Special Session, Frankfort, February 13, 1947

Speech to Meeting of Kentucky Petroleum Marketers Association, Louisville, February 26, 1947

Speech to Father-Son Banquet at Trinity Temple Methodist Church, Louisville, February 28, 1947

Speech to Daughters of American Colonists, Frankfort, March 11, 1947

Telegram Regarding Aid to Education, Frankfort, March 13, 1947*

Statement Regarding Education Record, Frankfort, March 13, 1947*

Speech to the DAR, Frankfort, March 13, 1947

Speech to Adath Israel Men's Club, Louisville, March 19, 1947

Speech to the Winchester Council of United Commercial Travelers, Winchester, March 23, 1947

Speech to Kentucky Hospital Association Dinner, Lexington, March 26, 1947

Statement Regarding Candidacy of Thruston Morton, Frankfort, March 30, 1947*

Remarks at Ground-breaking Ceremony for University of Kentucky Fieldhouse, Lexington, April 1, 1947

Speech to the Kentucky Bar Association, Louisville, April 3, 1947

Speech at Army Day, Fort Knox, April 7, 1947

Statement to U.S. Congress Asking for the Reduction of Government Regulation of Natural Gas, Frankfort, April 15, 1947

Speech to the State Capital Women's Republican Club, Frankfort, April 17, 1947

Welcoming Remarks to the Blue Grass Council of the Boy Scouts, Frankfort, April 18, 1947

Speech to the Louisville Automobile Club, Louisville, April 21, 1947

SPEECH ON TRAFFIC SAFETY, Maysville, April 22, 1947

SPEECH TO THE LOUISVILLE BUSINESSMEN'S CLUB, Louisville, April 24, 1947

ADDRESS TO LEXINGTON OPTIMIST CLUB, Lexington, May 2, 1947

ADDRESS AT DINNER FOR KENTUCKY COLONELS, Louisville, May 3, 1947

SPEECH AT DINNER FOR THE 1947 PHILHARMONIC PROGRESS FUND, Louisville, May 7, 1947

SPEECH TO NINTH DISTRICT MEETING OF REPUBLICAN WOMEN, Cumberland Falls, May 10, 1947

SPEECH AT COMMENCEMENT EXERCISES, LEWISPORT HIGH SCHOOL, Lewisport, May 12, 1947

SPEECH TO AMERICAN ASSOCIATION OF MOTOR VEHICLE ADMINISTRATORS, Louisville, May 13, 1947

WELCOMING SPEECH AT YMCA YOUTH AND GOVERNMENT CONFERENCE, Frankfort, May 16, 1947

SPEECH AT WAYNE COUNTY HIGH SCHOOL GRADUATION, Monticello, May 16, 1947

SPEECH AT COMMENCEMENT AT ESTILL COUNTY HIGH SCHOOL, Irvine, May 20, 1947

SPEECH TO LINCOLN CLUB, Louisville, May 21, 1947

100TH ANNIVERSARY OF KENTUCKY FEMALE ORPHAN SCHOOL, Midway, May 21, 1947*

SPEECH AT COMMENCEMENT EXERCISES AT KENTUCKY MILITARY INSTITUTE, Lyndon, June 1, 1947

SPEECH TO HIGHWAY SAFETY CONFERENCE, Louisville, June 6, 1947

SPEECH TO THE KENTUCKY TAX COMMISSIONERS ASSOCIATION MEETING, Lexington, June 11, 1947

KENTUCKY CHAMBER OF COMMERCE DINNER, Frankfort, July 10, 1947*

SPECIAL SESSION, Frankfort, July 10, 1947*

SPEECH OPENING THE JOHN FRED WILLIAMS CAMPAIGN FOR REPUBLICAN NOMINATION FOR GOVERNOR, Hazard, July 12, 1947

GROUND-BREAKING FOR VETVILLAGE, Cold Spring, July 13, 1947*

SPEECH TO RALLY OF JEFFERSON COUNTY BLACKS, Louisville, July 22, 1947

SPECIAL SESSION, Louisville, July 24, 1947*

INDEX